COMPUTER VISION

Springer
Singapore
Berlin
Heidelberg
New York
Barcelona
Budapest
Hong Kong
London
Milan
Paris
Santa Clara
Tokyo

Reinhard Klette • Karsten Schlüns • Andreas Koschan

COMPUTER VISION
Three-Dimensional Data from Images

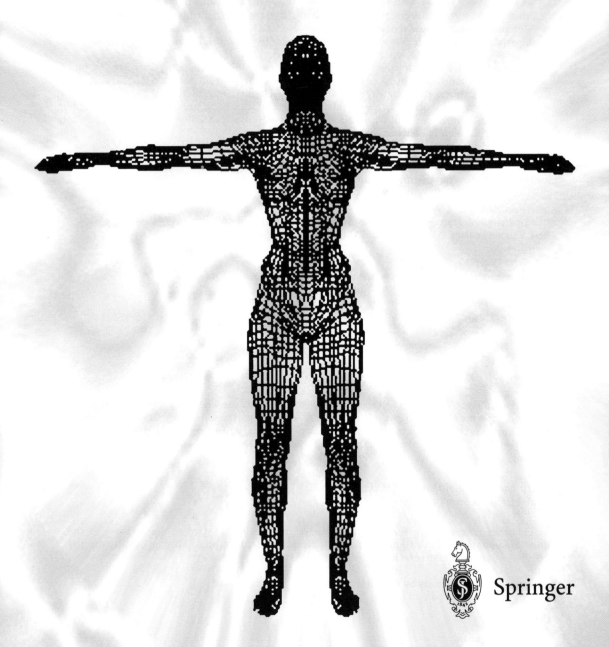

Springer

Prof. Dr. Reinhard Klette
Computing and Information
  Technology Research
Computer Science Department
Tamaki Campus
University of Auckland
Private Bag 92019, Auckland
New Zealand

Dr. Karsten Schlüns
Computing and Information
  Technology Research
Computer Science Department
Tamaki Campus
University of Auckland
Private Bag 92019, Auckland
New Zealand

Dr. Andreas Koschan
Computer Vision Group
Computer Science Department
Berlin Technical University
Franklinstraße 28/29
10587 Berlin
Germany

This book is a revised and extended version of the book originally published in the German language by Friedr. Vieweg & Sohn Verlagsgesellschaft mbH, D-65189 Wiesbaden, Germany, under the title "Computer Vision. 1. Auflage (1st Edition)".
Copyright 1996 by Friedr. Vieweg & Sohn Verlagsgesellschaft mbH, Braunschweig/Wiesbaden.

In the 1996 book, each co-author had main responsibilities: Reinhard Klette for Chapters 1, 3, and 5, Andreas Koschan for Chapters 2, 4, and 9, and Karsten Schlüns for Chapters 6, 7, and 8. Now, this new edition was completely revised and extended by Reinhard Klette and Karsten Schlüns at The University of Auckland, New Zealand. Parts of the book are completely modified in comparison to the 1996 edition. This book is based on a translation of the 1996 book into English by Kristian F. Klette (Auckland).

Library of Congress Cataloging-in-Publication Data

Klette, Reinhard.
  Computer vision : three-dimensional data from images / by Reinhard
Klette, Karsten Schlüns, Andreas Koschan
    p.   cm.
  ISBN 9813083719
  1. Computer vision. 2. Image reconstruction.   I. Schlüns, Karsten, 1966-
II. Koschan, Andreas, 1956- .   III. Title.
TA1634.K55 1998
006.3'7—DC21   98-13203
                                                    CIP

ISBN 981-3083-71-9

Typesetting: Camera-ready by Authors
SPIN 10676235   5 4 3 2 1 0

PREFACE

The reconstruction of object surfaces is a special discipline in *Computer Vision*. This discipline is directed towards the recovery of object shapes or recovery of distances between the camera and objects in a scene. This textbook is recommended for a one-semester university course at third or fourth year level in this field of surface reconstruction, for example in bachelor or master programs in Computer Science, in Applied Mathematics, or in Engineering.

The book provides a selection of fundamentals, often illustrated and explained by examples, and of comprehensible algorithmic solutions. Some of the recent results of the authors' research are included in this text. The exercises which follow each chapter are not only theoretic questions but are also directed towards practical applications. For these exercises it is recommended that the reader has a software system available which allows at least pixelwise write/read access to picture data. This will allow the reader to experience the discussed algorithms. Some image processing systems can be downloaded as public domain software from the Internet. Generally these systems are characterized by a certain number of basic procedures, e.g. picture enhancement, edge detection or picture representation. Information about such systems is available on the Internet.

The material in this book has been used during the last eight years for various courses in Computer Science at the *University of Auckland,* at the *University of Otago*, *Dunedin*, and at the *Berlin Technical University*. Section 4.3.2 is based on a text provided by *Georgy Gimel'farb* (University of Auckland). *Alan McIvor* (Industrial Research Ltd., Auckland) provided two figures for publication. We want to thank those colleagues who contributed to the manuscript with their comments: *Ryszard Kozera* (UWA Perth), *Richard Lobb* (University of Auckland), *Volker Rodehorst* (TU Berlin), *Horst Völz* (FU Berlin), and *Piero Zamperoni* (TU Braunschweig). Many of our students have contributed to the creation of this book. In particular, we would like to thank *Petra Bonfert, Peter Handschack, Tapani Hegewald, Wolfgang Huber, Richard Lewis-Shell, Greg Maddigan, Dirk Mehren, Arno Mitritz, Detlev Rumpel, Kathrin Spiller*, and *Matthias Teschner*.

Reinhard Klette   **Karsten Schlüns**   **Andreas Koschan**

SYMBOLS

This is a list of often used symbols with their default interpretation:

$\mathbf{C}$	color image
$C^{(n)}$	a class of functions (see page 83)
E, $E(x,y)$	image or image irradiance, image value at point $\mathbf{p} = (x,y)$
E_0	irradiance of a light source
f	effective focal length (see page 48)
fg	coordinate system of the stereographic projection plane
$\mathbf{F}\alpha$	α-functional (e.g. smoothness functional $\mathbf{F}s$)
G_{max}	maximal image value (maximal gray value)
λ	weight parameter, run variable, or wave length
L	scene radiance
M, N	image parameter, $1 \leq x \leq M$ and $1 \leq y \leq N$
$\mathbf{n}$, $\mathbf{n}°$	normal, unit normal
$\mathbf{O}$	origin, e.g. of the camera coordinate system
pq	coordinate system of the gradient space
p, q	surface slope in X- or in Y-direction
$\mathbf{p}$, $\mathbf{q}$, ...	points in the image plane
$\mathbf{P}$, $\mathbf{Q}$, ...	points in the three-dimensional space
ρ	albedo
$\Re^2$, $\Re^3$	Euclidean plane, Euclidean space
R	reflectance map
RGB	coordinate system of the color cube
$\mathbf{R}$ and $\mathbf{T}$	rotation matrix and translation vector
$\mathbf{s}$	direction to the light source, illumination direction
t	time variable
σ, θ	slant, tilt (see page 92)
$\xi\psi$	coordinate system of local displacement vectors
uv	coordinate system of the optical flow
$\mathbf{v}$	direction to the viewer, or velocity in the image plane
xy	coordinate system in the (undistorted) image plane
XYZ	camera coordinate system in the three-dimensional space

CONTENTS

DICHTER

Oft, wenn es erst durch Jahre durchgedrungen,
Erscheint es in vollendeter Gestalt.
Was glänzt, ist für den Augenblick geboren;
Das Echte bleibt der Nachwelt unverloren.

LUSTIGE PERSON

In bunten Bildern wenig Klarheit,
Viel Irrtum und ein Fünkchen Wahrheit,
So wird der beste Trank gebraut,
Der alle Welt erquickt and auferbaut.

DIREKTOR

Der Worte sind genug gewechselt,
Laßt mich auch endlich Taten sehn!

Johann Wolfgang von Goethe in *Faust - Der Tragödie erster Teil,* 1808

1 INTRODUCTION

The *reconstruction of object surfaces* is a special discipline in computer vision. This discipline is directed towards the recovery of object shapes or towards the calculation of distances between the sensor, i.e. the camera, and objects in a scene. Data acquired with one or more cameras constitute the initial information. Possible areas of application of *shape recovery*[1] are computer modeling of three-dimensional objects (e.g. architecture, mechanical engineering, surgery), distance measurements or roughly estimated positions of obstacles (e.g. vehicle control, robotics), surface inspections (e.g. quality control), approximate or exact estimates of the location of three-dimensional objects (e.g. automated assembly), or fast location of obstacles without recognition demand (e.g. navigation).

The process of shape reconstruction of three-dimensional objects often also contains procedures of image processing (image filtering, image restoration, image enhancement and others) or pattern analysis (edge detection, picture segmentation, feature identification and others). This book covers the procedures for image processing and pattern analysis only to a small extent.[2] For example, this introductory chapter deals with a special algorithm for edge detection (LoG operator) and provides two models for the representation of color images.

Two cameras with an ideal coplanar alignment to each other are used as an introductory example for the task of determining the position of a few surface points. This topic will be further described later in the sections about stereo analysis (Chapters 4 and 5). A first student assignment (Exercise 5 in Section 1.6) is suggested for the analysis of stereo color image pairs, where the determination of corresponding picture points is based on the utilization of edge images. Each chapter contains at least one proposal for such a student assignment.

---

[1] The term *shape* is used for the description of object surfaces (e.g. shape can be characterized in this sense by a set of surface normals). The *gestalt theory* of psychology (e.g. visual grouping of point patterns) or the *shape theory* of mathematical analysis (e.g. characterization of mathematical surfaces in different dimensions) are further areas where the term *shape* plays a central role, but are not covered in this textbook.

[2] For these areas of computer vision various textbooks are listed under the references in Section 1.5.

1.1   SHAPE RECONSTRUCTION

In computer vision shape reconstruction of three-dimensional objects is treated on the basis of visual data. This data is obtained by *visual sensors* (one or more cameras), which reproduce a static or a dynamic scene. In a *static scene* neither object movements occur in the time interval of taking the pictures nor changes in lighting or in camera parameters. For a *dynamic scene* such changes or motions are possible during this time interval. As an example, during the time interval of taking pictures of a dynamic scene the camera(s) can be spatially fixed and the intrinsic camera parameters (e.g. the focal length) can be changed (e.g. computer controlled). If a movement of the camera cannot be ruled out then this is also known as *dynamic image acquisition*.

1.1.1   Tasks and Tools

For problems in computer vision the projected scene can be a natural environment like a street scene or aerial photographs of developed land taken at low altitude. These are called *outdoor scenes*. The pictures can also be taken in industrial environments, for example in workshops or in laboratories. In this case they are called *indoor scenes*. Tasks of *scene analysis* differ clearly from problems of two-dimensional *pattern analysis* because in scene analysis three-dimensional images have to be interpreted. Scene objects can be very different, e.g. rigid or soft, opaque or transparent.

Informally speaking an *object face* of a scene object may be seen as a bounded set of surface points surrounded by some object edges. An *object edge* is a discontinuous change of orientations in surface points.[3] A sphere does not have object edges, and therefore has exactly one object face.[4] The whole of the object's surface points make up the *object surface*.

Problems of *shape reconstruction* are often oriented towards the reconstruction of object faces (*surface reconstruction*), which can only be calculated approximately (e.g. not necessarily true to scale) for certain applications. On the other hand, these problems can be characterized by an analysis of the depth values or the distance to individual points on the object surfaces (*range data analysis*).

The problems of surface reconstruction are usually relevant for indoor scenes or objects in indoor scenes. Figure 1.1 visualizes the result of a surface reconstruction of a human hand. This surface reconstruction, which may be done re-

---

[3]   The term *surface point of a scene object* is defined in Section 1.1.3. *Orientations at surface points* are covered in Chapter 3 (see index).

[4]   In Chapter 3 object surfaces are modeled by surface functions or respectively approximated by facets.

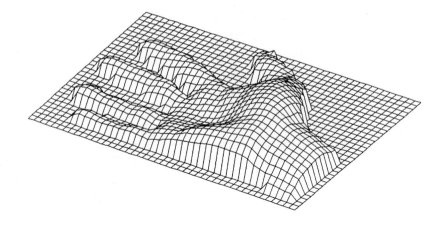

Figure 1.1: Reconstruction of the surface of a human hand (using photometric stereo analysis, see Chapter 8).

peatedly during a hand movement, can be of interest for computer graphics animations. Tasks of range analysis of individual surface points are typical for outdoor scenes. The task of measuring the distance to all visible surface points, and the reconstruction of all visible faces are geometrically almost equivalent problems.

Figure 1.2 presents typical tools for the shape reconstruction process of indoor scenes. Here lighting conditions and object movements can be controlled, the latter for example by the use of a turntable or conveyor belt.

Which tool of shape reconstruction we use depends on the kind of application. Can the object be placed on a turntable? Are object movements inevitable? Which object data do we have to calculate (and to what accuracy) to solve the problem? The task of shape reconstruction is usually very complicated, so pointless subtasks should be logically ruled out. For the reconstruction of a plaster statue it is not needed to reconstruct the surrounding objects as well. For distance measurements between vehicles a few reliable values are sufficient, i.e. the surface of the vehicle driving in front does not have to be reconstructed.

For the surface reconstruction and the range analysis, a technical and an application context needs to be considered for a concrete application. The analysis method which can be used is determined by the sensors available for capturing image data (cameras), the available tools for varying of measured gray value or image value distributions (e.g. lighting equipment), altogether the available image acquisition equipment, as well by the given objects in the scene which are to analyze, their movements or their arrangement. The designing of the context, i.e. the selection of scenes, of the lighting, of the cameras, of the computer hardware, of

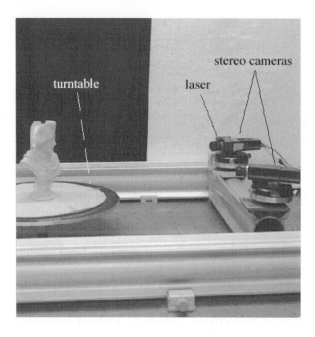

Figure 1.2: Laboratory set-up for shape reconstruction: an object ("Alter Fritz") on the turntable, and a pair of stereo cameras and a laser light source on profiles for device translation (on an optical bench).

the possible feedbacks etc., is complementary to the selection of usable techniques of shape reconstruction.

In the course of discussions of defined situations some assumptions, like *Lambertian surfaces*[5] for scene objects, can seem very restrictive for some readers. But such mathematically unique assumptions are needed for the description of concrete procedures, and often extendible to general situations.

Generally, the influences and possibilities of the third dimension need to be modeled for shape reconstruction. Here a new quality of problems has to be respected. In comparison to pattern analysis there is not just a further dimension added to the problem. For example, the lighting and the distance influence the surface texture, and texture can be used to analyze lighting or distance. Shadow formations or object movements make it possible to draw conclusions about the object geometry. Biologists managed to reconstruct the physical shape of dinosaurs on the basis of context knowledge from fossilized footprints.[6] For shape recon-

---

[5]   This surface property is defined in Chapter 6.
[6]   An illustration chart in the Phyletic Museum of Jena says: In 1824 fossilized, hand-shaped tracks of unknown animals were found in sandstone of the Trias in England. Fossilized tracks

struction using computer vision the context information has to be correctly deduced and used.

For the recovery of object surfaces several active and passive image acquisition techniques exist, which are directly oriented towards range determinations, or which at least allow for distance determinations.[7]

Range relevant or surface relevant data can be specifically embedded in the generated image information by means of *active image acquisition techniques*. For example, this can be done using controllable projected and reflected energy (e.g. ultrasound, laser), to make use of the differences between the sender and the receiver for generating range images (e.g. measuring of the phase difference, time of flight measurement). Other active image acquisition techniques were developed for mo- or binocular image acquisition and the application of *structured lighting*. For instance, line or grid patterns are projected into the scene (e.g. simply by using a slide projector) and distance measurements are performed by means of triangulation. Active image acquisition techniques can also be based on variations of the illumination (e.g. *photometric stereo analysis*), on variations of the focus (*shape from focus*), or on controlled object or camera movements (*shape from motion* or *shape from occluding boundaries* using calibration results).

Image acquisition techniques are distinguishable into *monocular* (one camera), *binocular* (two cameras), or *polyocular* (several cameras) techniques depending on the number of cameras involved.

Active or passive techniques usually require certain *calibrations* (exact parameter determination for the image acquisition situation) to base the acquisition process on models which are as exact as possible.

1.1.2　Formal Specification of the Basic Task

For a formal specification of the task of shape recovery a general comparison with the problem of projective optics can be drawn. A few fundamental concepts have to be explained first. *Scenes s* are defined in camera coordinates or world coordi-

---

obviously of the same origin were found later at different locations, such as near Hildburghausen/Thuringia in 1834. These tracks were interpreted to be tracks of marsupials by A. v. Humboldt (1769 - 1859) in 1835. In the year 1924 a shape reconstruction of these animals, who left the prints, could be given after a careful track analysis. According to that the animals were not marsupials, but specimen of Thecodontia, a class of giant dinosaurs. They carried the main burden of their bodies on their hind legs. These reptiles of the Trias were approximately 4-5 m (13-16 feet) long and are historically related to crocodiles. Up to now all that is known of these animals are their tracks.

[7]　The active image acquisition process should not be confused with the field of active image analysis (*active computer vision, animate computer vision*), which deals with the unity of aim and method (*purposive vision*).

nates *XYZ* of the three-dimensional space $\Re^3$. For a *position vector* $\mathbf{a} = (X, Y, Z)^T$ from the origin $\mathbf{O} = (0, 0, 0)$ to the point (X, Y, Z) assume $s(\mathbf{a})$ to be the *scene value* over the three-dimensional environment of the visual sensor. This vector has to be measured from $\mathbf{O}$ in direction $\mathbf{a}$. A scene s is the environment of a visual sensor at a certain moment. A *scene space* is made up of all the scenes that are assumed to be potential surroundings of the visual sensor. A scene space roughly corresponds to an application area of scene analysis.

In the case of a *CCD camera* as the visual sensor the scene values are measured gray values or color values. Distance values (for example measurable with a *laser range finder*) can also be seen as possible scene values. However, in this textbook we will generally assume cameras to be the image generating technology.

The projective *images E* of scenes are defined in image coordinates *xy* of the two-dimensional plane $\Re^2$. They are only defined for a limited array in this *image plane*, for instance for $1 \le x \le M$ and $1 \le y \le N$. The *image values* $E(x, y)$ correspond to scene values $s(\mathbf{a})$ according to a given projective mapping.[8]

An *optical mapping A* is a certain projection of a scene s on an image E,

$$E = A(s).$$

The image E represents the physical objects in the image plane by *irradiance values* (see Chapter 6 for a discussion of radiance and irradiance). The general task of projective optics consists of the implementation of mapping A. There, specific assumptions for A have to be considered such as no distortions, no shading and so on.

This textbook discusses the task that three-dimensional data of scene objects have to be reconstructed just based on a certain set of input images E using shape recovery techniques. Formally this is an inversion of the above sketched mapping A in the case of surface reconstruction (that means complete reconstruction of the surface structure) or, in the case of *depth analysis* (that means depth or range value calculation for only a few surface points) a partial inversion of this mapping A above, which means our interest is directed towards the mapping

$$s = A^{-1}(E).$$

So the general task of surface reconstruction consists of the implementation or the characterization of the mapping A^{-1}. But almost all the time it is only partially

---

[8] Coordinates (i, j) are used instead of (x, y) if it is appropriate to point out the discrete nature of the image coordinates.

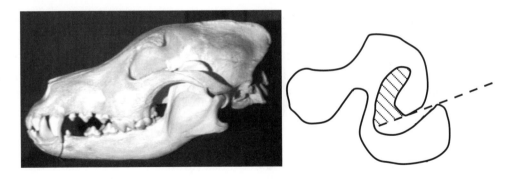

Figure 1.3: An object with surface areas not visible from the outside.

solvable: just a few faces (only of interesting objects, not the entire scene) up to only a few surface points (in the case of the depth analysis) can be determined.

In 1923, J. S. Hadamard (1865-1963) suggested the following characterization of problems: A mathematical problem is *well-posed* if a solution exists, if this solution is unique, and if this solution is continuously dependent on the input data ("robust against noise").[9]

The problems of projective optics for the implementation of the mapping A are usually well-posed. Compared with that the inverse problems of shape reconstruction are *ill-posed*. A unique mapping $s = A^{-1}(E)$ assumes a one-to-one relationship defined by the mapping A into the scene space, that means each scene s could only be assigned exactly one image E by A. However, for natural scene spaces this can practically be ruled out. Small changes in the images of scenes can often abruptly lead to alternative interpretations.

1.1.3   Three Straightforward Limitations for Shape Reconstruction

Under the sole point of view of *shape,* a scene object can be characterized at any time as a topological connected set of points of $\Re^3$, which is topologically compact (that means closed and bounded) and which is invariant with respect to Euclidean geometric mappings. The dependence of the shape on time is irrelevant for *rigid objects*. Further object characteristics, like surface texture, surface color, and surface reflection, are not contained in such a geometrically topologic approach for shape description.

We also mention a formal definition of scene objects for Euclidean space (for those readers interested in a mathematical model at this point):

---

9   See A. K. Louis: *Inverse und schlecht gestellte Probleme.* Teubner, Stuttgart, 1989.

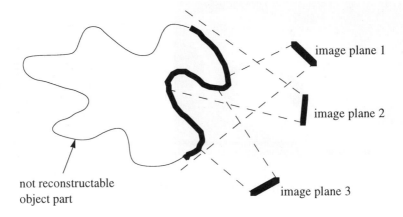

Figure 1.4: Only projected object surfaces can be reconstructed. This means usually a restriction to a $2\frac{1}{2}$D - surface representation.

An object in 3D Euclidean space $\Re^3$ is a connected compact set. A *compact set* is characterized by two properties: any infinite sequence of points of this set contains a convergent subsequence, and the set is closed with respect to the topology of the Euclidean space. An object in three-dimensional space may be characterized to be either one-dimensional, two-dimensional, or three-dimensional. A one-dimensional object in $\Re^3$ is a curve. A two-dimensional object in $\Re^3$ has no internal points (with respect to the 3D topology), i.e. it is a surface in $\Re^3$. A *3D object* is a connected compact set in $\Re^3$ which has internal points with respect to the 3D topology. Furthermore we can often assume that the 3D objects of interest are restricted to be simply-connected. A *simply-connected set* is homeomorphic (i.e. topologically equivalent) to a unit ball. Let us consider such a 3D object Θ. A point lies outside the object, if it does not lie in the corresponding closed set of points Θ. A point $\mathbf{P}$ in the three-dimensional space is a *surface point* of an object, if $\mathbf{P}$ is contained in the corresponding closed set of points Θ, and if at least one point exists outside of Θ in any ε-environment of $\mathbf{P}$, $\varepsilon > 0$.

The reconstruction of three-dimensional object faces based on two-dimensional visual mappings is only possible for visible (potentially, under a certain viewing direction and at some time slot) object faces, see Fig. 1.3. This is trivial, but it should not be forgotten for a concrete application. An object is *entirely visible from outside*, if there exists a ray to each point $\mathbf{P}$ on the surface, that intersects the object only at point $\mathbf{P}$. So a complete surface reconstruction can only be done for objects entirely visible from outside. Image acquisition methods that also allow a

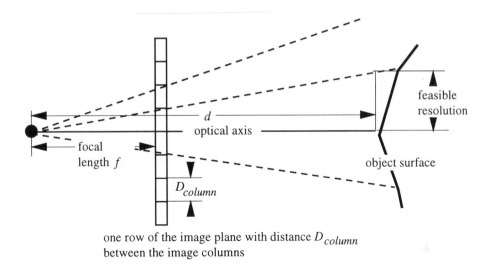

one row of the image plane with distance D_{column}
between the image columns

Figure 1.5: Analysis of the possible spatial resolution on an object surface in the projected scene.

look into the interior of the object (e.g. computer tomography) are not dealt with in this textbook.

The objects of interest are usually only projected from one or a small number of viewing directions. Correspondingly, objects can only be interpreted as $2\frac{1}{2}D$ *objects* for surface reconstruction, using only the reconstructable object faces or three-dimensional features, which are visible from the selected projection direction, see Fig. 1.4. The term "$2\frac{1}{2}D$ reconstruction" informally describes an incomplete 3D spatial information about an object (for example surface points with their gradients).

For the digitization of images the distance between the object surface and the camera as well as the *focal length* of the camera (= the distance between image plane and the projection center) need to be considered for analyzing the possible *spatial resolution* on the object surface. According to the image resolution and the distance between the camera and the object, only a limited spatial resolution is feasible on the object surface. Therefore certain limits are set for the accuracy of surface reconstruction.

The feasible *geometric resolution in the scene* can be easily calculated by applying the fact (*ray theorem*) that all lines coming from a point are cut by a pair of parallel lines in a certain ratio, see Fig. 1.5. The used camera is assumed to be a CCD matrix camera. Let D_{column} be the geometric width of an image column or respectively the distance between two neighboring image points (grid points) of one image row of a CCD matrix. Let f be the effective focal length and d be the distance from the image plane (CCD sensor matrix) to the projected surface point. Then it holds that

$$\frac{D_{column}}{f} = \frac{\text{feasible resolution}}{d}$$

or

$$\text{feasible resolution} = \frac{D_{column} \cdot d}{f} .$$

For $f = 15$ mm and $D_{column} = 10$ μm a feasible spatial resolution of 2 mm would result from a camera-object-distance of 3 m. It holds approximately that

width of the pictured scene = feasible resolution $\times$ number of image columns.

For an assumed number of 512 image columns, a scene domain with a width of 1.024 m would be projected when the scene domain is 3 m away from the camera.

Surely, further obvious restrictions can be named. Theoretically some limitations can be overcome by including object recognition into the surface recovery process. But object recognition is not a topic of this book, and is often also a more difficult task in comparison to surface recovery.

1.1.4   Utilization of Context Knowledge

For shape reconstructions good results can be achieved, if *limiting conditions* or *limiting constraints* about the image acquisition situation, the scene, and the scene objects can "skillfully" be included into the analysis process. Basically this will be the subject of this textbook. How useful are two cameras in comparison to just one camera? Does it help to switch several lightsources on and off? Do we need knowledge about the positions of the light sources? What use can we make of the controlled movement of an object?

Object surfaces can be modeled for the scene objects using functions of a certain complexity (see Chapter 3). The simplest approach that only "small" surface patches (*facets*) have to be reconstructed piecewise means to assume linear functions. For this, the objects are assumed to be approximately polyhedrons (with "many" small facets). With the theoretically unlimited reduced size of these *surface patches* any accuracy can be achieved for surface approximation using polyhedrons. This way the reconstruction can generally be oriented towards surface patches. Here the "additional knowledge" is given by the chosen approach of object modeling by planar faces.

The pre-definition of possible shape classes of scene objects (e.g. only convex polyhedrons) can also be considered to be used during the analysis process. Such shape restrictions can be applied during the reconstruction process using geometric constraints (e.g. "There exist no self shadows on scene objects"). This leads to an area of future research. For shadow analysis of concrete object shapes first results were achieved some years ago (*shape from shadows*). However, the application of these results is critical with respect to the numerical stability of the supported reconstruction algorithms.

Surface characteristics of scene objects can be used for a restriction of possible interpretations (e.g. reflection characteristics for photometric stereo analysis or for *shape from shading*). For this a variety of methods exists for surface reconstruction which are based on reflection models. The use of surface textures could be a further possible way (*shape from texture*). First results exist for shape from texture which still have to be further refined for deriving practically relevant solutions.

Natural or forced behavioral rules for image objects allow us to look at certain standard positionings or typical movement patterns. For example, surface points, which were analyzed during the sequence of movements, could theoretically be used for object reconstructions or for distance measurements (*shape from motion*). But in practice the problem of precise movement analysis of surface points has to be solved (e.g. *object tracking* or *optical flow techniques*).

Some methods were chosen for this textbook from this briefly sketched variety of methods for shape reconstruction, which could also be extended further according to the current level of progress in computer vision. These selected techniques are relevant to many practical applications. "Additional knowledge" can be gained by using specific image acquisition techniques (static and dynamic stereo analysis in Chapters 4 and 5, light plane projections in Chapter 9) and by using reflection models (Chapter 7) or respectively reflection models and a multiple lighting of the scene (Chapter 8).

1.2   GRAY VALUE AND COLOR IMAGES

The textbook does not only look at gray value images but also occasionally at color images, e.g. because of better correspondence analysis for static stereo analysis, for the visual output of calculated features or for the (partial) elimination of surface highlights. After the introduction of the *RGB* model and the *HSI* model the algorithmic transition between these two models is presented for color images in this Section. The *HSI* model, for instance, is very suitable for feature representation.

1.2.1   Image Parameters and Two Color Models

An *image* is defined for image points, which are assumed to be in the real plane or which can be elements of a discrete set of points. The image E always assumes a uniquely determined *image value* $E(\mathbf{p}) = E(x, y)$ [10] in each *image point* $\mathbf{p} = (x, y)$. The image value can be a signal value of a certain measured size, or a numerical *gray value* u which represents a certain gray tone. Formally this can be written as $E(x, y) = u$. The triple $(x, y, E(x, y)) = (x, y, u)$ is called a *pixel* (from: *picture element*). The coordinates x, y are the row position and the column position of the computer internal storage of the given image. [11]

A digital image is distinguished by discrete image points and discrete image values. The coordinates x and y of the image points (x, y) of digital images are assumed to be integers. Their value intervals are assumed to be $1 \leq x \leq M$ and $1 \leq y \leq N$. The values M and N mark the *image resolution*. The value $A = M \cdot N$ identifies the *image size*.

$G_{max} + 1$ gray values ($G_{max} \geq 1$) are assumed for the possible image values $E(x, y)$ of a digital image E. The mapping of (continuously distributed) image values or shades of gray into a limited number of gray values is called *quantization*. For the $G_{max} + 1$ gray values a connected interval of non-negative integers is assumed. For an integer gray value u it holds

$$0 \leq u \leq G_{max}.$$

Usually the values $G_{max} > 1$ (*gray value image*) or $G_{max} = 1$ (*binary image*) are used in image processing. The default value for gray value images is $G_{max} = 255$.

Additive color systems are used for displaying *color images* on computer screens. Almost all colors can be represented by a weighted sum of three primary colors. The wavelengths of such primary colors are internationally standardized. Often the spectral colors with the wavelengths 700 nm (**R**ed), 546 nm (**G**reen) and 435 nm (**B**lue) are selected to act as primary colors. This defines an *RGB model* for color images. The computational treatment of RGB color images is defined by calculations in three intensity images for the red, the green and the blue channel.

---

[10] For simplification double parentheses are omitted in $E(\mathbf{p}) = E((x, y))$ for $\mathbf{p} = (x, y)$.

[11] In Chapter 2 various coordinate systems for images are discussed, which correspond to certain image acquisition situations (a projected image in the image plane, an image distorted by lens distortions, and so on). In the sense of Chapter 2, x and y are the coordinates in the image plane. The points in the image plane are converted by the image acquisition equipment into integer, equipment dependent coordinates of the row and column positions. But in this introductory chapter no distinction between the different coordinate systems is made.

For a (three channel) color image $\mathbf{C}$ three intensity values R, G, B have to be given for each image point (x, y),

$$\mathbf{C}(x, y) = (R, G, B).$$

These values are called *tristimulus values*. The colors, represented by the value combinations R, G, B are relative, equipment dependent entities. A standardized color value can be defined on a specific discrete integer value scale $0, 1, ..., G_{max}$ formally denoted as a triple (R, G, B). The rational numbers

$$r = \frac{R}{R + G + B}, \quad g = \frac{G}{R + G + B}, \quad b = \frac{B}{R + G + B}$$

are the color value components normalized with respect to the intensity.

The primary colors Red $(G_{max}, 0, 0)$, Green $(0, G_{max}, 0)$, Blue $(0, 0, G_{max})$ and the complementary colors Yellow $(G_{max}, G_{max}, 0)$, Magenta $(G_{max}, 0, G_{max})$, Cyan $(0, G_{max}, G_{max})$ and also the gray tones White $(G_{max}, G_{max}, G_{max})$ and Black $(0, 0, 0)$ are the corners of the *color cube* that is formed by the possible value combinations of R, G, B.

Any integer triple (R, G, B) with $0 \le R, G, B \le G_{max}$ characterizes one color in the *RGB* model. This color cube is represented in Fig. 1.6. All gray tones lie on the main diagonal (u, u, u), with $0 \le u \le G_{max}$.

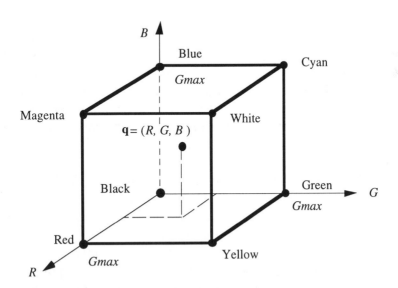

Figure 1.6: In the *RGB* model every point $\mathbf{q} = (R, G, B)$ inside the color cube characterizes exactly one color, where $0 \le R, G, B \le G_{max}$ and R, G, B are integers. Here $(G_{max} + 1)^3$ colors can be represented by points $\mathbf{q}$. For instance, for $G_{max} = 255$ these are 16 777 216 colors.

The *RGB* model is the common computer-internal representation of color images. With different cameras or scanners non-identical color images are generated for identical objects because of camera or scanner specific behavior, e.g., due to varying primary colors.

For computer vision and computer graphics further color representation models are of interest which can emulate the human color perception behavior. In the *HSI model*, **hue**, **saturation** and **intensity** are used as the coordinate axes. This model is very useful for working with color images to define visually inter-pretable local features.

Let a color $\mathbf{q} = (R, G, B)$ be given in the *RGB* model. The *hue* H of the color $\mathbf{q}$ characterizes the dominant color in $\mathbf{q}$. Red is assumed to be the "reference color". Therefore $H = 0°$ or $H = 360°$ correspond to the color Red. Besides the gray tone case $R = G = B$ the hue H is defined and given by

$$H = \begin{cases} \delta & \text{if } B \le G \\ 360° - \delta & \text{if } B > G \end{cases}$$

with

$$\delta = arccos\left(\frac{\dfrac{(R-G)+(R-B)}{2}}{\sqrt{(R-G)^2 + (R-B)\cdot(G-B)}} \right).$$

For example, for $G = B = 0$ and $R \ne 0$ it holds $\delta = arccos(1)$, i.e. $H = \delta = 0°$.

The *saturation* S of the color $\mathbf{q}$ is a measure of the purity of the color. This parameter is dependent on the number of wavelengths that contribute to the color perception. The wider the range of the wavelengths, the lower the purity of the color; the narrower the range of the wavelengths, the higher the purity. The extreme case of $S = 1$ is only valid for a pure color, and we have $S = 0$ for a gray tone $R = G = B$. Assume $R + G + B > 0$. Then S is given by

$$S = 1 - 3 \cdot \frac{min(R, G, B)}{R + G + B}.$$

For $R = G = B \ne 0$, for instance, indeed it always follows that $S = 0$. For $R = 0$ or $G = 0$ or $B = 0$, but $R + G + B \ne 0$ it follows that $S = 1$.

The *intensity* I of the color $\mathbf{q}$ corresponds to the relative brightness in the sense of a gray value image. The extreme case $I = 0$ corresponds to the color black. The intensity is already defined for the real values 0 to G_{max} according to

$$I = \frac{R + G + B}{3}$$

and only needs to be rounded to an integer for quantization (value I).

Therefore, for the color $\mathbf{q} = (R, G, B)$ in the *RGB* model a representation (H, S, I) of this color in the *HSI* model is given. This conversion is (except for rounding inaccuracies and with the exception of a few singularities) uniquely invertible. In the following section the inverse transformation is given as Algorithm 1.2.

Image processing boards exist for PCs and workstations which convert a PAL video image or an *RGB* image in real-time into an *HSI* image.

1.2.2   Conversion Between These Color Models

This section describes two algorithms which can easily be implemented. This textbook contains several algorithms which are specified at first by an exact task definition, then by comments regarding the task, or regarding the derivation of a solution algorithm, then by a somewhat informal representation of an algorithm (i.e. no formal program), and finally (optional) by some concluding comments regarding the algorithm, for example about the required computing time or about the treatment of special cases.

The algorithm descriptions incorporate informal descriptions. These descriptions are meant for the human reader, not for the computer.

(Task 1.1) A color image $\mathbf{C}$ is to be transformed from the *RGB* model into the *HSI* model. *RED*, *GREEN* and *BLUE* are the three input channels. Values in the three output channels *HUE*, *SATURATION* and *INTENSITY* have to be calculated. The output values have to be integers again and have to be in the interval $0, 1, ..., G_{max}$.

(Solution 1.1) The transformation formulas were given in Section 1.2.1. The special cases of singularities lead to the output "not defined". Here special values could also be generated.

(Algorithm 1.1) Assume a procedure *ADJUST* mapping real numbers into the permissible value range $0, 1, ..., G_{max}$. The procedure

$$ADJUST(q : real, \text{ var } u : gray\_value)$$

first carries out a rounding of q to the closest integer for any integer or real input number q,

$$q := integer(q + 0.5),$$

and then provides the value

$$u := min\{G_{max}, \, max\{0, \, q\}\} .$$

$M = M\_image$ and $N = N\_image$ characterize the size of the input image and thus the size of the six channels *RED*, *GREEN*, *BLUE*, *HUE*, *SATURATION* and *INTENSITY*. The algorithm is presented in Fig. 1.7.

Figure 1.8 visualizes the six channels *RED*, *GREEN*, *BLUE* respectively *HUE*, *SATURATION* and *INTENSITY* as gray value images of Color Image 1 (a picture of the Macbeth ColorChecker). The color images are given in the appendix.

Usually color images are provided in the *RGB* model. The presentation of color images in the *HSI* model is of interest for image segmentations, feature cal-

---

begin

    for $y := 1$ **to** N_image **do begin**

        for $x := 1$ **to** M_image **do begin**

           $u_1 := RED(x, y)$; $u_2 := GREEN(x, y)$; $u_3 := BLUE(x, y)$;

           $Z := \big((u_1 - u_2) + (u_1 - u_3)\big)/2$;

           $n := sqrt\big((u_1 - u_2)^2 + (u_1 - u_3)(u_2 - u_3)\big)$;

           if $(n \neq 0)$ **then** $delta := arccos(Z/n)$

                                            { *delta* in radians, $0 \leq delta < \pi$ }

                    else *delta* is undefined;

                                             { $u_1 = u_2 = u_3$ }

           if $(u_3 \leq u_2)$ **then** $H := delta$ **else** $H := 2\pi - delta$;

           $w := H \cdot (G_{max} + 1)/2\pi$;

                        { $G_{max} + 1$ is the number of gray values }

           call $ADJUST\big(w, HUE(x, y)\big)$;

           $SUM := u_1 + u_2 + u_3$; $MIN := min\{u_1, u_2, u_3\}$;

           if $(SUM \neq 0)$ **then** $S := 1 - 3 \cdot (MIN/SUM)$

                    else S is undefined;

                                        { $u_1 = u_2 = u_3 = 0$ }

           $w := S \cdot (G_{max} + 1)$;

           call $ADJUST\big(w, SATURATION(x, y)\big)$;

           $w := SUM/3$;

           call $ADJUST\big(w, INTENSITY(x, y)\big)$

        end {*for*};

    end {*for*}

end

Figure 1.7: Conversion of *RGB* images into *HSI* images. A substitute value can be arranged instead of "undefined".

culations, image stitching etc. in the area of computer vision. In the area of shape reconstruction the input images can be used either in the *RGB* model or in the *HSI* model as initial data, e.g. for calculating corresponding points in different color channels of stereo image pairs.

(**Task 1.2**) A color image **C** has to be transformed from the *HSI* representation into the *RGB* representation. For the integer input data a range

$$0 \leq HUE, SATURATION, INTENSITY \leq G_{max}$$

is assumed. *HUE*, *SATURATION* and *INTENSITY* are the three input channels. Values have to be calculated in the three output channels *RED*, *GREEN*, and *BLUE*. The output data have to be integers again in the range $0, 1, ..., G_{max}$.

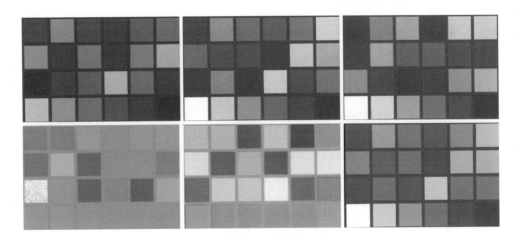

Dark Skin	Light Skin	Blue Sky	Foliage	Blue Flower	Bluish Green
Orange	Purplish Blue	Moderate Red	Purple	Yellow Green	Orange Yellow
Blue	Green	Red	Yellow	Magenta	Cyan
White	Neutral 8	Neutral 6.5	Neutral 5	Neutral 3.5	Black

Figure 1.8: Visualization of the six color channels of a color image of the Macbeth ColorChecker, see Color Image 1 in the appendix. Upper image row: *RED*, *GREEN* and *BLUE*, lower image row: *HUE* (with blue as reference color), *SATURATION* and *INTENSITY*. The table shows the color or gray value denotations corresponding to the standardized color patches of the Macbeth ColorChecker.

```
begin
   for y:= 1 to N_image do begin
      for x:= 1 to M_image do begin
         u₁:= HUE(x, y)·360/Gmax;                  { 0°≤ u₁ ≤ 360° }
         u₂:= SATURATION(x, y)/Gmax;           {real number, 0 ≤ u₂ ≤ 1 }
         u₃:= INTENSITY(x, y)/Gmax;             {real number, 0 ≤ u₃ ≤ 1 }
         if (u₂ = 0)  then                              {gray tone}
            R:= u₃ ;      G:= u₃;       B:= u₃
         else
            rt3:= 1/sqrt(3);
            if (0 ≤ u₁ < 120)      then                  { B is minimum}
               B:= (1−u₂)·u₃ ;     H:= rt3·tan(u₁ − 60);
               G:= (1.5+1.5·H)·u₃ − (0.5+1.5·H)·B;
               R:= 3·u₃ − G − B
            else
               if (120 ≤ u₁ < 240)  then               { R is minimum}
                  R:= (1−u₂)·u₃;     H:= rt3·tan(u₁ − 180);
                  B:= (1.5+1.5·H)·u₃ − (0.5+1.5·H)·R;
                  G:= 3·u₃ − B − R
               else                                     { G is minimum}
                  G:= (1−u₂)·u₃;
                  H:= rt3·tan(u₁ − 300);
                  R:= (1.5+1.5·H)·u₃ − (0.5+1.5·H)·G;
                  B:= 3·u₃ − R − G
               end {if}
            end {if}
         end {if}
         w:= R·Gmax ;      call ADJUST(w, RED(x, y));
         w:= G·Gmax ;      call ADJUST(w, GREEN(x, y));
         w:= B·Gmax ;      call ADJUST(w, BLUE(x, y))
      end {for}
   end {for}
end
```

Figure 1.9: Conversion of color images from the *HSI* representation into an *RGB* representation.

(**Solution 1.2**) The color image models were introduced in Section 1.2.1. The transformations arise from the inversion of the given formulas. The integer input data are first converted into angles (for *HUE*) respectively into reals in the interval $[0,1]$ (for *SATURATION* and *INTENSITY*). For the special cases of singularities the output is again generated as "undefined".

(**Algorithm 1.2**) The algorithm is presented in Fig. 1.9. The procedure *ADJUST* as introduced in Algorithm 1.1 is used for generating integer outputs in the default gray value interval.

After the transformation of an *RGB* image into an *HSI* image, Algorithm 1.2 will provide (usually with the exception of a few inaccuracies due to singularities) the back transformation into the *RGB* image. Generally these singularities can be ignored in applications.

1.3 EDGE DETECTION

Edges are important features of images which can, for instance, be used to support correspondence analysis of stereo image pairs. In this section, at first image edges are characterized and then an (illustrative) special method for edge detection is dealt with. For color images such an edge operator can repeatedly be used in the individual channels.

Figure 1.10: The gray value arrays for the two labeled windows in the image of the laboratory scene are numerically presented on the right. The "bottle window" shows a "homogeneous gray value pattern" and the "milk carton window" depicts an "edge".

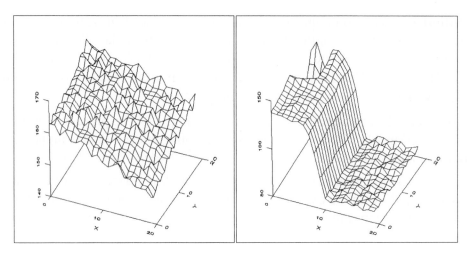

Figure 1.11: Gray value distributions of the two windows from Fig. 1.10. Left: lower window (gray value edge), right: upper window ("diagonally decreasing" homogeneous gray value distribution).

1.3.1   Edges in Gray Value Images

Figure 1.10 presents a gray value image onto which two windows were drawn. The windows contents (numerical gray values) are given on the right. The "gray value structure" of the gray value image can be looked at like through a magnifying glass. The upper image window is characterized by a relatively homogeneous gray value distribution. A strong discontinuity runs through the lower image window. The gray value pattern shows a clear increase in the gray values. An *image value edge* respectively *gray value edge* runs orthogonal to this increase.

The term *gray value relief* is illustrated by the 3D grid of gray value distributions which is presented in Fig. 1.11. This intuitive term describes the assumption, that gray values in the digital image do not differ very much from each other locally and therefore form plateaus, slopes, or valleys. The gray value relief does not have any "caves or overhangs". In an accurate mathematical sense these can be called *image value functions*, which uniquely represent individual (discrete) height values of a three-dimensional surface.

A digital gray value image can be transformed into a continuous image value distribution by a continuous approximation or interpolation of these discrete image values. For the continuous function $z = E(x, y)$ in two variables x and y the *gradient* respectively the *gradient vector*

$$grad(E) = \left(\frac{\partial E}{\partial x}, \frac{\partial E}{\partial y} \right)^T$$

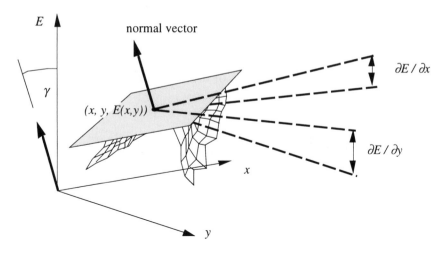

Figure 1.12: Representation of an image value function, of a tangential plane to a pixel $\big(x, y, E(x, y)\big)$, of the corresponding normal vector $\mathbf{n}_+$ and of the direction angle γ (see *slant* in Chapter 3) with the E-axis.

of E characterizes the "height change" of the function in the xyz space (object surface gradients are also dealt with in Subsection 3.1.2). In each pixel $\big((x, y), E(x, y)\big)$ of the image value function exactly one tangential plane is defined, to which the *normal vectors*

$$\mathbf{n}_- = \left(\frac{\partial E}{\partial x}, \frac{\partial E}{\partial y}, -1\right)^T \quad \text{respectively} \quad \mathbf{n}_+ = \left(-\frac{\partial E}{\partial x}, -\frac{\partial E}{\partial y}, +1\right)^T$$

are perpendicular. The normal vector is uniquely defined except for the sign of the components. The direction of this vector is determined by the angles α, β, γ to the xyz axes. The direction angle γ to the z axis (see Fig. 1.12) characterizes the slope of the image value function in the point $\big((x, y), E(x, y)\big)$ relative to the xy plane. So this direction angle can be very useful to describe transitions between constant gray value plateaus and gray value slopes (e.g. gray value edges). The absolute value of the gradient,

$$\|grad(E)\| = \sqrt{\left(\frac{\partial E}{\partial x}\right)^2 + \left(\frac{\partial E}{\partial y}\right)^2},$$

respectively of the normal vectors $\mathbf{n} = \mathbf{n}_-$ or $\mathbf{n} = \mathbf{n}_+$,

$$\|\mathbf{n}\| = \sqrt{\left(\frac{\partial E}{\partial x}\right)^2 + \left(\frac{\partial E}{\partial y}\right)^2 + 1},$$

takes on the extreme value of zero for a constant gray value plateau (in the ideal case $E(x, y) = const$ close to (x, y)). Therefore these values are useful to characterize the shape of the image value function.

For the direction angles α, β, γ of the vector $\mathbf{n}_+$ with the axes it holds

$$cos(\alpha) = \frac{\frac{\partial E}{\partial x}}{\|\mathbf{n}\|}, \quad cos(\beta) = \frac{\frac{\partial E}{\partial y}}{\|\mathbf{n}\|} \quad \text{and} \quad cos(\gamma) = \frac{1}{\|\mathbf{n}\|}.$$

Therefore for the especially interesting angle $\gamma = arccos(1/\|\mathbf{n}\|)$ it follows that [12]

$$\gamma = arctan(\|grad(E)\|).$$

For example, gray value edges may also be modeled with respect to large local changes in γ. Practically approximate values are used for the modeling of gray value edges which are easier (and generally more robust) to calculate, like the ratios of directional changes of the image value function in the direction of x and y, which are represented by the quotients

$$\frac{\partial E}{\partial x} \bigg/ \frac{\partial E}{\partial y} \quad \text{respectively} \quad \frac{\partial E}{\partial y} \bigg/ \frac{\partial E}{\partial x}.$$

The absolute value of the gradient of an image value function is invariant relative to translation of the xy-coordinate system. This also holds for the square of this value,

$$\|grad(E)\|^2 = \left(\frac{\partial E}{\partial x}\right)^2 + \left(\frac{\partial E}{\partial y}\right)^2,$$

for the _Laplace derivation_, called the _Laplacian_, of the image E,

$$\nabla^2 E = \frac{\partial^2 E}{\partial x^2} + \frac{\partial^2 E}{\partial y^2},$$

and for the _quadratic variation_,

$$\left(\frac{\partial^2 E}{\partial x^2}\right) + 2\left(\frac{\partial^2 E}{\partial x \partial y}\right)\left(\frac{\partial^2 E}{\partial y \partial x}\right) + \left(\frac{\partial^2 E}{\partial y^2}\right).$$

---

[12] $\quad arccos\left(\dfrac{1}{\|\mathbf{n}\|}\right) = arc\,cot\left(\dfrac{1}{\sqrt{\|\mathbf{n}\|^2 - 1}}\right) = arc\,cot\left(\dfrac{1}{\|grad(E)\|}\right) = arctan(\|grad(E)\|)$

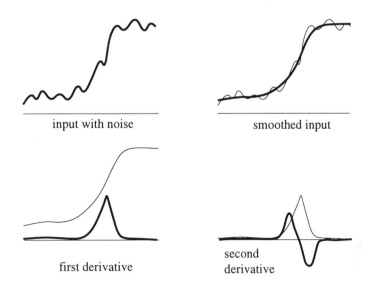

Figure 1.13: Representation of different one-dimensional curves (visualizing gray value distributions in a single image row or column).

In digital images the derivatives $\partial E/\partial x$ and $\partial E/\partial y$ can only be approximately determined (for instance by using the *Sobel operator*, which also performs a smoothing parallel to the edge that was sought after). New image value functions can be calculated approximating a multiple derivation of a given gray value function and by appropriate arithmetic combinations. These calculated images represent particular local gray value situations which may be interpreted with respect to the process how they were generated.

A simple general model of gray value edges is illustrated by Fig. 1.13. In the upper left corner, a curve of "noisy input data" (a one-dimensional cross section through a gray value image) is shown. First, this can be transformed into a smooth image ("input with reduced noise"), for example using a convolution with the Gaussian function (see Section 1.3.2). For this smooth image (upper right corner) the results of the first and the second derivatives are shown below.

Following this simple model an edge can be approximately identified by local maxima of the first derivative (i.e. the absolute value of the gradient) or by the *zero crossings* of the second derivatives (e.g. of the Laplace derivation or of the standard deviation). Accordingly, discrete operators can be designed for edge calculation. For completeness, one example of an edge operator (which usually works relatively well) will be given in the following.

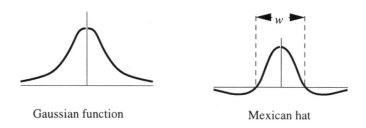

Gaussian function   Mexican hat

Figure 1.14: The Gaussian function and the Laplace derivation (multiplied by -1) of the Gaussian function ("Mexican hat").

1.3.2   Laplacian-of-Gaussian Edge Detector

The Laplace operator will be used on a Gauss-smoothed image for the calculation of the second derivative of a given ("noisy") image. The result of the smoothing and the second derivative afterwards can also be computed more time efficiently through a single-step convolution of the original (noisy) input with the Laplace derivation of the Gaussian function. Because of its shape this convolution kernel is also called the *Mexican hat*, see Fig. 1.14. The size of the convolution window should be about $3w \times 3w$ as a default where w is shown in Fig. 1.14 and explained below.

The convolution with the Mexican hat kernel may be followed by an absolute value calculation. For an ideal edge this should lead to the generation of two "parallel bright stripes" lying closely together with a "dark stripe" between as a consequence of the previous zero-crossing (i.e. the location of the original gray value edge).

The just outlined *LoG filter* (*Laplacian-of-Gaussian*) carries out a Gaussian smoothing and after that a Laplace derivation for an input image $E(x, y)$,

$$\nabla^2(GAUSS*E),$$

where *GAUSS* is the error distribution function of the two-dimensional normal distribution,

$$GAUSS(x, y, \sigma) = \frac{1}{2\pi\sigma^2} exp\left(-\frac{x^2 + y^2}{2\sigma^2}\right) = \frac{1}{2\pi\sigma^2} \cdot e^{-\frac{x^2+y^2}{2\sigma^2}},$$

and the symbol $*$ denotes the convolution operation. The variable σ specifies the standard deviation and σ^2 is the variance. In the continuous case it generally holds that

$$\nabla^2(GAUSS * E) \;=\; \nabla^2(GAUSS) * E.$$

So the LoG filtering can be done by a single convolution with the convolution kernel

$$\nabla^2 GAUSS(r, \sigma) = -\left(1 - \frac{r^2}{\sigma^2}\right) \cdot exp\left(-\frac{r^2}{2\sigma^2}\right)$$

where $r^2 = x^2 + y^2$. For discrete images $E(x, y)$ actually a certain "non-linearity" should be taken into consideration, but this can often be disregarded.

(Task 1.3) For images E the convolution $\nabla^2(GAUSS) * E$ has to be calculated approximately (i.e. for a discrete array of input data) and the resulting zero-crossings have to be represented.

(Solution 1.3) The convolution kernel $c(x, y)$ is separable for continuous local coordinates x, y,

$$c(x, y) = c_1(x) \cdot c_2(y) + c_2(x) \cdot c_1(y),$$

where $c_1(t)$ and $c_2(t)$ are one-dimensional functions

$$c_1(t) = \left(1 - \frac{t^2}{\sigma^2}\right) \cdot exp\left(-\frac{t^2}{2\sigma^2}\right) \text{ and } c_2(t) = exp\left(-\frac{t^2}{2\sigma^2}\right).$$

These two one-dimensional (initially continuous) convolution kernels $c_1(t)$ and $c_2(t)$ characterize the "Mexican hat" and a Gaussian function, respectively.

Approximate discrete convolution kernels have to be chosen for these continuous convolution kernels. An important issue in this context is the determination of the right size of these discrete kernels (arrays). Let $w = 2\sqrt{2} \cdot \sigma$ be the diameter of the circle where the Mexican hat function has non-negative values, as shown in Fig. 1.14. Assume that during quantization of an interval w there are W values selected as discrete samples. In general it is sufficient to restrict the infinite domain set of the Mexican hat function to a convolution window of size $3w \times 3w$ (centered with respect to the origin), i.e. there are $3W \times 3W$ discrete values in the discrete convolution kernel approximating the Mexican hat function.

For analyzing such a transition from continuous to discrete convolution kernels let us assume that the sampling interval (i.e. for example the physical image point distance in the CCD matrix array of the camera) satisfies the *sampling theorem* (which is well-known in signal theory) with regard to the pictured image data. As a rough "rule of thumb" this means that there are at least two sampled values for each detail of minimum size, e.g. across digitized lines of minimum width. Based on this assumption we can derive an empirical estimate of at least $W \approx 3.8$ sample points in an interval of width w. So a discrete convolution kernel of a minimum size of 12×12 would be reasonable.

```
for  y:= k +1 to  N_image − k do begin              { with restriction  k ≤ kmax }
                                    { first run through the image "in window width" }
        for  j:= −k to  k do
            for  x:= k +1 to  M_image − k do begin
```
$$v_1:= c_1(0)\cdot E(x,y+j); \qquad v_2:= c_2(0)\cdot E(x,y+j);$$
```
                for  i:= 1 to  k do begin
```
$$v_1:= v_1 +\big(E(x-i,y+j)+E(x+i,y+j)\big)\cdot c_1(i);$$
$$v_2:= v_2 +\big(E(x-i,y+j)+E(x+i,y+j)\big)\cdot c_2(i)$$
```
                end {for};
```
{ arrays $U_1\big[1...M\_image,-k_{max}...k_{max}\big]$, $U_2\big[1...M\_image,-k_{max}...k_{max}\big]$

will act as temporary storage of the first run }
$$U_1(x,j):= v_1; \qquad U_2(x,j):= v_2$$
```
            end {for};
```
{ initializing of two one-dimensional arrays }
```
        for  x:= 1 to  M_image do begin
```
$$H_1(x):= 0; \qquad H_2(x):= 0$$
```
            end {for};
```
{ second run "in window width" }
```
        for  j:= −k to  k do
            for  x:= 1 to  M_image do begin
```
$$H_1(x):= H_1(x)+U_1(x,j)\cdot c_2\big(|k+1-j|\big);$$
$$H_2(x):= H_2(x)+U_2(x,j)\cdot c_1\big(|k+1-j|\big)$$
```
            end {for};
```
{ two versions of the representation of zero-crossings }
```
        if "shift of the zero-crossing" by  Gmax/2 then
```
$$H(x,y):= G_{max}/2+\big(H_1(x)+H_2(x)\big)/2$$
```
        else                                    { output as absolute value }
```
$$H(x,y):= \big|H_1(x)+H_2(x)\big|;$$
```
    end {for}
```

Figure 1.15: Convolution procedure of the LoG operator. An input image E is transformed into a resulting image H. In H the zero-crossings are represented either by gray value $G_{max}/2$ or by means of absolute value calculation as dark middle line between two bright lines.

The indicated separability of the kernel is of advantage to save computing time for an implemented operator. For the algorithm, the coefficients of the two one-dimensional discrete convolution kernels $c_1(t)$ and $c_2(t)$ have to be determined, for integer values t in the range from $-1.5 \cdot W$ to $1.5 \cdot W$. Furthermore, the coefficients $c_1(t)$ and $c_2(t)$ have to satisfy the two following constraints,

$$C_1 := \sum c_1(t) = 0 \quad \text{and} \quad C_2 := \sum c_2(t) = 1,$$

so that for the band pass $c_1(t)$ the resulting gray value is equal to zero for an assumed constant gray value distribution in the operator window, and that an assumed constant gray value distribution remains unchanged if smoothed by a Gaussian low pass $c_2(t)$.

Hence all the calculated coefficient values for $c_1(t)$ and for $c_2(t)$ must be corrected by addition of value $S_1 := -C_1/3W$ or of value $S_2 := (1 - C_2)/3W$, respectively.

For the convolution kernel entity $\approx 3W$ it is assumed that it is an odd number $n = 2k + 1$. Let k_{max} be an upper bound for k.

(Algorithm 1.3) In the initializing phase a temporary entity n can be entered and then the calculation of the related filter coefficients for $k := (n-1)/2$ can take place:

$$c_1(0) := 1; \qquad c_2(0) := 1;$$
$$S_1 := 1; \qquad S_2 := 1;$$

for $t := 1$ **to** k **do begin**
$$c_1(t) := \left(1 - 8(3t/n)^2\right) \cdot exp\left(-4(3t/n)^2\right);$$
$$c_2(t) := exp\left(-4(3t/n)^2\right);$$
$$S_1 := S_1 + 2 \cdot c_1(t);$$
$$S_2 := S_2 + \left(12/n\sqrt{\pi}\right) \cdot c_2(t)$$
end {for};

Because of $c_1(-t) = c_1(t)$ and $c_2(-t) = c_2(t)$, only half of the coefficients need to be calculated for $t = 1, ..., k$. Then the additive adjustment of the filter coefficients can be done according to the following instructions:

$$S_1 := S_1/n; \qquad S_2 := (1 - S_2)/n;$$

for $t := 1$ **to** k **do begin**
$$c_1(t) := c_1(t) - S_1;$$
$$c_2(t) := c_2(t) + S_2$$
end {for}

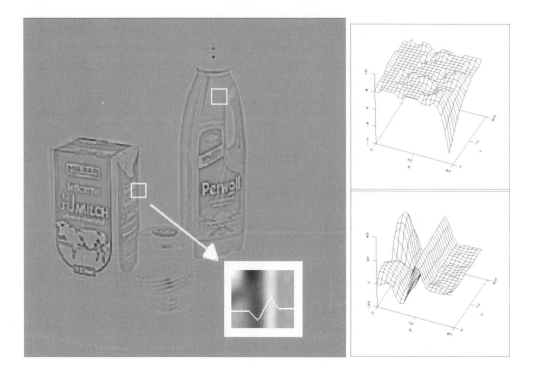

Figure 1.16: The resulting gray value distributions of the LoG operator for the two windows in Fig. 1.10 are shown on the right (note: also the negative values). The lower window contains a typical zero-crossing as an indication of an edge. The result of the LoG operator for the image in Fig. 1.10 is represented in the picture on the left using an increase of the calculated values by $(G_{max}+1)/2$. In the enlarged window the gray values were transformed linearly to improve the contrast.

After this preliminary phase the edge detection for the input image E can take place using these prepared values of the window parameters.

Figure 1.15 indicates the transformation procedure. For every y value first the linear convolutions are carried out for all x in the x-direction. There, two arrays U_1 and U_2 are used for temporary storage. After that the convolution of these arrays takes place in the y-direction.

(Comment 1.3) The zero-crossings have to be detected after this LoG transformation. The algorithm contains two simple variants. A local operation can also be used which detects those image points for which at least one "significant" negative value and at least one "significant" positive value were calculated in a local environment. Figure 1.16 presents the result of a certain application of the LoG operator.

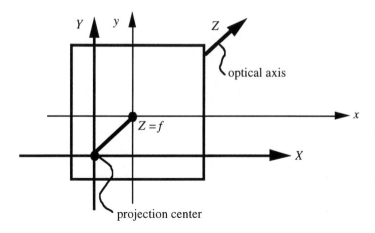

Figure 1.17: Assumed orientation of the XYZ-coordinate system (with respect to the left camera in case of a binocular image acquisition situation).

1.4   AN INTRODUCTORY EXAMPLE - STATIC STEREO IMAGE ANALYSIS

Chapter 4 is devoted to the technique of static stereo image analysis. However this section already presents an algorithm for stereo image analysis that allows a first illustration of the task and of a few problems of distance or range measurement in computer vision.

1.4.1   Coplanar Stereo Image Geometry

Often the camera can be modeled quite well by the so-called *pinhole camera model*. An image plane is assumed in distance f with respect to a projection center. This image plane lies between the projection center and the projected scene points. The projection center is physically defined by the *focal point* or *optical center* of the camera and the distance f by the (*effective*) *focal length* of the camera. The projected image is a bounded array (rectangle) in the image plane. The *optical axis* of the camera intersects the image plane approximately [13] in the center of the projected image.

In the following two cameras (one on the left and one on the right) are assumed for a discussion of static stereo analysis (*binocular image acquisition*). It is sufficient to align one XYZ-coordinate system for the three-dimensional space of

---

[13]   Chapter 2 looks more accurately at this intersection of the optical axis and the image plane.

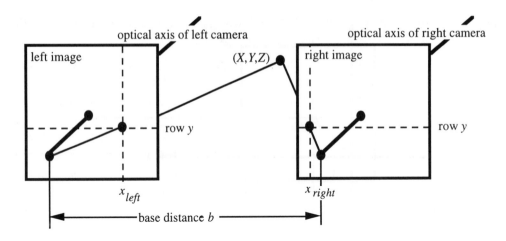

Figure 1.18: The standard stereo geometry for two camera is characterized by identical focal length of the left and of the right camera, parallel optical axes (into the same direction), and row-identical orientation of the images. A scene point $\mathbf{P} = (X, Y, Z)$ is projected onto an image point $\mathbf{p}_{left} = \left(x_{left}, y\right)$ in the left image plane and onto a corresponding image point $\mathbf{p}_{right} = \left(x_{right}, y\right)$ in the right image plane under these circumstances. The two projection centers are located in focal separation b (the *base distance*) which can roughly be understood as being the distance between the two cameras.

the scene points with one of these two cameras, for example with the camera on the left (see Fig. 1.17).

The Z-axis is identified to be the optical axis of the camera. For the orientation of this axis we assume that it is directed towards the space of the scene objects. Furthermore for the left-handed, orthogonal XYZ-coordinate system it is assumed that the focal point (the projection center) lies in the XY-plane and that the xy image coordinate axes run parallel to the XY-axes. The focal length f defines the orthogonal distance between the projection center and the image plane. The special plane equation $Z = f$ defines the xy-image plane in the XYZ coordinate system.

A pinhole camera projects scene points $\mathbf{P}$ which lie in front of the image plane into image points $\mathbf{p}$ according to a *central projection*. From the fact that all lines coming from a point are cut by a pair of parallel lines in a certain ratio it follows directly that a point $\mathbf{P} = (X, Y, Z)$ is projected onto a point

$$\mathbf{p} = (x, y) = \left(\frac{f \cdot X}{Z}, \frac{f \cdot Y}{Z} \right).$$

It is assumed that $Z > f$, see Fig. 1.17. For the second camera of a stereo image acquisition system this projection equation has to be modified while considering the positioning of the camera in the XYZ space. As an example we consider the so-called *standard stereo geometry* of two cameras:

Two cameras are assumed in positions as shown in Fig. 1.18. The XYZ-coordinate system is oriented at the left camera. The focal point of the left camera lies at the origin $\mathbf{O} = (0, 0, 0)$ and the focal point of the right camera lies at distance b on the X axis at the point $(b, 0, 0)$. The two optical axes are parallel and oriented towards the scene objects. Both cameras have the same focal length f. The images of both cameras are located in the same image plane $Z = f$. The x-axes of both images are identically oriented, i.e. a row y in the left image and the corresponding row y in the right image are always *collinear* (i.e. lie on the same straight line). Therefore we can refrain from giving the image rows special indices like *left* or *right*.

In general it holds for a stereo image acquisition system that a scene point $\mathbf{P} = (X, Y, Z)$ is projected onto two *corresponding image points*

$$\mathbf{p}_{left} = \left(x_{left}, y_{left}\right) \text{ and } \mathbf{p}_{right} = \left(x_{right}, y_{right}\right)$$

in the left respectively in the right image plane assuming, of course, that the scene point is not hidden in one of the projection directions, i.e. it is visible from both projection centers. With respect to variable $\mathbf{p}_{left} = \left(x_{left}, y_{left}\right)$ the *disparity* (or *parallax*) is a vector

$$\Delta\left(x_{left}, y_{left}\right) = \left(x_{left} - x_{right}, y_{left} - y_{right}\right)^T$$

between the two corresponding image points $\mathbf{p}_{left} = \left(x_{left}, y_{left}\right)$ in the left image respectively $\mathbf{p}_{right} = \left(x_{right}, y_{right}\right)$ in the right image (if they exist). Under the standard stereo geometry assumption it suffices to calculate a *scalar disparity*

$$\Delta_{ssg}\left(x_{left}, y_{left}\right) = \sqrt{\left(x_{left} - x_{right}\right)^2 + \left(y_{left} - y_{right}\right)^2} \ .$$

A *disparity map* $\Delta(x, y)$ is defined by these values, or the value "undefined" at image points where the correspondence problem has no, or no unique solution.

A row equality $y = y_{left} = y_{right}$ is satisfied in case of the ideal assumption of the standard stereo geometry of the two cameras. For the left camera the central projection equation can be used directly,

$$x_{left} = \frac{f \cdot X}{Z} \text{ and } y = \frac{f \cdot Y}{Z} \ .$$

For the right camera while considering the shift on the X axis by b it holds that

$$x_{right} = \frac{f \cdot (X - b)}{Z} \text{ and } y = \frac{f \cdot Y}{Z} \ .$$

Because of the identity in row coordinates of corresponding points, here the scalar disparity (or scalar parallax) of a pair of corresponding points is equal to

$$\Delta_{ssg}\left(x_{left}, y_{left}\right) = \left|x_{left} - x_{right}\right| = x_{left} - x_{right},$$

as $x_{left} \geq x_{right}$ is always satisfied because of the chosen arrangement of the cameras, and therefore the absolute value does not have to be determined. Let us consider this standard stereo geometry model in the sequel.

The disparity values $x_{left} - x_{right}$ of corresponding image points allow to reconstruct the coordinates of the projected points **P** within the three-dimensional XYZ-space, where the parameters f and b are assumed to be known. From the two central projection equations (left and right camera) it follows that

$$Z = \frac{f \cdot X}{x_{left}} = \frac{f \cdot (X - b)}{x_{right}}$$

and therefore

$$X = \frac{b \cdot x_{left}}{x_{left} - x_{right}}.$$

With this X value it follows that

$$Z = \frac{b \cdot f}{x_{left} - x_{right}}.$$

We substitute this result into the projection equation for y and finally it follows that

$$Y = \frac{b \cdot y}{x_{left} - x_{right}}.$$

The disparity $\Delta\left(x_{left}, y_{left}\right)$ is the entity that has to be measured for each pair of corresponding points to infer 3D coordinates or surface point positions of visible scene points from a given stereo image pair. The image coordinates are integers, i.e. disparities are restricted to be integers as well. Practically this means that the disparities will only have values in a relatively small range of integers. Note that a disparity value is inversely proportional to the coordinate values X, Y and Z. For points **P** close to the two cameras the disparity is relatively large and the XYZ-coordinates can be determined relatively accurate in this case. The accuracy of the distance measurement can also be improved with increasing the focal separation b. However, a larger focal separation means that less scene points are visible in both images.

The focal length f and the focal separation b can be expressed in units of the image plane. For example, for an assumed resolution in the image plane of 10 μm (e.g. the physical length of a grid edge or side length of a CCD matrix cell, see also Section 2.1 for the problem to specify the physical distance between image points) and a focal length of 16 mm it follows that "$f = 1600$ pixel widths". Finally the "pixel width" can be used as uniform scale in all calculations.

Of course, only those points **P** can be located in 3D space that were projected into both images (according to the visibility) and for which the corresponding point pairs $\mathbf{p}_{left} = \left(x_{left}, y \right)$ and $\mathbf{p}_{right} = \left(x_{right}, y \right)$ were determined accurately. The latter is the *correspondence problem*, here specified for a special binocular image acquisition situation. Assume for example that a white sheet of paper is projected into the left and the right image. Then corresponding points can (possibly) be determined for the corner points of the sheet, but certainly not within the interior area of the sheet.

The following algorithm illustrates the general problem of calculating corresponding points. This is a special feature-based technique where the idea is to calculate edges at first as candidate locations for further correspondence analysis. We will assume the standard stereo geometry of the cameras. So we can restrict our search for corresponding points on searching in the same image row $y = y_{left} = y_{right}$. The disparities computed with this algorithm can then be used (as indicated above) for the calculation of XYZ-coordinates (assuming that focal length f and focal separation b are known).

1.4.2   Shirai Algorithm

A more elaborate discussion of the correspondence problem will follow later in Chapter 4. For the time being an algorithm (which is relatively easy to explain) shall be provided as a first solution that also can be used for the suggested student assignment project in Section 1.6 for the analysis of color stereo images. If the parameters f and b are available for the given image pairs then this allows even a certain reconstruction of visible surface points in the three-dimensional scene space.

(**Task 1.4**) Calculate corresponding image points and a disparity map for pairs of gray value stereo images. The standard stereo geometry is assumed for the given images, i.e. it is sufficient to restrict the search for a corresponding point on the identical row in the second image. Furthermore it is assumed that the search always starts at an edge pixel only (because only these pixels are a-priori assumed to be candidates for positive search results).

(**Solution 1.4**) W.l.o.g. we calculate the edge image for the left image, i.e. the search always starts with an initial point in the left image. For example, Algorithm 1.3 can be used for this step. Every edge pixel

for (every pixel $\left(\mathbf{p}, E_{left}(\mathbf{p})\right)$ of the left image E_{left}) **do**

    if $\left(\left(\mathbf{p}, E_{left}(\mathbf{p})\right)\right.$ is an edge pixel) **then begin**

        initialize the window parameter k and the search interval I;

        loop

        set the window size $n = 2k + 1$ and the new search interval I;

        calculate the similarity measure $SIMILARITY(\mathbf{p}, \mathbf{q})$

            for fixed pixel $\left(\mathbf{p}, E_{left}(\mathbf{p})\right)$ in the left image and

            for every pixel $\left(\mathbf{q}, E_{right}(\mathbf{q})\right)$ of the search interval;

                        { profile analysis }

        if (there is a unique minimum smaller than d_1) **then begin**

            set the disparity value for point $\mathbf{p}$ in the disparity map;

            exit the loop

            end {then}

        else if (all similarity values are larger than d_2) **then begin**

            a disparity assignment is not possible;

            exit the loop

            end {then}

        else if (the window already has maximum size) **then begin**

            a disparity assignment is not possible;

            exit the loop

            end {then}

                     { preparation of a next search run }

        else begin

            reduce the interval size using d_3;

            $k := k + 1$ { i.e. increase the window size }

            end {else}

        end {loop}

    end {if}

Figure 1.19: Shirai algorithm for a stereo pair E_{left} and E_{right} of scalar images (e.g. of a stereo gray value image pair, or of a stereo pair of related color channels of a stereo color image pair).

$$\left(\mathbf{p}, E_{left}(\mathbf{p})\right) = \left(\left(x_{left}, y\right), E_{left}\left(x_{left}, y\right)\right)$$

of the left image initializes a search process for a corresponding pixel

$$\left(\mathbf{q}, E_{right}(\mathbf{q})\right) = \left(\left(x_{right}, y\right), E_{right}\left(x_{right}, y\right)\right)$$

in the right image. For this it can generally be assumed that

$$x_{right} \leq x_{left}$$

(see Fig. 1.18). It is sufficient to search for a corresponding pixel with value x_{right} in the search interval $\left[1, x_{left}\right]$.

During the search a *similarity measure SIMILARITY*$(\mathbf{p}, \mathbf{q})$ is calculated for every pixel $\left(\mathbf{q}, E_{right}(\mathbf{q})\right)$ in the left image that is a possible candidate according to the search interval. The gray value patterns in certain image windows $\mathbf{F}\left(E_{left}, \mathbf{p}\right)$ respectively $\mathbf{F}\left(E_{right}, \mathbf{q}\right)$ of the left respectively the right image are compared with each other for determining this similarity measure. Y. Shirai (1989) suggested the following function *SIMILARITY*$(\mathbf{p}, \mathbf{q})$ for the similarity measure (This is actually a dissimilarity measure. But we will stay with the original name for historic reasons.).

In the left image a fixed image window $\mathbf{F}\left(E_{left}, \mathbf{p}\right)$ acts as a comparison matrix. During the search the image window $\mathbf{F}\left(E_{right}, \mathbf{q}\right)$ is compared at all possible positions of the search row y (according to the current search interval) with the fixed image window using the *square error*

$$SE(\mathbf{p}, \mathbf{q}) = \sum_{i=-k}^{k} \sum_{j=-k}^{k} \left(E_{left}\left(x_{left} + i, y + j\right) - E_{right}\left(x_{right} + i, y + j\right)\right)^2.$$

This comparison is normalized with respect to

$$VARIANCE(\mathbf{p}) = \frac{1}{(2k+1)\cdot(2k+1)} \sum_{i=-k}^{k} \sum_{j=-k}^{k} \left[E_{left}\left(x_{left} + i, y + j\right) - AVERAGE(\mathbf{p})\right]^2$$

$$= \frac{1}{(2k+1)\cdot(2k+1)} \sum_{i=-k}^{k} \sum_{j=-k}^{k} E_{left}\left(x_{left} + i, y + j\right)^2 - AVERAGE(\mathbf{p})^2$$

what is the (estimated) value of the variance of the fixed image window in the left image. Here the value $AVERAGE(\mathbf{p})$ denotes the arithmetic mean of the image window $\mathbf{F}\left(E_{left}, \mathbf{p}\right)$ and, as a consequence, an estimate of the expected value of the gray value variable in this image window. Finally, Shirai's similarity measure is defined as

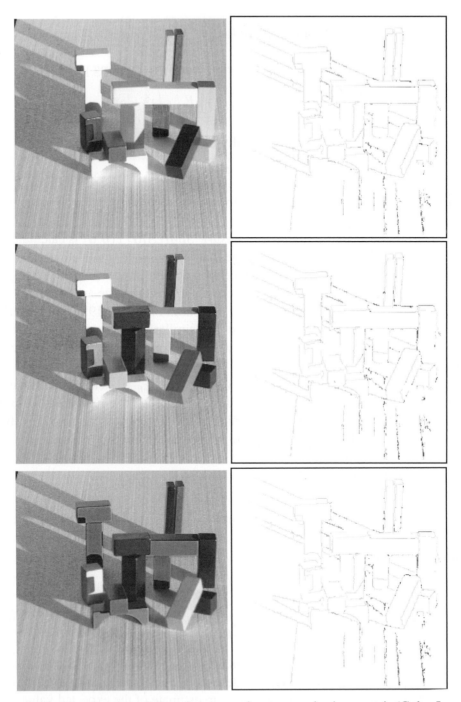

Figure 1.20: Visualization of disparity maps of a stereo color image pair (Color Image 2 in the Appendix). Above: blue channel, middle: green channel, below: red channel. The parameters $d_1 = 25$, $d_2 = 50$, $d_3 = 75$, $k_{min} = 1$ and $k_{max} = 9$ were used.

$$SIMILARITY(\mathbf{p,q}) = \frac{SE(\mathbf{p,q})}{VARIANCE(\mathbf{p})+1} .$$

If both windows are identical then the square error is zero, i.e. this function takes value zero. Otherwise the function values are always positive.

(**Algorithm 1.4**) Figure 1.19 shows a certain informal sketch of the algorithm. At the beginning of the search the window parameter k is initialized with value k_{min}, and the search interval I is initialized with value $[k, x_{left}]$.

The algorithm determines that point $\mathbf{q}$ in the right image as a corresponding image point where the similarity measure takes a global minimum within the search interval, and this global minimum must be smaller or equal to an a-priori specified threshold d_1. If such a global minimum $\leq d_1$ does not exist within the search interval then it has to be decided,

at first - whether to continue the search: If all of the values $SIMILARITY(\mathbf{p,q})$ are greater or equal to an a-priori specified threshold $d_2 > d_1$, then the search is abandoned and the next edge pixel $(\mathbf{p}, E_{left}(\mathbf{p}))$ is selected in the left image (on an edge) for the initialization of a further search process.

at second - how to modify the search process if it is continued: For the continuation of the search the search interval is examined for a possible reduction where all points $\mathbf{q}$ are excluded for future comparisons for which it holds $SIMILARITY(\mathbf{p,q}) \geq d_3$, and d_3 is an a-priori specified threshold $\geq d_2$. To simplify this interval reduction, the interval is only reduced at both ends.

A larger window $\mathbf{F} = \{(i,j): \ -k \leq i, j \leq k \}$ of size $(2k+1) \times (2k+1)$ is chosen with the intention to ensure a more accurate calculation of the similarity measure, as long as $k \leq k_{max}$ holds.

(**Comment 1.4**) A program implementing this method can be inefficient with respect to computing time. It is important to think carefully about efficient programming (e.g. selection of the edge operator, application of a-priori knowledge to limit the initial search intervals).

Figure 1.20 represents resulting disparity maps (note: defined values exist only at edge positions) for the stereo pair of color image 2 in the Appendix. An *optimal difference recursive filter*[14] was used as edge operator. The disparities are gray value encoded: the darker it is the larger the disparity value, i.e. the closer the surface point to the camera). On the left a scalar image of a separate color channel (of the left image of the stereo pair) is represented, and on the right the encoded disparity map is shown as calculated for this channel.

---

[14] J. Shen, S. Castan: Further results on DRF method for edge detection. in: Proceedings 9th IAPR conf., Rome, 1988.

The results repeat themselves relatively stable in the individual color channels. However this can generally not be expected for stereo color images.

1.5   REFERENCES

The following books are generally recommended as introductory readings for the field of computer vision:

Marr, D.: *Vision - A Computational Investigation into the Human Representation and Processing of Visual Information.* W. H. Freeman & Co., San Francisco, 1982,

Overington, I.: *Computer Vision - A Unified, Biologically-Inspired Approach.* Elsevier, Amsterdam, 1992 and

Watt, R.: *Visual Processing - Computational, Psychophysical and Cognitive Research.* Lawrence Erlbaum, Hove, 1988.

The book also incorporates recent research results of the authors as reported in

Klette, R., Koschan, A., Schlüns, K., Rodehorst, V.: *Surface reconstruction based on visual information*, TR 95/6, July 1995, Perth, The University of Western Australia, Computer Science,

Klette, R., Koschan, A., Schlüns, K., Rodehorst, V.: *Evaluation of surface reconstruction methods,* Proceed. Image and Vision Conference of New Zealand, keynote, IVCNZ'95, Christchurch, August 1995, pp. 3 - 12, and

R. Klette: *Progress in surface capturing and analysis - towards integration into IT applications.* Proceed. Image and Vision Conference of Australia and New Zealand, plenary talk, DICTA/IVCNZ'97, Albany, December 1997, pp. 219 - 227.

This textbook follows in notation and algorithm representation the style as specified in

Klette, R., Zamperoni, P.: *Handbook of Image Processing Operators.* Wiley & Sons, Chichester, 1996.

The cited handbook offers a variety of edge detection techniques and deals with image transformations in general, also for multi-channel images.

Furthermore for the fields of *image processing*, *pattern analysis*, or *scene analysis* the reader is referred to the text books (just to cite a few)

Gonzalez, R.C., Woods, R. E.: *Digital Image Processing*, 3rd ed., Addison-Wesley, Reading, 1992,

Haberäcker, P.: *Digitale Bildverarbeitung*, 4. Auflage. Carl Hanser Verlag, Munich, 1991,

Haralick, R.M., Shapiro, L. G.: *Computer and Robot Vision*, Volumes I, II. Addison-Wesley, Reading, 1992 (vol. I) / 1993 (vol. II),

Horn, B. K. P.: *Robot Vision*. The MIT Press, Cambridge, Massachusetts, 1986 and 1992,

Jain, A. K.: *Fundamentals of Digital Image Processing*. Prentice Hall, Englewood Cliffs, 1990,

Pitas, I.: *Digital Image Processing Algorithms*. Prentice Hall, Hertfordshire, 1993,

Radig, B. (Hrsg.): *Verarbeiten und Verstehen von Bildern*. Oldenbourg, Munich, 1993,

Rosenfeld, A., Kak, A. C.: *Digital Picture Processing*, Vol. I and Vol. II. Academic Press, New York, 1982,

Shirai, Y.: *Three-dimensional Computer Vision*, Springer, Berlin, 1987,

Sonka, M., Hlavac, V., Boyle, R.: *Image Processing, Analysis and Machine Vision*. Chapman & Hall, London, 1993,

Voss, K., Süsse, H.: *Praktische Bildverarbeitung*. Carl Hanser Verlag, Munich, 1991,

Wahl, F. M.: *Digital Image Processing*, Artech House, Norwood, 1987 and

Zamperoni, P.: *Methoden der digitalen Bildsignalverarbeitung*, 2. Edition Vieweg, Braunschweig, 1991.

This list represents only a small selection of the available literature. The books of B. K. P. Horn and Y. Shirai are particularly recommended for additional reading in conjunction with this textbook.

For further reading about color image models that were specially dealt with in this introductory chapter the reader is, for example, referred to

Pratt, W. K.: *Digital Image Processing*, 2nd ed., John Wiley & Sons, New York, 1991.

Algorithms for the conversion of color image models can also be found in computer graphic textbooks (see a few references in Section 3.5). The discrete and continuous geometry of scene objects (modeling of object surfaces, digital geometry in 3D, approximations of surfaces, topology of 3D objects etc.) is dealt with in

Klette, R., Rosenfeld, A., Sloboda, F. (eds.): *Advances in Digital and Computational Geometry*. Springer, Singapore, 1998.

See also Chapter 3 for a more detailed discussion of surfaces or the geometry of scene objects.

1.6   EXERCISES

(1) Consider the pure colors Red and Yellow (colors at corner points of the RGB color cube). What are the values *SATURATION*, *HUE* and *INTENSITY* for these two colors?

(2) Assume a "modified LoG filter kernel" restricted to the smaller size $w \times w$ instead of the $3w \times 3w$ filter kernel of the discussed LoG operator. What influence does this have on the calculated transformed image?

(3) Assume two cameras in the standard stereo geometry arrangement. Let the focal separation be $b = 5$ cm, let the focal length be $f = 16$ mm, let the horizontal and the vertical pixel width be uniformly $\mu = 17\ \mu m$. Assume two scene points $\mathbf{P}_1$ and $\mathbf{P}_2$ for which correctly determined corresponding image point pairs are given,

$$\left(x_{1,left}, y_{1,left} \right) = (80, 30) \text{ and } \left(x_{1,right}, y_{1,right} \right) = (30, 30), \text{ and}$$
$$\left(x_{2,left}, y_{2,left} \right) = (81, 30) \text{ and } \left(x_{2,right}, y_{2,right} \right) = (30, 30).$$

What are the Euclidean distances between these points $\mathbf{P}_1$ and $\mathbf{P}_2$ and the focal point of the left camera? What are the differences ΔX, ΔY and ΔZ of these two points in the three-dimensional space of the scene objects ?

Outline the related depth values (i.e. the distances to the focal point of the left camera) for varying integer disparity values in the interval $[20, 80]$ for the specified parameters.

(4) Consider a modification of the standard stereo geometry: Derive formulas for the calculation of 3D coordinates (X, Y, Z) utilizing disparity values under the assumption that the two cameras have different focal lengths f_1 and f_2.

(5 - Assignment) Implement and apply the Shirai algorithm as described in Section 1.4.2 for the analysis of binocular stereo *RGB* color images. Visualize and discuss the calculated disparity maps.

Hints: First of all the following procedure is repeated identically for all three *RGB* color channels. Consider the left and the right image of a selected color channel as input data for the Shirai algorithm. Implement a decision criterion for pixels in the left image whether they are edge pixels or not, e.g. based on the LoG operator as discussed in Section 1.3.2, or based on another already available edge operator. Calculate all of the defined scalar disparity values using the Shirai algorithm for scalar images. These integer values are written into a disparity map, i.e. into an array of the size $M\_image \times N\_image$.

Note that this correspondence analysis technique can be very time consuming if possible run-time optimizations are not considered.

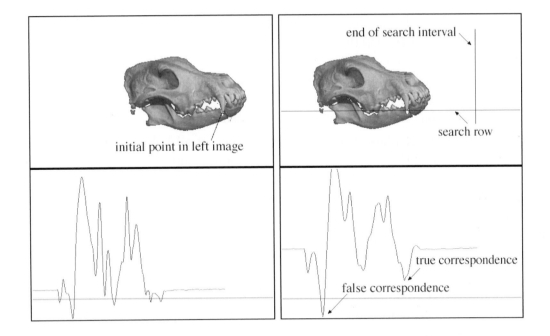

Figure 1.21: Above: Stereo gray value image pair illustrating a selected initial point in the left image, and the corresponding search row and the right end of the search interval in the right image. Below: Graphs of two similarity functions $SIMILARITY(\mathbf{p}, \mathbf{q})$ for a small (left) and a larger (right) search window. Below the shown threshold d_1 there exist several local minima on the left, and exactly one local minimum on the right (however at a false position).

A function for displaying the graph of the function $SIMILARITY(\mathbf{p}, \mathbf{q})$ is suggested for the interactive specification of a-priori values d_1, d_2, d_3, where $\mathbf{q}$ varies in the search interval I (see Fig. 1.21, here a local minimum in the window below, on the right, indicates the true correspondence, i.e. at the correct position. However, the global minimum specifies a false correspondence. This misbehavior might be solved by starting with a larger window parameter k_{min}.

Finally the disparity maps that were generated for the three different color channels must be unified into a single resulting disparity map. Different approaches may be considered for this unification process, e.g. the mean of the (maximally three) defined disparity values for all positions for which a disparity was found in at least one of the color channel.

Visualize the resulting disparity maps (for example, color encoded) and discuss these results with respect to accuracy, diversity, and density of defined values in the disparity maps.

(6) As possible extension of the assignment (5) a comparison can be carried out of the obtained disparity map (unified for three color channels) with results of modified approaches:

(a) Calculate a disparity map just based on scalar (i.e. single channel) image data, e.g. only use the *INTENSITY* channels of both images for a disparity map calculation. Thus the input data are reduced to one third.

(b) Instead of calculating separate edge images in all color channels (what makes the disparity unification process even more complicated) now calculate only a single edge image (this can be calculated for the *INTENSITY* channel), and use this uniformly for all three *RGB* color channels.

(c) Use the three channels of the *HSI* color model instead of the *RGB* color model.

Compare the obtained disparity values that were computed with two different approaches. For example: Can you verify quantitatively that the disparity analysis has improved if complete color information is used instead of just scalar image data? The true disparity values (the "ground truth") are hardly available for real-world stereo image pairs. Comparative verifications may be the way to go.

2   IMAGE ACQUISITION

The generation of digital images is normally the first step in a chain of image processing tasks. Subsequent processing and analysis of the images can incorporate physical and geometrical parameters characterizing the capture of the image data. First of all, the resulting function values of the digital image function depend on the material and reflection characteristics of the object surfaces in the recorded scene. Secondly, the resulting image function is also directly influenced by the sensor characteristics of the camera, the optical characteristics of the lens, the digital scanning of the analog image signal, the characteristics of the light source, and last but not least the geometric laws which the image acquisition process is subject to.

This chapter explains the latter influence factors. The main points here are camera geometry and sensor characteristics. The exact knowledge of the camera geometry is needed, for example, for the surface reconstruction using static or dynamic stereo analysis (Chapters 4 and 5) and for techniques using structured lighting (Chapter 9). The knowledge of the photometric (and for the use of a color camera also of the colorimetric) characteristics of the camera sensor is of great significance for the measurement and description of the surface reflection (Chapter 6) as well as for the surface reconstruction through photometric stereo analysis (Chapter 8) or for a "shape from shading" technique (Chapter 7). This chapter introduces techniques for the determination of these parameters that are relevant within the process of image generation.

2.1   GEOMETRIC CAMERA MODEL

The projection of an object surface point of a three-dimensional scene into the two-dimensional image plane can essentially be described as either central (i.e. perspective) or parallel projection. The projective relationship between the concerned coordinate systems (world coordinates, camera coordinates, ideal image coordinates etc.) is of importance for techniques for object surface reconstructions. This section briefly introduces the mathematical (idealized) projection

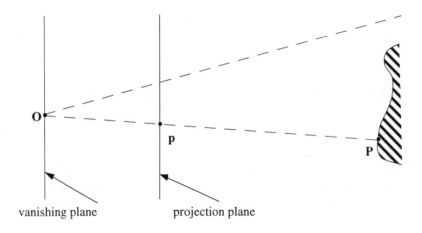

vanishing plane   projection plane

Figure 2.1: Central projection of a point **P** onto a point **p**.

models first. Then two variants of camera modeling and one related calibration technique for each of them are given to be able to determine the parameters of each camera model. The first technique is methodically easier but generally also less accurate.

2.1.1   Central and Parallel Projection

The *central projection* (also called *perspective projection*) and the *(orthogonal) parallel projection* (also called *orthographic projection*) are idealized models of the projection of scenes s onto images E. These two models are used throughout this textbook.

Section 1.1.2 discussed a general projection $E = A(s)$ into the image plane for scenes s. This projection was specified further by Section 1.4.1 where a pinhole camera with camera constant f was assumed (see Fig. 1.16).

For the assumed (ideal) pinhole camera the projection of scene points $P = (X, Y, Z)$ of the XYZ-space onto image points $p = (x, y)$ of the xy-image plane is a central or perspective projection. If the coordinate system of the XYZ-space is defined to be the *camera-centered coordinate system* (focal point = projection center, optical axis = Z-axis) then the projection equations are given by

$$x = \frac{f \cdot X}{Z} \quad \text{and} \quad y = \frac{f \cdot Y}{Z} .$$

These equations can be derived directly from the ray theorem of geometry.

If the origin of the coordinate system is positioned in the image plane (*image-centered coordinate system*), then the projection equations are given accordingly by

$$x = \frac{f \cdot X}{f + Z} \quad \text{and} \quad y = \frac{f \cdot Y}{f + Z} .$$

For a central projection, a *projection center* and a *projection plane* have to be specified (see Fig. 2.1). The points $\mathbf{P} = (X, Y, Z)$ of $\mathfrak{R}^3$ are projected onto points $\mathbf{p}$ in the *xy*-projection plane. Points $\mathbf{P}$ of the *vanishing plane* (the plane incident with the projection center, and parallel to the projection plane, see Fig. 2.1) would be projected onto points at infinity in the projection plane.

Homogeneous coordinates are suitable for a general simple treatment of the central projection, although these may look a bit excessive at this point in the textbook. For the sake of completeness projective or homogeneous coordinates are mentioned here briefly. Actually the formally simpler model of inhomogeneous *XYZ*-coordinates can be used to a large extent for the tasks of image analysis as discussed in this textbook because for the scene points it can always be assumed that $Z > f$.

The real space $\mathfrak{R}^3$ respectively the *XYZ*-space is described by homogeneous coordinates as the *projective space* $\mathbf{P}^3$. The homogeneous coordinates

$$(t, u, v, w)$$

of *projective points* in this projective space have to be interpreted as follows:

Case $w \neq 0$: The projective point (t, u, v, w) is identified by the point

$$(X, Y, Z) = (t/w, u/w, v/w)$$

of the *XYZ*-space. The values $X = t/w$, $Y = u/w$, and $Z = v/w$ are the inhomogeneous coordinates of the projective point (t, u, v, w).

Case $w = 0$: A projective point $(t, u, v, 0)$ is identified by a *point at infinity* of the *XYZ* space. The set of points $(t, u, v, 0)$ of the projective space forms the *plane at infinity* with the plane equation $w = 0$.

If a point of the *XYZ* space has to be given in projective coordinates then any value $w \neq 0$ can be chosen in principle. A plane

$$Z = pX + qY + r ,$$

for example, has the projection

$$v = pt + qu + rw$$

in homogeneous coordinates. For $w = 0$ we receive the plane at infinity of $\mathbf{P}^3$.

The projective transformations of $\mathbf{P}^3$ in the $\mathbf{P}^3$ are all linear transformations (also called *collineations*)

$$\left(t',u',v',w'\right)^T = \mathbf{A} \cdot \left(t,u,v,w\right)^T,$$

where $\mathbf{A}$ is a non-singular[1] 4×4 matrix of real numbers. The most important advantage of projective or homogeneous coordinates is that the projective transformations can be described uniformly by such 4×4 matrices. In this textbook, however, only two special transformations are of interest of the projective space $\mathbf{P}^3$ into the projective space $\mathbf{P}^2$:

(i) The above mentioned (camera centered) central projection of the space $\Re^3$ of the scenes into the image plane $\Re^2$ is such a special projective transformation. Assume that the camera constant f is the distance between the projection plane and the vanishing plane. Then a scene point

$$(X,Y,Z) = (t/w, u/w, v/w)$$

is projected into the image point (x,y,f) according to the general homogeneous central projection equation

$$\left(t',u',v',w'\right)^T = \begin{pmatrix} 1 & 0 & 0 & 0 \\ 0 & 1 & 0 & 0 \\ 0 & 0 & 1 & 0 \\ 0 & 0 & \frac{1}{f} & 0 \end{pmatrix} \cdot \left(t,u,v,w\right)^T$$

with

$$x = \frac{t'}{w'} = \frac{t}{v/f} = \frac{f \cdot X}{Z}, \quad y = \frac{u'}{w'} = \frac{u}{v/f} = \frac{f \cdot Y}{Z}, \quad \frac{v'}{w'} = \frac{v}{v/f} = f.$$

For this central projection of $\Re^3$ into the image plane $\Re^2$ the origin $(0,0,0)$ of $\Re^3$ was assumed to be the projection center (see Fig. 1.16). The image centered projection model is the subject of Exercise (1) in Section 2.8.

The general homogeneous central projection equation, i.e. a model of transformations of $\mathbf{P}^3$ into $\mathbf{P}^3$, can be simplified because often only projections $\mathbf{P}^3$ into $\mathbf{P}^2$ are of interest. The resulting, more specialized projection equation

$$\left(t',u',w'\right)^T = \begin{pmatrix} f & 0 & 0 & 0 \\ 0 & f & 0 & 0 \\ 0 & 0 & 1 & 0 \end{pmatrix} \cdot (X,Y,Z,w)^T$$

---

[1] i.e. the determinant is not zero respectively the inverse exists.

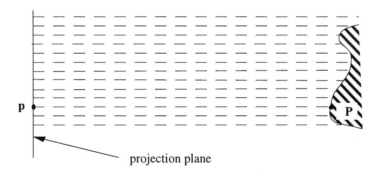

Figure 2.2: Orthogonal parallel projection (orthographic projection) of a point **P** onto a point **p**.

leads again to

$$x = \frac{t'}{w'} = \frac{f \cdot X}{Z}, \quad y = \frac{u'}{w'} = \frac{f \cdot Y}{Z}.$$

This **P**³ into **P**² projection model is normally used in the calibration literature.

(ii) Often it is appropriate to use an (orthogonal) parallel projection (also called orthographic projection) as an approximation of the realized scene projection. For the parallel projection every point $\mathbf{P} = (X, Y, Z)$ of $\Re^3$ is projected unambiguously onto a point $\mathbf{p} = (x, y)$ of the image plane (projection plane), with the projection equations

$$x = X \text{ and } y = Y.$$

Here, the projection center turned into a point at infinity (see Fig. 2.2). For the corresponding general parallel projection equation

$$(t', u', v', w')^T = \begin{pmatrix} 1 & 0 & 0 & 0 \\ 0 & 1 & 0 & 0 \\ 0 & 0 & 0 & f \\ 0 & 0 & 0 & 1 \end{pmatrix} \cdot (t, u, v, w)^T$$

in homogeneous coordinates a scene point

$$(X, Y, Z) = (t/w, u/w, v/w)$$

is projected into the image point (x, y, f), with

$$x = \frac{t'}{w'} = \frac{t}{w} = X, \quad y = \frac{u'}{w'} = \frac{u}{w} = Y, \quad \frac{v'}{w'} = \frac{f \cdot w}{w} = f \ .$$

In fact only the projection $\mathbf{P}^3$ into $\mathbf{P}^2$ is normally of interest, and the more specialized homogeneous parallel projection equation

$$(t', u', w')^T = \begin{pmatrix} 1 & 0 & 0 & 0 \\ 0 & 1 & 0 & 0 \\ 0 & 0 & 0 & 1 \end{pmatrix} \cdot (t, u, v, w)^T$$

leads again to

$$x = \frac{t'}{w'} = \frac{t}{w} = X, \quad y = \frac{u'}{w'} = \frac{u}{w} = Y.$$

The assumption of a parallel projection is especially relevant when the projected scene objects are close to the camera but very small compared to the camera constant (e.g. microscopic structures), when the scene objects are relatively far away from the camera or when telephoto lenses (with large focal length) are used. Another motivation can also be that all scene objects lie approximately in one plane $Z = const$ for the use of the parallel projection model.

In both mentioned general 4×4 homogeneous projection equations the matrices are singular. This is a mathematical characterization of the fact that neither the central nor the (orthogonal) parallel projection of $\mathbf{P}^3$ into $\mathbf{P}^2$ are unambiguously inversible.

2.1.2   A Camera Model for Central Projection

In the following the XYZ-coordinate system that is adjusted with the camera is called a *camera coordinate system* and is labeled by an index k. In addition to this $X_k Y_k Z_k$ camera coordinate system a $X_w Y_w Z_w$ *world coordinate system* is assumed which is adjusted with a selected object (like a so-called *calibration object*) that is positioned in the three-dimensional space of the scenes.

The *camera constant* [2] (also called *effective focal length*) describes the orthogonal distance between the center of the camera lens and the image plane (compare Fig. 1.5: this figure depicts actually the camera constant). We denote the camera constant by f_k instead of f in distinction to the focal length of the lens. Up to now the pinhole camera model (note: a lens was not assumed for this simple model) was used for camera modeling. Another (but still approximate because inaccurate) description of a camera is given by the following *optical-lens camera model*. Here the optical system consists of an ideal lens with focal length f instead

---

[2] A common term in photogrammetry.

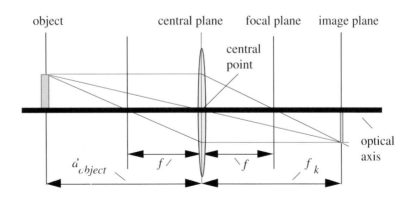

Figure 2.3: Object point and image plane for a thin lens.[3]

of a pinhole diaphragm. The focal length of the lens is defined as the distance of the central point of the (thin) lens to its focal point (see Fig. 2.3). An *ideal lens* is defined as a lens without any projection error.

Geometrically both camera models, pinhole model and optical-lens model, have about the same characteristics. In both cases we may consider the central projection, that was discussed in Section 2.1.1, as a model for the projection of real scene points **P** into the image plane of the camera.

A difference between the two models is that a lens only projects those scene points sharply (focused) into the image plane which are located on a specific plane which is in a defined distance to the camera. The distance of this plane from the camera (exactly: from the center point of the lens along the Z_k coordinate of the camera coordinate system) is called the *object width*. In physical optics the distance between the center point of the lens and the image plane is called the *image width* and corresponds to the (photogrammetric) term of a camera constant. The connection between the image width respectively the camera constant f_k, the focal length f of the lens, and the object width d_{object} is given by the famous *Gaussian lens formula* (see Fig. 2.3). It holds that

$$\frac{1}{f} = \frac{1}{f_k} + \frac{1}{d_{object}} .$$

If an object point is projected into infinity, then $d_{object} = \infty$ and therefore $f = f_k$, i.e. in this case the focal length of the lens is equal to the camera constant. In all

---

[3] Elaborate explanations of geometric optics can, for instance, be found in E. Hecht: *Optics*, 2nd ed., Addison-Wesley, Reading, 1990, or in P. Mouroulis, and J. MacDonald: *Geometrical Optics and Optical Design*, Oxford Univ Press, 1996.

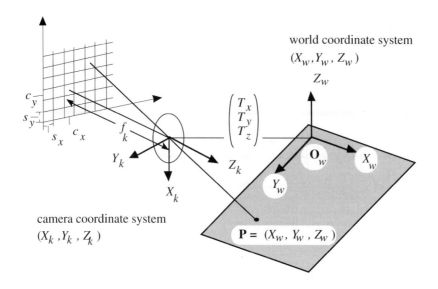

Figure 2.4: World coordinates, camera coordinates, and image coordinates.

other cases the focal length and the camera constant differ slightly. For instance, if a camera with a lens with a fixed focal length of $f = 50$ mm is adjusted such that a scene point 2 m away from the camera is projected sharply into the image plane, then, according to the Gaussian lens formula, it holds that

$$\frac{1}{50} = \frac{1}{f_k} + \frac{1}{2000} \text{ , i.e. } f_k = \frac{2000}{39} \approx 51.28.$$

The camera constant is 1.28 mm larger than the focal length in this example. In general the focal length of the lens can be used as a rough estimate of the camera constant. Nevertheless in many applications, such as accurate distance measurement in close range, the camera constant has to be determined separately for every focus adjustment of the camera using a certain calibration technique.

In the following the term (effective) *focal length* is uniformly used (for consistency reasons with the literature) in projective camera models for characterizing the distance between projection center and image plane although the term *camera constant* would be more accurate.

Figure 2.4 outlines the general image acquisition situation as it is assumed in the following discussion. Here the image plane is (as opposed to Fig. 1.16) assumed to be behind the $X_k Y_k$ plane in a distance of f_k. World coordinates and camera coordinates can be transformed into each other through a simple Euclidean transformation (namely translation followed by rotation). Figure 2.4 also shows the translation vector.

Let x_b and y_b be the coordinates of pixels in the digital image buffer where these pixels may be considered to be the final result of an image acquisition process. Altogether, object points $\mathbf{P} = (X_w, Y_w, Z_w)$ in world coordinates are projected into digital image points $\mathbf{p} = (x_b, y_b)$ specifying row and column indices in the digital image buffer (or in the frame grabber, or in the image memory etc.) during image acquisition. This mapping can be split into several coordinate transforms and mappings (see below), and is described by the following linear transformation

$$\begin{pmatrix} x_b - c_x \\ y_b - c_y \\ -f_k \end{pmatrix} = \begin{pmatrix} r_1 & r_2 & r_3 \\ r_4 & r_5 & r_6 \\ r_7 & r_8 & r_9 \end{pmatrix} \cdot \begin{pmatrix} X_w - X_0 \\ Y_w - Y_0 \\ Z_w - Z_0 \end{pmatrix}. \tag{2.1}$$

In this equation

(x_b, y_b) denotes the (digital) image buffer coordinates of the projected points (X_w, Y_w, Z_w),

(c_x, c_y) are the coordinates of the principal point (i.e. the intersection point of the optical axis with the image plane) according to the image coordinate system,

f_k is the distance between the lens center and the image plane (effective focal length),

r_i are the coefficients of the rotation matrix $\mathbf{R} = \mathbf{R}_x \cdot \mathbf{R}_y \cdot \mathbf{R}_z$ of the Euclidean transformation (world into camera coordinates),

(X_w, Y_w, Z_w) are the world coordinates of the projected scene point, and

(X_0, Y_0, Z_0) are the coordinates of the projection center in world coordinates.

The transformation of a point parametrization (X_w, Y_w, Z_w) in world coordinates into a point parametrization (X_k, Y_k, Z_k) in camera-centered coordinates is described by a rotation $\mathbf{R}$ and a preceding translation $\mathbf{T}$,

$$\begin{pmatrix} X_k \\ Y_k \\ Z_k \end{pmatrix} = \mathbf{R} \cdot (\begin{pmatrix} X_w \\ Y_w \\ Z_w \end{pmatrix} + \mathbf{T}) , \text{ with } \mathbf{T} = \begin{pmatrix} T_x \\ T_y \\ T_z \end{pmatrix} = \begin{pmatrix} -X_0 \\ -Y_0 \\ -Z_0 \end{pmatrix}.$$

Here $\mathbf{T}$ denotes the 3D translation vector and $\mathbf{R}$ denotes the 3D rotation matrix. The matrix $\mathbf{R}$ represents three partial transformations $\mathbf{R}_x$, $\mathbf{R}_y$ and $\mathbf{R}_z$ with

$$R = R_x \cdot R_y \cdot R_z = \begin{pmatrix} r_1 & r_2 & r_3 \\ r_4 & r_5 & r_6 \\ r_7 & r_8 & r_9 \end{pmatrix} .$$

The matrix R_x describes a rotation about the X_k axis by a certain angle α (*pan angle*). It holds that

$$R_x(\alpha) = \begin{pmatrix} 1 & 0 & 0 \\ 0 & cos(\alpha) & sin(\alpha) \\ 0 & -sin(\alpha) & cos(\alpha) \end{pmatrix}.$$

The matrix R_y describes a rotation about the Y_k axis by a certain angle β (*tilt angle*). It holds

$$R_y(\beta) = \begin{pmatrix} cos(\beta) & 0 & -sin(\beta) \\ 0 & 1 & 0 \\ sin(\beta) & 0 & cos(\beta) \end{pmatrix}.$$

The matrix R_z describes a rotation about the Z_k axis by a certain angle γ (*roll angle*). Here it holds that

$$R_z(\gamma) = \begin{pmatrix} cos(\gamma) & sin(\gamma) & 0 \\ -sin(\gamma) & cos(\gamma) & 0 \\ 0 & 0 & 1 \end{pmatrix}.$$

For an unambiguous definition of such a transformation of a Cartesian coordinate system into another we specify that a 3D rotation about the origin is carried out after the 3D translation. In calibration situations the parameters for the matrix R and the vector T have to be determined to solve the first calibration problem - how are world and camera coordinates related to each other? The parameters of this Euclidean transform define the *extrinsic parameters* of the camera.

Furthermore, the *intrinsic parameters* of the camera determine the projective behavior of the camera. These parameters are, e.g., the principal point, and the camera constant (the effective focal length) in equation (2.1). The *principal point* is defined as the intersection point of the optical axis and the image plane. The principal point is not identical with the *image center* which is the origin in the image plane. The accuracy of a camera may be evaluated by the (normally small) distance between principal point and the translated image center (translated by an ideal vector as, e.g., half of the image size in both directions).

2.1.3 Calibration by Direct Linear Transformation

A direct measurement of the extrinsic parameters, and of the intrinsic parameters of a given and positioned camera in 3D scene space is usually technically impossible or not feasible (in general, the development of required physical measurement devices seems be to impossible). For that reason the parameters are calculated indirectly in practice using a suitable *calibration technique*. The aim is to achieve the best possible correspondence between the used camera model (parameterized by the observed or calculated parameters) and the realized image acquisition with the given camera.

A calibration technique is based on known space coordinates (e.g. in the world coordinate system) of geometrically configured points (*calibration points*) which are physically realized by marks (*calibration marks*) on a certain *calibration object*. A calibration technique takes the resulting locations (as a result of image acquisition: taking pictures of the calibration object) of such calibration marks on the image plane as input data.

See Fig. 2.5 for some examples of calibration marks (as suggested in the photogrammetry literature). Under specific conditions the automated calculation of locations of calibration marks can be a solvable task in digital image analysis, e.g. assuming that lighting conditions, and coloring of the faces of the calibration object and the coloring of the marks on these faces supports easy detection of projected marks as "blobs" in the digital image. The marks may be filled circles (first mark on the left in Fig. 2.5), and sub-pixel accurate localizations of the projected calibration points (midpoints of the marks) can be found based on calculating centroids (e.g., use of weighted moments) of these "blobs" in the digital image.

For an example of a calibration object ("open cube") see Fig. 2.6. Calibration objects are commercially available.

For an accurate determination of the calibration parameters it is of benefit that the calibration marks are evenly spread within the scene and the taken digital image as good as possible. Figure 2.6 shows such a situation. Therefore the size of the calibration object has to be in a certain relation to the working range of the camera. For example, if the aim of the image processing task consists in the measurement and the analysis of objects within a distance of about 2 or 3 meters

Figure 2.5: Examples of calibration marks for camera calibration.

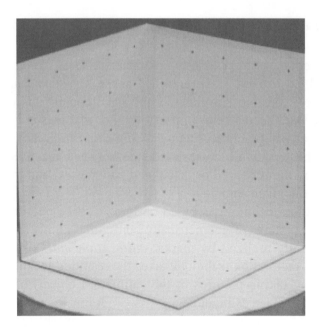

Figure 2.6: Example of a calibration object ("open cube") with three planar configurations of 25 points in each of these planes. [4]

to the camera then such a calibration object has to be chosen that it is projected onto the whole digital image from this distance to the camera.

The use of a *Direct Linear Transformation* (DLT) is one possibility of specifying a calibration technique. This method was suggested by Y.I. Abdel-Aziz and H.M. Karara (1971). It has the advantage that almost only linear equations have to be solved.

First, we take a picture of the calibration object, i.e. of the marks of the geometrically configured calibration points. The geometric configuration of these calibration points has to be known. Next, the device dependent row and column positions (x_b, y_b) (if possible, in sub-pixel accuracy) are determined for every calibration point having a visible projected mark in the image. This may be done interactively or based on an automated image analysis solution. Note that an automatic determination of these point positions in the image also requires to specify a one-to-one mapping between the different detected positions of calibration points in the image, and a subset of calibration points in the known geometric configuration on the surface of the calibration object.

---

[4] Notice: Figure 2.6 is an example for a visual concave-convex conflict (compare Section 8.1.1). The human visual system is generally not able to deal with this ambiguity. In fact, the image shows the (concave) interior view of three sides of a cube from slantly above.

From the vector equation (2.1) we obtain the following linear equations for $x_b - c_x$ and for $y_b - c_y$:

$$x_b - c_x = -f_k \cdot \frac{r_1(X_w - X_0) + r_2(Y_w - Y_0) + r_3(Z_w - Z_0)}{r_7(X_w - X_0) + r_8(Y_w - Y_0) + r_9(Z_w - Z_0)} \text{ and} \qquad (2.2)$$

$$y_b - c_y = -f_k \cdot \frac{r_4(X_w - X_0) + r_5(Y_w - Y_0) + r_6(Z_w - Z_0)}{r_7(X_w - X_0) + r_8(Y_w - Y_0) + r_9(Z_w - Z_0)} \cdot \qquad (2.3)$$

These equations (2.2) and (2.3) can be rewritten in the form

$$\begin{pmatrix} X_w & Y_w & Z_w & 1 & 0 & 0 & 0 & 0 & x_b X_w & x_b Y_w & x_b Z_w \\ 0 & 0 & 0 & 0 & X_w & Y_w & Z_w & 1 & y_b X_w & y_b Y_w & y_b Z_w \end{pmatrix} \cdot \begin{pmatrix} L_1 \\ L_2 \\ \vdots \\ L_{11} \end{pmatrix} = \begin{pmatrix} X_w \\ Y_w \end{pmatrix} \cdot$$

For a mathematically unambiguous solution at least six calibration points (X_w, Y_w, Z_w) and the corresponding image coordinates of the centers of their projected calibration marks are required to solve this system with respect to the eleven unknown transformation parameters $L_1, \ldots, L_{11}$. In the case of six points we have twelve linear equations. In general (six points or more) this leads to an over-determined system of linear equations. Also with respect of stability of the calculated solution more points are required, typically at least 100 points.

The pseudo-inverse matrix of such an over-determined system of linear equations (*Moore-Penrose-inverse*, see W.H. Press et al (1992) in Section 2.4) allows to calculate the eleven transformation parameters $L_1, \ldots, L_{11}$.

These transformation parameters "contain" the intrinsic and extrinsic parameters. The principal point is determined by

$$c_x = \frac{L_1 \cdot L_9 + L_2 \cdot L_{10} + L_3 \cdot L_{11}}{L_9^2 + L_{10}^2 + L_{11}^2}$$

and

$$c_y = \frac{L_5 \cdot L_9 + L_6 \cdot L_{10} + L_7 \cdot L_{11}}{L_9^2 + L_{10}^2 + L_{11}^2} \cdot$$

The effective focal length f_k can be calculated with respect to its components

$$f_{kx}^2 = -c_x^2 + \frac{L_1^2 + L_2^2 + L_3^2}{\left(L_9^2 + L_{10}^2 + L_{11}^2\right)^2},$$

and

$$f_{ky}^2 = -c_y^2 + \frac{L_5^2 + L_6^2 + L_7^2}{\left(L_9^2 + L_{10}^2 + L_{11}^2\right)^2} \ ,$$

with respect to both axes of the image coordinate system, respectively. It holds

$$f_k = (f_{kx} + f_{ky})/2.$$

The extrinsic camera parameters can also be determined from $L_1, ..., L_{11}$. The calculation of the angles in the transformation matrices $\mathbf{R}_x$, $\mathbf{R}_y$ and $\mathbf{R}_z$ is possible in two steps. In the first step, the unknown coefficients in the general rotation matrix $\mathbf{R} = (r_i)$, $i = 1, ..., 9$, are calculated based on the equations for $L_1 - L_3$, $L_5 - L_7$, and $L_9 - L_{11}$. In the second step, the individual angles for slant, tilt, and roll can be determined from the values of the coefficients r_i of this matrix $\mathbf{R}$.

Next, the coordinates of the projection center (X_0, Y_0, Z_0) can be determined from the equations (2.2) and (2.3). By solving these equations for X_0, Y_0 and Z_0 two equations with three unknowns arise. Therefore, the problem can be solved by analyzing two calibration points and their projected marks. It holds that

$$\begin{pmatrix} a_1 & a_2 & a_3 \\ b_1 & b_2 & b_3 \end{pmatrix} \cdot \begin{pmatrix} X_0 \\ Y_0 \\ Z_0 \end{pmatrix} = \begin{pmatrix} A \\ B \end{pmatrix}$$

with

$$a_1 = (c_x - x_b) \cdot r_7 - f_k \cdot r_1 , \qquad b_1 = (c_y - y_b) \cdot r_7 - f_k \cdot r_4 ,$$
$$a_2 = (c_x - x_b) \cdot r_8 - f_k \cdot r_2 , \qquad b_2 = (c_y - y_b) \cdot r_8 - f_k \cdot r_5 ,$$
$$a_3 = (c_x - x_b) \cdot r_9 - f_k \cdot r_3 , \qquad b_3 = (c_y - y_b) \cdot r_9 - f_k \cdot r_6 .$$

$$A = X_w \cdot \left((c_x - x_b) \cdot r_7 - f_k \cdot r_1\right) +$$
$$Y_w \cdot \left((c_x - x_b) \cdot r_8 - f_k \cdot r_2\right) +$$
$$Z_w \cdot \left((c_x - x_b) \cdot r_9 - f_k \cdot r_3\right) ,$$

$$B = X_w \cdot \left((c_y - y_b) \cdot r_7 - f_k \cdot r_4\right) +$$
$$Y_w \cdot \left((c_y - y_b) \cdot r_8 - f_k \cdot r_5\right) +$$
$$Z_w \cdot \left((c_y - y_b) \cdot r_9 - f_k \cdot r_6\right) .$$

The parameters that are needed for the linear transformation (2.1) are determined after solving all of the above equations.

2.1.4 A Camera Model with Radial Lens Distortion

In the preceding sections the camera model was based on an ideal optical system as approximately realized by especially designed camera systems in photogrammetry. However, common cameras are often characterized by a somehow distorted projection behavior, e.g. due to radial lens distortions. These effects can be described mathematically and can therefore be taken into account in the camera model. The influence of the lens distortions on the image geometry also varies with the quality of the used camera lens and can not be generally predicted.

A camera model with perspective projection and radial lens distortion is used in the following. Figure 2.7 shows the camera geometry with the utilized left-handed camera and world coordinate systems. The projection center $\mathbf{O}_k$ is the origin of the camera-centered coordinate system. The Z-axis Z_k in the camera-centered coordinate system coincides with the optical axis. The projection of a point (X_w, Y_w, Z_w) given in world coordinates into a device-dependent digital

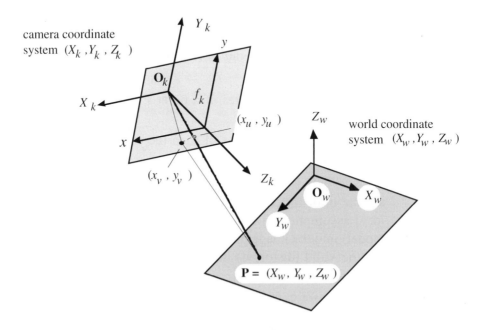

Figure 2.7: Camera geometry with perspective projection and radial lens distortion.

transformations	components	coordinates
	(X_w, Y_w, Z_w)	world coordinates
coordinate transformation		
	(X_k, Y_k, Z_k)	camera centered coordinates
central projection		
	(x_u, y_u)	projection plane coordinates
lens distortion		
	(x_v, y_v)	valid projection plane coordinates
shift of principal point		
	(x_s, y_s)	sensor coordinates
storage of the sensor array		
	(x_b, y_b)	image memory coordinates

Table 2.1: Calculation steps within a geometric model of the image acquisition process: the left column specifies the mathematical or device-dependent transformation of a component (see column in the middle) into the next component below. The components (i.e. points) are given in different coordinate systems which are listed in the right column.

image array position (x_b, y_b) is carried out in five transformation steps. In these steps,

(X_w, Y_w, Z_w) denote the 3D coordinates of a point **P** in the *world coordinate system,*

(X_k, Y_k, Z_k) denote the 3D coordinates of **P** in the *camera centered coordinate system ,*

f_k is the camera constant (i.e. the effective focal length),

(x_u, y_u) are the **u**ndistorted image coordinates of (X_k, Y_k, Z_k) under the ideal assumption of a central projection (ideal pinhole camera model) into the image plane,

(x_v, y_v) are the **v**alid (distorted) image coordinates under consideration of a radial lens distortion,

(x_s, y_s) are the sensor coordinates under consideration of the shift of the principal point (assumed to be at the image center), and

(x_b, y_b) are the (final) device-dependent digital image buffer coordinates.

Figure 2.7 sketches the geometric relation between the world, camera, and image coordinate systems whereas the positions (x_s, y_s) and (x_b, y_b) are not shown in this figure. Table 2.1 outlines a sequence of operations modeling an image acquisition process which may also considered to be the sequence of calculation steps for the transformation of points **P** given in the world coordinate system (e.g. calibration points physically represented by a certain calibration object) into the final device-dependent digital image array coordinates. Next these transformations are explained more in detail.

(i) Transformation of world coordinates into camera centered coordinates

The Euclidean transformation of a point (X_w, Y_w, Z_w) given in world coordinates into a point (X_k, Y_k, Z_k) in camera-centered coordinates is, as mentioned before in Section 2.1.2, described by

$$
\begin{pmatrix} X_k \\ Y_k \\ Z_k \end{pmatrix} = \mathbf{R} \cdot \left(\begin{pmatrix} X_w \\ Y_w \\ Z_w \end{pmatrix} + \mathbf{T} \right) , \text{ with } \mathbf{T} = \begin{pmatrix} T_x \\ T_y \\ T_z \end{pmatrix} = \begin{pmatrix} -X_0 \\ -Y_0 \\ -Z_0 \end{pmatrix}.
$$

Here **T** denotes the 3D translation vector and **R** denotes the 3D rotation matrix that arises from the three partial transformations $\mathbf{R_x}$, $\mathbf{R_y}$ and $\mathbf{R_z}$. The parameters for the orthogonal matrix **R** and the vector **T** have to be determined during a process of camera calibration.

(ii) Projection into the image plane

Under the assumption of (ideal) central projection the transformation of the camera coordinate system (X_k, Y_k, Z_k) into the undistorted image coordinate system (x_u, y_u) is described by the projection equations

$$
x_u = \frac{f_k \cdot X_k}{Z_k} \text{ and } y_u = \frac{f_k \cdot Y_k}{Z_k}
$$

which follow from the famous geometrical ray theorems (compare Section 2.1.1). The camera constant f_k must be known for modeling of this transformation.

(iii) Transformation of undistorted into distorted image coordinates

Radial lens distortions generally occurs with common cameras. Figure 2.8 shows the influence of this distortion on the acquired image. The effects of the radial lens distortion can be described mathematically. However, an ideal modeling of the lens distortion leads to an infinite number of distortion coefficients. In practice we already have a good approximation for these distortions when only the first

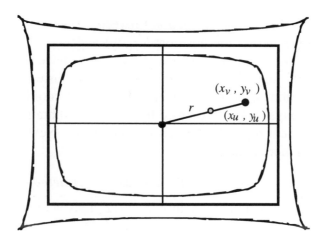

Figure 2.8: Deformation of the ideal image by radial lens distortion.

two coefficients κ_1 and κ_2 are considered. A positive value for κ_1 or κ_2 means that the corners in the image are projected towards the image center. In such a case the image has to be "stretched" towards the corners. On the other hand, a negative value for κ_1 or κ_2 means the inverse situation and transformation, respectively.

The distortedly projected, valid image coordinates (x_v, y_v) can be determined from undistorted image coordinates (x_u, y_u) using the equations

$$x_v = x_u - D_x \quad \text{and} \quad y_v = y_u - D_y$$

where it holds that

$$D_x = x_v \cdot \left(\kappa_1 r^2 + \kappa_2 r^4 \right), \quad D_y = y_v \cdot \left(\kappa_1 r^2 + \kappa_2 r^4 \right) \quad \text{and} \quad r = \sqrt{x_v^2 + y_v^2} \, .$$

The distortion coefficients κ_1 and κ_2 have to be calibrated. Starting with the valid image coordinates (x_v, y_v) a correction of locations of image points can be calculated using these equations as specified above.

However, for the inverse calculation (from ideal to valid coordinates) the algebraic transformation of these equations of the parameters κ_1 and κ_2 leads to a system of nonlinear equations. Based on these equations,

$$x_{vi} = \frac{x_u}{1 + \kappa_1 r_{i-1}^2 + \kappa_2 r_{i-1}^4}, \quad y_{vi} = \frac{y_u}{1 + \kappa_1 r_{i-1}^2 + \kappa_2 r_{i-1}^4}$$

$$\text{with} \quad r_i = \sqrt{x_{vi}^2 + y_{vi}^2} \, , \quad \text{for} \quad i \in \{1, \dots, n\},$$

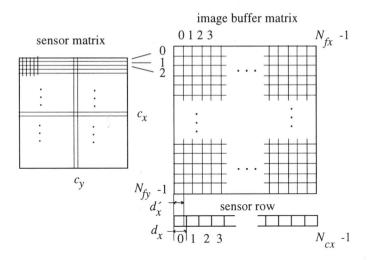

Figure 2.9: Conversion of the principal point centered sensor coordinates into digital image buffer coordinates.

the distortion of ideal coordinates (x_u, y_u) can be determined iteratively as follows:

We initialize the iteration with a start value of $r_0 = \sqrt{x_u^2 + y_u^2}$. This allows to calculate a first approximation for (x_v, y_v) based on these equations. Iteratively improved radii r_i and thus once more improved values for (x_v, y_v) can be calculated using the same set of iteration equations.

The demands of accuracy and computing speed determine the maximum number of iterations (note that no mathematical proof of convergence is provided). By experience a good approximation is achieved within less than eight iterations.

(iv) Transformation of the distorted image coordinates into digital image coordinates under consideration of the shift of the principal point

As already mentioned before it holds that the principal point is not necessarily identical with the image center. If the two points are different then the principal point exhibits a circular motion in the image plane while the focus of the camera lens is altered. Therefore the actual position of the principal point (c_x, c_y) in the image plane has to be calibrated with respect to the current adjustment of the camera lens to be able to determine the *principal point centered sensor coordinates*. Finally these coordinates have to be transformed into digital image buffer coordinates (x_b, y_b).

Therefore, the principal point centered sensor coordinates are scaled (normally based on the available data sheet of the sensor array) and finally converted into row and column positions of the stored digital image (compare Fig. 2.9). These image buffer coordinates can be determined directly from the distorted image coordinates by

$$x_b = \frac{s_x x_v}{d'_x} + c_x \quad \text{and} \quad y_b = \frac{y_v}{d_y} + c_y .$$

Here

(c_x, c_y)	denotes the principal point,
N_{cx}	is the number of sensor elements in one image row,
N_{fx}	is the number of pixels in one row of the final digital image,
$d'_x = d_x \dfrac{N_{cx}}{N_{fx}}$	is the horizontal distance between two image pixels,
d_x	is the horizontal distance between two sensor elements,
d_y	is the vertical distance between two sensor elements, and
s_x	is the horizontal scaling factor.

The scaling factor s_x has to be calibrated. The parameters d_x, d_y, N_{cx} and N_{fx} are normaly included in the manufacturer data sheets for the camera and the image digitization unit (*frame grabber*).

The extrinsic parameters of the image acquisition process are determined by the rotation matrix **R** and the translation vector **T** (compare Section 2.1.2) as described in the first transformation step (*i*). The intrinsic parameters of the image acquisition process are given by the effective focal length f_k, the lens distortion coefficients κ_1 and κ_2, the scaling factor s_x, and the principal point (c_x, c_y). A special approach (a calibration procedure) for the determination of these extrinsic and intrinsic parameters is described in the following section.

2.1.5   Tsai's Calibration Method

A number of techniques for geometric calibration of CCD cameras is known from the computer vision literature which include the treatment of lens distortion. At this point one of these techniques is exemplary chosen and explained. A comparison or evaluation of different computer vision techniques is not the intention of this chapter, and not of this textbook in general. However, the evaluation and the further development of calibaration techniques is a very important topic in computer vision.

The calibration technique by R.Y. Tsai (1986) was chosen for this section because of its frequent application in computer vision applications and because of our own good practical experiences with this approach. Unlike the DLT method described in Section 2.1.3 it also includes the determination of the coefficients κ_1 and κ_2 of the radial lens distortion, and of the scaling factor s_x. The method requires at least seven non-coplanar, accurately detected calibration points which were given in any arbitrary but known geometric configuration. In the following the seven processing steps of the method are explained.

(i)   Calculation of the sensor coordinates from the image buffer coordinates

At first an image of the calibration object is taken. The same remarks can be made about the benefit of uniform distribution of calibration marks on the calibration object, and in the taken image as made for the DLT method in Section 2.1.3. The digital image is assumed to be stored in an image buffer. We define that the position (0, 0) is located in the lower left corner of the image, and we assume a left-handed coordinate system. This ensures positive image buffer coordinates . At next the row and column positions (x_b, y_b) are (interactively) determined (if possible, in sub-pixel accuracy) for all calibration marks which have projected "blobs" in this image buffer.

We assume that the number N_{cx} of sensor elements in one image row, the number N_{fx} of pixels in one image row, the horizontal distance between two pixels d'_x, and the vertical distance between two sensor elements d_y can be read in the manufacturer data sheets.

First the principal point (c_x, c_y) is assumed to be at the image center so it holds that $(x_s, y_s) = (x_v, y_v)$. The corresponding sensor coordinates (x_s, y_s) are calculated for all (centers of) calibration marks by

$$x_s = \frac{(x_b - c_x) \cdot d'_x}{s_x} \quad \text{and} \quad y_s = (y_b - c_y) \cdot d_y.$$

The scaling factor s_x is initially set to the value one and is determined explicitly later in Step *(iv)*.

(ii)   Calculation of seven parameters for the transformation of sensor coordi-nates into world coordinates

The projection of marks of calibration points (X_w, Y_w, Z_w) in the world coordinate system onto corresponding image points (x_s, y_s) in sensor coordinates is characterized by the following linear equation. It holds

$$x_s = (y_s X_w, \ y_s Y_w, \ y_s Z_w, \ y_s, \ -x_s X_w, \ -x_s Y_w, \ -x_s Z_w) \cdot \mathbf{L}$$

with

$$\mathbf{L} = \left(\frac{r_1 s_x}{T_y}, \ \frac{r_2 s_x}{T_y}, \ \frac{r_3 s_x}{T_y}, \ \frac{T_x s_x}{T_y}, \ \frac{r_4}{T_y}, \ \frac{r_5}{T_y}, \ \frac{r_6}{T_y} \right)^T \quad \text{for } T_y \neq 0.$$

Here T_x and T_y denote the components of the translation vector $\mathbf{T}$, and the r_i-values represent the elements of the rotation matrix $\mathbf{R}$. The use of more than seven calibration points leads to an over-determined set of equations which can be solved for $\mathbf{L}$ using the pseudo-inverse technique (*Moore-Penrose inverse*) as follows. It holds

$$\mathbf{L} = (\mathbf{M}^T\mathbf{M})^{-1}\mathbf{M}^T\mathbf{X},$$

where $\mathbf{M}$ and $\mathbf{X}$ are determined by

$$\mathbf{M} = \begin{pmatrix} y_{s1}X_{w1} & y_{s1}Y_{w1} & y_{s1}Z_{w1} & y_{s1} & -x_{s1}X_{w1} & -x_{s1}Y_{w1} & -x_{s1}Z_{w1} \\ y_{s2}X_{w2} & y_{s2}Y_{w2} & y_{s2}Z_{w2} & y_{s2} & -x_{s2}X_{w2} & -x_{s2}Y_{w2} & -x_{s2}Z_{w2} \\ \vdots & \vdots & \vdots & \vdots & \vdots & \vdots & \vdots \\ y_{sn}X_{wn} & y_{sn}Y_{wn} & y_{sn}Z_{wn} & y_{sn} & -x_{sn}X_{wn} & -x_{sn}Y_{wn} & -x_{sn}Z_{wn} \end{pmatrix}$$

and $\mathbf{X} = (x_{s1},\quad x_{s2},\quad \dots,\quad x_{sn})^T$, for n calibration points.

(*iii*)   *Calculation of the Y-component of the translation vector*

The components of the solution vector $\mathbf{L}$ will be described in the following by the abbreviations a_1 to a_7 :

$$a_1 = \frac{r_1 s_x}{T_y},\ a_2 = \frac{r_2 s_x}{T_y},\ a_3 = \frac{r_3 s_x}{T_y},\ a_4 = \frac{T_x s_x}{T_y},\ a_5 = \frac{r_4}{T_y},\ a_6 = \frac{r_5}{T_y},\ a_7 = \frac{r_6}{T_y}.$$

All parameters a_1 to a_7 were already determined in Step (*ii*). From the orthonormality property of $\mathbf{R}$ and the definition of a_5, a_6 and a_7 it follows that:

$$\left(a_5^2 + a_6^2 + a_7^2\right)^{-1/2} = \left(\left(T_y^{-1}r_4\right)^2 + \left(T_y^{-1}r_5\right)^2 + \left(T_y^{-1}r_6\right)^2\right)^{-1/2}$$

$$= \left|T_y\right| \cdot \left(r_4^2 + r_5^2 + r_6^2\right)^{-1/2} = \left|T_y\right|.$$

Thus, the value of T_y is calculated by

$$\left|T_y\right| = \frac{1}{\sqrt{a_5^2 + a_6^2 + a_7^2}}.$$

For determining the sign of T_y that object point $\mathbf{P}$ in the world coordinate system (X_w, Y_w, Z_w) is chosen from the set of projected calibration points whose image position (x_b, y_b) lies as far away from the principal point (c_x, c_y) as possible. First the sign of T_y is assumed to be positive. Next the parameters

$$r_1 = \left(\frac{r_1}{T_y}\right) \cdot T_y, \; r_2 = \left(\frac{r_2}{T_y}\right) \cdot T_y, \; r_4 = \left(\frac{r_4}{T_y}\right) \cdot T_y, \; r_5 = \left(\frac{r_5}{T_y}\right) \cdot T_y \text{ and } T_x = \left(\frac{T_x}{T_y}\right) \cdot T_y$$

are calculated using the components of the solution vector **L** already determined in Step (*ii*) (so far s_x was set equal to one in Step (*ii*)). The calculated position

$$x = r_1 X_w + r_2 Y_w + T_x, \qquad y = r_4 X_w + r_5 Y_w + T_y$$

of the projected point **P** is compared to the actual position (selected before). If the parameters x and x_b as well as y and y_b of the selected calibration point have the same signs, then T_y stays the same, otherwise $sgn(T_y) = -1$.

(*iv*) *Determination of the scaling factor* s_x

Because of the orthonormality property of **R** and the fact that for an assumed scanning orientation of the image from left to right s_x is always positive it holds that

$$\sqrt{a_1^2 + a_2^2 + a_3^2} \cdot |T_y| = \sqrt{\left(T_y^{-1} s_x r_1\right)^2 + \left(T_y^{-1} s_x r_2\right)^2 + \left(T_y^{-1} s_x r_3\right)^2} \cdot |T_y|$$

$$= s_x \cdot \sqrt{r_1^2 + r_2^2 + r_3^2} = s_x.$$

Therefore the image scaling factor s_x can be determined using the equation

$$s_x = |T_y| \cdot \sqrt{a_1^2 + a_2^2 + a_3^2}.$$

(*v*) *Calculation of the 3D rotation matrix and of the X-component of the translation vector*

From the definition of $a_i, i = 1, \ldots, 7$ in Step (*iii*) it follows immediately that the components $r_1, \ldots, r_6$ of the 3D rotation matrix **R** are given by

$$r_1 = a_1 \cdot \frac{T_y}{s_x}, \quad r_2 = a_2 \cdot \frac{T_y}{s_x}, \quad r_3 = a_3 \cdot \frac{T_y}{s_x},$$

$$r_4 = a_5 \cdot T_y, \quad r_5 = a_6 \cdot T_y \text{ and } r_6 = a_7 \cdot T_y.$$

Furthermore the X-component of the translation vector can also be determined by

$$T_x = \frac{a_4 \cdot T_y}{s_x}.$$

The still missing components r_7, r_8 and r_9 are calculated with the inner vector product of the first two rows of the rotation matrix **R** and using the orthonormality property $r_7^2 + r_8^2 + r_9^2 = 1$.

(*vi*) *Approximation of the focal length and of the Z-component of the translation vector with disregard to the lens distortion*

The linear equation

$$\left(y, \ -y_s\right)\begin{pmatrix} f_k \\ T_z \end{pmatrix} = w \cdot y_s$$

is formulated for every calibration point with

$$y = r_4 X_w + r_5 Y_w + r_6 \cdot 0 + T_y \text{ and } w = r_7 X_w + r_8 Y_w + r_9 \cdot 0 \ .$$

Assuming more than two calibration points an over-determined set of equations results which can be solved, for example, for the unknowns f_k and T_z using the pseudo-inverse technique: it holds that

$$\begin{pmatrix} f_k \\ T_z \end{pmatrix} = \left(\mathbf{M}^T\mathbf{M}\right)^{-1}\mathbf{M}^T\mathbf{X},$$

where $\mathbf{M}$ and $\mathbf{X}$ are calculated using n calibration points with

$$\mathbf{M} = \begin{pmatrix} y_1 & -y_{s1} \\ y_2 & -y_{s2} \\ \vdots & \vdots \\ y_n & -y_{sn} \end{pmatrix} \quad \text{and} \quad \mathbf{X} = \begin{pmatrix} w_1 y_{s1} \\ w_2 y_{s2} \\ \vdots \\ w_n y_{sn} \end{pmatrix}.$$

(*vii*) *Calculation of exact solutions for the focal length, the Z-component of the translation vector, and the radial distortion coefficients*

The utilization of a standard optimization technique allows (more) accurate calculations of the camera constant f_k, of the depth T_z and of the distortion coefficients κ_1 and κ_2. The already determined approximations of f_k and T_z act as the starting values. Zero is assumed as the initial value for the radial distortion coefficients.

In the following the steepest descent method is used for optimization. Nevertheless, a different optimization method could also be used. The equations

$$x_{u1} = f_k \cdot \frac{r_4 X_w + r_5 Y_w + r_6 Z_w + T_x}{r_7 X_w + r_8 Y_w + r_9 Z_w + T_z} \text{ and } y_{u1} = f_k \cdot \frac{r_4 X_w + r_5 Y_w + r_6 Z_w + T_y}{r_7 X_w + r_8 Y_w + r_9 Z_w + T_z}$$

can, for example, be used for the determination of the parameters. These equations describe the transformation of a world coordinate point $\left(X_w, Y_w, Z_w\right)$

into the camera-centered coordinate system assuming perspective projection in-between.

On the other hand, projected ideal image points can also be generated by an radial rectification of the actually projected, valid image points (x_v, y_v). Therefore, the values

$$x_{u2} = x_v \cdot \left(1 + \kappa_1 r^2 + \kappa_2 r^4\right) \text{ and } y_{u2} = y_v \cdot \left(1 + \kappa_1 r^2 + \kappa_2 r^4\right) \text{ with } r = \sqrt{x_v^2 + y_v^2}$$

are calculated. For a search in a four-dimensional vector space the error function

$$\mathcal{E}\left(\kappa_1, \kappa_2, f_k, T_z\right) = \sqrt{\left(x_{u2} - x_{u1}\right)^2 + \left(y_{u2} - y_{u1}\right)^2}$$

arises from the Euclidean distance between a pair of ideal image points that were calculated in different ways. The gradient of $\mathcal{E}$,

$$\nabla\mathcal{E} = \left(\frac{\partial\mathcal{E}}{\partial\kappa_1}, \frac{\partial\mathcal{E}}{\partial\kappa_2}, \frac{\partial\mathcal{E}}{\partial f_k}, \frac{\partial\mathcal{E}}{\partial T_z}\right)^T$$

is calculated with the partial derivatives

$$\frac{\partial\mathcal{E}}{\partial\kappa_1} = \frac{r^2 \cdot \left(\left(x_{u2} - x_{u1}\right) \cdot x_v + \left(y_{u2} - y_{u1}\right) \cdot y_v\right)}{\mathcal{E}},$$

$$\frac{\partial\mathcal{E}}{\partial\kappa_2} = \frac{r^4 \cdot \left(\left(x_{u2} - x_{u1}\right) \cdot x_v + \left(y_{u2} - y_{u1}\right) \cdot y_v\right)}{\mathcal{E}},$$

$$\frac{\partial\mathcal{E}}{\partial f_k} = -\frac{\left(x_{u2} - x_{u1}\right) \cdot \left(r_1 X_w + r_2 Y_w + r_3 Z_w + T_x\right)}{\mathcal{E} \cdot \left(r_7 X_w + r_8 Y_w + r_9 Z_w + T_z\right)}$$

$$-\frac{\left(y_{u2} - y_{u1}\right) \cdot \left(r_7 X_w + r_8 Y_w + r_9 Z_w + T_y\right)}{\mathcal{E} \cdot \left(r_7 X_w + r_8 Y_w + r_9 Z_w + T_z\right)}$$

and

$$\frac{\partial\mathcal{E}}{\partial T_z} = \frac{f_k \cdot \left(x_{u2} - x_{u1}\right) \cdot \left(r_1 X_w + r_2 Y_w + r_3 Z_w + T_x\right)}{\mathcal{E} \cdot \left(r_7 X_w + r_8 Y_w + r_9 Z_w + T_z\right)^2}$$

$$+\frac{f_k \cdot \left(y_{u2} - y_{u1}\right) \cdot \left(r_7 X_w + r_8 Y_w + r_9 Z_w + T_y\right)}{\mathcal{E} \cdot \left(r_7 X_w + r_8 Y_w + r_9 Z_w + T_z\right)^2}.$$

This gradient allows to specify the direction of the steepest increase of the error function $\mathcal{E}$. The optimum has to be analyzed contrary to the direction of the gradient because a minimum error is needed.

The determination of the principal point (c_x, c_y) is also possible with this optimization method if the image point in sensor coordinates is replaced by

$$x_s = \frac{d'_x \cdot (x_b - c_x)}{s_x}, \qquad y_s = d_y \cdot (y_b - c_y)$$

in this error function $\mathcal{E}$, and if the gradient $\nabla \mathcal{E}$ is adjusted accordingly.

At the beginning of the calibration it was assumed that the principal point is identical with the image center. Yet, if the result of the optimization method shows a shift of the principal point, then the whole calculation process can be repeated with the updated parameters (c_x, c_y) to improve the accuracy of the calibration results.

2.2   SENSOR MODEL

Modern cameras suitable for image processing are usually based on semiconductor sensors the so-called CCD (*charge coupled device*) chips. The interline transfer architecture and the frame transfer architecture are the two major concepts for CCD chip design. They differ in the way how the charge is transferred out of the light sensitive sensor elements.

An *interline transfer sensor* contains light sensitive sensor elements that are arranged in columns. Every column is connected to an adjacent vertical shift register through a transfer gate (compare Fig. 2.10). The vertical shift registers store the charge coming from the light sensitive elements. In a subsequent step the charge is shifted from the vertical shift registers row by row to the horizontal readout register. In a *frame transfer sensor* the light sensitive elements and the shift registers are not arranged in columns but in two separate grids. The advantage of the frame transfer architecture is that the light sensitive elements are also horizontally adjacent to each other and hence less image distortions arise. Interline transfer sensors have the advantage that they do not need a mechanical shutter.

Because of the increasing significance of color image processing the following section will introduce the generation of color images. Color images can be generated with black and white cameras (B/W cameras) using color filters, with inexpensive single chip CCD cameras, and with high-quality and more expensive three chip CCD cameras. Besides, a color image generation can also be done using scanners.

2.2.1   Camera Hardware for Color Image Acquisition

The cheapest way to generate color images is to use a B/W camera in conjunction with *color filters*. The spectral sampling of the color signal is done in a sequential manner. A static scene must be assumed because the filters have to be changed mechanically. This method does not influence the spatial resolution of the images. The advantage of this sequential method is that an arbitrary number of color filters can be chosen and hence more than three color channels can be acquired if necessary. Furthermore, we are free to select an optimal set of color filters.

When using B/W cameras special attention has to be paid concerning white balance (see Section 2.3.2) and chromatic aberrations. Chromatic aberrations are caused by the lens since light of different wavelengths has different indices of refraction. The lens refracts light of longer wavelengths less than light of shorter wavelengths. In other words, the focal length is a function of the wavelength. This physical effect has to be considered in particular if a B/W camera and color filters are employed for color image acquisition whereas lenses of color cameras can cope with this problem to a certain degree by using a special optics to reduce these effects.

A color camera is needed if the application of the sequential method is not suitable, e.g. if dynamic scenes have to be digitized. We can distinguish between single chip cameras (1-CCD cameras) and three chip cameras (3-CCD cameras). In a 1-CCD camera a filter mask covers the light sensitive area. There exist three different variants: primary color mosaic filters, complementary color mosaic filters, and color stripe filters.

An arrangement of red, green, and blue filters attached on the CCD chip as shown in Fig. 2.11 (left) is used in *primary color mosaic filter* cameras. Four

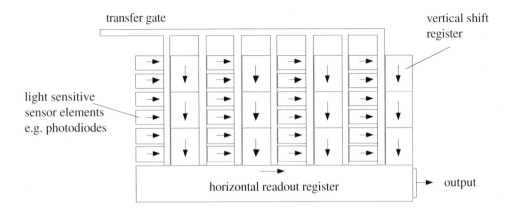

Figure 2.10: The interline transfer architecture.

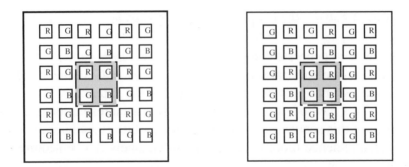

Figure 2.11: Primary color filters of 1-CCD cameras. The left hand side illustrates a mosaic filter, and the right hand side shows a stripe filter. The four shaded CCD elements form a 2×2 macro pixel, respectively.

elements form a 2×2 macro pixel. A macro pixel consists of two green elements, one red element, and one blue element. The emphasis of green light takes the spectral sensitivity of the human eye into account which is most sensitive to wavelengths of about 560 nm. The macro pixels reduce the spatial resolution in vertical and in horizontal direction.

Vertical red, green, and blue stripes cover the sensor area (see Fig. 2.11, right) in a *color stripe filter* camera. Here, the vertical resolution is not reduced but the horizontal resolution is affected as for primary color mosaic filters. The

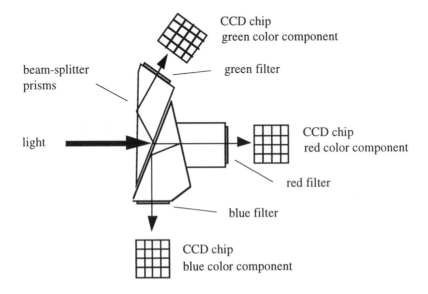

Figure 2.12: Light beam splitting by using prisms in a standard 3-CCD camera.

color stripe filter technique is used in the 1-CCD camera Sony XC-711, for example. Besides cameras with additive color filters 1-CCD cameras which use complementary color patterns are popular, as well. Such cameras employ a so-called *complementary color mosaic filter* (or *Ye-Cy-Mg-G color mosaic filter*). Each macro pixel comprises a yellow, cyan, magenta, and green filter. Such cameras do not provide separate RGB signals, but a complementary filter increases the sensitivity of the image acquisition. On the other hand, the color reproduction decreases slightly. The Sanyo camera VCC-3770 is an example for a camera using a complementary color mosaic filter.

1-CCD cameras tend to show color deviations due to color Moiré effects. They are caused by color signals containing high spatial frequencies, when not all CCD elements of a macro pixel are uniformly illuminated.

In order to reduce these distortions more expensive 3-CCD cameras are employed. They produce images of much better quality, since prisms split the incoming light into three separate parts. These prisms are called *beam-splitter prisms*. They cast the separated light onto three spatially separated CCD chips (see Fig. 2.12). Besides the much higher price of 3-CCD cameras the corresponding digitization unit (frame grabber) is more complex, since three color signals have to be processed.

2.2.2 Photometric Sensor Model

Generally, the following *sensor model* is applied to describe the generation of a color image:

$$
\begin{aligned}
\rho_k &= \int_{\lambda_l}^{\lambda_h} E(\lambda) \cdot R(\lambda) \cdot S_k(\lambda) \; d\lambda \\
&= \int_{\lambda_l}^{\lambda_h} C(\lambda) \cdot S_k(\lambda) \; d\lambda, \qquad \text{with } C(\lambda) = E(\lambda) \cdot R(\lambda).
\end{aligned}
\tag{2.4}
$$

The function $E(\lambda)$ is the *spectral power distribution* of the illumination and $R(\lambda)$ is the *spectral reflectance factor* of the surface material. The function $S_k(\lambda)$ is the *spectral sensitivity* (or *spectral response curve*) of the subsensor k, and ρ_k is its *response*[5]. The interval of integration $[\lambda_l, \lambda_h]$ describes the measuring range with respect to the wavelength. The product of the functions $E(\lambda)$ and $R(\lambda)$ is called the

---

[5] We adopt the notation and symbols of the existing literature in this specific field. The symbol E should not be mixed up with the image irradiance. The (sensor) responses are the components of the color image **C**, see Section 1.2.1.

color signal $C(\lambda)$, hence $C(\lambda)$ describes the radiation reflected from the object that reaches the sensor[6].

The spectral quantities $E(\lambda)$, $R(\lambda)$, $C(\lambda)$, and $S_k(\lambda)$ can be measured by using physical devices. This implies that only a finite number of measurements can be taken. Normally wavelength subintervals $\Delta\lambda$ in a range between 2 and 10 nm are used. For example, interference filters have such narrow transmittance bands. The smaller the interval, the less energy reaches the sensor which means that there exist physical limitations in measuring small wavelength intervals. The equation

$$\rho_k = \sum_{i=1}^{n} E(\lambda(i)) \cdot R(\lambda(i)) \cdot S_k(\lambda(i))$$

$$= \sum_{i=1}^{n} C(\lambda(i)) \cdot S_k(\lambda(i)), \qquad \text{with } C(\lambda(i)) = E(\lambda(i)) \cdot R(\lambda(i))$$

approximates the integral as a finite sum. The function $\lambda(i)$ maps the i-th value of the n measurements onto the corresponding wavelength subinterval $\Delta\lambda$. If suitable, the quantities $E(\lambda)$, $R(\lambda)$, $C(\lambda)$, and $S_k(\lambda)$ can be represented as vectors. If the sensor response ρ_k is described by an integral the vectors are of infinite dimension, whereas the description by a finite sum leads to finite dimensional vectors. In vector representation the above equation can be rewritten as

$$\rho_k = \mathbf{c}^{\mathrm{T}} \cdot \mathbf{s}_k \ ,$$

where "$\cdot$" denotes the inner vector product (scalar product) of two vectors. The column vectors $\mathbf{c}$ and $\mathbf{s}_k$ are of dimension n. They represent the color signal $C(\lambda)$ and the spectral sensitivity $S_k(\lambda)$, respectively. Using these vectors, equation (2.4) can be equivalently represented as

$$\rho_k = \mathbf{e}^{\mathrm{T}} \cdot diag(\mathbf{R}(\lambda(i))) \cdot \mathbf{s}_k = \mathbf{e}^{\mathrm{T}} \cdot \mathbf{R} \cdot \mathbf{s}_k \ ,$$

where the spectral reflectance factor $R(\lambda)$ is described as diagonal matrix $\mathbf{R}$ of dimension $n \times n$ containing the elements $\mathbf{R}(\lambda(i))$. The n-dimensional column vector $\mathbf{e}$ is the spectral power distribution of the illumination. Instead of representing the spectral reflectance factor $\mathbf{R}(\lambda(i))$ as a diagonal matrix we could also describe $\mathbf{E}(\lambda(i))$ by a diagonal matrix of dimension $n \times n$:

$$\rho_k = \mathbf{r}^{\mathrm{T}} \cdot diag(\mathbf{E}(\lambda(i))) \cdot \mathbf{s}_k = \mathbf{r}^{\mathrm{T}} \cdot \mathbf{E} \cdot \mathbf{s}_k \ ,$$

---

[6] The color signal $C(\lambda)$ should not be mistaken for the color image $\mathbf{C}$, since $C(\lambda)$ is not yet evaluated by the camera sensor.

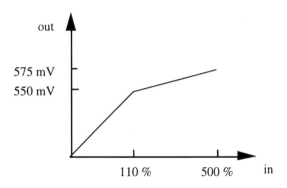

Figure 2.13: Example of pre-kneeing to preserve the dynamic range.

where **r** is the n-dimensional reflectance vector. The m sensor responses can be written as one m-dimensional row vector ρ. Similarly, all m column vectors $\mathbf{s}_k$ can be represented by a single $n \times n$-matrix **S**. It follows that

$$\rho = \mathbf{c}^T \cdot \mathbf{S} \; , \; \rho = \mathbf{e}^T \cdot \mathbf{R} \cdot \mathbf{S} \; , \; \text{and} \; \rho = \mathbf{r}^T \cdot \mathbf{E} \cdot \mathbf{S} \tag{2.5}$$

when the sensor response is represented as a vector.

2.2.3 Pre-kneeing, Clipping, and Blooming

Attenuation of the color signal occurs if more photons fall on the CCD chip than the image acquisition system is able to process. This can be caused by different factors when the image signal is processed in analog form (voltages) in the camera or when the signal is digitized in the frame grabber. One reason of attenuation is the limited *dynamic range* of the components in the imaging system. Special attention has to be paid to this problem in color image processing. The analog component of the camera system causes an attenuation if the electric signal is processed by a so-called *pre-knee-circuit*. Figure 2.13 shows the characteristics of the pre-knee-circuit of the Sony three chip camera DXC-930P. The voltage of the signal is linearly attenuated starting at a certain level of the input signal. The attenuation factor is 1 : 78. As a result, the signal is not longer globally linear. The advantage of a pre-knee-circuit is that the signal stays longer in the dynamic range.

Furthermore, *clipping* of the input signal occurs whenever the analog signal exceeds the highest processable voltage, e.g. when the analog signal is converted to a digital signal (a gray value for each color channel) in the frame grabber. For example, the gray value 255 would be the upper output limit for a 8-

intensity factor	RGB original			RGB clipping			H in degrees	S in %
	R	G	B	R	G	B		
× 1	0.8	0.4	0.2	0.8	0.4	0.2	19.1	57.1
× 2	1.6	0.8	0.4	1.0	0.8	0.4	40.9	45.5
× 4	3.2	1.6	0.8	1.0	1.0	0.8	60.0	14.3

Table 2.2: Example of hue and saturation distortion caused by a color clipping. The clipping level is 1.0.

bit analog/digital converter (ADC). Light signals of higher intensity are clipped to gray value 255 in the ADC. Usually, the clipping level (*white level*) of the ADC can be controlled by programming the frame grabber.

Linear attenuation and clipping can lead to severe deviations from the expected color. If the intensity of the light in all color channels is above the clipping level, the output is white, i.e. (255, 255, 255). If only one or two channels are affected, the output has incorrect but still defined hue and saturation values (see Sect. 1.2.1). An example will illustrate this problem.

Let us assume that the electric signal of the colored light falling on the CCD chip can be expressed by the RGB vector (0.8, 0.4, 0.2) and the clipping level is 1.0. In this case, the color signal is not subjected to clipping. The hue value H and the saturation value S of the color signal are 19.1° and 57.1%, respectively (compare Tab. 2.2). Now let us change the iris setting of the camera. For example we can decrement the f-stop[7] of the camera lens from f8 to f5.6. This scales the light signal arriving at the CCD chip by factor 2 and hence the red channel is affected by clipping. Table 2.2 shows the distortion in H and S. When we open the iris even more, for example by changing the f-stop from f5.6 to f4 (further scaling by factor 2), not only the red channel but also the green channel is affected by clipping.

If the intensity of the incoming light at a CCD cell exceeds a certain level which is several times higher than the clipping level, it happens that the CCD cell is not able to accumulate more charge per time unit any longer. The additional charge is spread into the neighboring CCD cells. This effect is called *blooming* and appears as a white streak or blob around the affected pixels in the image. Blooming is particularly noticeable in scene analysis when specular highlights occur on the surface of the object that has to be reconstructed. Figure 2.14 shows

---

[7] F-stops are logarithmic. Examples are: f1.4, f2, f2.8, f4, f5.6, f8, f11, f16, f22. In this order, the next f-stop admits only half of the light entering the camera than the previous one, since the area of the circular opening of the iris is reduced by factor 2.

Figure 2.14: Blooming at a corner of a rectangular metallic surface as an effect of intensive illumination.

blooming caused by a specular highlight on a rectangular, metallic surface. For interline transfer sensors blooming starts at about 600 % overload according to R. Lenz (1989).

2.3   PHOTOMETRIC CALIBRATION

A linear behavior of the imaging sensor is assumed in many methods of digital image processing. This is especially true for shading based techniques such as shape from shading or photometric stereo which will be discussed in Chapters 7 and 8. For these techniques it is assumed that the gray values (or the color values) in the image have a *direct linear relation* to the image irradiances (the radiation entering the camera lens). Furthermore, most of the methods applied in color image processing often require a linear sensor. In the following some reasons for nonlinear camera behavior are explained and afterwards a sketch of a linearization technique is given. Note that also signal attenuation caused by a pre-knee-circuit, clipping, and blooming as discussed in the previous section lead to a nonlinear camera response.

2.3.1   Gamma Re-Correction

In principle CCD chips possess the property of having a high linearity because photons are transformed directly into charge in a CCD cell. But CCD cameras usually delinearize the signal for display requirements. It has to be guaranteed that

	PAL	NTSC	SECAM	Monitors
gamma value	2.8	2.2	2.8	2.35..2.55

Table 2.3: Gamma values for television systems and computer monitors.

the light received by the camera is transformed into a proportional amount of light emitted by a monitor screen. The input voltage U of a cathode ray tube in a monitor and the emitted radiant intensity I have the exponential relationship

$$I \propto U^{\gamma},$$

where γ is the so-called *gamma value*. Therefore, a circuit is integrated in the camera for the *gamma correction*. The circuit adjusts the *linear* CCD camera signal to the *nonlinear* monitor characteristic. This adjustment in the camera can be written as

$$U_{out} = U_{max} \cdot \left(\frac{U_{in}}{U_{max}} \right)^{1/\gamma} = U_{max}^{(1-1/\gamma)} \cdot U_{in}^{1/\gamma} \, ,$$

where U_{max} is the maximum voltage. The gamma value γ depends on the monitor and the video standard of the television system. Generally the gamma values of monitors lie between 2.0 and 3.0. Table 2.3 shows the gamma values for the three common television systems and computer monitors. These are the PAL system (*Phase Alternation Line*) developed in Germany, the SECAM system (*Séquentiel Couleur à Mémoire*) developed in France, and the NTSC system (*National Television System Committee*) used in North America and Japan. Details of these systems are described in CCIR standards.

　　Therefore, the gamma correction has to be inverted to linearize the camera characteristic. This gamma *re-correction* can be done through substituting γ by $1/\gamma$ if the gamma value of the camera is known. This leads to the equation

$$E_{out} = G_{max} \cdot \left(\frac{E_{in}}{G_{max}} \right)^{\gamma} = G_{max}^{(1-\gamma)} \cdot E_{in}^{\gamma}$$

which transforms the image irradiance values (gray values) from E_{in} to E_{out}. For most scientific CCD cameras it is possible to switch the gamma value through the camera control unit to 1. This avoids a gamma re-correction procedure.

　　If neither the gamma value is known nor the gamma correction can be switched off then the gamma value has to be calculated by using a calibration image. A calibration image for this purpose usually contains a number of gray patches of known reflection properties. The reflection properties are described by the spectral reflectance factor $R(\lambda)$, see Section 2.2.2. Color Image 1 in the Appendix shows an image of such a calibration object, called the *GretagMacbeth ColorChecker®*.

This color rendition chart contains 24 matte color patches including six gray patches. The spectral reflectance factors $R(\lambda)$ of the gray patches of the ColorChecker are constant over the visible wavelength interval of the light. That is the reason why they appear gray. The constant reflectance factors can be represented as percentages[8] which describe how much light the gray patches reflect. The percentages are as follows (from left to right in Color Image 1): 90%, 59.1%, 36.2%, 19.8%, 9%, and 3.1%. Note that these values are properties of the patches and are independent from the illumination and the camera. The relationship between these percentages and the measured image irradiances describes directly the camera behavior with respect to linearity. Since a model of the nonlinear characteristic of the camera is known (see above) the gamma value can be determined.

2.3.2 Black Level and White Balance

Besides the gamma correction which causes a nonlinear camera behavior the so-called black level has to be considered. A CCD cell generates electrons even if no light (photons) are falling on the light sensitive area which arise from thermal energy within the CCD chip. The current generated by these electrons is called *dark current*. The ADC transforms the associated voltage into an image gray value (measured image irradiance). The gray value which is a result of the dark current is called *black level* [9]. It can be modeled as being an additive offset to the camera signal and must be subtracted from the gray values. Actually the black level does not lead to a nonlinear characteristic but the goal is to produce a camera curve that is directly linear that means a totally black gray patch having 0% reflection should generate the gray value 0. In other words, the camera curve should pass through the origin of the coordinate system spanned by the reflectance factor and the measured image irradiance. Often the black level can be adjusted by a knob at the camera control unit called *master black control*.

A further factor playing an important role with respect to color reproduction is the overall scaling of the three color channels. A gray object taken under white illumination produces a gray image, hence the color channels have

---

[8] In Chapter 6, Section 6.2.4, we will introduce the term *albedo* as the correct name for this percentage.
[9] The corresponding analog signal is also called black level.

identical gray values *v*. Therefore, the gray value triple **C** = (*v*, *v*, *v*) is assigned to each pixel when we assume idealized image acquisition. Although called "white", the color of white light sources, such as daylight, fluorescent lamps, and tungsten lamps (usual light bulbs) produce different white tones, expressed in color temperature values. To get "white" for these different light sources a so-called *white balance* has to be performed. A manual white balance is done by exposing a white object to the color camera and pushing the white balance button at the camera control unit.

When using a B/W camera in conjunction with color filters the white balance is even more important. Normally, the color channels differ to such an extent that a set of neutral density filters is necessary for balancing. Neutral density filters can be used to attenuate the light without changing its spectral distribution. A subsequent fine-balancing can be done by scaling the color channels.

2.4   REFERENCES

The general architecture of semiconductor cameras and the advantages and disadvantages of the individual technologies are, for example, summarized in

Hashimoto, Y., Yamamoto, M., Asaida, T.: *Cameras and display systems*. Proc. IEEE **83** (1995), pp. 1032-1043,

Lahe, D.: *Solid state color cameras: tradeoffs and costs now*. Advanced Imaging April 1996, pp. 63-66, and

Lenz, R.: *Image data acquisition with CCD cameras*. In: Gruen, A., Kahmen, H.: *Optical 3-D Measurement Techniques*, Wichmann, Karlsruhe, Germany, 1989, pp. 22-34.

The DLT method for camera calibration that was presented in Section 2.1.3 was introduced in

Abdel-Aziz, Y.I., Karara, H.M.: *Direct linear transformation into object space coordinates in close-range photogrammetry*. Proc. ASP Symposium on Close-Range Photogrammetry, Urbana, Illinois, USA, 1971, pp. 1-18.

An interesting survey on different techniques for geometric calibration of CCD cameras is given in

Tsai, R.Y.: *An efficient and accurate camera calibration technique for 3D machine vision*. Proc. International Conference on Computer Vision and Pattern Recognition, Miami Beach, Florida, USA, 1986, pp. 364-374.

The geometric calibration technique (after Tsai) that was described in Section 2.1.5 can be found in the above article, as well, and in more detail in

Tsai, R.Y.: *A versatile camera calibration technique for high-accuracy 3D machine vision metrology using off-the-shelf TV cameras and lenses*. IEEE Journal of Robotics and Automation **3** (1987), pp. 323-344.

More recent approaches for geometric camera calibration can be found in

Robert, L.: *Camera calibration without feature extraction*. Computer Vision and Image Understanding **63** (1996), pp. 314-325 and in

Heikkilä, J., Silvén, O.: *A four-step camera calibration procedure with implicit image correction*. Proc. Int. Conf. on Computer Vision and Pattern Recognition 1997, San Juan, Puerto Rico, 1997, pp. 1106-1112.

An overview of optimization techniques and methods for determining the pseudo inverses as well as their implementation in different programming languages (FORTRAN, PASCAL, C) is given in

Press, W.H., Teukolsky, S.A., Vetterling, W.T., Flannery, B.P.: *Numerical Recipes in C (FORTRAN, PASCAL)*. 2nd Edition, Cambridge University Press, Cambridge, USA, 1992.

The spectral reflectance factors of the GretagMacbeth ColorChecker® are presented graphically in

McCamy, C.S., Marcus, H., Davidson, J.G.: *A color-rendition chart*. Journal of Applied Photographic Engineering **2** (1976), pp. 95-99 and

Meyer, G.W.: *Wavelength selection for synthetic image generation*. Computer Vision, Graphics and Image Processing **41** (1988), pp. 57-79.

The ColorChecker is a product of GretagMacbeth based in Regensdorf, Switzerland, URL: http://www.gretagmacbeth.com/.

2.5   EXERCISES

(1) For the central projection of $\Re^3$ into the image plane $\Re^2$ discussed in Section 2.1.1 the origin $(0,0,0)$ was assumed to be the projection center (compare Fig. 1.16). Now assume that the projection center is located at the point $(0,0,-f)$ and accordingly the xy image plane corresponds to the XY plane of the XYZ space. Describe the projection equations of the central projection for this image centered projection model in terms of homogeneous coordinates.

(2) A camera has to be calibrated for a work range of 2 to 4 meters. The position of the camera is fixed. What has to be kept in mind for the selection of the calibration marks?

(3) The calibration marks that are actually projected in the image have to be determined with subpixel accuracy in order to reach a high quality calibration. Design an algorithm for the subpixel accurate detection of the calibration marks. (Hint: Moments

$$m_{ij} = \sum_x \sum_y x^i y^j \cdot E(x, y)$$

allow to calculate the centroid of areas in irradiance images E).

(4 - Assignment) Implement the DLT method for the geometric calibration that was described in Section 2.1.3. To solve the overdetermined system of linear equations use the pseudo inverse. An algorithm is given in the book by W.H. Press et al. which was referred in Section 2.4. Furthermore, compare the end of Section 5.3.1.

(5) Visualize the differences between the saturation and the intensity of a color (compare Section 1.2.1 for the definition of the HSI space). Choose a fixed hue (e.g. $H = 0$) and generate a synthetical image that visualizes intensities in the columns and saturation in the rows. To solve the task the intensity can, for example, be divided into 256 intervals and the saturation can be divided into 100 intervals. Then, the resulting image has the size 256×100 pixels on the monitor. Use a color map having a depth of at least 16 bits to allow a good visualization.
Generate a similar image by varying the hue and the saturation. Set the intensity to the maximum value (e.g. $I = 255$). The hue can, for instance, be divided into 360 intervals and the saturation can be divided into 100 intervals. Visualize the resulting image of size 360×100 pixels on the monitor.

(6) Consider the consequences if a gamma re-correction is not applied to an image acquired by a color camera. Calculate the corresponding HSI values for several RGB triples with and without gamma re-correction. A synthetical, gamma corrected image can be generated by adapting the formula from Section 2.3.1 that models the conversion of the voltages.

3 GEOMETRY OF OBJECT SURFACES

This chapter provides geometric fundamentals for the scene objects that have to be reconstructed. Later Chapter 6 addresses aspects of surface reflection which is a further essential characterization of the surfaces of the scene objects. Chapter 3 looks at the "pure" geometric representations of object faces without taking any surface textures or shading in mind. The geometric issues in this chapter are relevant later in the book in the context of different methods for shape reconstruction. However, we refrain from giving pre-references.

3.1 FUNCTIONAL REPRESENTATIONS

This section deals with two different surface models for *rigid objects*. Basic functional terms like normal, gradient (compare also Section 1.3.1), Taylor expansion, or solid angle are provided for these surface models.

3.1.1 Facets or Differentiable Functions

An *object surface* can generally be seen as a union of several faces in the three-dimensional space $\Re^3$. In the following a functional description in terms of the XYZ camera coordinates is assumed for these faces.

Consider a functional representation $F(X,Y,Z) = 0$ of surface points $\mathbf{P} = (X,Y,Z)$. This is a conditional equation which generally does not allow a unique solution for Z, for given values X and Y of a defined range $\mathbf{M}$. On the other hand, a function $Z = Z(X,Y)$ provides a unique representation of height or depth values Z over a defined range $\mathbf{M}$. For instance, cube faces that are orthogonal to the XY plane cannot be represented as a function in X and Y. But they can be defined by conditional equations of the form $aX + bY + c = 0$ and by specifying a possible range of Z values.

Two options for modeling faces of the three-dimensional space $\mathfrak{R}^3$ are provided in this section to discuss methods for surface reconstruction. In the *facet model* object faces are represented through piecewise linear approximations. The individual planar segments can theoretically be assumed to be arbitrarily small so that approximations of the object faces are possible with any arbitrary accuracy. A second option for modeling object faces is the use of *continuous functions*. Certain characteristics of object surfaces concerning continuity and differentiability are modeled (locally) by the use of $C^{(n)}$ functions (defined below), i.e. by the specification of the value of n for these classes of functions.[1]

In the *facet model* object surfaces are approximated by linear faces, e.g. given by the so-called *slope-intercept equations* $Z = Z_\mathbf{P}(X,Y) = pX + qY + r$, on (e.g., a circular, or polygonal base set within) "small" local neighborhoods

$$\mathbf{M}_\varepsilon = \left\{ (X,Y): \quad \sqrt{(X - X_0)^2 + (Y - Y_0)^2} \le \varepsilon \right\},$$

for selected surface points $\mathbf{P} = (X_0, Y_0, Z_0)$.[2] Such an assumed planar segment is called a *facet* or a *linear surface patch*.

The function $Z_\mathbf{P}$ defines a plane in the Euclidean space $\mathfrak{R}^3$. The *slope* of the plane is defined by the values of p and q. The plane intersects the Z-axis in the point $(0,0,r)$, the *Z-intercept* of the plane. An object surface point $\mathbf{P} = (X_0, Y_0, Z_0)$ satisfies the slope-intercept equation of "its" plane, i.e. it holds specially that $Z_0 = Z_\mathbf{P}(X_0, Y_0) = pX_0 + qY_0 + r$.

Facets can be polygons, i.e. planar areas in $\mathfrak{R}^3$ that are bounded by a finite sequence of straight line segments, if a polygon is assumed to be the base set in the neighborhoods $\mathbf{M}_\varepsilon$ in the XY plane (e.g. a square, an equilateral triangle, or a hexagon). If only a finite number of object surface points is assumed, discretely distributed on the surface, then the object surface is approximated by a finite union of polygonal planar surface patches or facets. Geometric objects that are bounded by a finite number of polygons are well known as *polyhedrons*.

---

[1]   Beside these two modeling possibilities some more are dealt with in the literature about computer vision. For example there are *generalized cylinders*. A generalized cylinder is a "swept volume" defined by a generating axis (a curve in $\mathfrak{R}^3$), by a generating two-dimensional set (a planar face, e.g. a rectangular or a circular bounded planar region) "sweeping along" the generating axis (usually the axis be normal to the cross section), and by a parametrization function (parameters of the generating face depending on a point position on the generating axis defining the specific cross section at this point). Informally speaking, the generating face is swept along the generating axis while it changes its shape according to the parametrization function (defining the different cross sections). The generalized cylinder is the union of all points that are contained in these cross sections at a certain moment.

[2]   This corresponds to a local Taylor expansion (compare Section 3.1.3) of the surface function where the non-linear terms are neglected.

However, the facet model is generally not used in the sense of such a polyhedral approximation but in the sense of a local linear approximation of object surfaces. The classes of $C^{(n)}$ *functions* are very suitable to describe *curved surfaces*. These classes model certain continuity respectively differentiability assumptions. Every function that can be differentiated in a point is also continuous at that point. The reverse is not always true, i.e. there are functions that are continuous but cannot be differentiated. This applies, for example, for the function

$$h(X,Y) = \begin{cases} 0, & \text{for} \quad X \leq 0 \\ X, & \text{for} \quad X > 0 \end{cases}$$

in all points $(0, Y)$.

Generally $C^{(n)}(\mathbf{M})$ denotes the class of all functions that are defined on a set $\mathbf{M}$, for $n \geq 0$. These functions are continuous, and their derivatives exist up to and including the nth order and are continuous as well. Analogously, $C^{(\infty)}(\mathbf{M})$ denotes the class of functions which are defined on $\mathbf{M}$, which are continuous, and which have continuous derivatives of any order. The above function h is, for example, contained in the class $C^{(0)}(\Re^2)$ but not in the class $C^{(1)}(\Re^2)$. Generally the inclusion (proper inclusion for non-trivial sets $\mathbf{M}$)

$$C^{(n+1)}(\mathbf{M}) \subseteq C^{(n)}(\mathbf{M})$$

holds for $n \geq 0$. In this textbook either the real plane $\Re^2$ or a bounded subset of this plane is assumed to be the definition domain $\mathbf{M}$. Accordingly often we refrain from stating the definition domain. Furthermore only the sets $C^{(0)}$ (facets or polyhedrons), $C^{(1)}$, or $C^{(2)}$ are relevant in the textbook. Functions of the two latter sets are called $C^{(1)}$-*continuous* respectively $C^{(2)}$-*continuous surface functions*.

A surface function $Z = Z(X,Y)$ is also characterized by the validity or invalidity of the *integrability condition*

$$\frac{\partial^2 Z(X,Y)}{\partial X \partial Y} = \frac{\partial^2 Z(X,Y)}{\partial Y \partial X},$$

for all $(X,Y) \in \mathbf{M}$, i.e. over the relevant definition domain $\mathbf{M}$. If this condition is satisfied then the mixed second derivatives are independent from the order of differentiation. The validity of this condition is "approximately equivalent" to the $C^{(2)}(\mathbf{M})$-continuity according to the following theorem (known from mathematics).

First let us introduce some terms to prepare the formulation of this theorem. A set $\mathbf{M}$ is (topologically) *simply connected* if it can be mapped continuously onto a circular region, i.e. if it is an area "without holes". A (bounded) rectangular region or the (unbounded) real plane are, for instance, simply connected sets.

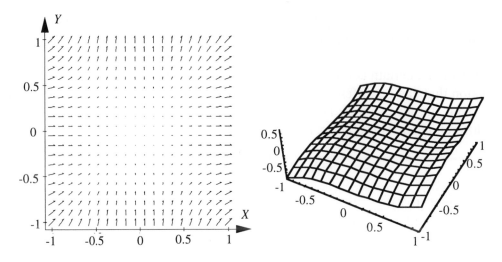

Figure 3.1: A vector field $\mathbf{w}(X,Y)=\left(X^2,Y^2\right)^T$ over $\mathbf{M}=[-1,1]\times[-1,1]$ and a corresponding antiderivative $Z(X,Y)=X^3/3+Y^3/3-1/3$.

A *vector field* over a set $\mathbf{M}$ is a set of vectors where exactly one vector is assigned to every point in $\mathbf{M}$. Thus these vector fields can be seen as functions with the definition domain $\mathbf{M}$, i.e. the above specified terms of $C^{(n)}(\mathbf{M})$-continuity are applicable accordingly for the individual components of these vectors. As known from mathematical analysis the set of all antiderivatives of a given (integrable) function defines the *indefinite integral* of this function. A function $Z=Z(X,Y)$ is an *antiderivative* of a vector field $\mathbf{w}(X,Y)=\left(p(X,Y),q(X,Y)\right)^T$ over $\mathbf{M}$ if

$$p(X,Y)=\frac{\partial Z}{\partial X}(X,Y) \ \text{ and } \ q(X,Y)=\frac{\partial Z}{\partial Y}(X,Y)$$

hold, for all (X,Y) in $\mathbf{M}$. An antiderivative (if it exists) is determined uniquely up to an additive constant. A *conservative vector field* has an indefinite integral.

For example, the two functions X^2 and Y^2 are $C^{(\infty)}$ continuous over $\mathfrak{R}^2$ which are the components of the vectors (compare Fig. 3.1 on the left)

$$\mathbf{w}(X,Y)=\left(X^2,Y^2\right)^T.$$

It follows that this vector field is also characterized as being $C^{(\infty)}$ continuous over $\mathfrak{R}^2$. The general antiderivative (i.e. the indefinite integral) for this vector field is $Z(X,Y)=X^3/3+Y^3/3+const$ where *const* can be any real number.

In the following theorem the common abbreviating subscript notation for derivatives is used, which means

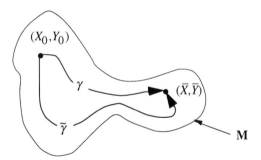

Figure 3.2: Two different integration paths γ and $\tilde{\gamma}$ inside a connected region **M** between an initial position (X_0, Y_0) and a "target" position $(\overline{X}, \overline{Y})$.

$$p_Y(X,Y) = \frac{\partial p}{\partial Y}(X,Y) \text{ respectively } q_X(X,Y) = \frac{\partial q}{\partial X}(X,Y)$$

in this context. In this abbreviating notation the integrability condition for a function $Z(X,Y)$ is as follows: it holds $Z_{XY} = Z_{YX}$ on **M**. If a non-differentiable function only depends on one variable (in Chapter 5 this is, for instance, the time t), then the *dot notation* is also used for the derivatives. For example, we write

$$\dot{y} = \frac{df}{dt} \text{ or } \ddot{y} = \frac{d^2 f}{dt^2}$$

for the first or second derivative of the function $y = f(t)$.

Theorem 3.1:[3] *Let* $\mathbf{w}(X,Y) = \left(p(X,Y), q(X,Y) \right)^T$ *be a* $C^{(1)}(\mathbf{M})$*-continuous vector field on a simply connected set* **M**. *Then a* $C^{(2)}(\mathbf{M})$*-continuous antiderivative* $Z(X,Y)$ *exists to this vector field if* $p_Y(X,Y) = q_X(X,Y)$ *is true for every* (X,Y) *in* **M**, *i.e.* $Z(X,Y)$ *satisfies the integrability condition on* **M**.

Furthermore, mathematical analysis offers (in principle) ways to calculate such an antiderivative. For example, the integration of vector fields can be based on arbitrarily specified *integration paths*, i.e. on piecewise $C^{(1)}$-curves

$$\gamma: \ [a,b] \to \Re^2, \ \ \gamma(t) = \left(\gamma_1(t), \gamma_2(t) \right) = \left(X(t), Y(t) \right)$$

that lies inside the region **M**, with $a < b$, $\gamma(a) = (X_0, Y_0)$ and $\gamma(b) = (\overline{X}, \overline{Y})$. For such a curve γ from (X_0, Y_0) to $(\overline{X}, \overline{Y})$, and for a selected antiderivative Z (i.e. with a specified additive constant) it holds that

---

[3] A special corollary from Frobenius' theorem in mathematical analysis.

$$Z(\overline{X},\overline{Y}) = Z(X_0,Y_0) + \int_\gamma p(X,Y)\,dX + q(X,Y)\,dY$$

$$= Z(X_0,Y_0) + \int_a^b \left[p(\gamma_1(t),\gamma_2(t)) \cdot \dot{\gamma}_1(t) + q(\gamma_1(t),\gamma_2(t)) \cdot \dot{\gamma}_2(t) \right] dt,$$

where the result at position $(\overline{X},\overline{Y})$ is independent from the curve γ, the integration path (compare Fig. 3.2 and Exercise (7) in Section 3.6).

Exercise (4) in Section 3.6 provides an example to illustrate the fact of "almost equivalence" of integrability condition and $C^{(2)}(\mathbf{M})$-continuousity in Theorem 3.1.

The shape reconstruction context will influence the decision whether facets or $C^{(n)}(\mathbf{M})$-continuous (for a small value of n) surface functions are used for surface modeling. Object faces can be characterized by their absolute location in the three-dimensional space, or just by partial descriptions, e.g. by their orientations in specific surface points.

3.1.2   Normals and Gradients

A *tangent plane* (compare Section 1.3.1) is defined at an object surface point $\mathbf{P} = (X,Y,Z(X,Y))$. Assume that the surface satisfies a specific conditional equation $F(X,Y,Z) = 0$ in the local neighborhood of point $\mathbf{P}$, and that this equation is partially differentiable with respect to X, Y and Z. Equivalently, we also can assume that the local neighborhood is characterized by a surface function

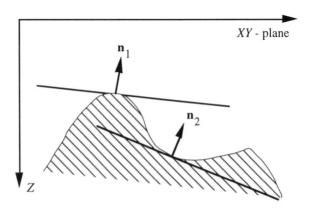

Figure 3.3: Tangents on curves characterize the two-dimensional situation which are analogous to the tangent planes. The normal vectors are perpendicular to these tan–gents.

$Z = Z(X, Y)$ that is partially differentiable with respect to X and Y. Both assumptions ensure an unambiguous definition of the tangent plane at point **P**.

The tangential plane is incident with the corresponding surface point **P** (i.e. it contains this point) and it is perpendicular to the *normal*

$$\mathbf{n}(\mathbf{P}) = \left(n_X, n_Y, n_Z\right)^T$$

in this surface point, compare Fig. 3.3. The normal is defined by

$$\mathbf{n}(\mathbf{P}) = \left(\frac{\partial F}{\partial X}, \frac{\partial F}{\partial Y}, \frac{\partial F}{\partial Z}\right)^T = \left(\frac{\partial Z}{\partial X}, \frac{\partial Z}{\partial Y}, -1\right)^T.$$

Because of the value -1 for the Z-coordinate of the surface function the normal is inversely directed to the Z-axis. The *unit normal*

$$\mathbf{n}°(\mathbf{P}) = \left(n_1, n_2, n_3\right)^T$$

has the same direction as the normal but it is normalized to be a vector of length 1, i.e. it holds

$$\mathbf{n}°(\mathbf{P}) \quad = \frac{\mathbf{n}(\mathbf{P})}{\|\mathbf{n}(\mathbf{P})\|} = \frac{\left(\dfrac{\partial F}{\partial X}, \dfrac{\partial F}{\partial Y}, \dfrac{\partial F}{\partial Z}\right)^T}{\sqrt{\left(\dfrac{\partial F}{\partial X}\right)^2 + \left(\dfrac{\partial F}{\partial Y}\right)^2 + \left(\dfrac{\partial F}{\partial Z}\right)^2}} \quad = \frac{\left(\dfrac{\partial Z}{\partial X}, \dfrac{\partial Z}{\partial Y}, -1\right)^T}{\sqrt{\left(\dfrac{\partial Z}{\partial X}\right)^2 + \left(\dfrac{\partial Z}{\partial Y}\right)^2 + 1}}.$$

The normal respectively the unit normal uniquely characterizes the *orientation* of the facet or of the tangent plane at the given surface point.

The *gradient* is the vector

$$grad(Z)(X, Y) = \left(\frac{\partial Z}{\partial X}, \frac{\partial Z}{\partial Y}\right)^T$$

in the point (X, Y), for a surface function $Z = Z(X, Y)$. Evidently, gradient and normal (respectively unit normal) are vectors that define themselves mutually uniquely up to a scaling factor.

Gradients combine the derivatives of a surface function in X-direction and in Y-direction. Generally a derivative of the surface function $Z = Z(X, Y)$ can be analyzed in any direction α within the XY plane. Let α be an angle to the X-axis (in counterclockwise measurement). The *directional derivative*

$$m(\alpha) \quad = \quad \frac{\partial Z}{\partial X} \cdot cos(\alpha) \quad + \quad \frac{\partial Z}{\partial Y} \cdot sin(\alpha)$$

characterizes the slope of the surface $Z = Z(X, Y)$ in direction α. For $\alpha = 0$ this is the slope in X-direction and for $\alpha = \pi/2$ it is the one in Y-direction.

The definition of gradients can be extended for one-dimensional objects as vectors, straight lines, or line segments in the three-dimensional XYZ space. This extension can be advantageous for certain gradient studies (e.g. for the analysis of the gradient of a straight line in relation to the gradients of those planes which are incident with that straight line, i.e. which contain this line). For a vector $\mathbf{a} = (a_1, a_2, a_3)^T$ the gradient of this vector $\mathbf{a}$ is defined by

$$grad(\mathbf{a}) = \left(\frac{a_1}{-a_3}, \frac{a_2}{-a_3} \right)^T .$$

It is assumed that $a_3 \neq 0$. Thus parallel vectors (i.e. having the same or the inverse orientation; note $grad(\mathbf{a}) = grad(-\mathbf{a})$) have the same gradients.

The gradient of a straight line can therefore be uniquely identified by any arbitrary vector that is parallel to this straight line. Finally the gradient of a line segment is defined uniquely by the gradient of that straight line which is incident with the line segment. It follows immediately that parallel straight lines, or parallel line segments have the same gradient.

Example 3.1 (*plane*): We illustrate the introduced terms especially for planes in $\Re^3$ respectively for facets incident with such planes (i.e. being a subset of such planes). Just to specify our preferred notation, a *plane* $\mathcal{E}(X, Y)$ is the set of all points (X, Y, Z) which satisfy equations of the form

$$aX + bY + cZ + d = 0 \quad \text{or} \quad Z = pX + qY + r .$$

The functional plane representation is only possible if the plane $\mathcal{E}$ is not orthogonal to the XY-plane. In this functional representation r is the distance between the intersection of the plane with the Z-axis and the origin. The point $(0, 0, r)$ was already named the Z-intercept of the plane (see Section 3.1.1). The slope of the plane $\mathcal{E}$ relatively to the XY-plane is characterized by p and q. Accordingly this plane representation is also called the *slope-intercept equation*. The vector

$$\mathbf{n} = (p, q, -1)^T$$

is the (universal or global) normal of the plane $\mathcal{E}$. The unit normal is

$$\mathbf{n}° = \frac{(p, q, -1)^T}{\sqrt{p^2 + q^2 + 1}} ,$$

and $grad(\mathcal{E}) = (p, q)^T$ is the gradient of the plane $\mathcal{E}$. The directional derivative of

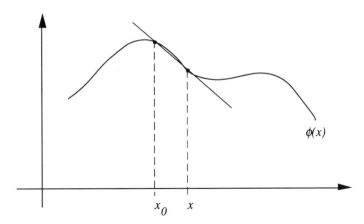

Figure 3.4: Linear approximation of a unary function in the interval $\left[x_0, x\right]$.

the plane in direction α is equal to $m(\alpha) = p \cdot cos(\alpha) + q \cdot sin(\alpha)$. The slope in X-direction is equal to p and the slope in Y-direction is equal to q.

For the gradient $grad(\mathcal{E})$ of a plane and the gradient $grad(\mathbf{n})$ of the normal $\mathbf{n}$ of this plane it holds that

$$grad(\mathcal{E}) = grad(\mathbf{n})$$

since $grad(\mathbf{n}) = (p, q)^T$ for the normal $\mathbf{n} = (p, q, -1)^T$ of this plane. {end of example 3.1}

In the case of curved object surfaces the equation $grad(\mathcal{E}) = grad(\mathbf{n})$ also holds for a tangent plane $\mathcal{E}$ that is (by definition) orthogonal to the normal in the selected surface point.

Normals allow the definition of object edges or specific points on the object surface. Normals also allow to specify features in digital images (see Section 1.3.1), however, this is not the topic in this chapter.

An *orientation edge* of the object surface is a certain curve (defining the geometric location of the edge) on this surface characterized by discontinuities of normals at all points along this curve on the object surface. These object edges "exist" by the object itself, they are not defined by an image acquisition configuration.

On the other hand, the *rim* of an object is defined with respect to a specific projection of this object into the image plane (see Section 2.1.1 for parallel or central projection): It consists of all points $\mathbf{P} = (X, Y, Z)$ on a $C^{(1)}$ object surface where the projection ray $\mathbf{v}(\mathbf{P})$ from point $\mathbf{P}$ into the image plane is perpendicular to the surface normal $\mathbf{n}(\mathbf{P})$. The *occluding boundary* (or *occlusion edge, apparent contour, profile*, or *silhouette*) is the rim projected into the image plane.

3.1.3   Taylor Expansion

Occasionally this textbook refers to the Taylor expansion[4] for local approximations of $C^{(n)}$-surface functions, or for local approximations of gray value image
functions E that are assumed to be differentiable.[5] The basic idea of the Taylor
expansion is to characterize functions based on their derivatives.

   For a brief sketch of the geometric interpretation of this expansion (only
up to derivatives of first order) see Fig. 3.4 for a unary function. Assume that the
unary function $\phi = \phi(x)$ is differentiable. For the approximation of the difference
quotient

$$\frac{\phi(x) - \phi(x_0)}{x - x_0} = \frac{\phi(x_0 + \delta x) - \phi(x_0)}{\delta x}$$

it may be assumed that the function ϕ behaves approximately linearly from x_0 to
x. The difference quotient is equal to the slope of the straight line that passes
through the points $(x_0, \phi(x_0))$ and $(x, \phi(x))$. If ϕ is exactly this line then the
slope of the line is equal to the differential quotient respectively equal to the
derivative

$$\frac{d\phi(x)}{dx} \text{ respectively } \frac{d\phi}{dx}(x) \text{ respectively } \frac{d\phi(x)}{dx}(x)$$

(these are three equivalent notations) at the position x_0. Therefore the difference
quotient and the differential quotient

$$\frac{\phi(x) - \phi(x_0)}{x - x_0} \text{ and } \frac{d\phi(x)}{dx}$$

can be identified under the *linearity assumption*. In the case of an almost linear
function follows

$$\frac{\phi(x) - \phi(x_0)}{x - x_0} \approx \frac{d\phi(x_0)}{dx}$$

and therefore

$$\phi(x) = \phi(x_0) + (x - x_0) \cdot \frac{d\phi(x_0)}{dx} + e,$$

---

[4] Named after the mathematician Brook Taylor (1685 - 1731).
[5] Mathematically correctness would require to consider only functions which are in $C^{(\infty)}$.

for an insignificant error e. This may be written as

$$\phi(x_0 + \delta x) \approx \phi(x_0) + \delta x \cdot \frac{d\phi(x_0)}{dx} \, .$$

The linearity assumption is very practical since it can be used to rule out derivatives of higher order as required of a general Taylor expansion

$$\phi(x) = \sum_{i=0,1,2,\dots} \frac{1}{i!} \cdot (x - x_0)^i \cdot \frac{d^i \phi(x_0)}{d^i x}$$

of $C^{(\infty)}$ functions.

Now let ϕ be a binary function with two arguments u and v (e.g., a scalar image). Here the formula

$$\phi(u, v) = \phi(u_0, v_0) + \left((u - u_0) \cdot \frac{\partial \phi(u_0, v_0)}{\partial u} + (v - v_0) \cdot \frac{\partial \phi(u_0, v_0)}{\partial v} \right) + e$$

can be used as a linear approximation if the value of e is insignificant. Usually this can be assumed for given data in computer vision applications, e.g. if the step size is small in comparison to the frequency of the data. For an assumed small step size from $(u, v) = (u_0 + \delta u, v_0 + \delta v)$ to (u_0, v_0) the notation

$$\phi(u_0 + \delta u, v_0 + \delta v) \approx \phi(u_0, v_0) + \delta u \cdot \frac{\partial \phi(u_0, v_0)}{\partial u} + \delta v \cdot \frac{\partial \phi(u_0, v_0)}{\partial v}$$

expresses this possibility of a linear approximation.

3.1.4 Sphere and Solid Angles

The *sphere* is repeatedly used in the following as a means of description. Some terms and functions are provided in this section. Assume a sphere in an *xyz* Cartesian coordinate system. The sphere center coincides with the origin. Let the radius be equal to r. The surface points $\mathbf{P} = (x, y, z)$ of the sphere satisfy the conditional equation

$$x^2 + y^2 + z^2 - r^2 = 0,$$

or at least one of the two surface functions

$$z = \phi_1(x, y) = \sqrt{r^2 - x^2 - y^2} \quad \text{or} \quad z = \phi_2(x, y) = -\sqrt{r^2 - x^2 - y^2},$$

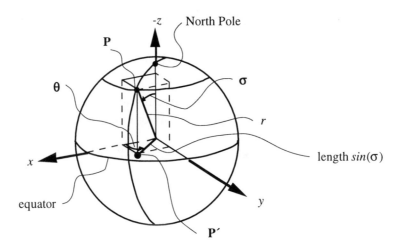

Figure 3.5: Representation of a surface point **P** on the Gaussian sphere through *slant* σ and *tilt* θ. The radius r is equal to 1. The point **P′** that is projected into the xy plane is characterized in the xy equatorial plane by the tilt θ and the distance $sin(\sigma)$ to the origin.

for the "invisible" (assume a viewing direction in the xyz coordinate system in direction of the z axis) or for the "visible" side of the sphere. For surface points $\mathbf{P} = (x, y, z)$ of the visible side ϕ_2 we obtain the unit normal

$$\mathbf{n}^\circ(x,y) = \left(n_1(x,y), n_2(x,y), n_3(x,y)\right)^T = \frac{1}{r} \cdot \left(x, y, -\sqrt{r^2 - x^2 - y^2}\right)^T .$$

A so-called *Gaussian sphere* is specified by $r=1$. Here, surface points $\mathbf{P} = (x, y, z)$ of the sphere can be uniquely defined by two *spherical coordinates* (or *Gaussian coordinates*) namely *slant* σ and *tilt* θ (compare Fig. 3.5).

Every point $\mathbf{P} = (x, y, z)$ on the surface of the Gaussian sphere represents a unit normal. The slant σ is the angle to the z-axis.[6] The tilt θ is an angle in the equatorial plane, defined by the point $\mathbf{P}' = (x, y, 0)$ and the x-axis. Generally the radius r could be used as the third coordinate. However, for the unit normals it holds $r=1$, i.e. these vectors are characterized uniquely by slant and tilt.

Every *great circle* (intersection of the sphere surface with a plane passing through the sphere center) defines two *Gaussian hemispheres*. Figure 3.6 shows a shaded great circle and a normal that corresponds to the generating intersecting plane.

The surface area of the whole surface of the Gaussian sphere is equal to 4π. Thus one Gaussian hemisphere has the surface area $A = 2\pi$.

---

[6] In astronomy the value $\pi/2 - \sigma$ is called the slant.

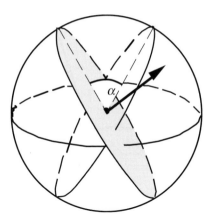

Figure 3.6: Intersection of two Gaussian hemispheres.

The intersection of two great circles defines four *spherical lunes*, compare Fig. 3.6. The surface area of a single spherical lune equals

$$A = 2 \cdot r^2 \cdot \alpha = 2\alpha, \text{ with } 0 \le \alpha \le \pi.$$

Note that the surface area of a spherical lune only depends on the smaller angle α defined by the two great circles.

Solid angles are an important means of characterizing three-dimensional lighting situations as they are described in Chapters 6 to 9. A *solid angle* Ω is defined analogously to the radian measure as follows: The ratio of the length of the arc to the radius of the circle defines the plane angle. Accordingly, the solid angle Ω is defined by the ratio of the surface area A of a sphere to the square of the radius r of the sphere (see Fig. 3.7):

$$\Omega = \frac{A}{r^2} .$$

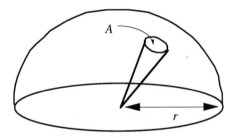

Figure 3.7: Entities for the definition of the solid angle.

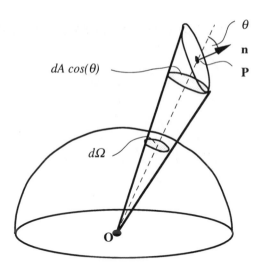

Figure 3.8: Solid angle of a tilted facet (surface patch).

The unit of measure of the solid angle is denoted by sr (*steradiant*). As an example, the solid angle of the whole sphere is equal to 4π steradiants.

Assume a face A in $\mathfrak{R}^3$ that has to be described with respect to the assumed sphere center. Assume that A is not incident with the sphere surface. Then this region A can be characterized with respect to the sphere center by a projected solid angle Ω as follows:

We consider a sphere with radius r. The sphere center lies at the origin $\mathbf{O}$ of the *xyz* coordinate system. Let dA be an infinitesimal surface element of the face A. Let $\mathbf{P}$ be a position vector in the *xyz* coordinate system, from the origin to a point in dA (compare Fig. 3.8).

Now let $\mathbf{n}$ be the normal of dA in point $\mathbf{P}$. Let θ be the angle between the position vector $\mathbf{P}$ and the normal $\mathbf{n}$,

$$\theta = \measuredangle\,(\mathbf{P}, \mathbf{n})\ .$$

Let $r = \|\mathbf{P}\|$. Then the solid angle $d\Omega$ under which the surface element dA is seen from the origin (i.e. center of the sphere) is equal to

$$d\Omega = \frac{\cos(\theta)\cdot dA}{r^2}.$$

A given face A can be decomposed into infinitesimal surface elements, and the sum of the corresponding solid angles $d\Omega$ defines the solid angle of A (with respect to the chosen decomposition).

3.2   PROJECTION AND RECONSTRUCTION

The *general shape reconstruction problem* (*general shape recovery problem*) consists of three major steps:

> A single viewing direction (projection direction) only allows a certain $2\frac{1}{2}D$-*reconstruction* of scene objects. The first step of a general shape reconstruction problem is formally defined by the task to generate partial or complete *depth maps* or *height maps* (arrays of scalar range data), or at least partial or complete *gradient maps* (vector fields, compare, for example Fig. 3.1, left), for all the visible surface points, and for a selected set of viewing directions.

> *Registration* of different maps (generated with respect to different viewing directions) defines a second step of a general shape reconstruction problem. This means that the different maps have to be mapped into a uniform coordinate system for the given scene, or for the given 3D object.

> *Integration* of registered maps defines the third step of a general shape reconstruction problem. This, finally, can lead to the generation of a complete 3D model of the given scene or of the given object.

Normally such a shape reconstruction problem is embedded in a specific context of a certain computer vision task. However this textbook is not oriented towards a specific application area. The focus is on the general fundamentals of the first major step in this general problem scheme, the problem of $2\frac{1}{2}D$-reconstruction.

Two projection models were introduced and discussed in Chapter 2. In this section the problem of $2\frac{1}{2}D$-reconstruction is formulated for these projection models and briefly discussed: Which geometric entities have to be calculated? Which relations do exist between these entities? How $2\frac{1}{2}D$-reconstruction results can be generated for synthetic objects (for purposes of comparison, evaluation etc.)? We start with having a closer look at the projection of surface points.

3.2.1   Range Image, Depth Map, Height Map, and Gradient Map

The projection center for the central projection is the origin $\mathbf{O} = (0,0,0)$ of the XYZ coordinate system[7]. From this point a *ray of projection*

$$\gamma(t) = \mathbf{O} + t(\mathbf{Q} - \mathbf{O}) = t \cdot \mathbf{Q} = (tx, ty, tf), \text{ with } t \geq 1$$

---

[7]   Often the index k is omitted for camera coordinates (X, Y, Z) if no further $3D$ coordinate systems are directly relevant in the given context. Analogously the index u is often omitted for undistorted image plane coordinates (x, y).

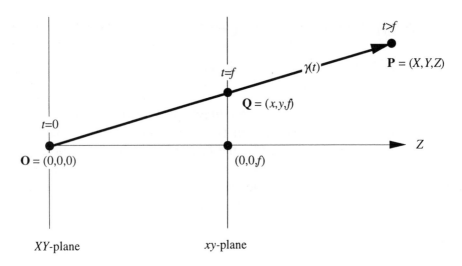

Figure 3.9: A ray of projection for the camera-centered central projection model.

emerges into the scene space that passes through a certain point $Q = (x, y, f)$ of the xy image plane (compare Fig. 3.9).

In the case of parallel projection the ray of projection into the scene space can be modeled as

$$\gamma(t) = (x, y, t), \text{ with } t \geq f.$$

This ray passes through a certain image point $Q = (x, y, f)$ and is parallel to the optical axis. In this case the projection center is a point at infinity.

Now assume that a certain projection model is chosen. A surface point $P = (X, Y, Z)$ is *projected into an image point* $p = (x, y)$ of the image plane if a ray of projection exists which intersects the object surface at $P = (X, Y, Z)$ "for the first time" (to be exact: for the smallest $t \geq 1$ respectively $t \geq f$) after passing through the image point $Q = (x, y, f)$.

The given definition of projection into the image plane specifies at most one surface point for each image point. This excludes situations as follows: In the case of a parallel projection all those object surface points with identical XY-coordinates are geometrically projected into the same point (x, y) (e.g. surface points on a face which is orthogonal to the image plane). Our definition specifies "the closest point" if there are "several candidates". In general (i.e. also covering central projection), if several surface points are incident with the same ray of projection then we select (in studies of image acquisition or in discussions of shape reconstruction techniques) that point with the smallest t-coordinate value. If a surface point is projected into an image point then this surface point is *visible* with respect to the chosen projection model.

This definition allows to deal with synthetic objects as follows: if a surface function is given (e.g. a synthetic model of a real-world object that is to be reconstructed) then the ray coordinates $\gamma(t)$ can be substituted into the given surface equation. The given equation in three variables X, Y, Z is transformed into an equation in one variable t. The solution(s) of this equation define the intersection point(s) of the ray of projection with the given surface. By specifying image coordinates (x, y) the relevant (projected) surface point(s) can be calculated. For such a computer graphics approach it can be assumed that the focal length f is given, and the generated images can be used to evaluate shape recovery techniques because the shape of the synthetic object (the *ground truth*) is known in this case. The evaluation of the accuracy of reconstructed object surfaces (for different recovery techniques, for different classes of scene objects etc.) is an important topic in recent computer vision research.

The depth map respectively the height map, and the gradient map are functions over the image grid $\{(x, y): 1 \leq x \leq M \wedge 1 \leq y \leq N\}$. The value distribution in depth maps or height maps can simply be visualized by gray value images. We use the following convention: "bright" corresponds to a "value of large magnitude" and "dark" corresponds to a "value of small magnitude".

In the ideal case at each point (x, y) a *depth map* $Z = Z(x, y)$ states the depth Z of those surface point $\mathbf{P} = (X, Y, Z)$ that is projected into the image point $\mathbf{p} = (x, y)$. For an example of a depth map, compare Fig. 3.10, above right.

A *height map* $H(x, y)$ is defined relatively to an assumed background plane (of height zero), which is parallel to the image plane. In the ideal case at each point (x, y) the value $H(x, y)$ is equal to the (scaled) height of those surface point $\mathbf{P} = (X, Y, Z)$ that is projected into the image point $\mathbf{p} = (x, y)$. Height is measured with respect to the chosen background plane. Visualizations of the depth map and the height map behave to each other approximately like a positive and a negative. Depth respectively height can be given absolutely or just be calculated as relative values (e.g. scaled with respect to an assumed distance between image and background plane). In the case of absolute values depth and height data are determining equivalently each other.

For visualizing or representing $2\frac{1}{2}$D-reconstructions the calculation of a *range image* is a third option. However the Euclidean distance

$$d_2(\mathbf{P}, \mathbf{O}) = \sqrt{X^2 + Y^2 + Z^2}$$

between the visible surface point $\mathbf{P} = (X, Y, Z)$ and the origin of the camera coordinate system, or the Euclidean distance

$$d_2(\mathbf{P}, \mathbf{Q}) = \sqrt{(X - x)^2 + (Y - y)^2 + (Z - f)^2}$$

between the visible point $\mathbf{P} = (X, Y, Z)$ and the projected point $\mathbf{Q} = (x, y, f)$ in the image plane are geometrically equivalent to depth Z (see Exercise (1) in Section 3.6).

In comparison to height, depth or range map the following is a somewhat "weaker" representation of object surfaces. In the ideal case at each image point (x, y) a *gradient map* states the gradient $(p, q)^T$ of those object surface point $\mathbf{P} = (X, Y, Z)$ that is projected into this image point (assuming, of course, that such a gradient is defined at the projected point). Thus a gradient map can be visualized by two gray value images depicting the functions $p(x, y)$ and $q(x, y)$.

The depth map respectively the height map on one hand, and the gradient map on the other hand are not geometrically equivalent representations of visible surface points. For instance, assume that a camera is directed towards a staircase so that it can only "see" faces coplanar to the image plane. All these surfaces have the same gradient, i.e. the gradient map would have an identical vector value in all of its positions. Of course, the stairs would appear as different depth or height values in the depth or height map. Gradient data can be approximated from given discrete height or depth maps (with different techniques, e.g. difference quotients for specific local neighborhoods). The generation of height or depth maps based on gradient information is more challenging, and is considered in a forthcoming section in this textbook.

Example 3.2 (*sphere*): Consider a sphere in the XYZ space (compare Section 3.1.4). The sphere center $(0, 0, a)$ is assumed to lie on the Z-axis. Let the radius be r. Points $\mathbf{P} = (X, Y, Z)$ on the sphere surface satisfy the functional equation

$$X^2 + Y^2 + (Z - a)^2 - r^2 = 0 \text{ , where } a - r > f$$

is assumed to assure that sphere and image plane do not intersect. The focal length f is the distance between the XY-plane and the image plane in the sense of the camera-centered coordinate system.

In the case of parallel projection $x = X$ and $y = Y$ an intersection point (X, Y, Z) of the sphere surface with a ray of projection $\gamma(t) = (X, Y, t)$ is defined by a real solution of the equation

$$X^2 + Y^2 + (t - a)^2 = r^2$$

for the unknown t. For at most two real solutions $t \geq f$ the minimum Z-value

$$Z(x, y) = t = a - \sqrt{r^2 - x^2 - y^2}$$

(note the sign $-$ in front of the root) is simply taken as depth map value. It holds that

$$grad(Z)(x,y) = \left(p(x,y),q(x,y)\right) = \left(\frac{x}{\sqrt{r^2 - x^2 - y^2}}, \frac{y}{\sqrt{r^2 - x^2 - y^2}}\right)$$

is the gradient function

The case of an assumed central projection model,

$$x = \frac{f \cdot X}{Z} \quad \text{and} \quad y = \frac{f \cdot Y}{Z},$$

is not as straightforward. The relevant intersections with the rays of projection $\gamma(t)$ arise here from the real solutions $t \geq 1$ of the equation

$$t^2 x^2 + t^2 y^2 + (tf - a)^2 = r^2.$$

Because of selecting the smaller value we receive the visible (with respect to the central projection) intersection point with the surface of the sphere for

$$t = \frac{af - \sqrt{r^2(x^2 + y^2 + f^2) - a^2(x^2 + y^2)}}{x^2 + y^2 + f^2},$$

and therefore the depth map $Z(x, y) = tf$. Insertion of the Z-values into the projection equations leads to the X-values and the Y-values, and therefore also to the gradient map $\left(p(x, y), q(x, y)\right)$. { end of Example 3.1 }

This simple example illustrates a general approach of generating depth or height maps from synthetic object data. A 3D object is mapped in a certain set of descriptive data in the image plane. However, the (general) object reconstruction problem in computer vision is exactly the opposite, i.e. 3D object faces have to be reconstructed from descriptive data. The calculation of "meaningful" descriptive surface data based on images is the main subject of this book. What information can be derived from a calculated depth map or from a calculated gradient map? To what extent are these maps "valuable" analysis aims inside of a complex reconstruction procedure? The following section gives a first answer.

3.2.2   Backprojection

Surfaces of scene objects are projected into the image plane by projections as discussed in Sections 2.1 and 3.2.1. The inverse mapping of projected object surfaces or projected faces into the 3D space is generally called *backprojection*. Depth maps (or height maps), and gradient maps provide important but differing information for such a back projection.

As an example of an object face that has to be reconstructed assume a facet or a planar surface segment in the plane $Z = pX + qY + r$ and assume central projection. Note that this assumption is actually very general; see the facet model for object surfaces in Section 3.1.1.

It is well-known that coordinates of three non-collinear points in the 3D space incident with a certain plane allow a unique characterization of this plane. However, here our input data are normally not this way. Our interest is often in back projecting of individual image points (x, y) into the 3D space. The "local knowledge around" this point should support a way to reconstruct the visible surface point (X, Y, Z) projected into this point, or a certain surface patch "around (X, Y, Z)".

In general it holds that the coordinates X, Y, Z of a visible point on an object surface can be calculated as functions of the image coordinates x, y, the facet parameters $p(x, y)$, $q(x, y)$, and $r(x, y)$, and the effective focal length f if the facet is not parallel to the rays of projection. The image coordinates x and y are known. The focal length f is (often) also given. Therefore, if a hypothetical image analysis technique would allow to calculate the gradient respectively the orientation values $p(x, y)$ and $q(x, y)$ as well as the Z-intercept value $r(x, y)$ at image points (x, y) then the visible surface can be uniquely (in the sense of a facet approximation) recovered in 3D space according to the following theorem.

Theorem 3.2 *(backprojection of a facet): For a central projection of a plane $Z = pX + qY + r$ into the xy-image plane it holds that*

$$X = \frac{rx}{f - qy - px}, \quad Y = \frac{ry}{f - qy - px} \quad and \quad Z = \frac{rf}{f - qy - px},$$

if f is the effective focal length and $f - qy - px \neq 0$.

Proof: Because of the assumed central projection all visible surface points (X, Y, Z) satisfy the equations

$$X = \frac{xZ}{f} = \frac{pxX + qxY + rx}{f} \quad and \quad Y = \frac{yZ}{f} = \frac{pyX + qyY + ry}{f}.$$

Thus, it holds that

$$Y = \frac{pyX + ry}{f - qy}$$

and therefore

$$(f - px)X = qxY + rx = qx \cdot \frac{pyX + ry}{f - qy} + rx,$$

or

$$(f - px - qy)X = rx \ .$$

This leads to the 3D coordinates of the theorem. Q.E.D.

In principle this theorem and the mentioned hypothetical image analysis technique (!) allow a back projection for all "visible object facets", i.e. facets which have a unique intersection at a visible surface point with at least one ray of projection. If several visible surface points on the same facet are projected into different image points then the same gradient values and the same Z-intercept value can be used for the recovery of these surface points. Because the mentioned hypothetical image analysis technique is not known so far in computer vision this theorem encourages the design of such a shape recovery technique in computer vision directed on calculations of gradients and Z-intercepts.

Instead of the hypothetical image analysis technique we may have just the gradient data (and the constant f), or range values at a few image points. These situations specify different back projection problems. In general we have to answer the question: how the calculated data can be used to support a certain back projection technique. Or even better: Specify a set of parameters which supports shape recovery (prove this as we did for the theorem above), and design a computer vision technique which ensures a "good quality" calculation of these parameters.

As a final note to the given Theorem 3.2: A general technique for the back projection of single object facets can also incorporate the analysis of neighboring object facets. Neighboring (polygonal) object facets intersect ("touch") in one straight line segment. Two straight line segments of a polygonal border, or three vertices on the border of a facet specify an equation of the facet's plane. Such interrelations can be used to support the reconstruction process; see Section 1.5 in the book by K. Kanatani (1990), cited in Section 3.5.

A *polyhedral scene object* is an obviously intended physical realization of a polyhedron (see Fig. 3.13 and Color Image 2 for examples of polyhedral scene objects). Many objects in real scenes can be interpreted to be polyhedral. These objects of the real world specify a certain "polyhedral world". Theorem 3.2 might be of use for designing a shape recovery technique for a polyhedral world where reconstructed face parameters can be optimized within each image segment, and the reconstruction of neighboring object faces (i.e. geometrical constraints between these segments) can be used to control the whole process. Orientation edges of the polyhedral scene objects arise as intersection lines of the reconstructed planes.

3.2.3   Visualization of Gradient Maps

So-called *needle maps* can be used to visualize gradient maps (see Fig. 3.10).
Known surface normals are entered into the needle map as line segments starting
at the image points where they were determined. A vectorial representation of the
surface normals (with arrowheads) is generally not useful because of the selected
image resolution since it will not be recognizable visually. Later (Chapters 7 and

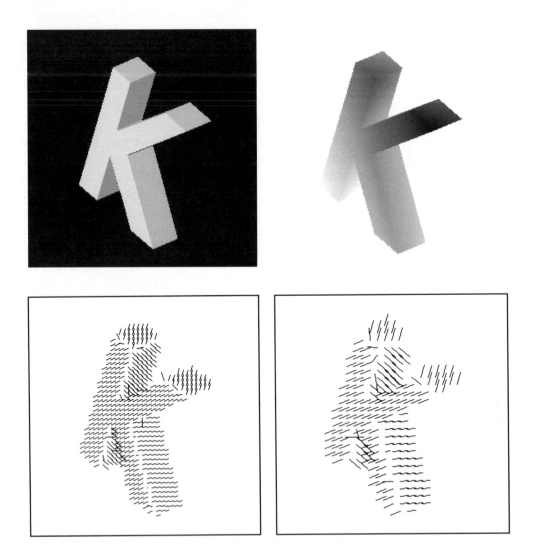

Figure 3.10: An image of a synthetic polyhedral scene, a depth map and two needle maps
(with different scaling) of this scene. All images have the resolution 256×256.

8) it will be shown under which conditions the (approximate) calculation of orientation information (i.e. gradients) is possible for object surface points. Computer vision allows the generation of dense needle maps in some cases.

(Task 3.1) Assume that values of calculated normals or gradients are given at image points (x, y) as input. These normals have to be represented on the screen as a needle map. The given normals are either assumed as normals of arbitrary length in *XYZ*-coordinates or as unit normals in coordinates of the Gaussian sphere (slant and tilt).

(Solution 3.1) We define that a needle represents a normal as a line segment. A given normal $\mathbf{n} = (n_X, n_Y, n_Z)^T$ in the *XYZ* coordinate system with a non-scaled length is represented by its unit normal $\mathbf{n}° = (n_1, n_2, n_3)^T$ since an unnormalized length would complicate the visual interpretation of the needle map. For the unit normal the representation of the Gaussian sphere (slant σ and tilt θ, see Fig. 3.5) is used as a basis for the representation. The direction of the line segment is determined by θ and the length of the line segment is determined by $sin(\sigma)$. Therefore for the coordinate differences that have to be calculated it holds that $\Delta x = n_1$ and $\Delta y = n_2$, with $0 \le \Delta x, \Delta y \le 1$.

Since these Δ-values lie inside the interval $[0,1]$ a scaling factor s, for example $s = 10$, is recommended for the length of the line segment. Then the line segment has to be drawn on the screen from the image point (x, y) that is the projective image of an object surface point $\mathbf{P}$ (the normal $\mathbf{n} = (n_X, n_Y, n_Z)^T$ was determined for this point $\mathbf{P}$) to an image point $(x + s \cdot \Delta x, y + s \cdot \Delta y)$. Furthermore, it is also sensible to draw only every rth line segment. For the algorithm let us assume that $r = s$ (i.e. same scaling of length and spatial distribution).

(Algorithm 3.1) It is assumed that for every image point (x, y) at most one surface normal starting at (x, y) has to be represented. The availability of a suitable graphics procedure is assumed to draw the line segments from (x, y) to $(x + s \cdot \Delta x, y + s \cdot \Delta y)$. This procedure has also to deal in particular with situations where line segments cross the border of the image window. The algorithm is shown in Fig. 3.11.

(Comment 3.1) For facets or object faces that are oriented parallel to the image plane (i.e. the normal is orthogonal to the image plane and $sin(\sigma) = 0$) the needles are dots. Facets or object faces that are almost orthogonal to the image plane (but still visible) are represented by needles of maximum length. If a color screen is available information like the length $sin(\sigma) = 0$ or the gradient direction can also be represented color encoded (e.g. the direction as color value *HUE* and the length as intensity).

Figure 3.10 illustrates the results of the specified technique for a synthetic scene. At the upper left a synthetic polyhedral object is shown. For such a synthetic object normals $\mathbf{n} = (n_X, n_Y, n_Z)^T$ can be calculated for all image points (except for edge and background positions). At the upper right the depth map is represented by gray values (bright encodes large depth values, and dark encodes smaller depth values). Figure 3.10 below shows two examples of needle maps (on the left with scaling factor $s = 10$ for the length of line segments and a representation of every fifth line segment, and on the right with $s = 20$ and a representation of every eighth line segment). Discontinuities in the distribution of normals are clearly visible in these two needle maps at projections of orientation edges.

---

for every image point $(x, y) = (r \cdot i, r \cdot j)$,
           in which a normal $\mathbf{n}$ was determined **do**
   begin
       if ($\mathbf{n}$ was determined in XYZ coordinates) **then**
          begin

$$\text{let } \mathbf{n} = (n_X, n_Y, n_Z)^T;$$
$$\|\mathbf{n}\| := \sqrt{n_X^2 + n_Y^2 + n_Z^2};$$
$$\text{if } \|\mathbf{n}\| = 0 \quad \textbf{then}$$

                             { error in the normal determination }
                    begin $\Delta x := 0; \quad \Delta y := 0$ **end** {then}
          else
               begin

$$\Delta x := n_X / \|\mathbf{n}\|; \quad \Delta y := n_Y / \|\mathbf{n}\|$$

               end {else}
          end {then}
       else   { $\mathbf{n}$ is a unit normal given in spherical coordinates σ, θ }
          begin

$$\Delta x := cos(\theta) \cdot sin(\sigma);$$
$$\Delta y := sin(\theta) \cdot sin(\sigma)$$

          end {else};
       $\Delta x := s \cdot \Delta x; \quad \Delta y := s \cdot \Delta y;$ { scaling }
       draw a line from $(r \cdot i, r \cdot j)$ to $(r \cdot i + \Delta x, r \cdot j + \Delta y)$
   end {for}

Figure 3.11: Algorithm for the needle map generation (with uniform scaling of length and spatial distribution).

3.3   DEPTH MAPS FROM GRADIENT MAPS

A given depth or height map allows us to reconstruct object faces in 3D space within a subsequent computation step of a general back projection approach.[8] Then, e.g., these $2\frac{1}{2}$D surface representations can be visualized under different angles, with respect to different resolutions etc. Computer graphics also allows to visualize object surfaces just based on a given depth or height map (floating horizon technique, simple shading approaches, adding texture mapping etc. - see references in Section 3.5).

However, if (only) gradient values are available for a certain discrete set of visible points on object surfaces then in general it is useful to calculate a relative[9] depth or height map at first before going to the next step of a general backprojection approach.

3.3.1   Local Propagation Methods

Based on Theorem 3.2 the following simple technique could be suggested for polyhedral objects and an assumed central projection:

Starting with a given gradient map $(p(x, y), q(x, y))$ at first calculate the values $denom(x, y) = f - p(x, y) \cdot x - q(x, y) \cdot y$ for positions (x, y). Then the reconstruction of surface points in 3D space, or just the calculation of the depth or height map can be based on the formula

$$\mathbf{P} = (X, Y, Z) = r(x, y) \cdot \left(\frac{x}{denom(x, y)}, \frac{y}{denom(x, y)}, \frac{f}{denom(x, y)} \right).$$

Here the real problem is hidden in the coefficient $r(x, y)$. This local scaling factor is unknown if only the gradient map is given.

Under the relatively weak assumption of differentiability for the surface function the depth of the visible surface points can actually be determined very accurately up to a constant scaling factor. This reconstruction requires (complete) knowledge of the gradient map and a scene projection which can be modeled by central projection.

For the following theorem note that a step $(\delta x, \delta y)$ in the image plane corresponds to a step $(\delta X, \delta Y, \delta Z)$ in the 3D space. As before, a visible point (X, Y, Z) is projected into the point (x, y) in the image plane.

---

[8]   This step is often more difficult than it seems at the first glance. According to the uniformly scaled height map and the different local surface slopes the visible discrete points on the object surface are characterized by different densities.

[9]   "Relative" means generally "up to a certain additive constant or scaling factor".

Theorem 3.3 *(depth from gradients for central projection): For central projection and a differentiable surface function* $Z = Z(X, Y)$ *it holds that*

$$\frac{Z(X + \delta X, Y + \delta Y)}{Z(X, Y)} \approx 1 + c(x, y, p, q, \delta x, \delta y) \, ,$$

where $p(x, y)$ *and* $q(x, y)$ *are the gradient values for the image point* (x, y) *(i.e. for the visible surface point* $(X, Y, Z(X, Y))$ *projected into this image point) and* c *is a function which is explicitly specified in the proof.*

Proof: First we show that

$$\delta X \approx \frac{x \cdot \delta Z + \delta x \cdot Z}{f} \quad \text{and} \quad \delta Y \approx \frac{y \cdot \delta Z + \delta y \cdot Z}{f}$$

holds. To prove the "X-approximation" we consider

$$x = \frac{f \cdot X}{Z} \quad \text{and} \quad x + \delta x = \frac{f \cdot (X + \delta X)}{Z + \delta Z} \, .$$

It follows immediately that

$$\delta X = \frac{xZ + x\delta Z + \delta xZ + \delta x\delta Z - fX}{f} = \frac{x\delta Z + \delta xZ + \delta x\delta Z}{f} \, .$$

Now note that $\delta x \cdot \delta Z$ can be assumed to be insignificantly small for a small step $(\delta x, \delta y)$. Analogously the "Y-approximation" follows for δY.

According to the assumed central projection a function $z(x, y)$ is defined by

$$z(x, y) = Z\left(\frac{xZ}{f}, \frac{yZ}{f}\right) = Z(X, Y).$$

It holds that

$$Z(X + \delta X, Y + \delta Y) = Z(X, Y) + \delta Z = z(x + \delta x, y + \delta y) = z(x, y) + \delta Z \, .$$

The linear approximations of the Taylor expansion are

$$\delta Z \approx \frac{\partial Z}{\partial X} \delta X + \frac{\partial Z}{\partial Y} \delta Y \approx \frac{\partial z}{\partial x} \delta x + \frac{\partial z}{\partial y} \delta y \, .$$

Thus using the approximations for δX and δY it follows that

$$\delta Z \approx \frac{1}{f}\left(\frac{\partial Z}{\partial X}\delta x + \frac{\partial Z}{\partial Y}\delta y\right)\cdot Z + \frac{1}{f}\left(\frac{\partial Z}{\partial X}x + \frac{\partial Z}{\partial Y}y\right)\cdot\delta Z.$$

Therefore it holds that

$$\left(\frac{\partial Z}{\partial X}\delta x + \frac{\partial Z}{\partial Y}\delta y\right)\cdot Z \approx f\delta Z - \left(\frac{\partial Z}{\partial X}x + \frac{\partial Z}{\partial Y}y\right)\cdot\delta Z$$

$$= \left(f - \frac{\partial Z}{\partial X}x - \frac{\partial Z}{\partial Y}y\right)\cdot\delta Z$$

and it follows that

$$\left(\frac{\partial Z}{\partial X}\delta x + \frac{\partial Z}{\partial Y}\delta y\right)\cdot\frac{Z}{f - \dfrac{\partial Z}{\partial X}x - \dfrac{\partial Z}{\partial Y}y} \approx \delta Z$$

$$\approx \frac{\partial z}{\partial x}\delta x + \frac{\partial z}{\partial y}\delta y.$$

By comparing the factors of the independent values δx and δy on both sides of this equation it follows that

$$\frac{\partial z}{\partial x} \approx \frac{\dfrac{\partial Z}{\partial X}}{f - \dfrac{\partial Z}{\partial X}x - \dfrac{\partial Z}{\partial Y}y}\cdot Z$$

$$= \frac{p}{f - px - qy}\cdot Z = c_1(x, y, p, q)\cdot Z$$

and

$$\frac{\partial z}{\partial y} \approx \frac{\dfrac{\partial Z}{\partial Y}}{f - \dfrac{\partial Z}{\partial X}x - \dfrac{\partial Z}{\partial Y}y}\cdot Z$$

$$= \frac{q}{f - px - qy}\cdot Z = c_2(x, y, p, q)\cdot Z.$$

Note that we have just defined two functions c_1 and c_2. Altogether it holds that

$$\delta Z \approx c_1\cdot\delta x\cdot Z + c_2\cdot\delta y\cdot Z$$

$$= (c_1\cdot\delta x + c_2\cdot\delta y)\cdot Z = c\cdot Z.$$

The values δx and δy are known (in the image plane). From these formulas the explicit representation

$$c(x, y, p, q, \delta x, \delta y) = c_1(x, y, p, q) \cdot \delta x + c_2(x, y, p, q) \cdot \delta y$$
$$= \frac{p \cdot \delta x + q \cdot \delta y}{f - px - qy}$$

follows. Because of

$$Z(X + \delta X, Y + \delta Y) = Z(X, Y) + \delta Z = (1 + c) \cdot Z(X, Y)$$

we obtain the formula as stated in the theorem. Q.E.D.

The theorem concludes that the depth can be calculated up to a multiplicative scaling factor that is constant for the whole image if the surface gradients $(p(x, y), q(x, y))$ are known. Scene objects can be, for example, small and close, or big and far away. However, the visible object faces should not have any discontinuities since a $C^{(1)}$-function $Z(X, Y)$ was assumed for Theorem 3.3.

In the case of a parallel projection the depth can be calculated approximately up to an additive constant if the surface gradients $(p(x, y), q(x, y))$ are known. - As before note that a step $(\delta x, \delta y)$ in the image plane corresponds to a step $(\delta X, \delta Y, \delta Z)$ in 3D space.

Theorem 3.4 (*depth from gradients for parallel projection*): *For parallel projection and a differentiable surface function $Z = Z(X, Y)$ it holds that*

$$Z(X + \delta X, Y + \delta Y) - Z(X, Y) \approx c(p, q, \delta x, \delta y) ,$$

where $p(x, y)$ and $q(x, y)$ are the gradient values for image point $(x, y) = (X, Y)$ (i.e. for the surface point $(X, Y, Z(X, Y))$ projected into this image point). The function c is explicitly specified in the proof.

Proof: Since $(x, y) = (X, Y)$ the linearity assumption for the Taylor expansion yields

$$Z(X + \delta X, Y + \delta Y) - Z(X, Y) \approx \frac{\partial Z}{\partial X} \cdot \delta X + \frac{\partial Z}{\partial Y} \cdot \delta Y$$
$$= p \cdot \delta x + q \cdot \delta y$$

in this case. The left hand side of this equation specifies the function c of the Theorem. Q.E.D.

So the following algorithm is theoretically possible for calculating a depth or height map:

Initially a depth value is known at one image point. Then corresponding depth values are determined along different integration paths (see Fig. 3.2) using the gradients for depth value propagation. The gradients are assumed to be known.

However, this requires that the visible discrete surface points which are projected into the given discrete image points, "satisfy the $C^{(1)}$ assumption", and that the calculated gradients correspond to slopes between these discrete surface points. Such propagation algorithms have the serious drawback that they propagate errors without any control mechanism.

In the staircase example discussed in Section 3.2.1 (view "from the front", i.e. all visible faces are assumed to be coplanar to the image plane) the reconstructed surface would only be a plane! In general it is true that these gradient-based local propagation techniques are not suitable for polyhedral objects (note that their surface function is not in $C^{(1)}$).

Theorem 3.3, Theorem 3.4, or the more general remarks about integration paths in Section 3.1.1 can be cited as fundamentals to support *local integration techniques*:

Assume a scan algorithm which passes through all image points of the image grid (e.g. known under names as meander scan, Hilbert scan, or Peano scan etc.). Starting with initial depth values this algorithm can be used to propagate depth values according to a certain local approximation rule (e.g. based on the 4-neighborhood) using the given gradient data. Such a calculation of relative depth values can be done within repeated scans (i.e. using different scan algorithms). Finally resulting depth values can be determined by certain averaging operations. Initial depth values have to be assumed for the start positions of the different runs.

See Exercise (2) in Section 3.6 for a more detailed discussion of local integration techniques.

The following *global integration method* cannot be described that easily but leads practically to considerably better results for the task of calculating depth from gradients.

3.3.2 Frankot-Chellappa Algorithm

Assume a $C^{(2)}$-surface function $Z = Z(X, Y)$ that was projected into the xy image plane by parallel projection, and that has to be reconstructed. Thus, following the parallel projection equations $x = X$ and $y = Y$ we are looking for an explicit surface representation $Z = Z(x, y)$ (i.e. a depth map).

As given information about this function assume gradient values $\tilde{p}(x, y)$ and $\tilde{q}(x, y)$ which represent approximately (e.g. depending on the quality of the reconstruction technique for the calculation of surface gradients) the actual (unknown) surface slopes

$$p(x, y) = \frac{\partial Z(X, Y)}{\partial X} = \frac{\partial Z(x, y)}{\partial x} \text{ and } q(x, y) = \frac{\partial Z(X, Y)}{\partial Y} = \frac{\partial Z(x, y)}{\partial y}.$$

Two (global) optimization constraints are formulated to express this problem mathematically precise. First, a *smoothness constraint* specifies a functional dependence between increases in x-direction and in y-direction. As an example of such a constraint for the unknown surface function $Z = Z(x, y)$ it is assumed that this function satisfies the integrability constraint (as discussed in Section 3.1.1)

$$\frac{\partial^2 Z}{\partial x \partial y}(x, y) = \frac{\partial^2 Z}{\partial y \partial x}(x, y)$$

on the relevant definition domain in the real plane. Secondly, the function Z has to be determined in the set of all of those functions that satisfy the integrability condition such that the following *distance error* between given and (unknown) ideal gradients

$$\iint |p(x, y) - \tilde{p}(x, y)|^2 + |q(x, y) - \tilde{q}(x, y)|^2 \, dx \, dy$$

is minimized where the integral is calculated over the relevant (bounded) definition domain in the image plane.

For the solution of this *optimization problem* we can consider the surface function Z with respect to an expansion on a certain set of basis functions. Let us assume that the set of basis functions is the set of Fourier functions

$$\phi(x, y, u, v) = exp(i(x \cdot u + y \cdot v))$$

with the imaginary unit $i = \sqrt{-1}$. Thus assume the *Fourier expansion*

$$Z(x, y) = \sum_{(u,v) \in \Omega} Z^{(F)}(u, v) \cdot \phi(x, y, u, v)$$

for function Z where $Z^{(F)}(u, v)$ denotes a *Fourier coefficient* of Z for frequency (u, v), and Ω is the assumed frequency domain. For example, it is appropriate to select

$$\Omega = \{(u, v): \quad u = 2\pi x \quad \wedge \quad v = 2\pi y \quad \wedge \quad 0 \le x, y \le N - 1\}$$

for an image of size $N \times N$, i.e. $0 \le x, y \le N - 1$. [10]

Analogously this Fourier basis function expansion of Z also holds for the derivatives

$$p(x, y) = Z_x(x, y) = \sum_{(u,v) \in \Omega} Z^{(F)}(u, v) \cdot \phi_x(x, y, u, v)$$

with derivatives

$$\phi_x(x, y, u, v) = i \cdot u \cdot \phi(x, y, u, v)$$

of the basis functions, as well as for (the same Fourier coefficients!)

$$q(x, y) = Z_y(x, y) = \sum_{(u,v) \in \Omega} Z^{(F)}(u, v) \cdot \phi_y(x, y, u, v)$$

with the derivatives

$$\phi_y(x, y, u, v) = i \cdot v \cdot \phi(x, y, u, v)$$

of the basis functions. Now the corresponding Fourier expansions

$$\tilde{p}(x, y) = \sum_{(u,v) \in \Omega} \tilde{Z}_1^{(F)}(u, v) \cdot \phi_x(x, y, u, v)$$

and

$$\tilde{q}(x, y) = \sum_{(u,v) \in \Omega} \tilde{Z}_2^{(F)}(u, v) \cdot \phi_y(x, y, u, v)$$

are considered for the given gradient functions $\tilde{p}(x, y)$ and $\tilde{q}(x, y)$. Initially the Fourier coefficients $\tilde{Z}_1^{(F)}(u, v)$ and $\tilde{Z}_2^{(F)}(u, v)$ are unknown. However, the Fourier coefficients $\tilde{p}^{(F)}(u, v)$ and $\tilde{q}^{(F)}(u, v)$ can be determined for these functions using the *Fourier transformation* ,

$$\tilde{p}(x, y) = \sum_{(u,v) \in \Omega} \tilde{p}^{(F)}(u, v) \cdot \phi(x, y, u, v)$$

and

$$\tilde{q}(x, y) = \sum_{(u,v) \in \Omega} \tilde{q}^{(F)}(u, v) \cdot \phi(x, y, u, v).$$

Because of

$$\phi_x(x, y, u, v) = i \cdot u \cdot \phi(x, y, u, v) \quad \text{and} \quad \phi_y(x, y, u, v) = i \cdot v \cdot \phi(x, y, u, v)$$

---

[10] The image coordinates (x, y) start at 0 in this section since this corresponds to the common Fourier transformation notation.

it follows immediately that

$$\tilde{Z}_1^{(F)}(u, v) = \tilde{p}^{(F)}(u, v)/iu \quad \text{and} \quad \tilde{Z}_2^{(F)}(u, v) = \tilde{q}^{(F)}(u, v)/iv.$$

Now we are prepared to state an important theorem which is the theoretical fundamental for a global integration technique.

Theorem 3.5 *(R.T. Frankot and R. Chellappa, 1988): The stated optimization problem is solved when the values*

$$H(u, v) = \frac{P_x(u, v) \cdot \tilde{Z}_1^{(F)}(u, v) + P_y(u, v) \cdot \tilde{Z}_2^{(F)}(u, v)}{P_x(u, v) + P_y(u, v)}$$

are used as Fourier coefficients $Z^{(F)}(u, v)$ *(i.e. as approximations of* $Z^{(F)}(u, v)$*) in the Fourier expansion of function* Z *for* $(u, v) \neq (0, 0)$ *where*

$$P_x(u, v) = \iint |\phi_x(x, y, u, v)|^2 \, dx \, dy \approx u^2, \quad P_y(u, v) = \iint |\phi_y(x, y, u, v)|^2 \, dx \, dy \approx v^2.$$

A positive real number has to be used for the real part of $Z^{(F)}(0, 0)$ and the imaginary part of $Z^{(F)}(0, 0)$ is equal to zero.[11]
        The specified solution is optimal in the sense of the above stated error distance (i.e. of the quadratic error function) between the ideal and the given gradient values. But it only provides a relative height function up to an additive constant. The average height value is equal to the real part of $Z^{(F)}(0, 0)$. But exactly this value can not be calculated since the function H is singular at that point.
        This theorem completely establishes a global integration technique to reconstruct a relative depth map $Z = Z(x, y)$ based on given estimations $\tilde{p}(x, y)$ and $\tilde{q}(x, y)$ of the gradient functions.

(Task 3.2): Assume that for an image of size $N \times N$ estimated values $\tilde{p}(x, y)$ and $\tilde{q}(x, y)$ are given in as many image points as possible for the gradients of those object surface points that are projected into the image under an assumed parallel projection. Calculate a surface function $Z(x, y)$ (which can be sampled to obtain a depth map) which satisfies the integrability condition and which minimizes the quadratic error between the given gradient and the gradient of functions which satisfy the integrability condition.

(Solution 3.2): In principle, the solution was already specified above. The formula given in Theorem 3.4 can be simplified to

---

[11] The (necessary) special treatment of the null frequency is specified here as a supplement to the original reference of this algorithm.

{ initialization: entering p, q values of "normal size"
into the fields P, Q of complex numbers }

for $0 \le x, y \le N - 1$ **do**

  if (a gradient was calculated in (x, y) and it holds

    $\left| p(x, y) \right| < max\_pq$ and $\left| q(x, y) \right| < max\_pq$)   { slant $< \sigma$ }

  then begin

      $P1(x, y) := p(x, y);$ $P2(x, y) := 0;$

      $Q1(x, y) := q(x, y);$ $Q2(x, y) := 0;$

  end {then}

  else begin   { slant $\ge \sigma$, for example 0 or max_pq

                     with a corresponding sign as an assumed value }

      $P1(x, y) := 0;$ $P2(x, y) := 0;$

      $Q1(x, y) := 0;$ $Q2(x, y) := 0;$

  end {else};

{ FFT of the P field and the Q field "at that place" }

$FFT(P1, P2, N \times N, \text{ forward});$

$FFT(Q1, Q2, N \times N, \text{ forward});$

{ preparation of the back transformation }

for $(0 \le u, v \le N - 1$ and $(u, v) \ne (0, 0))$ **do begin**

    $H1(u, v) := \left(u \cdot P2(u, v) + v \cdot Q2(u, v) \right) / \left(u^2 + v^2 \right) ;$

    $H2(u, v) := \left(-u \cdot P1(u, v) - v \cdot Q1(u, v) \right) / \left(u^2 + v^2 \right)$

end {for};

$H1(0, 0) :=$ estimated average height of the object surface points;

$H2(0, 0) := 0;$

{ inverse FFT of the H-array "in place" }

$FFT(H1, H2, N \times N, \text{ backwards});$

{ read data from H-array }

for $0 \le x, y \le N - 1$ **do**

  $Z(x, y) := background\_depth\_value \ - \ H1(x, y)$

Figure 3.12: Frankot-Chellappa algorithm for the calculation of a depth map from gradient data. The final values $H1(x, y)$ specify a height map.

$$H(u,v) = \frac{u^2 \cdot \tilde{p}^{(F)}(u,v)/iu \quad + \quad v^2 \cdot \tilde{q}^{(F)}(u,v)/iv}{u^2 + v^2}$$

$$= \frac{-i \cdot u \cdot \tilde{p}^{(F)}(u,v) \quad - \quad i \cdot v \cdot \tilde{q}^{(F)}(u,v)}{u^2 + v^2}.$$

The corresponding calculations have to be carried out for complex numbers. A real-number arithmetic representation is chosen in the algorithm using the representations

$$H(u,v) = H1(u,v) + i \cdot H2(u,v) = \big(H1(u,v), \, H2(u,v)\big) \, ,$$

$$\tilde{p}^{(F)}(u,v) = P1(u,v) + i \cdot P2(u,v) = \big(P1(u,v), \, P2(u,v)\big) \, ,$$

$$\tilde{q}^{(F)}(u,v) = Q1(u,v) + i \cdot Q2(u,v) = \big(Q1(u,v), \, Q2(u,v)\big) \, .$$

Accordingly it holds

$$\big(u^2 + v^2\big) \cdot \big(H1(u,v), \, H2(u,v)\big)$$

$$= \big(u \cdot P2(u,v) + v \cdot Q2(u,v), \quad -u \cdot P1(u,v) - v \cdot Q1(u,v)\big).$$

As input data the gradient functions have to be read into the arrays of the real parts. The arrays of the imaginary parts are initialized with value zero at all positions. By Fourier transformation of these input arrays we initially obtain the Fourier transforms $(P1, P2)$ and $(Q1, Q2)$. After these two Fourier transformations we calculate $(H1, H2)$ according to the above formula. Note that the special case $(u, v) = (0, 0)$ has to be kept in mind.

An inverse Fourier transformation for $(H1, H2)$ leads to the desired height map in the real part of the resulting complex array. Note that during forward and backward Fourier transformation altogether all coefficients have to be divided by the size N^2 of the given gradient map. Otherwise the resulting height values have to be scaled, e.g. by a remaining scale factor during this final step of reading the real part $H1$ of the resulting complex array.

(**Algorithm 3.2**): Figure 3.12 presents the algorithm. For the read gradient estimations generally it has to be kept in mind that relatively large values of p or q represent such normal vectors which are approximately orthogonal to the optical axis, i.e. these gradients were determined at "strongly slanted" surface points. Here, the probability of erroneous values is generally very high. Accordingly we replace large p- and q-values. A slant-angle σ (i.e. an angular threshold) close to

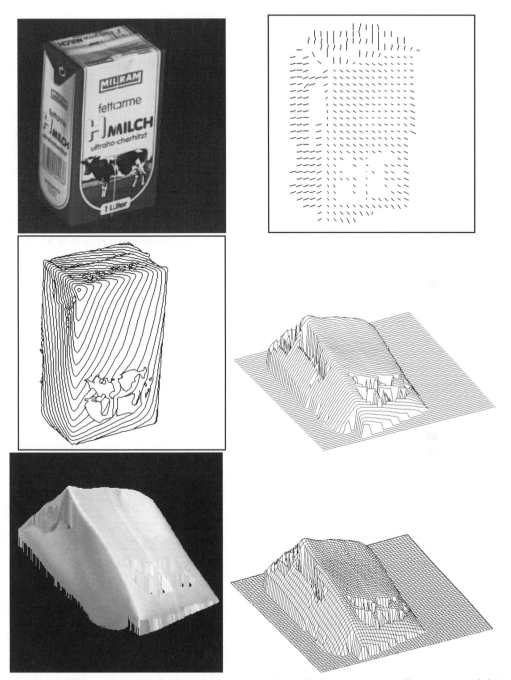

Figure 3.13: A scene (top left) and an estimated gradient map as a needle map (top right). Reconstruction results of the Frankot-Chellappa algorithm: a contour plot of the height map (middle left), a floating horizon representation of the height map (middle right), a shaded surface representation (bottom left: a Lambertian texture was generated for the lighting direction $p_s = q_s = 0$), and a grid representation (bottom right).

90° is selected to classify relatively large p- and q-values so that all pq-pairs which describe a slant angle between the angular threshold σ and 90° are replaced by a constant gradient vector value. For the algorithm in Fig. 3.12 the constant vector $(0,0)$ was chosen. As another option the value max_pq (with + or - sign) could be chosen instead of the value 0 for a slant $\geq \sigma$.

For $\sigma = 75°$ this angular threshold corresponds to a value max_pq which lies close to 4. The values $(p,q) = (\pm 12, 0)$ and $(p,q) = (0, \pm 12)$ represent orientations of approximately $\sigma = 85.2°$. These two examples illustrate that a value max_pq can be used in the algorithm (see Fig. 3.12) instead of an angular threshold.

For the Fourier transformation respectively the inverse Fourier transformation procedures can be taken from suitable libraries or hand books (FFT procedures, *Fast Fourier Transform*, see an example of a reference in Section 3.5). The background depth value or the average height of the object surface points (used to define $H1(0,0)$) can be adjusted to a certain application context. In general it is only necessary for the preparation of the back transformation to enter a certain positive real value into $H1(0,0)$.

(Comment 3.2): It is useful to classify the relative height values that have been calculated into object values and background values. To achieve a better ("more unperturbed") visual impression it is suggested to map all background values onto a constant (minimum) height value. A visualization of the depth or height map can be used for an interactive evaluation of such a background definition process (see Fig. 3.13).

Some references to applicable visualization techniques in computer graphics are given in Section 3.5. It is recommended to provide different visualization techniques in implementations of this approach for flexible (interactive) selection of a specific visualization.

In general note that many implementations of the fast Fourier transformation are especially time-efficient if N is a power of two. Symmetry properties of the Fourier coefficients can also be used to reduce computing time.

3.4   GRADIENT SPACE

The geometric distribution of normals on object faces offers useful ways of describing the shape of objects. This orientation information about the object's shape can be represented favorably and analyzed in the so-called gradient space. Consequently this section looks at some important properties of the gradient space.

3.4.1 Three Coordinate Systems

The *gradient space* is the Euclidean plane $\Re^2$ with the Cartesian coordinates p and q (compare Fig. 3.14). A point (p, q) in the gradient space specifies a gradient position in this plane. Such a gradient position represents the infinite family of planes in $\Re^3$ with the identical gradient $(p, q)^T$ but with any arbitrary distance r between the Z-intercept $(0, 0, r)$ of the plane and the origin $\mathbf{O}$. The vector $(p(\mathbf{n}), q(\mathbf{n}))^T$ denotes the corresponding surface gradient for a given normal $\mathbf{n} = (n_X, n_Y, n_Z)^T$ (not the gradient of the vector $\mathbf{n}$, compare Section 3.1.2). Thus it holds that

$$p(\mathbf{n}) = -n_X/n_Z \quad \text{and} \quad q(\mathbf{n}) = -n_Y/n_Z \ .$$

This pq-space is a special representation of values of gradients or normals. This representation has the general disadvantage that angular differences of the normal do not relate linearly to differences in pq-coordinates. Small differences in the pq-coordinates close to the origin correspond to relatively large angle differences of the normals, and large differences in the pq-coordinates far away from the origin correspond to small angle differences of the normals. This disadvantage becomes noticeable when smoothness constraints have to be formulated for gradients. The Gaussian sphere offers a better representation of gradient values concerning the angular distribution.

For the representation of the gradient values or normal values in spherical coordinates, first a normal $\mathbf{n} = (n_X, n_Y, n_Z)^T$ is transformed into the corresponding unit normal $\mathbf{n}° = (n_1, n_2, n_3)^T$ (see Section 3.1.2),

$$\mathbf{n}° = \frac{\mathbf{n}}{\|\mathbf{n}\|} = \left(\frac{n_X}{\sqrt{n_X^2 + n_Y^2 + n_Z^2}}, \frac{n_Y}{\sqrt{n_X^2 + n_Y^2 + n_Z^2}}, \frac{n_Z}{\sqrt{n_X^2 + n_Y^2 + n_Z^2}} \right)^T .$$

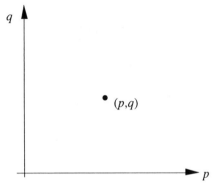

Figure 3.14: A Cartesian pq-coordinate system is assumed in the gradient space. A point (p, q) corresponds to the manifold of all planes that have $(p, q)^T$ as gradients.

This unit normal considered as a position vector (i.e. a vector with starting point at the origin) has a point **P** on the Gaussian sphere as its end point. This point

$$\mathbf{P} = (n_1, n_2, n_3) = \left(-sin(\sigma(\mathbf{n}°))cos(\theta(\mathbf{n}°)), -sin(\sigma(\mathbf{n}°))sin(\theta(\mathbf{n}°)), -cos(\sigma(\mathbf{n}°))\right)$$

is uniquely characterized by the spherical coordinates slant $\sigma(\mathbf{n}) = \sigma(\mathbf{n}°)$ and tilt $\theta(\mathbf{n}) = \theta(\mathbf{n}°)$. Thus it holds altogether that

$$\sigma(\mathbf{n}) = arccos\left(\frac{-n_Z}{\|\mathbf{n}\|}\right) = arctan\left(\frac{\sqrt{n_X^2 + n_Y^2}}{-n_Z}\right)$$

and

$$\theta(\mathbf{n}) = arccos\left(\frac{n_X}{sin(\sigma(\mathbf{n}))\cdot\|\mathbf{n}\|}\right) = arcsin\left(\frac{n_Y}{sin(\sigma(\mathbf{n}))\cdot\|\mathbf{n}\|}\right) = arctan\left(\frac{n_Y}{n_X}\right).$$

The normals of object surfaces can also be used for modeling the *surface curvature*. For example assume that unit normals could be determined for a certain set of neighboring image points. These unit normals are all identical for projected surface points of a planar object face, i.e. in this case they are all mapped onto the same point on the Gaussian sphere. On the other hand the corresponding points of the unit normals on the Gaussian sphere are spread over a larger region of the surface of the Gaussian sphere, if the local curvature of the object surface increases. The area of this region of the surface of the Gaussian sphere divided by the area of the segment of image points for which the unit normals were determined defines a measure of the curvature (*Gaussian curvature*).

The Gaussian coordinates also allow an adequate modeling of direction changes of the normals. But being spherical coordinates they are more complicated in their algorithmic treatment numerically as well as conceptionally than coordinates of a plane. The stereographic coordinates (f, g) offer themselves as a compromise.[12] These are defined in the plane and reflect "nearly linearly" the direction changes of the normals.

Since ancient times the *stereographic projection* and the *polar* (or *azimuthal,* or *gnomonic*) *projection* are used for the drawing of star maps (see Fig. 3.15). Here, the given points (i.e. the points that have to be projected) are assumed to lie on the surface of the Gaussian sphere for these projections. We are interested in the projection of all points of the southern hemisphere (i.e. the "visible directions" with respect to an assumed camera). The radius 1 of the Gaussian sphere

---

[12]   We assume that a confusion with the effective focal length f is out of question in a given context.

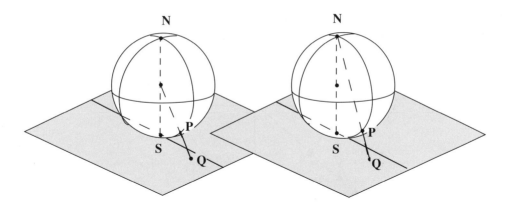

Figure 3.15: Polar, azimuthal or gnomonic projection (left) and stereographic projection (right) of surface points on the sphere into the plane.

is only selected for normalization reasons. Here we assume that the sphere center has the coordinates $(0,0,1)$ in the XYZ-coordinate system.

The given points are projected into the fg-plane by a central projection. The fg-plane is tangential to the south pole $\mathbf{S}$. For the polar projection the sphere center is equal to the projection center. Points on the equator are projected onto the straight line at infinity. For the stereographic projection the north pole $\mathbf{N}$ acts as the projection center. The fg-plane is assumed to be identical to the XY-plane.

The polar projection is not very useful to solve the problem of the "uniform angle representation of normals". For a plane with the gradient $(p,q)^T$ intersecting the sphere center a unit normal starting from the sphere center ends at a certain point on the surface of the southern hemisphere. This point is polar projected onto the point $(-p,-q)^T$ in the fg-plane. Therefore the projection plane can here be considered to be equivalent to the pq-space.

A stereographic projection allows to project the whole surface of the sphere into the fg-plane. The north pole $\mathbf{N} = (0,0,2)$ is projected onto a straight line at infinity. However, as mentioned above, we are only interested in surface points of the southern hemisphere.

Assume that $p(\mathbf{n})$ and $q(\mathbf{n})$ are the corresponding gradient values for a normal $\mathbf{n} = (n_X, n_Y, n_Z)^T$ that has to be projected into the fg-plane. The unit normal starts at the center of the sphere and ends at a certain point on the surface of the southern hemisphere. This end point of the unit normal is projected onto a point $(f(\mathbf{n}), g(\mathbf{n}))$ of the fg-plane. In this case it holds that

$$f(\mathbf{n}) = \frac{2p(\mathbf{n})}{1 + w(\mathbf{n})} \quad \text{and} \quad g(\mathbf{n}) = \frac{2q(\mathbf{n})}{1 + w(\mathbf{n})}$$

with the parameter $w(\mathbf{n}) = \sqrt{p(\mathbf{n})^2 + q(\mathbf{n})^2 + 1}$.

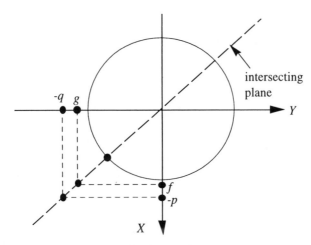

Figure 3.16: View of a sphere along the Z-axis illustrating stereographic projection.

For a proof of these projection equations consider a normal of the plane $Z = pX + qY + 1$. This plane intersects the Gaussian sphere that was used for the stereographic projection in its center $(0,0,1)$. A straight line **g** (not shown in Fig. 3.16) incident with the points $\mathbf{N} = (0,0,2)$ and $\mathbf{Q} = (f, g, 0)$ is assumed in an intersecting plane incident with the points **S**, **N**, and **Q** (i.e. perpendicular to the fg-plane, see Fig. 3.16). This straight line intersects the surface of the sphere in the point

$$\mathbf{P} = (0, 0, 1) + \frac{1}{w}(p, q, -1) \, ,$$

where

$$w = \sqrt{p^2 + q^2 + 1} \, .$$

To prove this equation simply add the corresponding unit vector to the center $(0,0,1)$ of the sphere. Thus the straight line **g** is also determined by the points **N** and **P**. The line **g** contains all points (X, Y, Z) with

$$(X, Y, Z) = \mathbf{N} + t(\mathbf{P} - \mathbf{N}) \, .$$

For the point **Q** on this line we obtain

$$(f, g, 0) = (0, 0, 2) + t\left((0, 0, 1) + \frac{1}{w}(p, q, -1) - (0, 0, 2)\right) = \left(\frac{tp}{w}, \frac{tq}{w}, 2 + t\left(-1 - \frac{1}{w}\right)\right).$$

This concludes

$$t = \frac{2w}{w + 1}$$

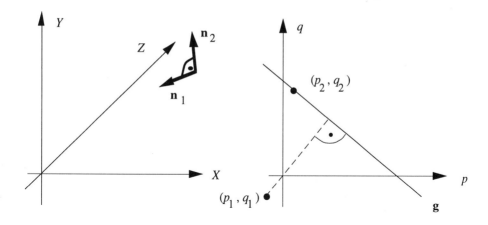

Figure 3.17: Two orthogonal vectors $\mathbf{n}_1$ and $\mathbf{n}_2$ of the *XYZ* space (left) and possible gradient positions (right). The gradient line **g** is the dual line to the gradient position $\left(p(\mathbf{n}_1), q(\mathbf{n}_1) \right) = (p_1, q_1)$.

and therefore the given stereographic projection equations.

With the stereographic projection all normals that are parallel to the *fg*-plane or to the *XY*-plane (i.e. the unit normal points on the equator of the Gaussian sphere) are projected onto points on a circle of radius 2. Thus all surface points on the southern hemisphere are projected stereographically into a circular region with radius 2.

3.4.2   Properties of the Gradient Space

Assume two orthogonal planes in the *XYZ* object space. An important property of the *pq*-space was proven for the (also orthogonal) normals $\mathbf{n}_1 = \left(p_1, q_1, -1 \right)^T$ and $\mathbf{n}_2 = \left(p_2, q_2, -1 \right)^T$ of such orthogonal planes. This property is used later on several times.

From the *orthogonality* of the two vectors it follows that their *scalar product* is zero. Thus it holds that

$$p_1 p_2 + q_1 q_2 + (-1)(-1) = 0 \quad \text{or} \quad (p_1, q_1) \cdot (p_2, q_2)^T = -1 .$$

This simply means that the product of both gradients (to be precise: a row vector times a column vector) is equal to a known constant, namely -1. That means if one normal respectively one gradient is given for these two normals or gradients, then the possible location of the second gradient is constrained by this equation to a straight line **g** in the gradient space (see Fig. 3.17).

Assume that $\left(p(\mathbf{n}_1), q(\mathbf{n}_1) \right) = (p_1, q_1)$ is the given gradient position. Then **g** is the *dual straight line* to this position. From the above line equation it follows that the dual straight line **g** does not intersect the quadrant in which the given point (p_1, q_1) lies, that the dual straight line **g** is orthogonal to the straight line passing through (p_1, q_1) and the origin, and that the two distances between the point (p_1, q_1) and the origin, or the straight line **g** and the origin are reciprocal to each other. The geometric location of the dual straight line **g** is uniquely defined by these three conditions, if a point (p_1, q_1) is given in the pq-plane. On the other hand, every straight line in the pq-plane determines uniquely a *dual point* (p_1, q_1).

As a second property of the gradient space we consider relations between two neighboring faces of polyhedrons, or of two neighboring polygonal facets, their linear edge (an orientation edge in the XYZ-space), and their corresponding gradients in the pq-space. Figure 3.18 shows two non-parallel planes. The planes E_1 and E_2 have the same intersection line **G** in the XYZ-space. Assume $\mathbf{n}_1 = (p_1, q_1, -1)^T$ and $\mathbf{n}_2 = (p_2, q_2, -1)^T$ to be the normal vectors of these planes E_1 and E_2. The line passing through the gradient positions (p_1, q_1) and (p_2, q_2) is a straight line **g** in the pq-space.

For the *cross product* (also called *outer vector product*) of both normals it holds that the vector

$$\mathbf{n}_1 \times \mathbf{n}_2 = (q_2 - q_1, p_1 - p_2, p_1 q_2 - p_2 q_1)^T$$

is parallel to the straight line **G**. Thus the parallel projection of this straight line **G** into the XY-plane is a straight line **G**′ which is parallel to the difference vector $(q_2 - q_1, p_1 - p_2)^T$. On the other hand the line **g** is defined by the direction vector

$$(p_1, q_1) - (p_2, q_2) = (p_1 - p_2, q_1 - q_2)^T$$

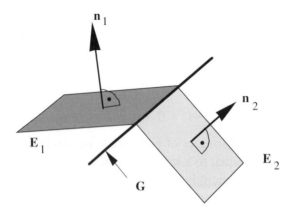

Figure 3.18: Two non-parallel planes and their normal vectors which point towards the XY plane, i.e. which are assumed to have a negative Z-component.

that is orthogonal to the difference vector $(q_2 - q_1, p_1 - p_2)^T$ (since the inner vector product of these two vectors is equal to 0). Altogether it follows that the parallelly projected line $\mathbf{G}'$ and the straight line $\mathbf{g}$ are orthogonal to each other.

As a third feature of the gradient space we consider the possible distinction between convex and concave orientation edges of polyhedral objects (see Fig. 3.19). The planar faces $\mathbf{E}_A$ and $\mathbf{E}_C$ are assumed to lie in one plane (i.e. to be coplanar). The faces $\mathbf{E}_A$ and $\mathbf{E}_B$ form a *convex orientation edge* $\mathbf{PQ}$ and the faces $\mathbf{E}_A$ and $\mathbf{E}_D$ form a *concave orientation edge* $\mathbf{PQ}$. The relevant object lies always behind the face pairs $\mathbf{E}_A \mathbf{E}_B$, $\mathbf{E}_A \mathbf{E}_C$, or $\mathbf{E}_A \mathbf{E}_D$ with respect to the viewer (camera).

Since $\mathbf{E}_A$ and $\mathbf{E}_C$ are coplanar it follows that the corresponding gradient positions A and C in the pq-space are identical. Because of the discussed second property of the gradient space it holds that the points A, B, D lie on a straight line $\mathbf{g}$ which is orthogonal to the parallel projection of the object edge $\mathbf{PQ}$.

Now we consider as an initial situation that an orientation edge does not exist, i.e. we assume faces $\mathbf{E}_A$ and $\mathbf{E}_C$. A convex orientation edge emerges when the surface $\mathbf{E}_C$ rotates towards $\mathbf{E}_B$. With such an rotation the gradient position moves continuously from C on the straight line $\mathbf{g}$ into one direction, namely relative to A "into the direction of the side $\mathbf{E}_B$ relative to the orientation edge $\mathbf{PQ}$". On the other hand, a concave edge emerges, if the surface $\mathbf{E}_C$ rotates into the direction of $\mathbf{E}_D$. In this case C moves continuously on the straight line $\mathbf{g}$ relative to A "opposite to the direction of the face $\mathbf{E}_D$ relative to the orientation edge $\mathbf{PQ}$".

Altogether it follows that for a linear orientation edge and a gradient position A (i.e. one fixed face) according to the second feature of the gradient space first a straight line $\mathbf{g}$ is uniquely defined orthogonal to the orientation edge $\mathbf{PQ}$

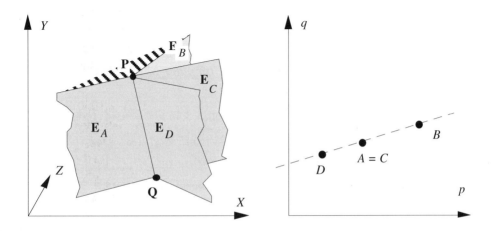

Figure 3.19: Convex and concave situations of orientation edges.

which is incident with *A* in the gradient space. Secondly, this line **g** is divided by point *A* into two rays. The gradient position of a second face is in one of these rays, and each ray characterizes a situation where the two faces form either a convex or a concave orientation edge with $\mathbf{E}_A$.

The second and third property of the gradient space can be used in object recognition processes for reasoning about procedural steps. The first property will later turn out to be very important for shading based image analysis (compare, for example, the direction to the light source in Lambertian reflectance maps, and the meaning of the dual straight line to this direction).

3.5   REFERENCES

The geometry of scene objects in connection with scene projections is discussed in

Kanatani, K.: *Group-Theoretical Methods in Image Understanding*. Springer, Berlin, 1990

in great detail. A facet model for image data controlled approximations of gray-value image functions is presented in

Haralick, R.M., Shapiro, L.G.: *Computer Vision, Volume* I. Addison-Wesley, Reading, 1992.

For Theorem 3.1 we refer to

Spivak, M.: *A Comprehensive Introduction to Differential Geometry,* Vol. 1. 2nd ed., Publish or Perish, Inc., Berkeley, 1979

(Chapter 7, page 298). The gradient space and properties of this space are studied in

Horn, B.K.P.: *Robot Vision*. The MIT Press, Cambridge, Massachusetts, 1986, Shafer, S.A.: *Shadows and Silhouettes in Computer Vision*. Kluwer Academic Publishers, Boston, 1985.

Relations between gradients and depth (Section 3.3.1) are considered in

Aloimonos, J., Shulman, D.: *Integration of Visual Modules: An Extension of the Marr Paradigm*. Academic Press, Boston, 1990.

The algorithm in Section 3.3.2 was formulated based on the paper

Frankot, R.T., Chellappa, R.: *A method for enforcing integrability in shape from shading algorithms*. IEEE Trans. on Patt. Anal. and Mach. Int. PAMI-**10** (1988), pp. 439-451.

A review on local and global integration techniques as well as a report on studies to evaluate integration techniques are contained in

> Klette, R., Schlüns, K.: *Height data from gradient fields*. Photonics East'96, Boston, 18-19 November 1996, SPIE Proceedings Vol. 2908, Machine Vision Applications, Architectures, and Systems Integration V, pp. 204-215.

FFT algorithms can be found in numerous books, for example in

> Klette, R., Zamperoni, P.: *Handbook of Image Processing Operators*. Wiley & Sons, Chichester, 1996,

especially with respect to image transformations.

The general literature of computer graphics can be referred to for *visualizations of object surfaces*. Useful techniques to visualize depth maps or height maps can be found under keywords like "floating horizon algorithm", "shaded surface representation", "texture mapping", "visible surface determination" or "Wright's algorithm for the reproduction of mathematical surfaces". The books

> Foley, J.D., van Dam, A., Feiner, S.K., Hughes, J.F.: *Computer Graphics - Principles and Practice*. 2nd ed., Addison-Wesley, Reading, Massachusetts, 1990,
>
> Plastock, R.A., Kalley, G.: *Computergrafik*. McGraw-Hill, Hamburg, 1987,
>
> Rogers, D.F.: *Procedural Elements for Computer Graphics*. McGraw-Hill, New York, 1988

are good examples of relevant literature in that respect. A further option for 3D visualization is given by autostereograms ("magic eye").

3.6   EXERCISES

(1) Show that depth and distance (see Section 3.2.1) are equivalent goals in scene analysis for parallel projection as well as for central projection, i.e. the distance can always be determined from the given depth and vice versa.

(2 - Assignment) Assume a correct reconstruction of a gradient map with respect to parallel projection, i.e. for a certain projected scene assume that the gradients of the parallelly projected surface points are always given at the discrete image points (x, y) (i.e. a dense gradient map can be assumed). As a first subtask visualize such a gradient map using a needle map (Algorithm 3.1). As a second subtask implement an algorithm that generates a depth map from a dense gradient map. The solution of the second subtask can be, for instance, a local integration technique, and this can be based on Theorem 3.4:

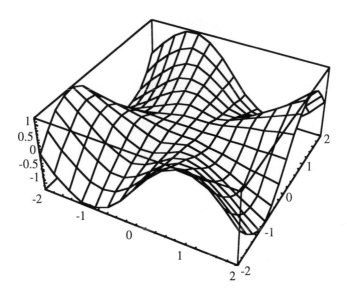

Figure 3.20: A function $f(x, y)$ that does not generally satisfy the integrability condition (see Section 3.1.1).

An integration process (for a given gradient map) should be based on several runs (scans) through the set of all image points (x, y). In each run the algorithm starts at a selected initial point and follows a certain scan order. Depth values are propagated through the array of image points (an initial depth value is assumed at the starting position) by continued addition of relative depth differences specified by the gradient data. Each run produces a single depth map. Finally these maps have to be transformed into a single resulting depth map.

As a third subtask, visualize the resulting depth map as a gray value image and save it as a gray value image. A more advanced solution of this third subtask would be to visualize depth maps in 3D (e.g. floating horizon algorithm).

Gradient maps have to be at your disposal as input for this assignment. These maps can be provided by special programs (e.g. sphere in Example 3.2). A gradient map consists of two channels, namely one channel for the p-components and one channel for the q-components. If the gradient is not defined at an image point, then this can be indicated in the p component by a special value *HUGE*.

(3) Figure 3.20 shows a 3D grid representation of the *Schwarz function*

$$f(x,y) = \begin{cases} \frac{xy(x^2-y^2)}{x^2+y^2}, & \text{for } (x,y) \neq (0,0) \\ 0, & \text{for } (x,y) = (0,0) \end{cases}.$$

This function does not satisfy the integrability condition at point $(0,0)$. Show that

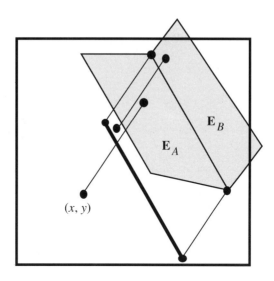

Figure 3.21: An assumed parallel projection into the image plane.

$$\frac{\partial^2 f}{\partial x \partial y}(0,0) = 1 \text{ and } \frac{\partial^2 f}{\partial y \partial x}(0,0) = -1.$$

(4) The relation between the validity of integrability condition and $C^{(2)}(\mathbf{M})$-continuity is characterized by Theorem 3.1. Consider the function

$$Z(X,Y) = \begin{cases} X^2, & \text{for } X \geq 0 \\ 0, & \text{for } X < 0 \end{cases}$$

for $\mathbf{M} = \Re^2$. This function satisfies the integrability condition but it is not $C^{(2)}(\mathbf{M})$-continuous. Prove these two statements. Why is this function not $C^{(2)}(\mathbf{M})$-continuous even though the integrability condition is satisfied?

(5) For the parallel projection of two faces into the image plane (sketched in Fig. 3.21) assume that the gradient value $A = (2,-1)$ was obtained as a correct measurement at the image point (x,y). It is known that the face $\mathbf{E}_B$ is orthogonal to the face $\mathbf{E}_A$. What can be said about the gradient of the surface $\mathbf{E}_B$?

(6) Differences in pq-coordinates in the gradient space are a poor illustration of relations between intersection angles of two planes. Assume one plane with gradient $(p,q) = (0,0)$ and a second plane with gradient $(p,q) = (p_0,0)$. What is the value of the intersection angle of these two planes? Characterize the change of this angle depending on changes of p_0?

(7) Figure 3.22 (on the left) shows two vector fields $\mathbf{w}_1(x,y) = (x,y)^T$ and $\mathbf{w}_2(x,y) = (y,x)^T$ as well as (on the right) the corresponding antiderivatives z.

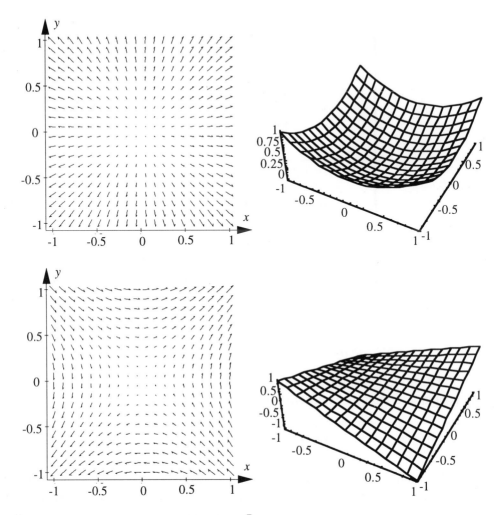

Figure 3.22: Vector field $\mathbf{w}_1(x, y) = (x, y)^T$ and an antiderivative (above, and a vector field $\mathbf{w}_2(x, y) = (y, x)^T$ and an antiderivative (below).

Calculate the values $z(\bar{x}, \bar{y})$ of these antiderivatives according to the integration formula

$$z(\bar{x}, \bar{y}) = z(x_0, y_0) + \int_\gamma p(x, y)\, dx + q(x, y)\, dy$$

(compare Section 3.1.1) where $(x_0, y_0) = (0, 0)$ and the integration paths

$$\gamma(t) = (t, t) \quad \text{or} \quad \tilde{\gamma}(t) = \left(t^2, t^2\right)$$

have to be used, for $0 \le t \le 1$ (i.e. $(\bar{x}, \bar{y}) = (1, 1)$ in both cases γ and $\tilde{\gamma}$) and for $0 \le t \le 2$ (i.e. $(\bar{x}, \bar{y}) = (2, 2)$ for the curve γ or $(\bar{x}, \bar{y}) = (4, 4)$ for $\tilde{\gamma}$).

4 STATIC STEREO ANALYSIS

Processes directed on understanding or analyzing three-dimensional visible object surfaces based on image data are denoted as *stereo vision* in different fields of science. Visual systems of animals and humans prove that stereo vision works in complex environments. In the human visual system two eyes perceive depth based on *stereopsis* (qualified as patent or qualitative stereopsis depending on disparity magnitude). This is known since mid of the 19th century. Even though a vivid perception of the surrounding environment can be obtained from a single eye, human vision is fundamentally a *binocular process* that transforms two images seen from slightly different viewpoints into a perception of the three-dimensional space.

The technical realization of binocular vision is the classical approach towards shape recovery has been used in *photogrammetry* for many decades. Interactive and expensive solutions allow highly accurate shape reconstructions (remote sensing, inverse engineering, architecture etc.). Computer vision approaches are directed on automated solutions. *Static stereo analysis* denotes a very active field of research in computer vision where it is assumed that at least two cameras capture a scene at the same time, or within a certain time interval. An important advantage of static stereo analysis is that apart from a second (or third etc.) camera neither further equipment (e.g. light sources) nor special projections of energy into the scene (e.g. structured lighting) are required. Basically static stereo analysis is the only shape recovery technique which can be called *passive* because of no required interaction with the 3D scene.[1]

For the static stereo analysis it is assumed that no object movements occur during the time interval of image acquisition of the two stereo images. If it is guaranteed that both images are obtained at exactly the same time, then this assumption is even satisfied if, for example, the cameras are mounted on a mobile robot or if the objects in the scene are moving.

---

[1] There are more proposals for passive techniques in computer vision which still have to prove to be of practical relevance. *Shape from shading* (Chapter 7) provides a good introduction into multi-source shading based shape recovery (e.g. Chapter 8), and limitations of shape from shading are discussed in Section 8.1. *Shape from texture* (not contained in this textbook) denotes an other idea how to derive 3D data from images without interaction with the 3D scene.

Compared to *dynamic stereo analysis* (see Chapter 5) the difference is that possible movements do not influence the calculations, and that static stereo analysis is often not directed on understanding motion. The aim of static stereo analysis techniques is rather the determination of depth information or shape recovery. In principle any static stereo approach covers more or less the following sequence of processing steps (*static stereo pipeline*):

Image acquisition: This process is affected by the environment (including light sources, computing facilities etc.) and the application context.

Camera modeling (or calibration, image orientation): The determination of the intrinsic and extrinsic parameters of the cameras was discussed in Chapter 2.

Feature extraction: The calculation of significant image features like edges (compare Section 1.3) is required in some techniques.

Correspondence analysis: Computer vision solutions are directed on automatic determinations of corresponding image points (see Section 1.4.1).

Triangulation: Starting with two corresponding image points in the right and the left image the corresponding depth value can be calculated characterizing a certain point in the 3D scene space.

Interpolation (or approximation): Often the calculated points in 3D scene space have to be transformed into a certain representation of an object surface in 3D space.

The main focus of this chapter is on the process of correspondence analysis for stereo image pairs. Section 1.4 already presented an example of a correspondence analysis algorithm for static stereo. The following sections discuss the problem of automated correspondence analysis in greater detail. Further examples are given of correspondence analysis algorithms. First, we consider the basic static stereo geometry for a more general situation in comparison to the (simple) standard stereo geometry (compare Fig. 1.18).

4.1 GEOMETRY OF STATIC STEREO

The so-called standard stereo geometry was discussed in Section 1.4.1. Again we assume two cameras with identical effective focal length f such that the distance between their focal points $\mathbf{O}_L$ and $\mathbf{O}_R$ is equal to b (compare Fig. 4.1). However, this time we assume that both cameras may be tilted towards each other. This allows that more object faces will be visible in both images. This benefit is "paid" with a few extra calculations.

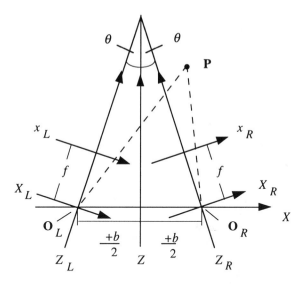

Figure 4.1: Geometry of a static stereo system with coplanar image rows.

To simplify our discussion we assume parallel Y-axes for both cameras. W.l.o.g. this allows to assume identical tilts (defined by angle θ in Fig. 4.1) for both cameras. The absolutely general case of static stereo camera geometry is characterized by arbitrary 3D viewing directions, and different effective focal lengths. However, our special set-up (Fig. 4.1) should be sufficient to demonstrate how to deal with the general case.

The line between the two optical centers $\mathbf{O}_L$ and $\mathbf{O}_R$ is called *base line* and value b is called *base distance*. Let the angle subtended by the two optical axes be 2θ. The coordinate systems $X_L Y_L Z_L$ and $X_R Y_R Z_R$ for the left and the right camera are defined as shown in Fig. 4.1. The coordinate system XYZ is defined such that the Z-axis exactly divides the angle subtended by the Z_L axis and the Z_R axis into two identical angles θ. The coordinate system XYZ can be transformed into the coordinate system $X_L Y_L Z_L$ through

a rotation by the angle $-\theta$ about the Y-axis

$$\begin{pmatrix} cos(-\theta) & 0 & -sin(-\theta) \\ 0 & 1 & 0 \\ sin(-\theta) & 0 & cos(-\theta) \end{pmatrix} = \begin{pmatrix} cos(\theta) & 0 & sin(\theta) \\ 0 & 1 & 0 \\ -sin(\theta) & 0 & cos(\theta) \end{pmatrix}$$

and a translation by $b/2$ to the left

$$
\begin{pmatrix} X - \frac{b}{2} \\ Y \\ Z \end{pmatrix}.
$$

Thus it holds altogether that

$$
\begin{pmatrix} X_L \\ Y_L \\ Z_L \end{pmatrix} = \begin{pmatrix} cos(\theta) & 0 & sin(\theta) \\ 0 & 1 & 0 \\ -sin(\theta) & 0 & cos(\theta) \end{pmatrix} \begin{pmatrix} X - \frac{b}{2} \\ Y \\ Z \end{pmatrix}. \tag{4.1}
$$

Analogously the coordinate system XYZ can be transformed into the coordinate system $X_R Y_R Z_R$ through

a rotation by the angle θ about the Y-axis and a translation by $b/2$ to the right. Therefore it holds that

$$
\begin{pmatrix} X_R \\ Y_R \\ Z_R \end{pmatrix} = \begin{pmatrix} cos(\theta) & 0 & -sin(\theta) \\ 0 & 1 & 0 \\ sin(\theta) & 0 & cos(\theta) \end{pmatrix} \begin{pmatrix} X + \frac{b}{2} \\ Y \\ Z \end{pmatrix}. \tag{4.2}
$$

Assume that a point $\mathbf{P} = (X, Y, Z)$ in 3D scene space is projected onto the points (x_L, y_L) and (x_R, y_R) in the image planes of the two cameras. For an assumed central projection it follows that

$$
x_L = \frac{f \cdot X_L}{Z_L}, \qquad y_L = \frac{f \cdot Y_L}{Z_L},
$$
$$
x_R = \frac{f \cdot X_R}{Z_R}, \qquad y_R = \frac{f \cdot Y_R}{Z_R}. \tag{4.3}
$$

We consider the case that the two corresponding image points (x_L, y_L) and (x_R, y_R) are correctly determined in the left and in the right image, respectively. Then the three-dimensional position of the point $\mathbf{P} = (X, Y, Z)$ can be calculated from the equations (4.1), (4.2) and (4.3). It holds that

$$
x_L = f \frac{cos(\theta)\left(X - \frac{b}{2}\right) + sin(\theta) \cdot Z}{-sin(\theta)\left(X - \frac{b}{2}\right) + cos(\theta) \cdot Z},
$$

$$x_R = f \frac{cos(\theta)\left(X + \frac{b}{2}\right) - sin(\theta) \cdot Z}{sin(\theta)\left(X + \frac{b}{2}\right) + cos(\theta) \cdot Z}$$

or

$$y_L = f \frac{Y}{-sin(\theta)\left(X - \frac{b}{2}\right) + cos(\theta) \cdot Z},$$

$$y_R = f \frac{Y}{sin(\theta)\left(X + \frac{b}{2}\right) + cos(\theta) \cdot Z}.$$

These equations have to be solved for X, Y, and Z. Through rearranging it follows that

$$\left[-x_L \cdot sin(\theta) - f \cdot cos(\theta)\right]X + \left[x_L \cdot cos(\theta) - f \cdot sin(\theta)\right]Z = -\left[\frac{b}{2} x_L sin(\theta) + \frac{b}{2} f\right],$$

$$\left[x_R \cdot sin(\theta) - f \cdot cos(\theta)\right]X + \left[x_R \cdot cos(\theta) + f \cdot sin(\theta)\right]Z = -\left[\frac{b}{2} x_R sin(\theta) - \frac{b}{2} f\right],$$

$$\left[-y_L \cdot sin(\theta)\right]X + \left[-f\right]Y + \left[y_L \cdot cos(\theta)\right]Z = \left[\frac{b}{2} y_L \cdot sin(\theta)\right], \quad \text{and}$$

$$\left[y_R \cdot sin(\theta)\right]X + \left[-f\right]Y + \left[y_R \cdot cos(\theta)\right]Z = -\left[\frac{b}{2} y_R \cdot sin(\theta)\right].$$

We substitute coefficients instead of the expressions in square brackets. Then the above equations can be rewritten as

$a_1 X + a_3 Z = a_0$,

$b_1 X + b_3 Z = b_0$,

$c_1 X + c_2 Y + c_3 Z = c_0$, and

$d_1 X + d_2 Y + d_3 Z = d_0$.

The coordinates X, Y, and Z can be determined by solving this system of linear equations (see Exercise 6 in Section 4.7). This process is called *triangulation*.

Example 4.1 (*ssg*): The standard stereo geometry (acronym *ssg*, see Section 1.4.1) is given if the angle θ in Fig. 4.1 subtended by the two optical axes of the cameras is equal to zero, i.e. if the camera coordinate systems are only translated parallel to each other. In this case it holds that $Z_L = Z_R = Z$ and the triangulation can be simplified further. Then the depth value Z is determined by

$$Z = \frac{f \cdot b}{x_L - x_R} ,$$

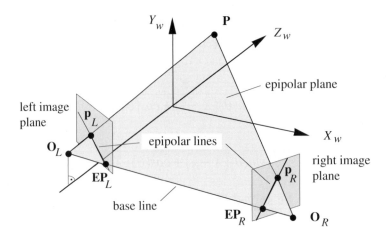

Figure 4.2: Two epipoles, two epipolar lines, and an epipolar plane. $\mathbf{O}_L$ and $\mathbf{O}_R$ are the optical centers of the two camera systems. $\mathbf{p}_L$ and $\mathbf{p}_R$ are the projections of point $\mathbf{P}$ into the image planes. $\mathbf{EP}_L$ and $\mathbf{EP}_R$ denote the epipoles.

for two corresponding points (x_L, y_L) and (x_R, y_R) in the left and in the right image ($y_L = y_R$, see Section 1.4.1). The depth is inversely proportional to the scalar disparity $\Delta_{ssg}(\mathbf{p}_L) = (x_L - x_R)$ since the effective focal length f of the two cameras and the base distance b between their projection centers are constant values in the above equation. Often more general geometric situations are geometrically transformed at first into this standard stereo geometry model (*rectification*). This spatial arrangement of the cameras leads to a significant simplification of the calculations. { end of Example 4.1 }

The following geometric constraint is useful for designing a time-efficient correspondence analysis process. As before we assume that a point $\mathbf{P}$ in the scene is projected onto the point $\mathbf{p}_L$ in the left image plane and onto the point $\mathbf{p}_R$ in the right image plane (compare Fig. 4.2). Assume we start a correspondence analysis process with one image point in one image plane, say $\mathbf{p}_L$. A search for the corresponding point $\mathbf{p}_R$ in the second image plane can be simplified significantly by utilizing the *epipolar geometry* underlying the binocular image acquisition situation. This will constrain the search space. Instead of a search in the whole image of the second camera we can restrict the search process onto the intersection line of this second image plane with the so-called epipolar plane.

The *base line* is incident with the projection centers $\mathbf{O}_L$ and $\mathbf{O}_R$. Generally the base line intersects each image plane in one point (i.e. if both image planes are not coplanar). These two intersection points are the *epipoles* of the given binocular camera set-up. If both image planes are coplanar then the epipoles are points at infinity, and they can be specified in homogeneous coordinates. The base line is also defined by the projection center of one of both cameras and the epipole in the image plane of this camera.

An *epipolar plane* is defined by a point $\mathbf{P}$ in the 3D space and both optical centers $\mathbf{O}_L$ and $\mathbf{O}_R$. The same plane is defined by the following two known (assuming that camera calibration was performed before) straight lines: for one straight line let us consider the ray of view which passes through the projection center $\mathbf{O}_L$ and the given image point $\mathbf{p}_L$ in the image plane of one camera. The base line incident with $\mathbf{O}_L$ and $\mathbf{O}_R$ can be taken as the second defining straight line (see Fig. 4.2). Thus a selected point $\mathbf{p}_L$ specifies the corresponding epipolar plane if the geometric camera calibration data (see Section 2.1) are at hand.

An *epipolar line* is the intersection of an epipolar plane with an image plane. All object points in the scene which lie on an epipolar plane defined by $\mathbf{p}_L$ are projected into the second image plane on points on this epipolar line. Note that the epipole of an image plane also lies on the epipolar line.

In compliance with the above described geometrical relations now the static stereo analysis task is reduced to the problem of *matching* or *assigning corresponding image points* in the left and in the right image. Before this *correspondence problem* is studied in greater detail the next section gives a number of general comments which illustrate the inherent complexity of a static stereo analysis system.

4.2 ASSUMPTIONS AND CONSTRAINTS

Generally, ambiguities occur during processes for the determination of corresponding image elements in stereo images. For a selected pixel of one image (i.e. left or right image) in general there exists more than one pixel in the other image which is a possible candidate for correspondence. The reduction of these ambiguities can be based, for example, on a-priori knowledge about the parameters of the scene objects, or about value ranges of the object parameters. If, for instance, it is known that the scene objects are polyhedral, or that they have curved surfaces then this information can be used directly for the design of a correspondence analysis process.

However, generally this a-priori knowledge is either not available or the complexity of the object geometry should not be restricted at all. Nevertheless also for these cases it is possible to derive a number of constraints to reduce the ambiguities for the correspondence analysis processes. A first illustration was given with the epipolar geometry in the section before. Such constraints arise from models of image generation, for example based on projective geometry or photometric properties, and also from the study of object characteristics in our natural environment. The study of image generation models or processes allows to formulate geometric constraints for

1. the location of the epipolar lines (*epipolar constraint*),

2. the uniqueness of the assignment (*uniqueness constraint*),

3. the compatibility of image intensity values (*photometric compatibility constraint*), or

4. the geometrical similarity of certain features (*geometric similarity constraint*).

Based on properties of scene objects further constraints may arise for

5. the order of the projected points in the images (*ordering constraint*),

6. the continuity of the disparities (*continuity constraint*),

7. the continuity along the orientation edges (*figural continuity constraint*),

8. the compatibility of certain features (*compatibility constraint*),

9. the *disparity limit*, or

10. the *disparity gradient limit*.

Based on this classification the following subsections give an overview about possible assumptions and constraints which might be helpful for the design of correspondence analysis processes in stereo image analysis[2]. Certainly not all of these constraints can be considered for a single algorithm simultaneously. They are stated at this point for overview purposes. Besides the reduction of the number of ambiguities in correspondence analysis processes such constraints can also speed-up computations.

4.2.1   Epipolar Line Constraint

The number of possible correspondence candidates can be reduced considerably by analyzing the geometric image acquisition model. These constraints are not based on assumptions about the object scene but they are solely based on geometrical laws. Section 4.1 already described the epipolar geometry of a binocular stereo system. This allowed to deduce the following rule:

---

[2] This overview is based on work done by Carsten Schröder at the University of Hamburg, see also the cited reference L. Dreschler-Fischer (1993) in Section 4.6.

Epipolar constraint: A point $\mathbf{p}_L$ in the left image can only correspond to such a point in the right image which lies on the corresponding epipolar line in the right image which is uniquely defined by $\mathbf{p}_L$.

For a given image point $\mathbf{p}_L$ this rule reduces the search for a corresponding image point from a two-dimensional problem to an one-dimensional problem.

For the general binocular geometric model (see discussion at the beginning of Section 4.1) the determination of formulas for these epipolar lines requires either a geometrically calibrated image acquisition set-up or a set of (at least seven) matched point pairs.[3] The epipolar lines can be determined and stored (e.g. coefficients into a look-up table) for the use of a fixed camera set-up. Any change of the camera set-up requires an update of these epipolar line data structures. The standard stereo geometry characterizes a special camera set-up where the cameras are arranged parallel to each other. In this case we have the following simplified constraint:

Epipolar lines for standard stereo geometry: With the use of the standard stereo geometry the epipolar lines in the two image planes coincide with the horizontal scanning rows of the images.

No calculation of epipolar lines is necessary in this case. However, the practical applicability of this model is subject to some restrictions. For example, a mobile robot is often exposed to mechanical vibrations. This strongly detracts the precise positioning of the sensor arrays during image acquisition. The problem might be solved in that not a single image row is considered for the correspondence analysis but a certain interval of rows is used instead. In a laboratory environment both stereo cameras can be mounted sufficiently well so that problems with vibrations can be reduced significantly. The applicability of this epipolar constraint strongly depends on the application and the demands on the image acquisition system.

Another problem arises from scenes with mainly artificial, man-made objects (e.g. in cities or factories) where horizontal lines often occur. In the standard stereo geometry model all points of a certain horizontal orientation edge of a scene object are projected onto the same epipolar line in the image plane. Because of that the occurring ambiguities in the correspondence analysis process may be expected to be very numerous depending on the chosen method for correspondence analysis.

Improvements of correspondence assignments may be achieved by first acquiring the stereo images with any arbitrary (calibrated) camera set-up followed

---

[3] See the fundamental matrix and self-calibration in O. Faugeras (1993) or in G. Xu and Z. Zhang (1996), cited in Section 4.6.

by a *rectification* (i.e. a transformation into the standard geometry model)[4] of the images using knowledge about the intrinsic and extrinsic camera parameters (see Section 2.1). Rectification is carried out such that the epipolar lines in the resulting images coincide with the horizontal image lines.

4.2.2   Uniqueness, Compatibility, and Similarity

In contrast to the epipolar constraint the following assumptions may be part of some image acquisition models and not of others. These assumptions depend upon the shape of the scene objects, the scene illumination, distances between objects and cameras, etc. The following assumptions may be checked whether they contribute to an appropriate model of a given situation or not.

Uniqueness assumption: Typically every pixel in one image of the stereo pair can only correspond to exactly one pixel in the other image.

Exceptions can occur during an image acquisition process when two (or more) surface points in a 3D scene lie on the same projection ray of one camera but the two points are projected into two (or several) different pixels in the second camera image. Another assumption for correspondence analysis procedures in binocular stereo analysis refers to the compatibility or similarity of intensity values.

Compatibility assumption for intensity values (*differential photometric compatibility constraint*): Two neighbors (x_{L1}, y_{L1}) and (x_{L2}, y_{L2}) in E_L, and two neighbors (x_{R1}, y_{R1}) and (x_{R2}, y_{R2}) in E_R can only correspond to each other if the absolute differences $|E_L(x_{Li}, y_{Li}) - E_R(x_{Ri}, y_{Ri})|$, $i = 1, 2$, between their intensity values are below a threshold, and the absolute difference $|(E_L(x_{L1}, y_{L1}) - E_L(x_{L2}, y_{L2})) - (E_R(x_{R1}, y_{R1}) - E_R(x_{R2}, y_{R2}))|$ between the intensity changes is below a threshold.

Apart from specularities on object surfaces (depending on viewer direction!) or different image value measurements for the left and right camera this assumption seems to be obviously satisfied in general. However, in practice single pixels cannot be checked for correspondence because of the sensitivity to noise and slightly different characteristics of the two cameras. Instead the intensity values in the local neighborhoods of pixels are included in the analysis process.

The term geometric similarity (*geometric similarity constraint*) usually summarizes the two following assumptions.

Angle criterion: A line segment S_L with orientation W_L in the left image only corresponds to a line segment S_R with orientation W_R in the right image if the difference $|W_L - W_R|$ is below a certain threshold.

---

[4] N. Ayache (1991) and O. Faugeras (1993) specify rectification methods (see Section 4.6).

Length criterion: A line segment S_L with length L_L in the left image only corresponds to a line segment S_R with length L_R in the right image if $|L_L - L_R|$ is below a certain threshold.

If the correspondence analysis also contains the comparison of image regions or contours then such geometric similarity assumptions can also be formulated for these image features.

4.2.3 Continuity of Disparities

The disparity was defined in Section 1.4.1 to be a vector pointing from $\mathbf{p}_L$ to the corresponding point $\mathbf{p}_R$. For objects of both outdoor and indoor scenes it can often be assumed that object surfaces are opaque and smooth. Under such circumstances it can be assumed that the disparities of corresponding point pairs $\mathbf{p}_L$ and $\mathbf{p}_R$ vary continuously almost everywhere in a given stereo image pair.

Continuity assumption for disparities (*continuity constraint, disparity smoothness constraint*): If two points (x_{L1}, y_{L1}) and (x_{R1}, y_{R1}) in the left and in the right image correspond to each other then a point (x_{L2}, y_{L2}) in the local neighborhood of the point (x_{L1}, y_{L1}) in the left image can (usually) only correspond to such a point (x_{R2}, y_{R2}) in the right image where the length of the difference vector of both disparity vectors,

$$\left| \sqrt{\left(x_{L1} - x_{R1}\right)^2 + \left(y_{L1} - y_{R1}\right)^2} - \sqrt{\left(x_{L2} - x_{R2}\right)^2 + \left(y_{L2} - y_{R2}\right)^2} \right|,$$

is below a certain threshold. In the case of standard stereo geometry and scalar disparities this means that $\left\| x_{L1} - x_{R1} \right| - \left| x_{L2} - x_{R2} \right\|$ has to be below a certain threshold.

Exceptions can be expected at surface points along the orientation edges. Normally projections of these surface points only cover a small fraction of an image.

Sometimes it is suggested to apply this continuity constraint just within image regions defined by an image segmentation process instead of within the whole image. However, often it cannot be ensured that a region or a closed contour in an image exactly represents a face of an object. Therefore, it can also not be guaranteed that the disparities vary continuously in an image region. Yet, sometimes the general assumption about the continuity of the disparities can be restricted to pixels on image edges for noise-filtered stereo images.

Continuity assumption for disparities along the edges (figural continuity constraint): If two edge points (x_{L1}, y_{L1}) and (x_{R1}, y_{R1}) in the left and in the right noise-filtered image correspond to each other then an edge point (x_{L2}, y_{L2}) in the local neighborhood of the point (x_{L1}, y_{L1}) in the left image can only correspond to such an edge point (x_{R2}, y_{R2}) in the right image where the length of the difference vector of both disparity vectors,

$$\left| \sqrt{(x_{L1} - x_{R1})^2 + (y_{L1} - y_{R1})^2} - \sqrt{(x_{L2} - x_{R2})^2 + (y_{L2} - y_{R2})^2} \right|,$$

is below a certain threshold. In the case of standard stereo geometry and scalar disparities this means that $\left\| |x_{L1} - x_{R1}| - |x_{L2} - x_{R2}| \right\|$ has to be below a certain threshold.

If this constraint can be included into the stereo image model then this means that the disparity values along the image edges can only vary slightly.

The *Shirai algorithm* in Section 1.4.2 utilizes the epipolar constraint (for standard stereo geometry), the uniqueness constraint, and the photometric compatibility constraint (in the form of using a special similarity measure for rectangular image windows). Because the algorithm contains edge detection as a subprocess it may also be modified (improved for a specific image acquisition context) to utilize the geometric similarity constraint as well. A more straightforward modification would be to include the continuity constraint. This constraint may lead to a modified procedure to select a disparity which corresponds to a local minimum of the calculated (dis)similarity measure, and which also satisfies the smoothness constraint, i.e. which is about the same as the disparity calculated for the previous pixel.

4.2.4 Compatibility of Features

Sometimes assumptions about the compatibility of intensity values can be extended to image features. Points on image edges were the subject of the figural continuity constraint. Now sets of pixels, e.g. an image edge, are considered in the following statement:

Compatibility assumption for features (feature compatibility constraint): Image features in images of a stereo pair can only correspond to each other if they have the same physical origin in the scene.

A restriction for the correspondence analysis can only be derived from this constraint if, for example, the features in the images can be classified according to their physical meaning. Section 1.3 characterizes edges in gray value images by 3D orientation changes in the gray value relief ("mountains and valleys"). Because of the geometric and photometric conditions in the scene edges in gray value images can have totally different causes.

Figure 4.3 sketches a few types of edges in images. A classification of edges in images can, for example, contain the following classes:

Orientation edges (object edges) arise from discontinuities of orientations on object surfaces (see end of Section 3.1.2).

Reflectance edges arise from discontinuities of the reflection characteristics (see Chapter 6) of object surfaces, e.g. from a change of the surface material,

Illumination edges (shadow edges) arise from discontinuities in the lighting of object surfaces.

Highlight edges are the boundaries of specularities. These specularities are caused by certain reflection characteristics of the surfaces and by a special spatial arrangement of the light source, the object surface, and the camera.

Occlusion edges (or occluding boundary, see end of Section 3.1.2) arise from profiles (silhouettes) of the objects in relation to the background or to other objects as projected by the camera.

Only orientation edges, reflectance edges, and illumination edges can be considered for applying a feature compatibility constraint in static stereo analysis. Highlight edges and occluding edges must not be assigned since they depend on the position of the camera. The example in Fig 4.4 illustrates that occlusion edges

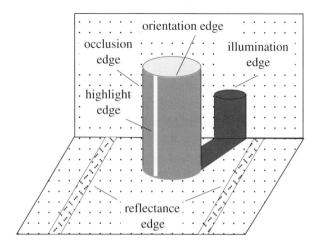

Figure 4.3: Classification of edges in an image of a scene.

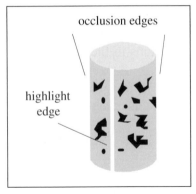
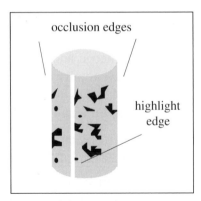

left stereo image   right stereo image

Figure 4.4: Example of occlusion edges and highlight edges in a pair of stereo images that depend on the position of the camera.

and highlight edges do not represent the same physical location in the scene in general. Furthermore, illumination edges must not be assigned in dynamic stereo analysis (compare Chapter 5).

Generally a unique assignment of orientation edges and calculated image edges is practically impossible. The problem in image edge classification is that it cannot just be done by using the information from the given image but at least a qualitative 3D reconstruction of the edges has to take place. On the other hand the 3D reconstruction could be supported by the classification of the image edges. Such a circular argument characterizes a special *bootstrap problem*, compare L. Dreschler-Fischer (1993).

4.2.5   Disparity Limit and Disparity Gradient Limit

Psychophysical research of the human visual system has shown that there is a maximum length of disparity vectors for the two images on the retinas for which visual fusion is still possible. This maximum value is called the *disparity limit.* In computer vision such a limit can be used to restrict the width of the search interval (see, e.g. Shirai algorithm) for the correspondence analysis.

Disparity limit: A maximum value d_{max} exists for the length of disparity vectors, for all corresponding points $\mathbf{p}_L = (x_L, y_L)$ and $\mathbf{p}_R = (x_R, y_R)$ in the left and in the right image, i.e. it holds

$$\|\Delta(x_L, y_L)\| = \sqrt{(x_L - x_R)^2 + (y_L - y_R)^2} < d_{max}.$$

In the case of the standard stereo geometry it holds that $|x_L - x_R| < d_{max}$.

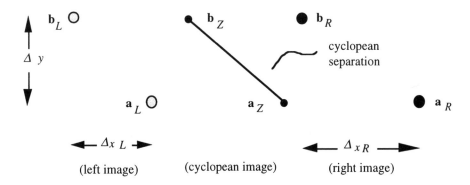

Figure 4.5: Definition of the disparity gradient assuming standard stereo geometry (after J. Mayhew and J. Frisby (1981)).

Note that setting a maximum value for the length of disparity vectors also means that a minimum distance between the scene objects and the camera system is defined at the same time. On the other hand a disparity limit can be derived directly using the a known minimum distance between the objects and the camera system (and the intrinsic and extrinsic camera parameters).

Psychophysical studies of the human visual system did also lead to the definition and understanding of disparity gradients. Let $\mathbf{a}_L$ and $\mathbf{a}_R$ as well as $\mathbf{b}_L$ and $\mathbf{b}_R$ be corresponding points in the left and in the right image (see Fig. 4.5). The *disparity gradient* $\Gamma(\mathbf{a}_L, \mathbf{b}_L)$ of such a pair of corresponding points is a vector defined by the difference vector $\Delta(\mathbf{a}_L) - \Delta(\mathbf{b}_L)$ of the disparities divided by their so-called *cyclopean separation* $d_{cs}(\mathbf{a}_L, \mathbf{b}_L)$,

$$\Gamma(\mathbf{a}_L, \mathbf{b}_L) = \frac{\Delta(\mathbf{a}_L) - \Delta(\mathbf{b}_L)}{d_{cs}(\mathbf{a}_L, \mathbf{b}_L)}.$$

The latter is defined by the Euclidean distance d_2 of the center points (here $\mathbf{a}_Z$ respectively $\mathbf{b}_Z$) between the two point pairs. For defining these center points assume a uniquely defined 3D coordinate system, say the XYZ-camera coordinate system with respect to the left camera. Then $\mathbf{a}_Z$ is the midpoint of the straight line segment connecting points $\mathbf{a}_L$ and $\mathbf{a}_R$, and $\mathbf{b}_Z$ is the midpoint of the straight line segment connecting points $\mathbf{b}_L$ and $\mathbf{b}_R$. Altogether we have

$$d_{cs}(\mathbf{a}_L, \mathbf{b}_L) = d_2\left(\frac{\mathbf{a}_L + \mathbf{a}_R}{2}, \frac{\mathbf{b}_L + \mathbf{b}_R}{2}\right).$$

Note that we have assumed the uniqueness constraint, i.e. $\mathbf{a}_L$ uniquely determines $\mathbf{a}_R$, and $\mathbf{b}_L$ uniquely determines $\mathbf{b}_R$.

As a special example let us consider the standard stereo geometry, see Fig. 4.5. In this case the disparity gradient $\Gamma(\mathbf{a}_L, \mathbf{b}_L)$ is given by

$$\Gamma(\mathbf{a}_L, \mathbf{b}_L) = \frac{|\Delta x_L - \Delta x_R|}{\sqrt{\frac{1}{4}(\Delta x_L - \Delta x_R)^2 + \Delta y^2}} \; ,$$

where Δx_L, Δx_R, and Δy denote the illustrated coordinate differences.

A further constraint for correspondence analysis in stereo images can be formulated using this disparity gradient. The experiments by P. Burt and B. Julesz (1980) showed that the binocular fusion in the human visual system is more strongly influenced by the disparity gradient than by the disparity value. If the absolute value of the disparity gradient exceeds a critical value γ_{max} (≈ 1), then no fusion did occur in their experiments.

Disparity gradient limit: For two consecutive[5] points $\mathbf{a}_L$ and $\mathbf{b}_L$ in the left image assume that $\mathbf{a}_L$ and $\mathbf{a}_R$ are corresponding points. Then $\mathbf{b}_R$ is a candidate to be a corresponding point to $\mathbf{b}_L$ if

$$\frac{\|\Delta(\mathbf{a}_L) - \Delta(\mathbf{b}_L)\|}{d_{cs}(\mathbf{a}_L, \mathbf{b}_L)} < \gamma_{max} \; ,$$

where γ_{max} is a specified disparity gradient limit.

Note that setting an upper threshold γ_{max} for the length of the disparity gradient vector also determines the maximum possible slope on the object surfaces in the scene in relation to the given camera geometry. In computer vision applications the disparity gradient limit is often used as a criterion to constrain the correspondence analysis process. Generally, disparity gradient limits are between 0.5 and 2.

4.2.6 Ordering of Projected Points in the Image Plane

A further reduction of the ambiguities in a correspondence analysis process can be achieved by an assumption about the order of the projected points along the corresponding epipolar lines in the images.

Ordering constraint: Points that lie on one epipolar line in a stereo image are projected onto the corresponding epipolar line of the other image in exactly the same order.

---

[5] Here, "consecutive" means in the order of a certain sequential vision process.

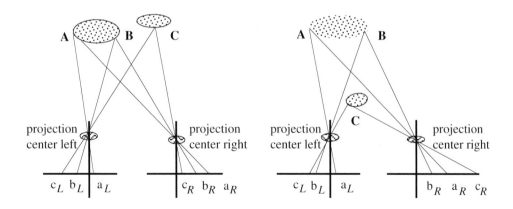

Figure 4.6: Examples of orders of the projected points along the corresponding epipolar lines in the images (see *ordering constraint*). On the left there are two objects with approximately the same distance to the image planes. The ordering constraint would be appropriate in this case. On the right the two objects have different distances to the image planes.

Figure 4.6 illustrates a valid and an invalid situation of geometric configurations for this assumption about the order of the projected points. Assuming that this constraint is applicable for a given stereo image acquisition situation means that all objects in the scenes have approximately the same distance to each of both cameras (what is invalid in Fig. 4.6 on the right), or the surface is continuous.

4.3 INTENSITY-BASED CORRESPONDENCE ANALYSIS

For correspondence analysis in stereo image pairs it is often assumed that corresponding pixels have a similar intensity value (*photometric compatibility constraint*, compare Section 4.2.2). However, identical intensity values occur in many points of a given image. Therefore, several neighboring pixels in an image window (e.g. a window of size 5×5 or 7×7) are defined as one *block* and the assignment of corresponding pixels is done using a *similarity measure* defined for the intensity values of these blocks (see also Shirai algorithm in Section 1.4.2 for a specific example). The literature refers to this technique as *area-based stereo*.

The application of these methods can either take place for all pixels of an image or only for selected pixels defined by extracted features, e.g. the edges in an image. Therefore, area-based stereo can be applied with feature extraction as well as without it. The essential difference to the feature-based techniques described later in Section 4.4 is that the stereo assignment is found based on the correlation between the intensity values. As a consequence we call area-based stereo also *intensity-based correspondence analysis* in the following.

For the practical application of this technique it has to be considered that high-frequency parts of the stereo image pairs are very sensitive to correlation errors. Therefore, a pre-processing step of the stereo images (e.g. a Gaussian smoothing) is recommended to improve the results. Furthermore, the quality of the results depends on the applied similarity measure as well as on the choice of a suitable window size.

Section 1.4.2 already introduced an intensity-based correspondence analysis technique for stereo image pairs. In this algorithm, first the edges in one of the given images are extracted and then the pixels along the edges are checked using a similarity measure. The result is a scalar disparity map which contains entries for assigned pixels along the edges (compare Fig. 1.20). In the following an intensity-based technique is described that basically determines a disparity value for every pixel in the stereo image pair. Of course, if an absolutely homogeneously colored object face is projected into a pair of stereo images then no correspondence analysis technique is able to calculate correct assignments in the interior of such an object face.

4.3.1   Block-Matching Method

The crucial component in recent encoding schemes for digital video sequences (MPEG standards) is motion compensation analysis. Basically images in the video sequence are generated from a selected subsequence of images by using motion vectors specifying shifts of image windows, and encodings of differences between image windows. A *motion vector* describes a change in the location of an image point (e.g. a center point of an image window) between two different images in the video sequence, compare Fig. 4.7a. The encoding of video image sequences is based on the detection, and the storage or the transmittance of such motion vectors.

(**Task 4.1**) Apply a method of motion estimation for solving the correspondence analysis problem in stereo image pairs. The temporal change between the images in the video sequence corresponds to the different image acquisition positions of the two cameras. Disparity vectors between the two images are determined instead of motion vectors. Under the assumption of the standard stereo geometry, only scalar disparities have to be determined in horizontal direction (i.e. in the same image row, see Fig. 4.7b).

(**Solution 4.1**) Motion estimation techniques are based on a similarity comparison of the gray value distributions between two identically sized blocks ($n \times m$ *search*

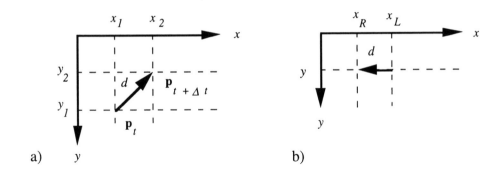

Figure 4.7 a) Motion vector of a pixel between the time slots t and $t + \Delta t$ of a video sequence. **b)** Representation of a disparity vector where standard stereo geometry is assumed.

window) and a specific search strategy (how to move the search window in the second image to detect a similar value distribution). Here first and second image (in the case of a video sequence) are the left and the right image. Because of the assumed standard stereo geometry the search strategy reduces to a search of a one-dimensional space (i.e. the same image row in the image on the right). However, the design of an efficient search strategy can also be suggested for this case instead of a simple one-pixel-move strategy within the given image row.

In this solution we discuss a specific two-step procedure: at first we calculate an initial draft of disparities just for subsampled image positions assuming that this helps to ensure that global image structures can be respected by allowing a reasonable large search window (block). In this first step the left image is divided into blocks, and all pixels inside the same block obtain the same (initial) disparity value, i.e., only one disparity value has to be determined for every block. The two-step technique is named after this first step. It is called *block matching*. A refinement of this technique is possible by designing a hierarchical block matching procedure for this first step: We start with a very large search window and a division of both images in just a few blocks of this window size. As a result we obtain corresponding blocks in the left and the right image (to speed up this process the search can be based on subsampled blocks in both images). Then the size of the search window is reduced and corresponding blocks are calculated within the corresponding blocks detected before for the larger window size, etc. However here we restrict the more detailed discussion on the non-hierarchical block matching step.

(Algorithm 4.1). At first we divide one of both images (for example the left image) into a constant number of identically sized blocks. The search for a corresponding block in the right image is only carried out for these blocks of the left image. The *mean square error* (*MSE*) can be used as a similarity measure to compare the intensity values of the pixels inside of blocks in the left and the right image.

The intensity functions of the left and the right image are denoted by E_L respectively E_R. The similarity measure (or more accurately, the dissimilarity measure) is defined by

$$MSE(x, y, d) = \frac{1}{m \cdot n} \sum_{i=0}^{m-1} \sum_{j=0}^{n-1} \left(E_L(x+i, y+j) - E_R(x-d+i, y+j) \right)^2 \qquad (4.4)$$

for a non-negative offset d (a multiple of m) which indicates the difference $(x_L - x_R)$ between the column positions in the left and in the right image and for a block size of $m \times n$ pixels. Note that this measure is only defined for blocks in the same image rows (because of the assumed standard stereo geometry). The parameter (x, y) always denotes the upper left corner (note: an coordinate system is assumed as shown in Fig. 4.7) of a block in the left image. The search interval in horizontal direction in the right image can be restricted by a disparity limit d_{max} (compare Section 4.2.5). The block of size $m \times n$ is shifted by d (a multiple of m) inside the search range.

The scalar disparity $\Delta_{ssg}(x, y)$ between two blocks in the left and in the right image is defined by the difference in column positions of that pair of blocks that possesses the minimum *MSE* value.

According to this definition the disparity value is only determined uniquely if the *MSE* function has a unique minimum in the search interval. In those cases where no unique minimum exists, the continuity constraint (compare Section 4.2.3) is assumed as an additional decision criterion: all disparity values for which the *MSE* function takes a minimum value are compared to the disparity value of the neighboring block on the left. We select the disparity with the smallest difference to the disparity of this neighboring block.

For image functions which contain regions with regular textures or regions with insignificant changes in the gray value distribution (homogeneous regions) a "correct" correspondence analysis result (what is "correct"?) is only possible if the block size is large enough to support a unique decision. A "good" block size depends upon the image size, the size of "object details" in the images, the surface texture of pictured objects etc.

The block-matching step calculates scalar disparities for all $\left(\frac{M}{m} \right) \times \left(\frac{N}{n} \right)$ positions of a 2D array *DISPARITY_OF_BLOCK*. This result is refined in a second step by calculating scalar disparities for all $M \times N$ pixels in the left image. The method by T. Reuter (1987) suggests three processes for this second step:

1. application of a median operator *MEDIAN* to the $\left(\frac{M}{m} \right) \times \left(\frac{N}{n} \right)$ disparity array *DISPARITY_OF_BLOCK* as a pre-processing step,

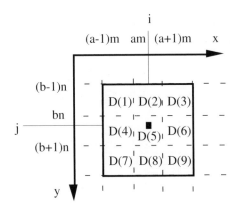

Figure 4.8: Assume a pixel position (i, j) inside of a block (a, b). Then $D(k)$, for $1 \le k \le 9$, lists the scalar block disparities of block (a, b) and of all blocks in the 8-neighborhood of this block (see the figure for an example of a numbering scheme).

---

begin
    segment left image into blocks of size $m \times n$;
                                      { block matching }

    for each block (a, b) of the left image **do**
        begin $min := MSE(am.bn, 0)$; $\Delta := 0$;
            for $d := 1$ **to** d_{max} **do**
                if $MSE(am, bn, d) < min$ **then**
                    begin $min := MSE(am, bn, d)$; $\Delta := d$
                    end {then}
                else if $MSE(am, bn, d) = min$ **then**
                    $\Delta :=$ scalar disparity with minimum distance
                        to scalar disparity of previous block;
            $DISPARITY\_OF\_BLOCK(a, b) := \Delta$
        end {for};
                { e.g. smooth the calculated array of scalar disparity values }
    pre-processing of $DISPARITY\_OF\_BLOCK$;
                              { define scalar disparities for pixels }
    for each point (i, j) in the left image ($D(k)$ as in Fig. 4.8) **do**
        begin for $k := 1$ **to** 9 **do**
                calculate $DIFF(k) = |E_L(i, j) - E_R(i - D(k), j)|$;
            $dis(i, j) := D(k)$, where $DIFF(k)$ is minimum;
        end {for}
    post-processing of dis {e.g. smoothing }
end

Figure 4.9: The block-matching method with the final step for specifying disparities for all pixels in the left image.

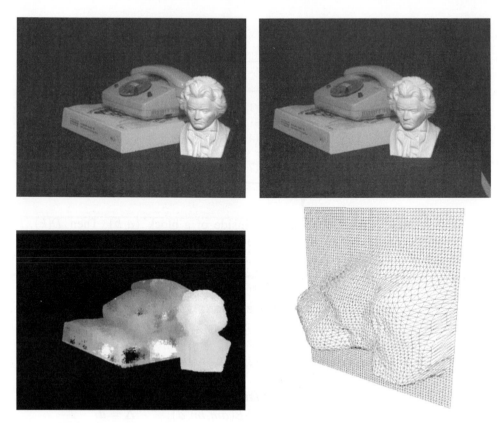

Figure 4.10: Top: The left and the right image of the stereo pair BEETHOVEN (752×566 pixel, PAL resolution). Bottom left: the gray value coded dense map of calculated scalar disparities; bottom right: a visualization of the scene BEETHOVEN based on this dense scalar disparity map.

2. definition of scalar disparities for all pixels in the left image (see Fig. 4.9), and
3. application of a median operator *MEDIAN* once again to the $M \times N$ disparity array *dis* that was determined in the second process.

A *median operator* determines that value in a set of given values which would take the center position in the ordered sequence of the given values. The first process eliminates outliers in the array of scalar block disparity values, and the third process eliminates outliers for the scalar disparity map for all pixels of the left image.

Both steps of the algorithm are sketched in Fig. 4.9 (instructions) and Fig. 4.8 (definition of local neighborhood for scalar block disparities). The second step of the algorithm leads to a disparity map *dis* with the original image size $M \times N$.

(**Comment 4.1**) The result of this algorithm differs fundamentally from the result of the Shirai algorithm described in Section 1.4.2 where only a sparse scalar disparity map was determined (scalar disparities along the edges). However, the Shirai algorithm is also an implementation of an intensity-based correspondence analysis method. A result of the specified block-matching method is visualized for a stereo image pair BEETHOVEN in Fig. 4.10. This figure shows the original stereo image pair BEETHOVEN, the calculated dense disparity map, and a reconstruction result.

4.3.2 Matching of Epipolar Lines using Dynamic Programming

In this section we assume that the stereo image pair is captured with a standard stereo geometry system, i.e. the conjugated epipolar lines in the left and in the right image possess identical y-coordinates.

The (dis)similarity measure (4.4) can be used to compare the intensity values for pixels along a conjugate pair of epipolar lines. For example, the intensity values of a block of size $m \times 1$ in the left image E_L can be compared with those of a block of size $m \times 1$ in the right image E_R if the matching process should be restricted to a single image row. In the simplest case we have

$$MSE(x_L, y, d) = |E_L(x_L, y) - E_R(x_L - d, y)| .$$

The calculation of scalar disparities d corresponds to the calculation of a scalar disparity function $\Delta_y(x_L) = \Delta_{ssg}(x_L, y)$. The scalar disparity function specifies the x-disparities between the corresponding pixels in the left and in the right images, see Section 1.4.1. It can be represented by the sequence of disparities,

$$\Delta_y = (\Delta_y(1), \Delta_y(2), ..., \Delta_y(M)) .$$

This scalar disparity function, for a pair of conjugated epipolar lines with a particular y-coordinate, represents an *epipolar profile* or cross-section of the observed 3D surface with an epipolar plane (specified by the particular y-coordinate). Figure 4.11 shows three examples of such scalar disparity functions.

Furthermore, we assume that the *ordering constraint* is valid for projected object surface points. In this case the calculation of scalar disparities corresponds to the calculation of a scalar disparity function which preserves the order of the corresponding pixels in both images:

$$x_{R1} = x_{L1} - \Delta_y(x_{L1}) \geq x_{R2} = x_{L2} - \Delta_y(x_{L2}) \text{ if } x_{L1} > x_{L2} . \tag{4.5}$$

Actually Fig. 4.11 shows three examples of order-preserving scalar disparity functions.

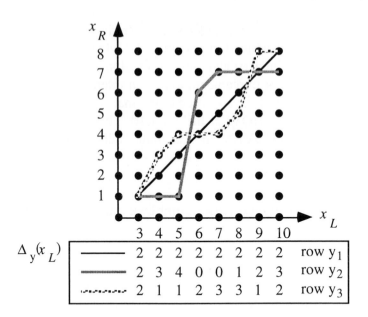

Figure 4.11: Examples of order-preserving scalar disparity functions Δ_y for three different y-coordinates. Note that $x_R = x_R(x_L) = x_L - \Delta_y(x_L)$ is monotonously increasing.

For image row y and a given scalar disparity function $\mathbf{d} = (d_1, d_2, ..., d_M)$ the *cumulative dissimilarity functional* is defined to be

$$DS_y(\mathbf{d}) = \sum_{x=1}^{M} MSE(x, y, d_x) .$$

(Task 4.2) The task consists in calculating such a scalar disparity function Δ_y which minimizes this functional DS_y. This is the given optimization problem what has to be solved.

(Solution 4.2) We assume that a minimum d_{min} and a maximum *disparity limit* d_{max} exists (see Section 4.2.5); the minimum limit d_{min} is equal to 0 in general. We assume that

$$d_{min} \le \Delta_y(x_L) \le d_{max} \tag{4.6}$$

holds, for all image points (x_L, y). Furthermore, the following technique is also based on the uniqueness assumption (Section 4.2.2) in the form that all pixels in the left image have a corresponding pixel in the right image, i.e.

$$1 \le x_L - \Delta_y(x_L) \le M . \tag{4.7}$$

From (4.6) and (4.7) it follows that

$$MIN(x_L) \leq \Delta_y(x_L) \leq MAX(x_L) \tag{4.8}$$

with $MIN(x_L) = max\{x_L - M, d_{min}\}$ and $MAX(x_L) = min\{x_L, d_{max}\}$. Furthermore, from (4.5) it follows that

$$\Delta_y(x_L) - \Delta_y(x_L - 1) \leq 1. \tag{4.9}$$

Note that the examples in Fig. 4.11 satisfy this equation. Finally, from (4.8) and (4.9) we conclude that

$$MINIMUM(x_L, \Delta_y(x_L)) \leq \Delta_y(x_L - 1) \leq MAX(x_L - 1) \tag{4.10}$$

holds, with $MINIMUM(x, d) = max\{d - 1, MIN(x - 1)\}$ and for $2 \leq x_L \leq M$. This specifies a dependency between the disparities of neighboring pixels (x_L, y) and $(x_L - 1, y)$.

    Dynamic programming is a general strategy for the design of efficient algorithms which requires such inter-dependencies between values which have to be calculated. We explain how the relation specified in inequality (4.10) can be used for designing a dynamic programming solution for disparity calculation.

    The given optimization problem is directed on minimizing the cumulative dissimilarity functional DS_y. For the dynamic programming approach we introduce a partial cumulative dissimilarity function $DSP_y(x, d)$ which is the partial sum of $DS_y(\mathbf{d})$ up to the given position x based on specified previously calculated disparity values $d_1, d_2, ..., d_{x-1}$ and a recent value d at position x.

    As initial value we define

$$DSP_y(1, d) := MSE(1, y, d)$$

where d is a disparity value in the set

$$\{\Delta : MIN(1) \leq \Delta \leq MAX(1)\},$$

see (4.8). For $2 \leq x \leq M$ and $MIN(x) \leq d \leq MAX(x)$ we define

$$DSP_y(x, d) := DSP_y(x - 1, backTrace(x, d)) + MSE(x, y, d)$$

where $backTrace(x, d)$ is that disparity d_{prev} which defines the minimum in the set

$$\{DSP_y(x - 1, d_{prev}) : MINIMUM(x, d) \leq d_{prev} \leq MAX(x - 1)\}.$$

see (4.8) and (4.10). The disparity value $backTrace(x, d)$ can be stored in position (x, d) in a two-dimensional array $backTrace$ of size $M \times (d_{max} - d_{min} + 1)$.

The value $backTrace(x,d)$ at position $x-1$ in this row is the potentially optimal value for the preceding position $x-1$ when the current position x has the disparity d. Only the partial dissimilarity value for the preceding position takes part in the computation for the current position. The values for more distant positions $x-2, x-3, \ldots$ do not need to be stored.

for each epipolar line y in the left and right image **do begin**
$\qquad\qquad\qquad\qquad\qquad\qquad$ { calculation of the $backTrace$ array }
$\quad$ **for** $d := MIN(1)$ **to** $MAX(1)$ **do begin**
$\qquad\qquad$ $DSP(1,d) := MSE(1,y,d)$; $\ backTrace(1,d) := stopLabel$;
$\quad$ **end** {*for*};
$\quad$ **for** $x := 2$ **to** M **do begin**
$\qquad$ **for** $d := MIN(x)$ **to** $MAX(x)$ **do begin**
$\qquad\qquad$ $min := bigValue$; $\ argMin := stopLabel$;
$\qquad\qquad$ **for** $d_{prev} := MINIMUM(x,d)$ **to** $MAX(x-1)$ **do**
$\qquad\qquad\qquad$ **if** $DSP\!\left(x-1, d_{prev}\right) < min$ **then begin**
$\qquad\qquad\qquad\qquad$ $min := DSP\!\left(x-1, d_{prev}\right)$; $\ argMin := d_{prev}$
$\qquad\qquad\qquad$ **end** {*if*};
$\qquad\qquad$ $DSP(x,d) := min + MSE(x,y,d)$;
$\qquad\qquad$ $backTrace(x,d) := argMin$
$\qquad$ **end** {*for*}
$\quad$ **end** {*for*};
$\qquad\qquad\qquad\qquad$ { calculation of the overall minimum dissimilarity value }
$\quad$ $min := bigValue$; $\ argMin := stopLabel$;
$\quad$ **for** $d := MIN(M)$ **to** $MAX(M)$ **do begin**
$\qquad$ **if** $DSP(M,d) < min$ **then begin** $\ min := DSP(M,d)$; $\ argMin := d$
$\qquad\qquad\qquad\qquad$ **end** {*if*}
$\quad$ **end** {*for*};
$\qquad\qquad\qquad$ { backward specification of the scalar disparity function }
$\quad$ $DS_y := min$; $\ \Delta_y(M) := argMin$;
$\quad$ **for** $x := M$ **to** 1 **do**
$\qquad$ $\Delta_y(x-1) := backTrace\!\left(x, \Delta_y(x)\right)$
end {*for*}

Figure 4.12: Gimel'farb algorithm for computing scalar disparities for all pixels along the epipolar lines.

Finally the partial dissimilarity values $DSP(M, d)$ are calculated for all values d with $MIN(M) \leq d \leq MAX(M)$. We select such a value d_M which has the minimal value $DSP(M, d)$. Starting with this value d_M the array *backTrace* allows to specify an optimum path $d_{M-1}, d_{M-2}, ..., d_1$ backward.

(**Algorithm 4.2**) A sketch of the algorithm (by Georgy Gimel'farb) is given in Fig. 4.12. Used values as *bigValue* or *stopLabel* have the obvious interpretation.

(**Comment 4.2**) The algorithm can be modified for symmetric (x, d)-coordinates $x_L = x + \frac{d}{2}$ and $x_R = x - \frac{d}{2}$, with $x = 0.5 \cdot (x_L + x_R)$ and $d = x_L - x_R$.

4.3.3 Block-Matching Method for Color Image Stereo Analysis

In static stereo analysis applications often robust and/or accurate solutions of the correspondence problem are necessary for automated, non-interactive uses of an implemented technique. One possibility for further improvement of robustness or of accuracy is the use and analysis of color information in the scene instead of just gray-value information to reduce the ambiguities in the correspondence analysis processes.

This approach is quite plausible since red pixel in the left image should not correspond to blue pixels in the right image. On the other hand, the digital intensity values in the gray value representations of both stereo images can be identical for the red and blue pixels. Thus color should allow refined discriminations. Actually, experiences with color stereo analysis have shown that in comparison to gray value methods an improvement of the results can be achieved in general. In comparison to gray-value images the amount of data increases by a factor of three (because we have three scalar channels in one color image), and the accuracy or robustness can increase by a certain percentage (for example, about 30%).

(**Task 4.3**) Design an extension of the block-matching method which was described in the previous section for color stereo analysis assuming standard stereo geometry.

(**Solution 4.4**) For every color image processing technique it is important to select a suitable color model. Section 1.2 introduced the computer hardware-oriented *RGB* model and the perception-oriented *HSI* model. We discuss the following color stereo technique for these two color spaces. After a color space is chosen the question arises how to describe the difference between two colors in this space. The *RGB* space is a 3D Euclidean space where known distance measures (e.g. the Euclidean metric d_2) can be used for the calculation of the color differences. We use the rational color value components

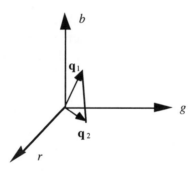

Figure 4.13: Two normalized color vectors $\mathbf{q}_1$ and $\mathbf{q}_2$ (i.e. $\|\mathbf{q}_1\|_1 = \|\mathbf{q}_2\|_1 = 1$) in the *rgb* space. The difference between both colors can be measured by the enclosed angle.

$$r = \frac{R}{R+G+B}, \quad g = \frac{G}{R+G+B}, \quad b = \frac{B}{R+G+B}$$

normalized with respect to the intensity, where it is assumed that $R+G+B>0$ holds (see Section 1.2.1). Note that always $\|(r,g,b)\|_1 = |r|+|g|+|b| = r+g+b = 1$. For the calculation of differences between normalized color values $\mathbf{q}_1 = (r_1,g_1,b_1)$ and $\mathbf{q}_2 = (r_2,g_2,b_2)$ (and analogously for the *RGB* model) we can use metrics as

$$d_1(\mathbf{q}_1,\mathbf{q}_2) = |r_1 - r_2| + |g_1 - g_2| + |b_1 - b_2|,$$

$$d_2(\mathbf{q}_1,\mathbf{q}_2) = \sqrt{(r_1 - r_2)^2 + (g_1 - g_2)^2 + (b_1 - b_2)^2} \quad \text{(the Euclidean metric)},$$

$$d_2^2(\mathbf{q}_1,\mathbf{q}_2) = (r_1 - r_2)^2 + (g_1 - g_2)^2 + (b_1 - b_2)^2 \quad \text{(as a simplification of } d_2 \text{), or}$$

$$d_\infty(\mathbf{q}_1,\mathbf{q}_2) = \max\left\{ |r_1 - r_2|, |g_1 - g_2|, |b_1 - b_2| \right\}.$$

The color distance $d_2(\mathbf{q}_1,\mathbf{q}_2)$ represents the angle subtended by the two normalized (with respect to the intensity) color vectors $\mathbf{q}_1$ and $\mathbf{q}_2$ in the *rgb* space (compare Fig. 4.13), and d_1, d_2^2, d_∞ can also be used to characterize color differences. Because of their simple calculation these metrics are also very common in color image processing. But there does not exist a relation between these distance measures and the human visual color perception. Apart from that, these formulas are also not suitable for determining differences in the *HSI* space (see Section 1.2.1). Instead the following distance measure is suggested for this color model.

For two color values $\mathbf{q}_1 = (H_1,S_1,I_1)$ and $\mathbf{q}_2 = (H_2,S_2,I_2)$ in the *HSI* space the color difference between them can be determined by

$$d_{HSI}(\mathbf{q}_1,\mathbf{q}_2) = \sqrt{(d_I)^2 + (d_C)^2}$$

with

$$d_I = |I_1 - I_2| \quad \text{and} \quad d_C = \sqrt{S_1^2 + S_2^2 - 2S_1 S_2 \cos\theta},$$

where

$$\theta = \begin{cases} |H_1 - H_2| & , \text{ for } |H_1 - H_2| \le \pi \\ 2\pi - |H_1 - H_2| & , \text{ for } |H_1 - H_2| > \pi. \end{cases}$$

Note that the hue value H was defined to be an angle in the interval $[0, 2\pi]$.

Now the proposed color metrics can be used to specify the similarity measure in the block matching step. If, for example, the RGB space and the color distance measure d_2^2 is chosen, then the similarity of two blocks can be estimated by extending the MSE function given in Section 4.3.1 (see equation (4.4)). Let $\mathbf{C}_L$ and $\mathbf{C}_R$ denote the normalized (with respect to intensity) left and right color image. Then a similarity measure MSE_{color} can be defined by

$$MSE_{color}(x, y, d) = \frac{1}{m \cdot n} \sum_{i=0}^{m-1} \sum_{j=0}^{n-1} d_2^2\left(\mathbf{C}_L(x+i, y+j), \mathbf{C}_R(x+i-d, y+j)\right)$$

$$= \frac{1}{m \cdot n} \sum_{i=0}^{m-1} \sum_{j=0}^{n-1} \Big(\left(r_L(x+i, y+j) - r_R(x+i-d, y+j)\right)^2$$

$$+ \left(g_L(x+i, y+j) - g_R(x+i-d, y+j)\right)^2$$

$$+ \left(b_L(x+i, y+j) - b_R(x+i-d, y+j)\right)^2 \Big)$$

for an offset d which indicates the non-negative difference $(x_L - x_R)$ between the column positions in the right and in the left image and for a block size of $m \times n$ pixels. Again (x, y) denotes the upper left corner of a block in the left image.

(Algorithm 4.3) The first step of the algorithm, the determination of the block disparities, is basically the same as in the gray value case (see Task 4.1 in Section 4.3.1), just a different measure is used to detect matching blocks. The second step (assignment of disparities to all pixels in the left image) in Algorithm 4.1 involves comparisons of pixel values. For comparisons of color values, i.e. for calculating the differences we can apply one of the given color metrics, e.g.

$$DIFF_{color}(k) = d_2^2\left(\mathbf{C}_L(i, j), \mathbf{C}_R(i - D(k), j)\right) \quad \text{with } k = 1,...,9.$$

This allows to calculate a dense disparity map for the whole image $\mathbf{C}_L$.

(Comment 4.3) The increase in accuracy and robustness, i.e. the improvement of the assignment results in comparison to the gray-value case, depends on the number of different colors in the image pair (more general: on the "dynamics of the color value distribution"). If a stereo image pair contains only a few colors, or like the image pair BEETHOVEN in Fig. 4.10 mainly gray values (Fig. 4.10 shows only the grayscale reproduction), then we can only expect a slight improvement from the analysis of the color information. On the other hand, matching results improve more significantly if more different colors are apparent in the image pair.

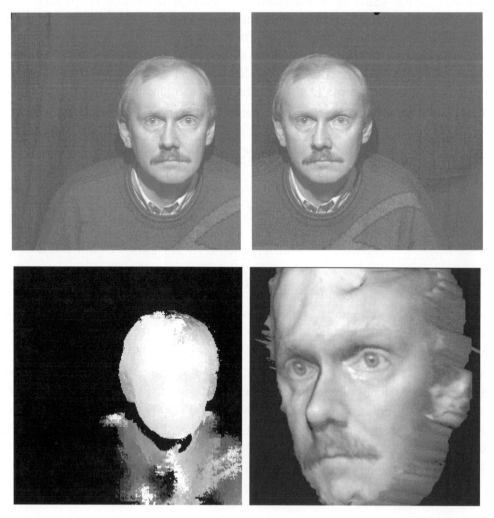

Figure 4.14: Top: gray value representation of the color stereo image pair ANDREAS. Bottom left: gray value coded representation of a calculated dense disparity map using the color variant of the block-matching method; bottom right: gray value representation (texture mapping) of this scene reconstructed using the shown dense disparity map.

Experiments with the block-matching method have shown that the average error (in pixels) for incorrectly calculated scalar disparity values can be reduced by about 20 to 25% if the color information is analyzed instead of just scalar images. In these experiments the choice of the color distance measure did not have a major impact on the assignment results. Therefore, to reduce computing time we recommend the use of the distance measures d_1 or d_2^2.

The color version of the block-matching method requires more computing time and more storage compared to the gray value method. While the storage requirement plays a minor role with sinking storage costs, computing time can be decisive for the applicability of the method. The application context is important to decide which technique should be selected. Figure 4.14 illustrates a dense disparity map determined using the color version of the block-matching method. This figure only shows gray value representations of the color stereo image pair (compare Color Image 3 in the Appendix).

The most errors in disparity calculation occur in homogeneous image regions. There, no unique assignment can be obtained for these pixels just using the given image values. Ambiguities can be partly dissolved if a colored pattern is projected into the scene. Through superpositioning of a colored pattern the object surfaces receives a texture that is (often) identifiable in both images. This technique is described later in Chapter 9.

4.4   FEATURE-BASED CORRESPONDENCE ANALYSIS

If a correspondence analysis technique for stereo images is not based on comparisons of intensity values of the image functions but instead on comparing image features then this technique is called *feature-based correspondence analysis (feature-based stereo)*. Particularly salient regions in the images like edges (see Section 1.3.1), "circular spots", "corners" etc. are used as features. The assignment is generally based on selected parameters of these features like the orientation or the length of the edges (compare the geometric similarity constraint in Section 4.2.2). Feature-based methods have the following advantages compared to intensity-based methods.

1. Ambiguities in correspondence analysis are significantly reduced for feature-based methods compared to intensity-based methods since the number of possible candidates for correspondence is considerably smaller.

2. The stereo assignment process is less sensitive with respect to the photometric variations during image acquisition since the features represent significant details of the scene.

3.   Often the disparities can be significantly more accurately determined, e.g. if the position of the features can be calculated with *subpixel accuracy* (i.e. more accurate than the camera resolution).

Feature-based methods are often also preferred because of the reduction of the required computing time. However, this is not true for every technique feature-based method. For some techniques the feature extraction process can be very time-consuming and far more lavish than the later assignment process of the features themselves. It is true that through reducing the features in the stereo images that have to be assigned the correspondence analysis is simplified considerably and thus generally the computing time for the assignment is also reduced. However, we cannot conclude from this that in every case the whole stereo analysis process is faster using a feature-based correspondence analysis than with an intensity-based correspondence analysis.

For the second advantage cited above for feature-based techniques note that photometric variations during image acquisition influence directly the result of an intensity-based technique. On the other hand they only have a small impact on the physical origin of features in the scene and therefore also on the results of feature-based techniques.

The third advantage describes the possibility of an increase in accuracy of the disparity determinations. This may allow that object surface points in three-dimensional space are calculated considerably more accurately. If three-dimensional object surfaces have to be described then disparity calculations with sub-pixel accuracies are inevitable.

In the following a histogram-based stereo analysis technique is described. This technique requires some extensive explanations and the run-time of its implementation was (so far) quite large. It was nevertheless chosen for this textbook because this technique allows good disparity results. Section 4.4.2 describes a simpler technique and its extension for color stereo analysis.

4.4.1   Stereo Analysis based on Zero-crossing Vectors

Y. Shirai and Y. Nishimoto (1985) suggest a technique for correspondence analysis in stereo image pairs which uses histograms of the disparities at different image resolution levels. This technique also includes considerations of two-dimensional pixel neighborhoods of potential correspondence candidates. The final assignment results from analyzing several resolution levels where a "best" resolution level (*channel*) is selected for every assignment. Histograms which reflect the frequency of the occurring disparity values in the neighborhood of a correspondence candidate serve as similarity measure. We assume standard stereo geometry. Thus the correspondence search can be restricted to a row-wise search (see epipolar line constraint in Section 4.2.1).

We use the LoG operator introduced in Section 1.3.2 at different resolution levels defined by values σ_1, σ_2, σ_3, ... for feature extraction. The zero-crossings (see end of Section 1.3.1) in the LoG filtered images form the features of the stereo assignment process. A *zero-crossing vector* is defined as a two-dimensional unit vector $e^{\sigma}(i,j)$ "along the line of neighboring zero-crossings" in the LoG filtered image starting at point (i,j). To be precise, let us assume that a decision criterion classifies image points to be a zero-crossing point in the LoG filtered image or not. If point (i,j) is not a zero-crossing point, then we select the zero vector, $e^{\sigma}(i,j) := (0,0)^T$, with $\left\| e^{\sigma}(i,j) \right\| = 0$. Otherwise let $E_x(i,j)$ and $E_y(i,j)$ denote the first derivatives in x- and in y-direction of the given scalar image E, and we define

$$e^{\sigma}(i,j) = \frac{1}{\sqrt{E_x^2(i,j) + E_y^2(i,j)}}\left(-E_y(i,j), E_x(i,j)\right) ,$$

with $\left\| e^{\sigma}(i,j) \right\| = 1$. Now assume that such vectors e_L^{σ} and e_R^{σ} are calculated for the left E_L and for the right image E_R.

A pair of zero-crossing vectors in the right and in the left image specifies a pixel pair of correspondence candidates if the directions of these two vectors do not differ by more than α_0 modulo 2π (see angle criterion in Section 4.2.2). The threshold α_0 stands for a small angle, e.g. $\alpha_0 = 30°$. This allows to define two binary assignment functions M_L^{σ} for the left image and M_R^{σ} for the right image. Assume that Δ is a non-negative number. If the vectors $e^{\sigma}(i,j)$ and $e_R^{\sigma}(i - \Delta, j)$ specify a pixel pair of correspondence candidates then it holds that $M_L^{\sigma}(i,j,\Delta) = 1$ and $M_R^{\sigma}(i - \Delta, j, \Delta) = 1$. Otherwise $M_L^{\sigma}(i,j,\Delta) = 0$ and $M_R^{\sigma}(i - \Delta, j, \Delta) = 0$.

Now we define a frequency table for all possible disparities (inclusive the "wrong" assignments). This frequency table is called a *global disparity histogram* and represents the distribution of all possible disparity values in the whole image. It is defined for the left image by

$$GDH_L^{\sigma}(\Delta) = \frac{\displaystyle\sum_{(i,j)\in\Omega} M_L^{\sigma}(i,j,\Delta)}{\displaystyle\sum_{(i,j)\in\Omega} \left\| e_L^{\sigma}(i,j) \right\|} ,$$

where $\Omega = \left\{ (i,j) : 1 \le i \le M \wedge 1 \le j \le N \right\}$ denotes the set of all image points.

Analogously GDH_R^{σ} can be defined for the right image. Because there are different numbers of zero-crossing vectors in the two images in general the

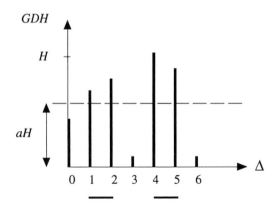

Figure 4.15: Two intervals $[1,2]$ and $[4,5]$ of a disparity candidate multi-interval.

histograms GDH_L^σ and GDH_R^σ are expected to be not identical. However, it is sufficient, to calculate just GDH_L^σ if we are only interested in a rough estimation of the disparity distributions in the given stereo pair. The global disparity histogram contains many wrong disparities.

Now let us assume that correct assignments specify certain peaks in these histograms. For complex scenes the location of such peaks can often be difficult because of the many different (correct) disparity values.

Starting from the GDH_L^σ a so-called *disparity candidate multi-interval* is determined. Let H^σ be the maximum value of all histogram values (this value may be taken at more than one disparity value). Then a disparity candidate multi-interval I_a^σ is defined by

$$I_a^\sigma = \left\{ \Delta \mid GDH_L^\sigma(\Delta) > a \cdot H^\sigma \right\},$$

where a is a constant value is with $0 < a < 1$. An "ideal" threshold value a is such that no incorrect (hopefully not very often appearing) disparity values lie in the interval and such that the multi-interval consists of several intervals where each interval corresponds to a class of objects in the scene which are in a specific distance to both cameras (see Fig. 4.15). If the image analysis task was just to analyze such clusters of objects in different "principal distances" to the two cameras then this might be the end of the solution process. Otherwise, if we are interested in calculating a (sparse) scalar disparity map then these values in the disparity candidate multi-interval are defined to be the possible values for the disparity map, and the assignment of these values to pixels (say, in the left image) remains as a task for the next step in the correspondence analysis process.

Now, local disparity candidates are determined through *local disparity histograms*. Basically this is the same as the global disparity histogram besides

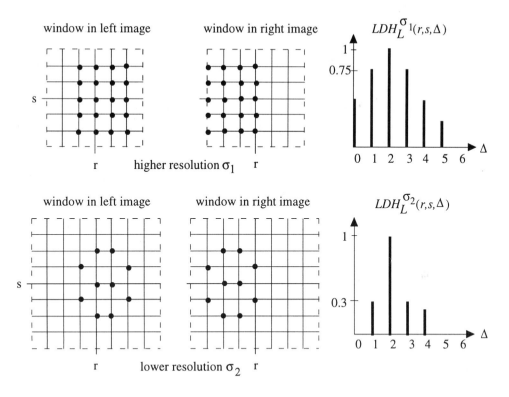

Figure 4.16: Examples of two local disparity histograms for different resolution levels.

that the whole image point array Ω is now replaced by a *placed image window* $\mathbf{F}(\mathbf{p})$ defined by a window $\mathbf{F}$ which is placed at image point $\mathbf{p}$. For example, let

$$\mathbf{F} = \{(x,y): 1 \le x \le m \wedge 1 \le y \le n\},$$

with a *reference point* $(x_0, y_0) = (\mathrm{int}(m+\tfrac{1}{2}), \mathrm{int}(n+\tfrac{1}{2}))$ in $\mathbf{F}$, and for $\mathbf{p} = (r,s)$ let

$$\mathbf{F}(\mathbf{p}) = \mathbf{F}(r,s) = \{(r - x_0 + x, s - y_0 + y): 1 \le x \le m \wedge 1 \le y \le n\}$$

be the window $\mathbf{F}$ placed at point $\mathbf{p} = (r,s)$. Now assume a square $n_\sigma \times n_\sigma$ window $\mathbf{F}^\sigma$ for the definition of local disparity histograms with $n_\sigma = \sqrt{2} \cdot \pi \cdot \sigma$, and σ denotes the standard deviation in the LoG operator (see Section 1.3.2).

The local disparity histograms are frequency tables of those disparities which occur in I_a^σ and in a placed image window $\mathbf{F}^\sigma(\mathbf{p})$ defined with respect to image E_L. Formally we use

$$LDH_L^\sigma(r,\mathrm{s},\Delta) = \frac{\displaystyle\sum_{(i,j) \in \mathbf{F}^\sigma(r,s)} M_L^\sigma(i,j,\Delta)}{\displaystyle\sum_{(i,j) \in \mathbf{F}^\sigma(r,s)} \left\| e_L^\sigma(i,j) \right\|} \quad, \text{ for } \Delta \in I_a^\sigma,$$

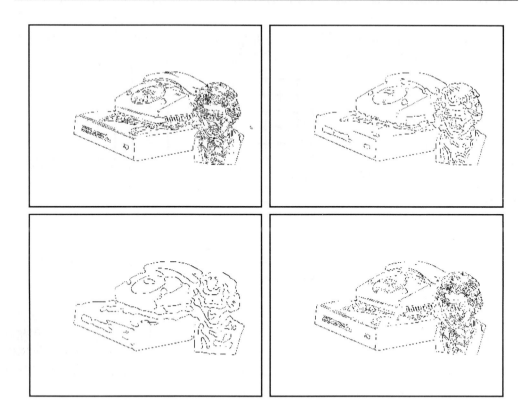

Figure 4.17: The detected edge points in the left stereo image BEETHOVEN (above left: with high resolution $\sigma_1 = 1.41$, above right: with medium resolution $\sigma_2 = 3.18$, below left: with low resolution $\sigma_3 = 6.01$) and (below right) those edge points in the left stereo image BEETHOVEN where a disparity value was assigned using parameter $a = 0.5$.

and the same histograms can be defined with respect to E_R as well. The histograms $LDH_L^{\sigma}(r,s,\Delta)$ and $LDH_R^{\sigma}(r-\Delta,s,\Delta)$ can differ greatly if an image value edge is passing through the local window $\mathbf{F}^{\sigma}(\mathbf{p})$ in the left image, or through the local window $\mathbf{F}^{\sigma}(r-\Delta,s)$ in the right image. But generally $LDH_L^{\sigma}(r,s,\Delta)$ and $LDH_R^{\sigma}(r-\Delta,s,\Delta)$ will be "similar".

Different standard deviations, for example for $w = 2\sqrt{2} \cdot \sigma$ and $w = 4,9,17$ use $\sigma_1 = \sqrt{2}$, $\sigma_2 = 3.18$ and $\sigma_3 = 6.01$, define different resolutions. Smaller values of σ specify higher resolutions. After local disparity histograms are determined for different resolutions, a "best" resolution is determined for every position (r,s) comparing the largest and the second-largest values in the local disparity histograms $LDH_L^{\sigma}(r,s,\Delta)$. That resolution $\sigma(r,s)$ is chosen to be the best for point (r,s) having the maximum difference between these two values. Now assume that $LDH_L^{\sigma(r,s)}(r,s,\Delta_L^{r,s,1})$ is the maximum value for this resolution $\sigma(r,s)$

for disparity $\Delta_L^{r,s,1}$, and that $LDH_L^{\sigma(r,s)}(r,s,\Delta_L^{r,s,2})$ is the second-largest value for disparity $\Delta_L^{r,s,2}$. This specifies a difference value

$$L(r,s) = \Delta_L^{r,s,1} - \Delta_L^{r,s,2} \ .$$

Similarly we define $LDH_R^{\sigma(r,s)}(r - \Delta_L^{r,s,1}, s, \Delta_R^{r,s,1})$ and $LDH_R^{\sigma(r,s)}(r - \Delta_L^{r,s,2}, s, \Delta_R^{r,s,2})$ for the right image, and the difference value

$$R(r,s) = \Delta_R^{r,s,1} - \Delta_R^{r,s,2} \ .$$

An assignment is accepted if, and only if $L(r,s)$ and $R(r,s)$ exceed a given threshold and if $\Delta_L^{r,s,1}$ and $\Delta_R^{r,s,1}$ only differ slightly. In this case finally the scalar disparity

$$\Delta^*(r,s) = \frac{\Delta_L^{r,s,1} + \Delta_R^{r,s,1}}{2}$$

is calculated for an image point (r,s) in E_L. Otherwise no assignment is made for this image point. The original paper by Y. Shirai and Y. Nishimoto suggests a further "final adjustment" procedure at this stage.

A result of the described histogram-based correspondence analysis (which is a modification of the original Shirai-Nishimoto technique) is visualized in Fig. 4.17 for the stereo image pair BEETHOVEN. Figure 4.17 shows the edge points that were detected in the left stereo image at three different resolution levels and those edge points where finally scalar disparities were assigned.

4.4.2   Feature-Based Color Stereo Analysis

This section discusses how the results of a feature-based stereo analysis technique can be improved by utilizing color information. Because of the correlation between the color channels in general it can be expected that at least 90% of the image edges are identical in the scalar images defined by the intensity or the three color channels (compare Fig. 1.20). Exceptions occur, for example, when neighboring objects in the scene exhibit the same brightness but a different hue value. In such a case the edge cannot be detected in some of the scalar images. Therefore, by using a "good" color edge finder, the number of correctly detected edges can be increased by about 10% at most. In the technique described in Section 4.4.1 disparities can only be assigned to pixels on edges. We can only expect a small improvement of the results from utilizing a "good" color edge detector.

In this section it is illustrated how the ambiguities of the correspondence analysis process can be reduced by using color information in the edge detection process and how wrong assignments of edges which do not correspond to each other can be reduced this way. A stereo analysis technique that was suggested by J.R. Jordan III and A.C. Bovik (1988) is described.

We assume standard stereo geometry. Because of the location of the epipolar lines (see Section 4.2.1) the correspondence process can be restricted on a row-wise search strategy. Analogously to the method described in the previous section, the zero-crossing vectors in the two LoG filtered stereo images constitute the features for the stereo assignment process. The standard deviation $\sigma = \sqrt{2}$ can be suggested in general. Additionally a maximum disparity value, e.g. 20% of the image width, can be assumed (compare disparity limit, Section 4.2.5).

The algorithm is sketched at first for an assumed gray value stereo image pair. Starting with a zero-crossing vector in the left image the following two criteria are used in the assignment algorithm. For assigning a candidate in the right image we restrict the search on

(i)   corresponding zero-crossings (i.e. start points of zero-crossing vectors) in the right image which lie inside a search interval defined by the maximum disparity value; and assign two points if

(ii) both zero-crossing vectors have approximately the same orientation (for example, threshold $\alpha_0 = 30°$), see Section 4.4.1.

If the two criteria (i) and (ii) allow an unambiguous assignment then such an unambiguous combination is selected, and all the other candidates are rejected. This allows to calculate (a few) assignments between points in the left and in the right image. Note that an unambiguous assignment using these two criteria is not necessarily a correct assignment. Color information may help to improve this simple technique.

Color information can be used in the assignment algorithm in one of the following ways:

(A) the zero-crossings are determined for the red, the green, and the blue channel and the assignment algorithm is carried out separately for each pair of color channels, or

(B) the complete color information is used for the characterization of the zero-crossings in the different scalar images.

The first technique (A) is not efficient with respect to computing time since the assignment process has to be called three times. More critical, the zero-crossings in the color channels only differ slightly from the zero-crossings in the intensity image because of the high correlation of edge information between the spectral channels.

The second option (B) is more challenging. The color information (hue, saturation, intensity) at an image point can be used to specify a given zero-crossing in the intensity channel. Points on image value edges are often correlated to a change of the color type at this point. Therefore, a use of *color gradients* could be a useful idea. Such gradients can be defined by following different ways.

Consider difference functions between the normalized color components r,g,b of the *RGB* model, see Section 1.2.1. Let

$$D_{rg}(x,y) = r(x,y) - g(x,y) = \frac{R(x,y) - G(x,y)}{R(x,y) + G(x,y) + B(x,y)} \quad,$$

be the red-minus-green difference function, and further difference functions D_{gb} or D_{br} can be defined analogously.

Note that these difference functions can also have negative values. The gradient of such a difference function describes the direction of a zero-crossing vector (in the intensity channel) with respect to a specific component of the given color information. Different features can be derived. For example, assume that the values of gradient directions are specified to be in the interval $[-\pi,\pi)$. Then the sign of the direction is a simple feature of such a gradient. For a given image point a positive sign indicates a relative intensity increase from red to green, while a negative sign indicates a corresponding intensity reduction (with respect to a specified direction).

Features of the gradients of these difference functions can be used as attributes in the assignment process for the considered zero-crossing vectors. This should restrict false assignments, and support unique selections of the corresponding image point in the right image. A Gauss filter operation (see Section 1.3.2) can be suggested for these difference functions before calculating the gradient for purposes of noise removal. For example, the orientation of the difference color gradient can be calculated as

$$tan^{-1}\left(\frac{\dfrac{\partial}{\partial y}(GAUSS * D_{rg})}{\dfrac{\partial}{\partial x}(GAUSS * D_{rg})}\right)$$

as a value in the interval $[0,\pi)$.

Based on these considerations the assignment algorithm can now be competed by an additional selection criterion based on features of the color difference functions. For examples, this can be:

(iii) For assigning two pixels in the left and in the right image, the signs of the difference color gradients have to be the same for the red-minus-green, the green-minus-blue, and the blue-minus-red difference functions of the left and of the right image.

Unambiguous assignments are determined with this algorithm based on (i), (ii), and (iii), and ambiguous assignments are excluded. Table 4.1 shows percentage changes in the results arising from the extension of the assignment algorithm by

measured quantity	percentage change
number of zero-crossings for which one or more assignment candidates were found	-31.72
total number of assignment candidates	-48.80
number of unambiguous assignments	+78.40
percentage of correct assignments	+5.74

Table 4.1: Percentage changes of the results while using the color algorithm instead of the gray value algorithm averaged over three selected color stereo images, see J.R. Jordan III and A.C. Bovik (1988) as cited in Section 4.6.

selection criterion (iii) for color images. An obvious though small improvement compared to the gray value algorithm is apparent. This relatively small improvement results mainly from the simple assignment scheme which can only be used to assign edge points in a stereo image pair.

4.5   STEREO ANALYSIS WITH THREE CAMERAS

A simple extension of the binocular stereo geometry is achieved by the addition of a third camera. Three different camera set-ups are common for such a trinocular situation (see Fig. 4.18). For the right-angle and coplanar (a) and the collinear (b) camera arrangements the optical axes are parallel and the image planes are coplanar. Therefore, the epipolar lines and the horizontal scanning lines coincide (configuration b) or the epipolar lines coincide with the vertical scanning lines (one camera pair in configuration a). The disadvantage of the collinear arrangement is that horizontal lines in the scene are projected onto the same epipolar line in all three planes. This is does not provide additional support to resolve ambiguities in the correspondence analysis processes.

On the other hand, with the right-angle and coplanar arrangement the horizontal as well as the vertical scanning lines can be used for the correspondence analysis. The assignment of an edge can be done independently from its orientation in the image planes. The exact positioning of the cameras has to satisfy additional accuracy constraints in comparison to a binocular case.

With the use of an unconstrained camera arrangement the stereo assignment can be carried out solely based on geometric laws. This allows that restricting assumptions can be avoided. The disadvantage of this arrangement is

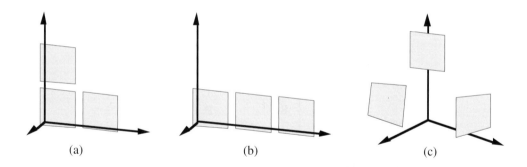

Figure 4.18: Trinocular camera arrangements (a) right-angle and coplanar arrangement, (b) collinear arrangement, (c) unconstrained arrangement.

that the epipolar lines do not correspond with the scanning lines in the image. They have to be re-determined for every camera arrangement. *Rectification* is one way to map this geometry into a standardized situation.

A trinocular camera arrangement can be extended further by including additional cameras. Camera arrangements with up to eight cameras are known from the literature. The restrictions arising from this are usually similar to those for the trinocular arrangement.

4.5.1 Assignment Strategies

For correspondence analysis strategies in principle two different approaches can be distinguished in case of an inclusion of another (e.g. a third) image:

(A) Only those pixels are assigned for which a correspondence was determined in all (e.g. all three) images.

(B) All pixels are assigned for which a correspondence was determined in at least two images.

The first approach (A) is to verify the assignments. It reduces the error rate significantly but at the same time also reduces the number of found assignments. This is especially true for edges which are occluded in one of the images.

On the other hand, the main motivation for selecting the second approach (B) is often based on the desire to be able to assign edges which are occluded in one of the (for example three) images. This increases the number of found assignments and therefore also the number of reconstructed 3D surface points which will be required later for the reconstruction of object surfaces.

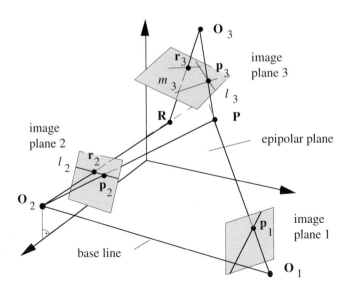

Figure 4.19: Illustration of geometric trinocular stereo analysis.

In the following, a technique is discussed where an additional third image is used to verify the assignment.

4.5.2   A Geometric Method

The principle of this geometric technique was proposed by M. Yachida, Y. Kitamura and M. Kimachi (1986) and is illustrated by Fig. 4.19.

(Task 4.4) Those image points that are visible in all three image planes have to be assigned uniquely using the geometric laws that hold for image acquisition with an unconstrained arrangement of the three cameras.

(Solution 4.4) O_1, O_2 and O_3 are the projection centers of the three cameras. The projections of a point P in the scene into the image planes 1 and 2 are denoted by p_1 respectively p_2. If the image point in the image plane 2 is sought which corresponds to p_1, then this point has to lie on the line l_2. The epipolar line l_2 is the projection of the line $O_1 p_1$ into the image plane 2. It can be determined as the intersection line between the image plane 2 and the epipolar plane that is formed by the base line $O_1 O_2$ and the line $O_1 p_1$ (compare Section 4.1).

   On the epipolar line l_2 lies not only the point p_2, but all points of the scene which lie on this epipolar plane are projected onto image points on the

---

begin

    determine edge points in all three images (as potential candidates for
        matching triples);

    for (every edge point **p** in image 1) **do**

        begin

        $A := \varnothing$;   { set of all correspondence candidates in image 3 }

        determine the epipolar line l_2 as projection of $O_1 p$ in image plane 2
            (with projection center O_2);

        determine the epipolar line l_3 as projection of $O_1 p$ in image plane 3
            (with projection center O_3);

        for (every edge point **q** on the epipolar line l_2 in image 2) **do**

            begin

            determine the epipolar line m_3 as projection of $O_2 q$ in image
                plane 3 (with projection center O_3);

            if (intersection point of l_3 and m_3 in image 3 is an edge point) **then**
                add this point to set A;

            end {*for*};

        if $A \ne \varnothing$ **then**

(*)   **if** **p**, **q**, and one (!) point in A form a triplet
              of corresponding points ("best match") **then**
                calculate the 3D position of the projected point
                    as intersection point of three epipolar planes;

        end {*for*}

    end

Figure 4.20: Sketch of procedure for geometric trinocular stereo analysis.

epipolar line l_2 (in the above described example let it be **P** and **R** with the projections p_2 and r_2, compare Section 4.1). Therefore, an unambiguous assignment cannot be done solely based on the epipolar geometry. For the correspondence analysis further assumptions are necessary, like they were introduced for the block-matching method (compare Section 4.3.1) or the method of histogram-based stereo analysis (compare Section 4.4.1).

    The solution of the correspondence problem can also be supported by including an additional third image. In Fig. 4.19 p_3 and r_3 are the projections of the points **P** and **R** into the image plane 3. Since p_3 is the projection of the point **P** it must lie on the epipolar line l_3 which represents the projection of the line

$\mathbf{O}_1 \mathbf{p}_1$ into the image plane 3. Nonetheless, the projections of the other points on the epipolar plane do not lie on l_3.

If $\mathbf{p}_2$ and $\mathbf{p}_3$ are corresponding points, then $\mathbf{p}_3$ must also lie on the epipolar line m_3 which represents the projection of the line $\mathbf{O}_2 \mathbf{p}_2$ in image plane 3. If all three cameras are well calibrated and $\mathbf{p}_1$ corresponds to $\mathbf{p}_2$, then the corresponding point $\mathbf{p}_3$ in image 3 lies exactly on the intersection of the epipolar lines l_3 and m_3. This is the case with the constellation in Fig. 4.19. Therefore the correspondence candidates in image 3 are just a subset on line l_3. The criterion (*) in Fig. 4.20 should allow to specify exactly one "best match". For example, parameters of edge points can be analyzed with respect to a consistent 3D interpretation (e.g. consider these edge segments as curves in 3D space).

(**Algorithm 4.4**) Figure 4.20 sketches the algorithm. The edge points can be determined in all three images, for example, with the LoG operator and subsequent search for zero-crossings (see Section 1.3.2). The epipolar lines can be determined once at the beginning of the algorithm and stored in a table because they are independent of the specific image values.

(**Comment 4.4**) Note that this method is not directed on the determination of disparity maps. The calculated results are surface points in three-dimensional world coordinates.

4.6   REFERENCES

A discussion of the computational stereo analysis problem with special consideration of the human visual system can be found in

Marr, D.: Vision: A Computational Investigation into the Human Representation and Processing of Visual Information. W.H. Freeman and Company, New York, USA, 1982.

A geometric view of the stereo analysis problem is presented in great detail in

Faugeras, O.: *Three-Dimensional Computer Vision: A Geometric Viewpoint.* MIT Press, Cambridge, Massachusetts, USA, 1993, and

Xu, G., Zhang, Z.: *Epipolar Geometry in Stereo, Motion and Object Recognition - A Unified Approach.* Kluwer, Dordrecht 1996.

For a historically first paper on dynamic programming applied to stereo image pair based surface reconstruction see

Gimel'farb, G., Marchenko, V., Rybak, V.: *An algorithm for automatic identification of identical sections on stereopair photographs.* Cybernetics (Kybernetica) **2** (1972), pp. 311-322 (English translation).

Recent work is reported in

Gimel'farb, G.: *Symmetric bi- and trinocular stereo - tradeoffs between theoretical foundations and heuristics.* Theoretical Foundations of Computer Vision (W. Kropatsch, R. Klette. F. Solina, eds.). Computing Supplement 11, Springer, Wien 1996, pp. 53-71.

Mobile robots are often equipped with a stereo camera system. A discussion of stereo analysis techniques that were especially designed for applications in robotics can be found in

Ayache, N.: *Artificial Vision for Mobile Robots: Stereo Vision and Multisensory Perception.* MIT Press, Cambridge, Massachusetts, 1991 and

Mayhew, J.E.W., Frisby, J. P. (eds.): *3D Model Recognition from Stereoscopic Cues.* MIT Press, Cambridge, Massachusetts, 1991.

A very interesting overview on the assumptions and constraints for the geometric scene reconstruction problem is compiled in

Dreschler-Fischer, L.: *Geometrische Szenenrekonstruktion.* In: Görz, G. (Hrsg.): *Einführung in die künstliche Intelligenz.* Addison-Wesley, Bonn, Germany, 1993, S. 681-711.

for the static as well as for the dynamic stereo analysis problem. Psychophysical research about binocular fusion in the human visual system can, for example, be found in

Burt, P., Julesz, B.: *Modifications of the classical notion of panum´s fusional area.* Perception **9** (1980), pp. 671-682 and

Mayhew, J., Frisby, J.: *Psychophysical and computational studies towards a theory of human stereopsis.* Artificial Intelligence **17** (1981), pp. 349-385.

The inclusion of color information into the correspondence analysis processes is studied in

Jordan, J.R. III, Bovik, A.C.: *Computational stereo vision using colo*r. IEEE Control Systems Magazine, June (1988), pp. 31-36,

Jordan, J.R. III, Bovik, A.C.: *Using chromatic information in edge-based stereo correspondence.* Computer Vision, Graphics, and Image Processing: Image Understanding **54** (1991), pp. 98-118,

Jordan, J.R. III, Bovik, A.C.: *Using chromatic information in dense stereo correspondence.* Pattern Recognition **25** (1992), pp. 367-383, and

Koschan, A.: *How to utilize color information in dense stereo matching and in edge-based stereo matching.* Proc. 3rd International Conference on Automation, Robotics and Computer Vision ICARCV´94, Singapore, 1994, Vol. 1, pp. 419-423.

Further research about the extension of the block-matching method for color stereo image analysis is described in

Koschan, A: *Chromatic block matching for dense stereo correspondence.* Proc. 7th Int. Conf. on Image Analysis and Processing 7ICIAP, Capitolo, Monopoly, Italy, 1993, pp. 641-648.

The procedures discussed as second step of block matching (in Section 4.3.1) in were suggested in

Reuter, T: *HDTV standards conversion.* Proc. IEEE-ASSP & EURASIP 5th Workshop on Multidimensional Signal Processing, Nordwijkerhouth, Netherlands, 1987, (reprint Heinrich-Hertz-Institute Berlin).

For the method of histogram-based stereo analysis we cite

Shirai, Y., Nishimoto, Y.: *A stereo method using disparity histograms of multi-resolution channels.* Proc. 3rd International Symposium on Robotics Research, Gouvieux, France, 1985, pp. 27-32.

Parallel implementations on different hardware architectures of block matching and histogram-based stereo analysis are described in

Koschan, A., Rodehorst, V.: *Towards real-time stereo employing parallel algorithms for edge-based and dense stereo matching.* Proc. IEEE Workshop on Computer Architectures for Machine Perception CAMP´95, Como, Italy, 1995, pp. 234-241.

The geometric trinocular stereo analysis method is discussed in

Yachida, M., Kitamura, Y., Kimachi, M.: *Trinocular vision: new approach for correspondence problem.* Proc. 8th International Conference on Pattern Recognition, Paris, France, 1986, pp. 1041-1044.

4.7   EXERCISES

(1) What does the term epipolar geometry mean? What are the definitions of an epipolar plane and an epipolar line? What is meant by standard stereo geometry?

(2) How does the location of the base line change compared to the standard stereo geometry when one (or both) stereo cameras are rotated such that the two optical axes intersect? Consider the case that the rotation centers for the two cameras are not identical with the projection centers. The rotation angles and the distances between the rotation center and the projection center are assumed to be known for both cameras. Does this allow to reconstruct a point in 3D based on a (correct) assignment of two image points in the first and in the second camera?

(**3**) State three ways how to improve the depth resolution of a static stereo analysis system. What are the advantages and disadvantages of these three options?

(**4**) Assume that a given stereo camera system is arranged according to standard stereo geometry in such a way that both lenses have an effective focal length of 50 mm and that the cameras are arranged with a base distance of 0.5 m between them. Which horizontal and vertical size (d_x and d_y, compare Section 2.1.4) can an element of the image sensor have at most to be able to measure an object at a distance of 2m to the camera system with an accuracy of 5mm $\pm$ 10%?

(**5**) Assume that the optical axes of a stereo system converge and intersect in the point (X_i, Y_i, Z_i). Also assume that the optical axes intersect the image planes of the cameras at their center point M (see Fig. 4.21). Now consider three points in 3D space,

$$\mathbf{P}_1 = (X_i, Y_i, Z_1) \text{ with } Z_1 = Z_i \,,$$

$$\mathbf{P}_2 = (X_i, Y_i, Z_2) \text{ with } Z_2 < Z_i \text{ and}$$

$$\mathbf{P}_3 = (X_i, Y_i, Z_3) \text{ with } Z_3 > Z_i \,.$$

Sketch the location of their projections in the left and in the right image.

(**6**) Section 4.1 introduced the equations

$$a_1 X + a_3 Z = a_0$$
$$b_1 X + b_3 Z = b_0$$

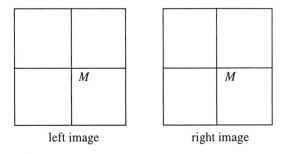

left image   right image

Figure 4.21: Illustration to Exercise (5).

$$c_1 X + c_2 Y + c_3 Z = c_0$$
$$d_1 X + d_2 Y + d_3 Z = d_0$$

for the determination of the coordinates X, Y and Z of a scene point, where a specific image acquisition geometry was assumed. Solve this equation system with respect to X, Y and Z.

(7) Which two classes of correspondence analysis methods for stereo images were discussed in this chapter? What are the general advantages and disadvantages for each of these classes?

(8) State two to three constraints that can be used to reduce the ambiguities of stereo assignments. For example, when does the ordering constraint not apply?

(9 - Assignment) Use the block-matching method described in Section 4.3.1 for implementing a correspondence analysis procedure for binocular gray value stereo images. Implement the algorithm as shown in Fig. 4.9. Generate a stereo image pair with standard stereo geometry and apply the technique to this image pair (synthetic image generation). Change the applied block size in this algorithm (e.g. 3×3, 5×5, 7×7 and 9×9) and visualize (e.g. gray value coded) the calculated disparity maps. Carry out the second step of the block-matching algorithm with or without median filtering and comment on the differences in the results.

(10) As a modification of the solution of exercise (9) extend the block-matching method for color images. Change the algorithm that was implemented in exercise (9) by using **(a)** the distance measure d_1 given in Section 4.3.2 in the *RGB* space and **(b)** the distance measure d_{HSI} in the *HSI* space. Visualize the results.

(11) Which object classes can not be reconstructed with a binocular stereo analysis method? Why not? Give examples.

(12) What geometric shape has the 3D set of all possible point locations for any arbitrary pair of corresponding stereo image points? Assume standard stereo geometry.

5   DYNAMIC STEREO ANALYSIS

This chapter almost exclusively considers motions of scene objects as causes of scene changes. Further options are moving cameras or modifications in lighting. According to the results of physiology, motion perception is an important cognitive element of the visual interpretation of our three-dimensional world by animals or humans. Geometric analysis of dynamic scene spaces proves that projected motion vectors can support the calculation of depth values or gradient vectors. In the ideal case the movement of the scene object in three-dimensional space (3D motion) corresponds to a 2D motion in a captured image sequence. These projected motions can be represented in the image plane as a *field of local displacement vectors*. If a technique allows the exact measurement of such fields of local displacements then a shape reconstruction can be carried out or supported on the basis of these local displacement vectors. For example, understanding of motions and shapes of the human body can be based on surface marks which allow an unambiguous pursuit of individual surface points as known from the *moving light displays* of G. Johannsson in the 1960's. This technique of tracking of surface marks is used in recent computer vision applications in sports sciences.

However, it is only partly possible to calculate almost error free sets of local displacement vectors. The main problem of the implementation of a dynamic stereo analysis approach is the correct measurement of projected motions and the analysis of partially distorted fields of local displacement vectors. Fields of local displacement vectors can be calculated approximately as optical flow fields (these will be defined in Section 5.2). A "classical" technique is introduced in this chapter in detail also with respect to evaluate results of algorithms for the detection of local displacement vectors. Optical flow fields allow rough estimations of the depth or distance, e.g. for navigation of robots or for tracking of moving objects in a scene.

5.1   DISPLACEMENT VECTORS AND RECONSTRUCTION

This section deals with selected theoretical fundamentals for dynamic stereo analysis. 3D motion of rigid objects is assumed to be not restricted, i.e. any arbitrary

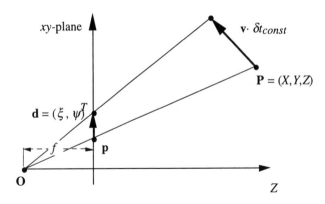

Figure 5.1: Relative or absolute motion of a 3D surface point **P** can only be analyzed on the basis of the motion of the projected point **p**. This requires that the corresponding projected positions during a 3D motion can be determined. The figure uses the camera-centered model of central projection.

translations and/or rotations are possible. Calibrated image acquisition situations are not supposed in this section. Under these general assumptions object normals can (theoretically) be calculated from local displacement vectors or restricted in their value range.

5.1.1 Local Displacement Vectors

Let an *image sequence* E_1, E_2, E_3, ... be generated by images E_i which were captured with a constant time interval δt_{const} in between. For static scenes *relative motions* can be observed in such an image sequence as a result of camera motion or changes in lighting between image E_i and image E_{i+1}. On the other hand, for dynamic scenes *absolute motions* resulting from object movements are projected in the image sequence. A correct projection of absolute motions assumes constant camera position and orientation, and constant lighting. Simultaneous camera motions, changes in lighting, and object movements, create the difficulty to separate relative and absolute motions. We will not consider such complex situations.

Assume rigid scene objects and no changes neither in lighting nor in camera parameters. The 3D motion of a surface point **P** that is visible in two subsequent images E_i and E_{i+1} is mapped onto a 2D motion vector in the image plane. The mapping depends on the chosen projection model. A surface point **P** is projected on image point $\mathbf{p}_{old} = (x,y)$ in image E_i and on $\mathbf{p}_{new}$ in E_{i+1}. The vector

$$\mathbf{d}_{xy}(t_i) = \mathbf{p}_{new} - \mathbf{p}_{old} = \delta t_{const} \cdot \left(\xi_{xy}(t_i), \psi_{xy}(t_i) \right)^T$$

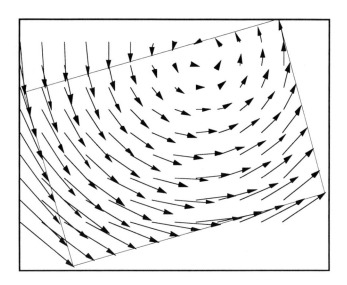

Figure 5.2: Some local displacement vectors for a rectangle that is rotating parallel to the image plane (with assumed parallel projection).

is defined for a discrete time slot $t_i = i \cdot \delta t_{const}$ and image point (x, y). It is assumed that the point motion can be differentiated with respect to time. Then

$$\mathbf{v}_{xy}(t) = \frac{d\mathbf{p}}{dt}(t) = \dot{\mathbf{p}}(t) = \left(\xi_{xy}(t), \psi_{xy}(t)\right)^T \quad \text{and} \quad \mathbf{d}_{xy}(t) = \delta t_{const} \cdot \mathbf{v}_{xy}(t)$$

are the *local velocity vectors* and *local displacement vectors,* for the projection of 3D surface point **P** into the image plane, respectively. The displacement vector represents the translation (normalized to the time unit δt_{const}) of the projected surface point in the image plane, between image E_i to image E_{i+1}, or at time slot t. There, ξ and ψ denote the velocities in the x-direction and in the y-direction, respectively. In the discrete case it holds that

$$\mathbf{p}_{new} = \mathbf{p}_{old} + \delta t_{const} \cdot \left(\xi_{xy}(t_i), \psi_{xy}(t_i)\right)^T = \left(x + \delta t_{const}\xi_{xy}(t_i), y + \delta t_{const}\psi_{xy}(t_i)\right)^T$$

and in the general case

$$\mathbf{p}_{new} = \mathbf{p}_{old} + \delta t_{const} \cdot \dot{\mathbf{p}}(t_i).$$

The local displacement vectors $\mathbf{d}_{xy}(t)$ represent the 3D motion in the image plane according to the given or assumed projection, compare Fig. 5.1. For rigid scene objects, a set of such vectors $\mathbf{d}_{xy}(t)$ defines a *local displacement field* [1] in the im-

---

[1] This is a vector field $\mathbf{w}(x, y)$ in the sense of Section 3.1.1 (i.e. also with discrete spatial coordinates). However, sometimes we still assume that the time variable is continuous.

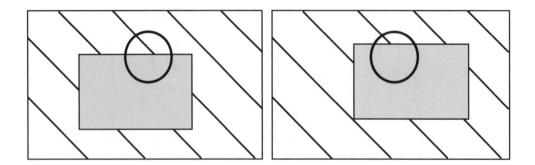

Figure 5.3: Illustration of the *aperture problem* for motion analysis: The movement of the object (here: a simple translation of the rectangle towards the upper right corner) cannot be determined uniquely by a local observation solely within the circular area (which can be identified with the aperture) in the two images of an image sequence. The motion component to the right cannot be recognized.

age plane. In the case of discrete time slots t_i the local displacement field is assigned to an image pair E_i and E_{i+1}. But it could, for example, also represent motions averaged over several pictures of the image sequence. Local displacement fields are often the initial data for investigations of the motion geometry in the case of object or camera motion.

The motions that have to be represented in the image plane are not just displacements (translations) of surface points of scene objects but also rotations. Nevertheless, the motion of a projected surface point between two image acquisitions can be approximately described locally in the image plane by a single displacement vector (compare Fig. 5.2). The *aperture problem* is given by the fact that locally limited apertures (e.g. the whole $M \times N$ image is also just a spatially limited projection of a scene) often do not provide sufficient information about a globally occurring object motion which is depicted in an image sequence (see Fig. 5.3 for an example). This means that our algorithms are always limited with respect to the scale of recoverable object motions.

Local displacement fields like the one in Fig. 5.2 can be calculated from image sequences if individual surface points can be tracked unambiguously in the image sequence. This is the *correspondence problem of dynamic stereo analysis*. Here, in principal the local correspondence comparisons that were discussed for static stereo analysis (compare Chapter 4) can also be applied. However, a reduction of the search interval for the corresponding image points (as it was possible for static stereo analysis by considering epipolar geometry) can only be based on information about 3D motion constraints. An exemplary discussion of reduced search ranges will take place later in Section 5.3.2 under the assumption that the dynamic of the scene objects is limited to a rotation on a turntable. The solution of the correspondence problem for dynamic stereo analysis can, for example, also be supported by using surface marks (as, e.g. in computer vision systems used in sports sciences where marks are attached to the skin of the athletes).

Section 5.1.2 specifies how 3D motion can be synthetically generated, e.g. for producing a set of test images. Sections 5.1.3 and 5.1.4 provide a first illustration of the value of calculated displacement fields assuming that correct local displacement vectors are available for further object shape analysis. Sections 5.2 and 5.3 deal with the calculation of such local displacement fields.

5.1.2   Object Motion and Local Displacement

The calculation of local displacement fields for geometric (synthesized) objects can be used, for example, to test reconstruction algorithms with these generated input data. First a projection model has to be specified for the projection of object movement into the image plane. Then for visible surface points the 3D motion vectors are projected into the image plane. These 3D motion vectors are not constant for a rigid object (e.g. translation and central projection). Let

$$\mathbf{v_P}(t) = \mathbf{v}_{XYZ}(t)$$

be the *velocity* in the surface point $\mathbf{P} = (X, Y, Z)$ at time t. The 3D motion vectors depend on the position (X, Y, Z) of the corresponding surface point and are equal to the product of a velocity vector $\mathbf{v_P}(t)$ and the time unit δt_{const} between two pictures of the image sequence.

$$\mathbf{d_p}(t) = \mathbf{d}_{xy}(t) = \delta t_{const} \cdot \left(\xi_{xy}(t), \psi_{xy}(t)\right)^T = \delta t_{const} \cdot \mathbf{v_p}(t)$$

denotes the local displacement vector of the projected point $\mathbf{p} = (x, y)$ in the image plane at time t.

The image plane is located in the XYZ space according to the camera centered projection model, i.e. at the distance f as the plane $Z = f$ "in front of the projection center". In the XYZ-coordinate system the points $\mathbf{P}$ and $\mathbf{p}$ have the coordinates $\mathbf{P} = (X, Y, Z)$ and $\mathbf{p} = (x, y, f)$. They are also identified with the position vectors $\mathbf{P} = (X, Y, Z)^T$ and $\mathbf{p} = (x, y, f)^T$, from the origin $\mathbf{O} = (0, 0, 0)$ to the corresponding point, respectively. It holds

$$\mathbf{v}_{XYZ}(t) = \frac{d\mathbf{P}}{dt}(t) = \dot{\mathbf{P}}(t) \quad \text{and} \quad \mathbf{d}_{xy}(t) = \frac{d\mathbf{p}}{dt}(t) = \dot{\mathbf{p}}(t) \ .$$

For the scalar product of $\mathbf{P}(t) = (X_t, Y_t, Z_t)^T$ and the unit vector $\mathbf{k} = (0, 0, 1)^T$ of the Z-axis it holds that $\mathbf{P}(t) \cdot \mathbf{k} = Z_t$. Furthermore, central projection and the camera centered coordinate system are assumed (compare Section 2.1.1). According to the formulas for central projection respectively directly from a ray theorem it follows that

$$\mathbf{p}(t) = \frac{f}{Z_t} \cdot \mathbf{P}(t) = \frac{f}{\mathbf{P}(t) \cdot \mathbf{k}} \cdot \mathbf{P}(t) \ .$$

By differentiating this equation with respect to the time it follows that

$$\mathbf{d}_{xy}(t) = \frac{d\mathbf{p}}{dt}(t) = f \cdot \frac{(\mathbf{P}(t) \cdot \mathbf{k}) \cdot \mathbf{v}_{XYZ}(t) - (\mathbf{v}_{XYZ}(t) \cdot \mathbf{k}) \cdot \mathbf{P}(t)}{(\mathbf{P}(t) \cdot \mathbf{k})^2}$$

$$= \frac{f}{Z_t^2} \cdot (\mathbf{P}(t) \times \mathbf{v}_{XYZ}(t)) \times \mathbf{k}$$

(hint: apply the quotient rule of differentiation). Also in this formula the general vector theorem

$$(\mathbf{a} \times \mathbf{b}) \times \mathbf{c} = (\mathbf{a} \cdot \mathbf{c}) \cdot \mathbf{b} - (\mathbf{b} \cdot \mathbf{c}) \cdot \mathbf{a}$$

was used for the *vector product*

$$(a_1, a_2, a_3)^T \times (b_1, b_2, b_3)^T = (a_2 b_3 - a_3 b_2, a_3 b_1 - a_1 b_3, a_1 b_2 - a_2 b_1)$$

to state a more simple formal representation of the result.

This result for the central projection model can be used to generate synthetic objects and a field $\mathbf{d}_{xy}(t)$ of local displacement vectors. For this, selected surface points $\mathbf{P} = (X, Y, Z)$ and their velocity vectors

$$\mathbf{v_P}(t) = \left(\dot{X}, \dot{Y}, \dot{Z} \right)^T$$

(e.g. in the discrete case standardized to the time unit δt_{const} between two pictures) have to be provided as input. On the other hand, with this representation of $\mathbf{d}_{xy}(t)$ a discussion of the behavior of local displacement vectors can be carried out relative to the object geometry in the scene. Neighboring object surface points have generally almost identical displacement vectors. Discontinuities in the field of local displacement vectors occur at occluding boundaries.

5.1.3 Object Motion and Gradients

For the characterization of the velocity $\mathbf{v_P}(t)$ in a surface point $\mathbf{P}$ assume that this point lies on a facet which is incident with a plane $Z = pX + qY + r$. Thus, for $\mathbf{P}$ it also holds especially $\mathbf{P} = (A, B, pA + qB + r)$, and the object surface has the gradient $(p, q)^T$ at point $\mathbf{P}$. The facet model specifies the surface gradient or the normal in surface point $\mathbf{P}$,

$$\left(p(\mathbf{P}), q(\mathbf{P}) \right)^T = (p, q)^T \quad \text{or} \quad \mathbf{n}(\mathbf{P}) = \left(n_X(\mathbf{P}), n_Y(\mathbf{P}), n_Z(\mathbf{P}) \right)^T = (p, q, -1)^T,$$

compare Section 3.1. Furthermore assume a combination of a rotation and a subsequent translation as uniform motion of the facet. For rigid objects this motion of a facet can be derived from global object motion parameters of a rotation and a translation (say, specified with respect to the centroid and principal axes of the object) and from the location of the point **P** or facet in object coordinates.

Let the rotation of the facet around the rotation center $(0, 0, r)$ be characterized by a vector $(\omega_1, \omega_2, \omega_3)^T$ whose direction describes the rotation axis and whose length represents the rotation velocity.[2] The subsequent translation is defined by a vector $(a, b, c)^T$ whose length represents the translation velocity (compare Fig. 5.4).

The velocity of a point $\mathbf{P} = (X, Y, pX + qY + r)$ on this facet is equal to

$$\mathbf{v_P}(t) = \begin{pmatrix} \dot{X} \\ \dot{Y} \\ \dot{Z} \end{pmatrix} = \begin{pmatrix} a \\ b \\ c \end{pmatrix} + \begin{pmatrix} \omega_1 \\ \omega_2 \\ \omega_3 \end{pmatrix} \times \begin{pmatrix} X \\ Y \\ Z - r \end{pmatrix} = \begin{pmatrix} a + p\omega_2 X + q\omega_2 Y - \omega_3 Y \\ b + \omega_3 X - p\omega_1 X - q\omega_1 Y \\ c - \omega_2 X + \omega_1 Y \end{pmatrix}$$

for $Z - r = pX + qY$. Subsection 5.1.2 already recalled of the definition of the vector product $\times$. If instead of $(0, 0, r)$ another point would be assumed as the rotation center then the constant r would go into the parametrization of the translation and would also have to be treated formally in the Z-component of the rotation.

For two vectors **a** and **b** the vector $\mathbf{a} \times \mathbf{b}$ is perpendicular to **a** as well as to **b** and its length $\|\mathbf{a} \times \mathbf{b}\|$ is proportional to $\|\mathbf{a}\|$ and to $\|\mathbf{b}\|$. Assume a cone with the rotation axis $(\omega_1, \omega_2, \omega_3)^T$ whose apex lies at the rotation center $(0, 0, r)$ and for which the point (X, Y, Z) is located on the cone surface. Then the vector $(\omega_1, \omega_2, \omega_3)^T \times (X, Y, Z - r)^T$ is tangential to this cone surface. Its length (i.e. the absolute value of the rotation velocity) is proportional to the absolute value of the velocity vector $(\omega_1, \omega_2, \omega_3)^T$ and also proportional to the distance of the point (X, Y, Z) to the rotation center $(0, 0, r)$. These explanations should provide an interpretation of the vector representation of $\mathbf{v_P}(t)$.

According to the individual motion parameters the velocity in a point $\mathbf{P} = (X, Y, pX + qY + r)$ can be developed in the following way:

$$\begin{pmatrix} \dot{X} \\ \dot{Y} \\ \dot{Z} \end{pmatrix} = a \cdot \begin{pmatrix} 1 \\ 0 \\ 0 \end{pmatrix} + b \cdot \begin{pmatrix} 0 \\ 1 \\ 0 \end{pmatrix} + c \cdot \begin{pmatrix} 0 \\ 0 \\ 1 \end{pmatrix} + \omega_1 \cdot \begin{pmatrix} 0 \\ -pX - qY \\ Y \end{pmatrix} + \omega_2 \cdot \begin{pmatrix} pX + qY \\ 0 \\ -X \end{pmatrix} + \omega_3 \cdot \begin{pmatrix} -Y \\ X \\ 0 \end{pmatrix}.$$

---

[2] The origin **O** or another point could also be assumed as the rotation center. The Z-intercept $(0, 0, r)$ of the facet plane is chosen to achieve a certain formal simplification later on.

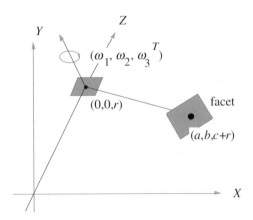

Figure 5.4: The rotation $(\omega_1, \omega_2, \omega_3)^T$ of a facet about the rotation center $(0, 0, r)$ and a subsequent translation $(a, b, c)^T$.

Altogether we have stated a few relations between 3D motions $\mathbf{v_P}(t)$ and local displacements $\mathbf{d_p}(t)$ on one hand (depending on the projection model), and between 3D motions $\mathbf{v_P}(t)$ and surface gradients $(p, q)^T$ on the other hand (independent from the projection model). If local displacement can be analyzed by image analysis then, for example, the question arises how surface gradients can be deduced from local displacement. Depth values can also be calculated from local displacements under the assumption of a calibrated image projection (compare the example later discussed in Section 5.3). But at first we are interested in the relationship between $\mathbf{d_p}(t)$ and $(p, q)^T$ for the non-calibrated case. This is the subject of the next subsection.

5.1.4   Local Displacements and Gradients

Let us consider a specific aim of shape reconstruction, the calculation of surface gradients from local displacements. The used projection model is important since it influences the relationships between 3D motions and local displacements.

For the projection models of the central projection and parallel projection it can be proven that every local displacement field

$$\mathbf{d}_{xy}(t) = \left(\xi_{xy}(t), \psi_{xy}(t) \right)^T$$

can be approximated by second order polynomials

$$\xi_{xy} = A_0 + A_1 \cdot x + A_2 \cdot y + \left(C_1 \cdot x + C_2 \cdot y \right) \cdot x,$$

$$\psi_{xy} = B_0 + B_1 \cdot x + B_2 \cdot y + \left(C_1 \cdot x + C_2 \cdot y \right) \cdot y,$$

at time t and in a local neighborhood of an observed image point **p**. There, A_k, B_k, and C_k are eight *displacement parameters*. The displacement field describes the motion situation in an image sequence at a particular time t. The local image point neighborhood can be identified with the projection of a surface facet. Such eight parameters can be calculated by local approximations of a given displacement field.

For example, the determination of the eight displacement parameters A_k, B_k, and C_k of a given local displacement field can be carried out as the solution of an optimization problem, where the error

$$\sum_{i=1,2,3,...} \left\{ \begin{array}{l} \left[A_0 + A_1 x_i + A_2 y_i + \left(C_1 x_i + C_2 y_i \right) x_i - \xi_{x_i y_i} \right]^2 \\ + \left[B_0 + B_1 x_i + B_2 y_i + \left(C_1 x_i + C_2 y_i \right) y_i - \psi_{x_i y_i} \right]^2 \end{array} \right\}$$

has to be minimized, for all image points $\left(x_i, y_i \right)$, $i = 1, 2, 3, ...$, of a local point neighborhood corresponding to a projected surface facet. Numerical techniques can be used for the determination of a least square error solution (LSE method).

Now these eight displacement parameters allow to specify some constraints for the six motion parameters a, b, c, ω_1, ω_2, ω_3 and for the three facet parameters p, q, r. At first assume central projection with an image-centered coordinate system arrangement, i.e. projection center in point $(0, 0, -f)$ of the XYZ-coordinate system, compare Section 2.1.1.

These nine unknown motion and facet parameters are constrained by eight *determination equations* according to the following theorem. Therefore, a solution always has at least one degree of freedom. The camera-centered model can also be used instead of the image-centered projection model. Of course, then the equations of the theorem have to be modified accordingly (compare Exercise (2) in Section 5.5).

Theorem 5.1 (K. Kanatani 1990): *In the case of central projection (image-centered projection model) the following relations exist between the displacement parameters, and the motion and facet parameters:*

$$A_0 = \frac{af}{f+r}, \qquad\qquad B_0 = \frac{bf}{f+r},$$

$$A_1 = p\omega_2 - \frac{ap+c}{f+r}, \qquad\qquad B_1 = -p\omega_1 + \omega_3 - \frac{bp}{f+r},$$

$$A_2 = q\omega_2 - \omega_3 - \frac{aq}{f+r}, \qquad\qquad B_2 = -q\omega_1 - \frac{bq+c}{f+r},$$

$$C_1 = \frac{1}{f}\left(\omega_2 + \frac{cp}{f+r} \right) \quad and \quad C_2 = \frac{1}{f}\left(-\omega_1 + \frac{cq}{f+r} \right).$$

Proof: For the image-centered coordinate system the central projection equations are given by

$$x = \frac{fX}{f+Z} \quad \text{and} \quad y = \frac{fY}{f+Z} \, .$$

By differentiating with respect to the time (hint: quotient rule) we obtain

$$\dot{x} = \frac{f \cdot \dot{X}}{f+Z} - \frac{f \cdot X \cdot \dot{Z}}{(f+Z)^2} = \frac{f \cdot \dot{X}}{f+Z} - \frac{x \cdot \dot{Z}}{f+Z}$$

and

$$\dot{y} = \frac{f \cdot \dot{Y}}{f+Z} - \frac{f \cdot Y \cdot \dot{Z}}{(f+Z)^2} = \frac{f \cdot \dot{Y}}{f+Z} - \frac{y \cdot \dot{Z}}{f+Z} \, ,$$

for the velocity $(\dot{x}, \dot{y})^T$ of the projected scene point in the image plane. From the representation of the velocity $\mathbf{v_P}$ (compare Section 5.1.3) it follows that

$$\dot{X} = a + p\omega_2 X + (q\omega_2 - \omega_3)Y \, , \quad \dot{Y} = b + (\omega_3 - p\omega_1)X - q\omega_1 Y \, ,$$

and

$$\dot{Z} = c - \omega_2 X + \omega_1 Y \, .$$

By substituting these values it follows that

$$\dot{x} = \frac{f \cdot a}{f+Z} + p\omega_2 x + (q\omega_2 - \omega_3)y - \frac{x}{f}\left(\frac{f \cdot c}{f+Z} - \omega_2 x + \omega_1 y\right)$$

and

$$\dot{y} = \frac{f \cdot b}{f+Z} + (\omega_3 - p\omega_1)x - q\omega_1 y - \frac{y}{f}\left(\frac{f \cdot c}{f+Z} - \omega_2 x + \omega_1 y\right).$$

Furthermore, for the backprojection of projected points $\mathbf{P} = (X, Y, pX + qY + r)$ of a plane $Z = pX + qY + r$ the equations

$$X = \frac{(f+r)x}{f - px - qy} \, , \quad Y = \frac{(f+r)y}{f - px - qy} \, , \quad \text{and} \quad Z = \frac{(px + qy + r)f}{f - px - qy}$$

arise for the image-centered coordinate system. The coefficient as they were stated above follow by substituting the equation for Z. Q.E.D.

Theorem 5.1 allows a derivation of the local displacement vectors $\left(\xi_{xy}, \psi_{xy}\right)$ with respect to the motion parameters $b_1 = a$, $b_2 = b$, $b_3 = c$, $b_4 = \omega_1$, $b_5 = \omega_2$, and $b_6 = \omega_3$,

$$\xi_{xy} = \sum_{i=1}^{6} b_i \cdot \xi_i(p, q, r, x, y) \text{ , and } \psi_{xy} = \sum_{i=1}^{6} b_i \cdot \psi_i(p, q, r, x, y) \text{ ,}$$

where the basis functions ξ_i and ψ_i depend on the facet parameters p, q, r of the facet which moves according to these motion parameters and which is projected into the image coordinates (x, y).

In the case of the camera-centered model of central projection these basis functions ξ_i and ψ_i are of the form

$$\xi_1(p, q, r, x, y) = \frac{f(f - px - qy)}{rf} \text{ ,} \qquad \psi_1(p, q, r, x, y) = 0,$$

$$\xi_2(p, q, r, x, y) = 0, \qquad \psi_2(p, q, r, x, y) = \frac{f(f - px - qy)}{rf} \text{ ,}$$

$$\xi_3(p, q, r, x, y) = \frac{-x(f - px - qy)}{rf} \text{ ,} \qquad \psi_3(p, q, r, x, y) = \frac{-y(f - px - qy)}{rf} \text{ ,}$$

$$\xi_4(p, q, r, x, y) = \frac{-xy}{f} \text{ ,} \qquad \psi_4(p, q, r, x, y) = -px - qy + \frac{y^2}{f} \text{ ,}$$

$$\xi_5(p, q, r, x, y) = px + qy + \frac{x^2}{f} \text{ ,} \qquad \psi_5(p, q, r, x, y) = \frac{xy}{f} \text{ ,}$$

$$\xi_6(p, q, r, x, y) = -y \text{ , and} \qquad \psi_6(p, q, r, x, y) = x \text{ .}$$

If the motion parameters of the individual facet would be known then the values of the basis functions ξ_i and ψ_i can be determined via a local expansion of the displacement field using these parameters. Thus we would obtain six equations for the facet parameters. Therefore, the shape of the surface can be derived completely from $3D$ motion and local displacement. However, the problem is that for the calculation of the motion parameters of a facet based on the motion parameters of a rigid object its surface shape (position of facet in object coordinates) has to be known. But at least this is a general statement that object shape can be derived from 3D and projected motion data.

Now we consider parallel projection. Again we assume the specified local approximation of displacement fields by second order polynomials. In this case the depth information about surface points is completely "erased" by the projection. So it is not surprising that compared to Theorem 5.1 only simplified determination equations can be stated:

Theorem 5.2 (K. Kanatani 1990): *In the case of parallel projection the following relations exist between the displacement parameters and the motion or facet parameters:*

$$A_0 = a , \qquad\qquad B_0 = b ,$$
$$A_1 = p\omega_2 , \qquad\qquad B_1 = -p\omega_1 + \omega_3 ,$$
$$A_2 = q\omega_2 - \omega_3 , \qquad\qquad B_2 = -q\omega_1 ,$$
$$C_1 = 0 , \quad \text{and} \qquad\qquad C_2 = 0 .$$

Parallel projection can be modeled by central projection where the effective focal length f converges towards infinity. Thus, the equations in Theorem 5.2 can be obtained as conclusions from Theorem 5.1. Here we have six non-trivial equations for the seven parameters a, b, ω_1, ω_2, ω_3, p, q. The parameters c (the translation component in Z-direction) and the Z-intercept r (i.e. the distance of point $(0,0,r)$ on the facet plane from the XY plane) remain completely undetermined. This is not surprising since the absolute depth information is lost with the parallel projection.

In the case of parallel projection, motion or parameters can be derived relatively easy from the differences of displacement vectors, or can be constrained in their value. Let us assume the following basic differences at time t:

$$\xi^{(x)}(x,y) = \xi_{x+1,y} - \xi_{xy} , \qquad\qquad \psi^{(x)}(x,y) = \psi_{x+1,y} - \psi_{xy} ,$$
$$\xi^{(y)}(x,y) = \xi_{x,y+1} - \xi_{xy} , \qquad\qquad \psi^{(y)}(x,y) = \psi_{x,y+1} - \psi_{xy} .$$

Then, from Theorem 5.2 we can conclude that in the case of $\omega_1 \neq 0$ and $\omega_2 \neq 0$ it holds that

$$p(x,y) = \frac{\omega_3 - \psi^{(x)}(x,y)}{\omega_1} = \frac{\xi^{(x)}(x,y)}{\omega_2} \qquad \text{and}$$

$$q(x,y) = \frac{\omega_3 + \xi^{(y)}(x,y)}{\omega_2} = \frac{-\psi^{(y)}(x,y)}{\omega_1}$$

for the parallel projection. However, the rotation parameters ω_1 and ω_2 are generally unknown. For the ratio of these rotation parameters it holds that

$$\frac{\omega_1}{\omega_2} = -\frac{1}{2\xi^{(x)}} \cdot \left(\xi^{(y)} + \psi^{(x)} \pm \sqrt{\left(\xi^{(y)} + \psi^{(x)}\right)^2 - 4\xi^{(x)}\psi^{(y)}} \right) .$$

These basic differences can also be used for the derivation of determination equations following Theorem 5.1. However, this leads to a polynomial of third order as determination equation for the "depth value" r of the facet plane.

5.1.5 Camera Rotation about the Projection Center

In distinction to the dynamic scene objects that were assumed up to now, this section supposes that a static scene is given (no object motions, no lighting changes etc.) and that the camera performs a (small) rotational motion. The projection center is assumed to be the rotation center. Practically this ideal identification of these two locations can only be achieved approximately, for instance with a rotation joint of the camera.

We assume the camera-centered model of central projection, i.e. the projection center is at the origin. Accordingly, the XYZ-coordinate system is transformed into a $X'Y'Z'$-coordinate system by a camera rotation about the projection center. This coordinate transformation is defined by a rotation matrix

$$\mathbf{R} = \begin{pmatrix} r_{11} & r_{12} & r_{13} \\ r_{21} & r_{22} & r_{23} \\ r_{31} & r_{32} & r_{33} \end{pmatrix}$$

which is an orthogonal matrix, with $det(\mathbf{R}) = \pm 1$ and $\mathbf{R}^T = \mathbf{R}^{-1}$. Thus, it holds

$$(X', Y', Z')^T = \mathbf{R} \cdot (X, Y, Z)^T .$$

There, r_{ij} is equal to the cosine of the angle subtended by the ith coordinate axis in the original coordinate system XYZ and the jth coordinate axis in the resulting coordinate system $X'Y'Z'$ (in the following order: X as the first, Y as the second, Z as the third coordinate axis).

The coordinate transformation that is given by the rotation $\mathbf{R}$ of the XYZ space converts the original xy-image plane $Z = f$ into a $x'y'$-image plane $Z' = f$. It holds that

$$x' = \frac{f \cdot X'}{Z'} = f \cdot \frac{r_{11}x + r_{12}y + r_{13}f}{r_{31}x' + r_{32}y' + r_{33}f} , \quad \text{and} \quad y' = \frac{f \cdot Y'}{Z'} = f \cdot \frac{r_{21}x + r_{22}y + r_{23}f}{r_{31}x + r_{32}y + r_{33}f}$$

for the resulting coordinate transformation in the image plane. So a (static) scene point $\mathbf{P}$ was projected onto the image point $\mathbf{p} = (x, y)$ before the camera rotation, and onto the image point $\mathbf{p}' = (x', y')$ after the rotation. On the assumption of an ideal static scene it follows that $E(x, y) = E_{\mathbf{R}}(x', y')$. There, E denotes the original image and $E_{\mathbf{R}}$ denotes the image after the camera rotation.

Therefore, corresponding image points do not need to be determined for a single camera rotation where it was assumed that the projection center and the rotation center coincide. The correspondence already arises from the rotation parameters and the effective focal length f. Now assume that the rotation parameters as well as the effective focal length are given. In this case, the local displacement vectors

$$(x', y') - (x, y) = \left(f \cdot \frac{r_{11}x + r_{12}y + r_{13}f}{r_{31}x + r_{32}y + r_{33}f} - x, \; f \cdot \frac{r_{21}x + r_{22}y + r_{23}f}{r_{31}x + r_{32}y + r_{33}f} - y \right)$$

are known for the image sequence $E_1 = E$ and $E_2 = E_R$. Object surface points that were not visible with respect to the previous projection center are also not projected with the new camera orientation. Of course, because of the restricted size of the taken pictures points which were outside of the bounded image domain before may be inside of the bounded image domain after the camera rotation. But no object shape parameters can be calculated from the displacement vectors of such an ideal camera rotation.

A camera rotation can still be of interest for problems of object recognition (what is not the subject of this textbook). In general the invariance relation

$$\iint_{\Re^2} E_R(x, y) \cdot J(x, y) \, dx \, dy = \iint_{\Re^2} E(x, y) \cdot J(x, y) \, dx \, dy$$

holds for the functional determinant (*Jacobian determinant*)

$$J(x, y) = \frac{f^3}{\sqrt{\left(x^2 + y^2 + f^2\right)^3}} \; ,$$

which corresponds to the coordinate transformation of the image plane onto the Gaussian sphere.

5.2   OPTICAL FLOW

Approximate calculations of local displacement fields can be based on analyzing the *optical flow* which is defined by the changes in image irradiances from image E_i to image E_{i+1} of an image sequence. Let us assume that these changes of image irradiances are caused by absolute object motions. On this assumption the optical flow allows approximations of local displacement fields. The "classical" Horn-Schunck method is explained in detail as an example of such a determination technique.

5.2.1   Solution Strategy

The optical flow can be analyzed for arbitrary image sequences, e.g. also for non-rigid scene objects like clouds in meteorological pictures or bacteria cultures in

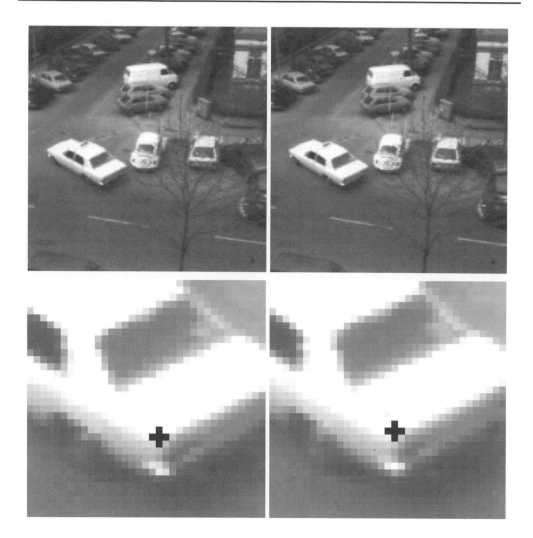

Figure 5.5: Visual comparison of the projection of a particular object surface point in two different images of an image sequence. Top: two original images of the "Hamburg taxicab" image sequence. Bottom: enlarged windows with labels at the same surface point. A comparison of these windows shows minor variations in the local gray value distributions around the labeled surface point which can be due to various causes during the image acquisition process.

biological microscope pictures. The optical flow is also, for example, of interest for calculating motion estimations in the area of *active vision*, or *animate vision* .[3]

---

[3] Compare, for example, Daniilidis, K.: *Attentive Visual Motion Processing - Computations in the Log-Polar Plane.* in: Theoretical Foundations of Computer Vision (eds.: W. Kropatsch, R. Klette, F. Solina), Computing Supplement 11, Springer, Vienna, 1996, pp. 1- 20.

The optical flow cannot be identified with local displacements. For example consider a sphere showing no surface texture that is rotating in front of a camera. No optical flow can be observed even though a motion of object points occurs, i.e. the field of local displacements is defined. Similar difficulties arise in general for motions of surfaces showing no surface texture. On the other hand, for a static sphere and changing lighting conditions an optical flow can be observed for the sphere surface although no motion of surface points takes place. The optical flow can also depend on instability of the camera sensor, on changing illumination, or on different surface appearance for different viewing directions (compare Fig. 5.5). Thus it is clear from the beginning that optical flow only allows to approximate local displacement fields.

Let the image irradiance of image E_i in point $\mathbf{p} = (x, y)$ be given by $E(x, y, t_i)$, for $i = 0, 1, 2, ...$, where $t_i = i \cdot \delta t_{const}$, and δt_{const} is the assumed constant time difference between capturing two pictures of the image sequence. Let us assume that the optical flow is uniquely defined (actually different optical flow models may specify different vector fields), and let

$$\mathbf{u}_i(x, y) = \left(u_i(x, y), v_i(x, y) \right)^T$$

be the optical flow from image E_i to image E_{i+1} which characterizes the change of image irradiances from image E_i to image E_{i+1}. In our optical flow model we assume that the equation

$$E\left(x + u_i(x, y), y + v_i(x, y), t_{i+1} \right) = E(x, y, t_i)$$

or

$$E\left(x + u_i(x, y), y + v_i(x, y), t_i + \delta t_{const} \right) = E(x, y, t_i)$$

has to be satisfied. Such an assumed *image value fidelity* of the optical flow alone cannot support the design of algorithms for the calculation of vectors $(u, v)^T$ since measured image irradiance values $0, 1, ..., G_{max}$ are always affected by noise. Further assumptions or constraints have to be formulated to support a solution strategy which allows to calculate a unique solution.

In general we expect that the calculated optical flow is highly correlated to the local displacement. Ideal correlation is given if the optical flow from picture to picture of a given image sequence, i.e. for different times $i = 0, 1, 2, ...$, is identical to the local displacements

$$\mathbf{d}_{xy}(t_i) = \dot{\mathbf{p}}(t_i) = \left(\xi_{xy}(t_i), \psi_{xy}(t_i) \right)^T$$

of projected image points $\mathbf{p} = (x, y)$, i.e. if the equations

$$\xi_{xy}(t_i) = u_i(x, y) \quad \text{and} \quad \psi_{xy}(t_i) = v_i(x, y)$$

hold at time t_i of the image sequence. Such an assumed identity which is called *motion fidelity* of the optical flow can be used for the definition of an error measure for evaluating the calculated optical flow as well as being an additional assumption for the derivation of a solution strategy for the optical flow.

5.2.2 Horn-Schunck Method

All image points will be treated equally, independent from the (unknown) distance of the projected object surface points to the image plane. This assumed situation corresponds to the projection model of the parallel projection.

Assume that the image function $E(x, y, t_i)$ can locally be represented by a Taylor expansion

$$E(x + \delta x, y + \delta y, t_i + \delta t)$$

$$= E(x, y, t_i) + \delta x \cdot \frac{\partial E}{\partial x}(x, y, t_i) + \delta y \cdot \frac{\partial E}{\partial y}(x, y, t_i) + \delta t \cdot \frac{\partial E}{\partial t}(x, y, t_i) + e$$

for a small step $(\delta x, \delta y, \delta t)$ (compare Section 3.1.3). We consider the Taylor expansion of $E(x, y, t_i)$ for a particular step $(u_i(x, y), v_i(x, y), \delta t_{const})$. From an assumed image value fidelity of the optical flow it follows that

$$0 = u_i(x, y) \cdot \frac{\partial E}{\partial x}(x, y, t_i) + v_i(x, y) \cdot \frac{\partial E}{\partial y}(x, y, t_i) + \delta t_{const} \cdot \frac{\partial E}{\partial t}(x, y, t_i) + e ,$$

or, in a formally more simplified form,

$$0 = u_i(x, y) \cdot \frac{\partial E}{\partial x}(x, y, t_i) + v_i(x, y) \cdot \frac{\partial E}{\partial y}(x, y, t_i) + \frac{\partial E}{\partial t}(x, y, t_i) ,$$

for $e = 0$ and $\delta t_{const} = 1$. This equation is called *Horn-Schunck constraint*. The normalization $\delta t_{const} = 1$ can be assumed w.l.o.g.

This way the Horn-Schunck constraint follows from the image value fidelity of the optical flow, and from the assumption that these optical flow vectors only describe small steps for which the linearity assumption for $E(x, y, t_i)$ is satisfied, i.e. for which $e = 0$ can be assumed (compare Section 3.1.3).

As a second alternative, the Horn-Schunck constraint can also be derived assuming the more appropriate motion fidelity constraint of the optical flow. For the Taylor expansion of the image function it is assumed at first that the error term e is approximately in the order of the aberration

$$E(x + \delta x, y + \delta y, t_i + \delta t) - E(x, y, t_i) .$$

Then we get the simplified equation

$$0 = \delta x \cdot \frac{\partial E}{\partial x}(x, y, t_i) + \delta y \cdot \frac{\partial E}{\partial y}(x, y, t_i) + \delta t \cdot \frac{\partial E}{\partial t}(x, y, t_i) \ .$$

Dividing by δt,

$$0 = \frac{\delta x}{\delta t} \cdot \frac{\partial E}{\partial x}(x, y, t_i) + \frac{\delta y}{\delta t} \cdot \frac{\partial E}{\partial y}(x, y, t_i) + \frac{\partial E}{\partial t}(x, y, t_i) \ ,$$

and $\delta t \to 0$ leads to the differential equation

$$0 = \dot{x}(i) \cdot \frac{\partial E}{\partial x}(x, y, t_i) + \dot{y}(i) \cdot \frac{\partial E}{\partial y}(x, y, t_i) + \frac{\partial E}{\partial t}(x, y, t_i) \ .$$

This way the Horn-Schunck constraint follows from this equation and an assumed motion fidelity of the optical flow.

The time scale factor $\delta t_{const} = 1$ is used in the following for formal simplification. In the following the values

$$t_i = i, \quad \text{for} \quad i = 0, 1, 2, \ldots, \quad \text{or} \quad t = 0, 1, 2, \ldots$$

specify the discrete times at which the individual pictures of the image sequence are taken.

For a certain moment in the image sequence the Horn-Schunck constraint has the form

$$u \cdot E_x + v \cdot E_y = -E_t \quad \text{or} \quad \left(E_x, E_y \right) \cdot (u, v)^T = -E_t$$

where u and v depend on (x, y) and where the derivatives E_x, E_y, and E_t of the image irradiance function depend on (x, y, t). The derivatives of the image irradiance functions are given by approximate values (i.e. values of local image operators calculating first order derivatives). Therefore, for a particular image point (x, y) the values of u and v are restricted by this linear equation (compare Fig. 5.6) if $E_x \neq 0$ or $E_y \neq 0$ holds at this image point. So far on this straight line in the uv-space (*velocity space*) any point could be chosen as a solution (u, v), e.g. the intersection point with that line $E_y \cdot u - E_x \cdot v = 0$ which is defined by the direction vector

$$\left(E_x, E_y \right)^T \ .$$

But a better way is to select the desired solution point on this straight line based on another (sensible) local or global assumption for the optical flow.

The ambiguity of a solution (u, v) on the line $u \cdot E_x + v \cdot E_y = -E_t$ corresponds to the aperture problem that was mentioned in Section 5.1.1 and is illustra-

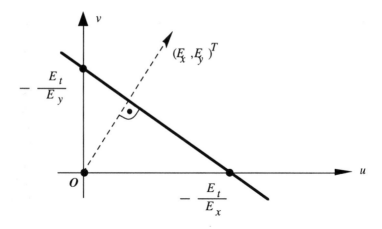

Figure 5.6: The Horn-Schunck constraint restricts the possible value range of the optical flow onto a straight line in the uv-space. The intersections of this line with the u-axis or with the v-axis are equal to $\left(-E_t/E_x, 0\right)$ or $\left(0, -E_t/E_y\right)$, respectively. The vector $\left(E_x, E_y\right)^T$ is perpendicular to the straight line.

ted in Fig. 5.3 (degrees of freedom for motion analysis if only local information is analyzed and/or available).

Starting with the perception that neighboring surface points of a dynamic, rigid object have approximately the same local displacement vectors, the *smoothness of the optical flow field* can be postulated as a global assumption. This smoothness is given if the first derivatives of the optical flow vector fields are "close to zero", i.e. if

$$u_x(x, y)^2 + u_y(x, y)^2 + v_x(x, y)^2 + v_y(x, y)^2$$

takes on a minimum value for the image points $\mathbf{p} = (x, y)$, for a given image sequence at a particular moment t. Let Ω be the set of all image points for which the optical flow has to be calculated. So this global optimization means that a functional [4]

$$\mathbf{F}s(u, v) = \iint_\Omega \left(u_x^2(x, y) + u_y^2(x, y) + v_x^2(x, y) + v_y^2(x, y)\right) dx dy$$

has to be minimized which indicates the *smoothness error* for a function pair $\left(u(x, y), v(x, y)\right)$. Since the Horn-Schunck constraint

$$u(x, y) \cdot E_x(x, y, t) + v(x, y) \cdot E_y(x, y, t) + E_t(x, y, t) = 0$$

---

[4] A *functional*, here denoted by $\mathbf{F}s$, $\mathbf{F}h$, ..., projects functions onto real numbers.

has to be satisfied at the same time for all image points $\mathbf{p} = (x, y)$ of the given image sequence for a moment t, a solution for (u, v) for this time t also has to minimize the functional

$$\mathbf{F}h(u, v) = \iint_{\Omega} \left(u(x, y) \cdot E_x(x, y, t) + v(x, y) \cdot E_y(x, y, t) + E_t(x, y, t)\right)^2 dxdy .$$

This functional indicates the error concerning the validity of the Horn-Schunck constraint for a function pair (u, v). The influence of the two functionals $\mathbf{F}s$ and $\mathbf{F}h$ can be weighted differently by a weighting parameter $\lambda \geq 0$. Altogether, a solution can be based on minimizing a combined error functional

$$\mathbf{F}c_{HornSchunck}(u, v) \;=\; \mathbf{F}s(u, v) + \lambda \cdot \mathbf{F}h(u, v) .$$

Note that the existing dependency of this functional value from the *weighting parameter* λ is not expressed explicitly (to simplify the formal denotation). The parameter λ can be large (say $\lambda \geq 10$) if the Horn-Schunck constraint is emphasized, and small (say, less than 1) if smoothness is very important.

Various strategies can be used to solve the optimization problem

$$\mathbf{F}c_{HornSchunck}(u, v) \rightarrow \text{minimum} .$$

The variation calculus (use of Euler equations) provides a pair

$$\nabla^2 u = \lambda \cdot \left(E_x \cdot u + E_y \cdot v + E_t\right) \cdot E_x ,$$

$$\nabla^2 v = \lambda \cdot \left(E_x \cdot u + E_y \cdot v + E_t\right) \cdot E_y$$

of partial elliptic second order differential equations for the solution. There, ∇^2 denotes the Laplace operator (compare Section 1.3.1). A system of partial differential equations has generally an infinite number of solutions. By specifying boundary conditions a unique solution can be determined. Numerical iteration techniques can be used for this solution strategy. A second solution strategy of the optimization problem is given with the use of a *discrete iteration scheme*, starting with some selected initial values. Such a discrete iteration scheme is explained in the sequel.

The discrete iteration is only performed in discrete image points with integer coordinates (i, j), with $1 \leq i \leq M$ and $1 \leq j \leq N$, and for integer times $t = 0, 1, 2, \dots$.

In the discrete case the smoothness error of the (discrete) optical flow field (u, v) in point (i, j) can be estimated by

$$F_s(i, j) = \tfrac{1}{4}\left(\left(u_{i+1, j} - u_{ij}\right)^2 + \left(u_{i, j+1} - u_{ij}\right)^2 + \left(v_{i+1, j} - v_{ij}\right)^2 + \left(v_{i, j+1} - v_{ij}\right)^2\right)$$

for a particular time t. [5] The error of the Horn-Schunck constraint can be estimated by

$$F_H(i, j) = \left(E_x(i, j, t) \cdot u_{ij} + E_y(i, j, t) \cdot v_{ij} + E_t(i, j, t) \right)^2.$$

Altogether the minimization problem

$$F_C = \sum_{(i,j) \in \Omega} \left(F_S(i, j) + \lambda \cdot F_H(i, j) \right) \to \text{minimum}$$

has to be solved for the combined error, for all points (i, j) of the considered image region Ω. The general solution strategy for such an minimization problem is as follows:

At first the combined error F_C is differentiated once with respect to the variables u_{ij} or v_{ij} in the given functions F_S and F_H. Then these derivatives are set equal to zero (note: this is a necessary condition for the minimization only, however there exists no maximum value). Finally, from the resulting equations the desired discrete functions u and v are determined for which F_C takes a minimum (note: there may be different arguments defining the same global minimum).

For the derivative of the combined error F_C with respect to variable u_{ij} we obtain

$$\frac{\partial F_S}{\partial u_{ij}}(i, j) = -\tfrac{1}{2} \left[\left(u_{i+1, j} - u_{ij} \right) + \left(u_{i, j+1} - u_{ij} \right) \right] + \tfrac{1}{2} \left[\left(u_{ij} - u_{i-1, j} \right) + \left(u_{ij} - u_{i, j-1} \right) \right]$$

$$= 2u_{ij} - 2 \left(\tfrac{1}{4} \left(u_{i+1, j} + u_{i, j+1} + u_{i-1, j} + u_{i, j-1} \right) \right)$$

$$= 2u_{ij} - 2\bar{u}_{ij}$$

for the error function F_S where it has to be considered that u_{ij} occurs more than once in F_S. Here, $\bar{u}_{ij}$ denotes the local arithmetic average (i.e. the mean) in the 4-neighborhood of the point (i, j). Altogether it holds that

$$\frac{\partial F_C}{\partial u_{ij}}(i, j) = 2 \left(u_{ij} - \bar{u}_{ij} \right) + 2\lambda \left(E_x(i, j, t)u_{ij} + E_y(i, j, t)v_{ij} + E_t(i, j, t) \right) E_x(i, j, t)$$

as well as analogously

$$\frac{\partial F_C}{\partial v_{ij}}(i, j) = 2 \left(v_{ij} - \bar{v}_{ij} \right) + 2\lambda \left(E_x(i, j, t)u_{ij} + E_y(i, j, t)v_{ij} + E_t(i, j, t) \right) E_y(i, j, t)$$

---

[5] Here, the first derivatives are approximated by simple differences of function values in neighboring image points.

for the derivatives of F_C with respect to variable v_{ij}. According to the general solution strategy of the minimization problem, these two derivatives of F_C have to be set equal to zero to determine the arguments at the minimum. This leads to the set of equations

$$\left(1 + \lambda \cdot E_x^2(i,j,t)\right) \cdot u_{ij} + \lambda \cdot E_x(i,j,t)E_y(i,j,t) \cdot v_{ij} = \bar{u}_{ij} - \lambda \cdot E_x(i,j,t)E_t(i,j,t)$$

$$\lambda \cdot E_x(i,j,t)E_y(i,j,t) \cdot u_{ij} + \left(1 + \lambda \cdot E_y^2(i,j,t)\right) \cdot v_{ij} = \bar{v}_{ij} - \lambda \cdot E_y(i,j,t)E_t(i,j,t)$$

or in short form,

$$\left(1 + \lambda \cdot E_x^2\right) \cdot u_{ij} + \lambda \cdot E_x E_y \cdot v_{ij} = \bar{u}_{ij} - \lambda \cdot E_x E_t$$

$$\lambda \cdot E_x E_y \cdot u_{ij} + \left(1 + \lambda \cdot E_y^2\right) \cdot v_{ij} = \bar{v}_{ij} - \lambda \cdot E_y E_t \ .$$

Thus, a pair of linear equations is given for every point (i,j). The coefficient matrix of this set of equations [6] has the determinant

$$det_{ij} = \left(1 + \lambda \cdot E_x^2\right) \cdot \left(1 + \lambda \cdot E_y^2\right) - \lambda^2 \cdot E_x^2 E_y^2 = 1 + \lambda\left(E_x^2 + E_y^2\right)$$

for (i,j). Accordingly the solution of the set of linear equations is equal to

$$u_{ij} = \frac{1}{1 + \lambda\left(E_x^2 + E_y^2\right)} \cdot \left[\left(1 + \lambda E_y^2\right) \cdot \bar{u}_{ij} - \lambda E_x\left(E_t + E_y \cdot \bar{v}_{ij}\right)\right] ,$$

$$v_{ij} = \frac{1}{1 + \lambda\left(E_x^2 + E_y^2\right)} \cdot \left[\left(1 + \lambda E_x^2\right) \cdot \bar{v}_{ij} - \lambda E_y\left(E_t + E_x \cdot \bar{u}_{ij}\right)\right] .$$

The combined error F_C takes on a minimum value for these values of discrete functions u and v (with respect to the used approximations). However in this given solution the values of u_{ij} and v_{ij} at the positions (i,j) also depend on the values of u and v in the 4-neighborhood of (i,j), i.e. the solutions cannot be determined simultaneously for the various image points just based on the given formulas. However these formulas support an iterative solution strategy. Altogether this specifies the *Horn-Schunck algorithm* for calculating optical flow fields.

(**Task 5.1**): Assume a given sequence of digital images, for example two consecutive $M \times N$ images $E(i,j,t)$ and $E(i,j,t+1)$ in this sequence, with $1 \le i \le M$ and $1 \le j \le N$. Calculate the optical flow field using the Horn-Schunck method. The

---

[6] A system of linear equations $ax + by = c$, $dx + ey = f$ with determinant $det = ae - bd$ of the coefficient matrix has the solutions

$$x = \frac{ec - bf}{det} \quad \text{and} \quad y = \frac{af - dc}{det} \ .$$

weighting factor λ and the iteration number are free parameters of the technique. Use simple local approximation formulas for the calculation of derivatives E_x, E_y, and E_t.

(**Solution 5.1**) At the beginning some initial values are specified, e.g.

$$u^0_{i,j} = 0 \quad \text{and} \quad v^0_{i,j} = 0,$$

or specific values on the straight line shown in Fig. 5.6. The calculation of the new values

$$u^{n+1}_{i,j} \quad \text{and} \quad v^{n+1}_{i,j}$$

in the iteration step $n+1$ is based on those arithmetic averages in the 4-neighborhood specified by previously calculated values in iteration step n. Thus altogether the iterative solution steps are given by the iteration formulas

$$u^{n+1}_{ij} = \bar{u}^n_{ij} - \frac{E_x(i,j,t)\bar{u}^n_{ij} + E_y(i,j,t)\bar{v}^n_{ij} + E_t(i,j,t)}{1 + \lambda\left(E^2_x(i,j,t) + E^2_y(i,j,t)\right)} \lambda E_x(i,j,t)$$

$$v^{n+1}_{ij} = \bar{v}^n_{ij} - \frac{E_x(i,j,t)\bar{u}^n_{ij} + E_y(i,j,t)\bar{v}^n_{ij} + E_t(i,j,t)}{1 + \lambda\left(E^2_x(i,j,t) + E^2_y(i,j,t)\right)} \lambda E_y(i,j,t)$$

where $n = 0, 1, 2, \ldots$ denotes the iteration step. In every iteration step the values of the optical flow are calculated at all image points (i, j).

For these formulas we have to specify procedures for the approximation of the derivatives $E_x(i,j,t)$, $E_y(i,j,t)$, and $E_t(i,j,t)$ of the given image irradiance functions. The obvious way to follow is to use *local difference operations*. For example,

$$E_x(i,j,t) = \tfrac{1}{4}\big(E(i+1,j,t) + E(i+1,j,t+1) + E(i+1,j+1,t) + E(i+1,j+1,t+1)\big)$$
$$-\tfrac{1}{4}\big(E(i,j,t) + E(i,j,t+1) + E(i,j+1,t) + E(i,j+1,t+1)\big),$$

$$E_y(i,j,t) = \tfrac{1}{4}\big(E(i,j+1,t) + E(i,j+1,t+1) + E(i+1,j+1,t) + E(i+1,j+1,t+1)\big)$$
$$-\tfrac{1}{4}\big(E(i,j,t) + E(i,j,t+1) + E(i+1,j,t) + E(i+1,j,t+1)\big),$$

$$E_t(i,j,t) = \tfrac{1}{4}\big(E(i,j,t+1) + E(i,j+1,t+1) + E(i+1,j,t+1) + E(i+1,j+1,t+1)\big)$$
$$-\tfrac{1}{4}\big(E(i,j,t) + E(i,j+1,t) + E(i+1,j,t) + E(i+1,j+1,t)\big)$$

are possible approximation functions. Even more simple approximation formulas are assumed in the forthcoming Example 5.1.

(Algorithm 5.1): A sketch of the described iterative technique is presented in Fig. 5.7.

(Comment 5.1): Altogether a technique is described to calculate the optical flow from an image sequence. Different options can be used to specify initial values, the weighting factor λ, and approximations for the functions E_x, E_y, and E_t. An alternative way of initialization is suggested in Section 5.5 in Exercise (6).

     The iteration depth can be controlled by an error measure (e.g. total deviation between the solutions of the iteration steps n and $n+1$). But in general it is suggested to use an a-priori defined termination level, e.g. $8 \le n \le 12$. The theoretical analysis of this algorithm (e.g. convergence) needs further work.

---

begin
      for $j:= 1$ **to** N **do** **for** $i := 1$ **to** M **do** **begin**
          calculate the values $E_x(i, j, t)$, $E_y(i, j, t)$, and $E_t(i, j, t)$ using
              a selected approximation formula;
                   { special cases for image points at the image border
                           have to be taken into account }
          initialize the values $u(i, j)$ and $v(i, j)$ with zero
      end {for};
      choose a suitable weighting value λ;   { e.g $\lambda = 10$ }
      choose a suitable number $n_0 \ge 1$ of iterations;   { $n_0 = 8$ }
      $n := 1$;   { iteration counter }
      while $n \le n_0$ **do begin**
          for $j:= 1$ **to** N **do** **for** $i := 1$ **to** M **do** **begin**

$$\bar{u} := \tfrac{1}{4}\big(u(i-1, j) + u(i+1, j) + u(i, j-1) + u(i, j+1)\big);$$

$$\bar{v} := \tfrac{1}{4}\big(v(i-1, j) + v(i+1, j) + v(i, j-1) + v(i, j+1)\big);$$

               { treat image points at the image border separately }

$$\alpha := \frac{E_x(i, j, t)\bar{u} + E_y(i, j, t)\bar{v} + E_t(i, j, t)}{1 + \lambda\big(E_x^2(i, j, t) + E_y^2(i, j, t)\big)} \cdot \lambda \ ;$$

$$u(i, j) := \bar{u} - \alpha \cdot E_x(i, j, t) \ ; \quad v(i, j) := \bar{v} - \alpha \cdot E_y(i, j, t)$$

        end {for};
          $n := n+1$
      end {while}
end;

Figure 5.7: Horn-Schunck method to calculate the optical flow.

5.2.3 Discussion

Usually, the motion fidelity that was postulated in Section 5.2.1 is not valid for the (calculated) optical flow. The introductory examples in Section 5.2.1 illustrate the differences between the optical flow and the local displacement field. But at least another statement can be generally verified for the calculated vector fields using Algorithm 5.1 in practice: The calculated optical flow corresponds (approximately) to the projection of the local displacement vector onto the image value gradient

$$\left(E_x(i,j,t), E_y(i,j,t)\right)^T$$

(compare Fig. 5.8). Let us assume that an image edge passes through the image point (i, j). If the local displacement vector (i.e. the projection of the 3D motion) is orthogonal to the image edge in this point then the optical flow vector and the local displacement vector coincide (i.e. the motion fidelity is satisfied). But if, for instance, the local displacement vector runs in the same direction as the image edge, i.e. this vector is parallel to the image edge, then the null vector is calculated as an optical flow vector. This inaccuracy of the calculated optical flow (compared to the aspired local displacement vectors) is a concrete expression of the aperture problem (compare Fig. 5.3). There is no general way to calculate the (unknown) local displacement vector from the calculated optical flow vector and the also calculable image value gradient. So the optical flow will always be only an approximation of the local displacement field. If the image value gradient is the null vector then the optical flow can also (approximately) be just the null vector.

Example 5.1: The behavior of the optical flow can be illustrated for an ideal im-

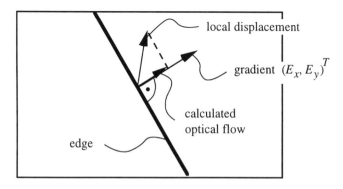

Figure 5.8: Projection of the local 2D displacement vector of a 3D object motion onto the image value gradient which is orthogonal to an image edge.

age edge. The image irradiance function (shown in Fig. 5.9) with gray values between 0 and 7 is an ideal linear edge in x-direction. Three different motion situations of the edge are considered. For simplification the forward differences

$$E_x(i, j, t) = E(i, j, t) - E(i+1, j, t),$$

$$E_y(i, j, t) = E(i, j, t) - E(i, j+1, t),$$

$$E_t(i, j, t) = E(i, j, t) - E(i, j, t+1)$$

are used in the Horn-Schunck algorithm for the approximation of the derivatives of the image irradiance function. According to the orientation of the edge at different moments t it always holds that $E_x(i, j, t) = 0$. Furthermore, it follows that $E_y(i, j, t) = 0$, if $j \le 3$ or $j \ge 11$, and $E_y(i, j, t) = -1$ for $4 \le j \le 10$. The value $\lambda = 10$ is chosen as the weighting factor. We use the initial values $u_{ij}^0 = 0$ and $v_{ij}^0 = 0$.

In case **(A)** assume that the true local displacement is equal to $\mathbf{d} = (0, 1)^T$ in all image points. Then $E_t(i, j, t) = 0$ for $j \le 4$ or $j \ge 12$, and $E_t(i, j, t) = 1$ for $5 \le j \le 11$. Three iteration steps are considered at a position (i, j) "on the edge". In x-direction it is always $u_{ij}^1 = 0$, $u_{ij}^2 = 0$, ... In y-direction it follows that

$$v_{ij}^1 = 0 - \frac{0 \cdot 0 + (-1) \cdot 0 + 1}{1 + 10 \cdot (0+1)} \cdot 10 \cdot (-1) = \frac{10}{11}$$

in the first iteration step, for $5 \le j \le 10$. So, for $6 \le j \le 9$ it is always $\bar{u}_{ij}^1 = 0$ and

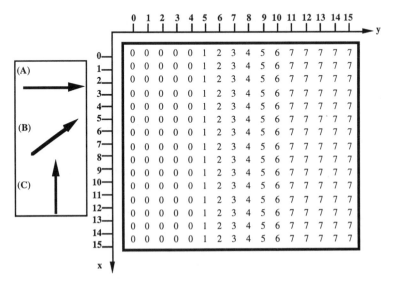

Figure 5.9: Assume constant local displacement vectors which run **(A)** in y-direction, **(B)** diagonally, and **(C)** in negative x-direction, for an ideal linear edge. Motion **(A)** can be represented adequately by the calculated optical flow.

$\bar{v}_{ij}^1 = \frac{10}{11}$. In the second iteration step it follows that

$$v_{ij}^2 = \frac{10}{11} - \frac{0\cdot0+(-1)\cdot\frac{10}{11}+1}{1+10\cdot(0+1)} \cdot 10 \cdot (-1) = \frac{120}{121} \,,$$

for $6 \leq j \leq 9$, and in the third iteration step it follows that

$$v_{ij}^3 = \frac{120}{121} - \frac{0\cdot0+(-1)\cdot\frac{120}{121}+1}{1+10\cdot(0+1)} \cdot 10 \cdot (-1) = \frac{1330}{1331} \,,$$

for $7 \leq j \leq 8$. Thus it holds here that $\left(u_{ij}^3, v_{ij}^3\right)^T \approx (0,1)^T = \mathbf{d}$.

In case **(B)** let be $\mathbf{d} = (-1,1)^T$ in all image points. Here the iteration values behave analogously to the just discussed Case **(A)**, for a point (i,j) "on the edge".

In case **(C)** assume $\mathbf{d} = (-1,0)^T$. In this case $(0,0)$ is calculated everywhere as the optical flow value at any level of iteration. { end of Example 5.1 }

Figure 5.10 illustrates the discussed behavior of the optical flow once again for a real image sequence (the Hamburg taxicab from Fig. 5.5). The car drives slowly up to the left. Accordingly, the flow vectors at edge positions are approximately

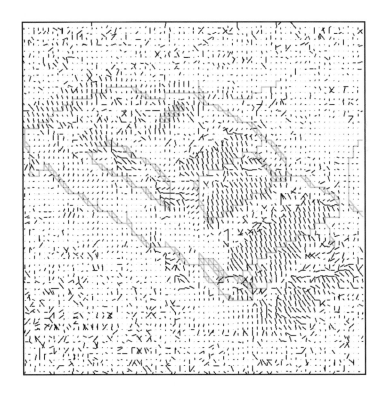

Figure 5.10: Representation of the calculated optical flow for an image window (Horn-Schunck algorithm) of the images given in Fig. 5.5, for $\lambda = 10$ and six iterations. Edges are overlaid as light gray pixels for a better visual identification of the image context.

correct if the edges run approximately orthogonal to the (non-calculable) local displacement vectors. However, optical flow vectors in this motion direction are also calculated for the shade edge behind the car even though actually there is no local displacement vector given there.

Figure 5.11: One image for each of the image sequences MYSINE, RUBIC, SQUARE, and TREES, for which convergence values are given in Table 5.1.

Table 5.1 illustrates the convergence behavior of the Horn-Schunck algorithm for various image sequences, see Fig. 5.11 (results are calculated for two consecutive images). The means of the deviations between an iteration level in comparison to the previous iteration level, of the calculated values of the optical flow fields are given as errors. The calculated vectors themselves are quite short (see row at the bottom of Tab. 5.1). In general an average deviation of less than 0.01 pixel units can already be observed after a few iteration steps. However, usually no convergence can be proved mathematically for this method (specifying initial values, weighting factor, and finite-difference based approximations of derivatives).

MYSINE		RUBIC		SQUARE		TAXI		TREES	
100×100		233×233		100×100		190×190		233×233	
254		255		255		251		174	
A	B	A	B	A	B	A	B	A	B
1.3812	1.1968	0.2361	0.2560	0.2369	0.2063	0.4149	0.3337	1.2670	0.9180
0.4713	0.4341	0.1103	0.0907	0.0235	0.0132	0.1649	0.1137	0.5067	0.3301
0.2347	0.2504	0.0569	0.0447	0.0165	0.0082	0.0697	0.0502	0.2211	0.1485
0.1614	0.1804	0.0400	0.0304	0.0138	0.0067	0.0418	0.0314	0.1327	0.0930
0.1155	0.1314	0.0280	0.0212	0.0120	0.0057	0.0264	0.0207	0.0851	0.0617
0.0850	0.0968	0.0219	0.0163	0.0108	0.0052	0.0183	0.0149	0.0593	0.0443
10.280	1.9886	13.981	3.8059	11.363	1.5812	22.409	8.7516	75.509	36.137

Table 5.1: Convergence behavior of the Horn-Schunck algorithm for $\lambda = 10$ and the simple forward differences from Example 5.1 (columns A) or the more complex approximations of the derivatives from Section 5.2.2 (columns B). The image size and the maximum irradiance value in the two input images are stated below the image names (see Fig. 5.11 for these images). The columns A and B give the average deviations of the calculated values of the optical flow between current and previous iteration step for the first six iterations. The bottom row shows the maximum values in one of both scalar components of the optical flow.

Various error functionals can be used for analyzing the calculated optical flow compared to the local displacement field. Synthetic input image sequences (see Section 5.1.2) allow that the correct values of the local displacement field (i.e. the *true* displacement field) are known. Let us assume that $\mathbf{d} = (\xi, \psi)$ is a true local displacement field in the image plane in real-valued accuracy.

Now assume a technique for calculating the optical flow which produces an optical flow $\mathbf{u} = (u, v)$ as the result. The normalized *sum of all relative errors* (SRE) between $\mathbf{d}$ and $\mathbf{u}$ is defined as the value

$$SRE(\mathbf{u}, \mathbf{d}) = \frac{1}{card(\Omega)} \cdot \sum_{(x,y) \in \Omega} \frac{\|\mathbf{u}(x, y) - \mathbf{d}(x, y)\|}{\|\mathbf{d}(x, y)\|},$$

where Ω is the definition domain of all discrete image points for which the optical flow is calculated. Examples of values of this error measure are shown in Fig. 5.12. Another possibility for defining an error measure is given with the normalized *sum of angular errors* (SAE),

$$SAE(\mathbf{u}, \mathbf{d}) = \frac{1}{card(\Omega)} \cdot \sum_{(x,y) \in \Omega} arccos \left(\frac{(\mathbf{d}(x, y), \delta t_{const}) \cdot (\mathbf{u}(x, y), \delta t_{const})}{\|(\mathbf{d}(x, y), \delta t_{const})\| \cdot \|(\mathbf{u}(x, y), \delta t_{const})\|} \right),$$

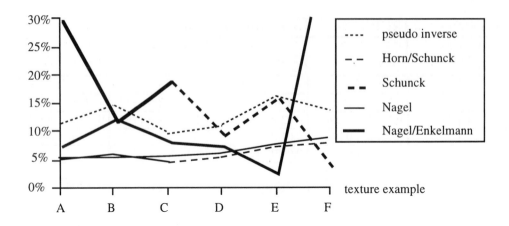

Figure 5.12: SRE-error measure values for differently textured (called textures A, ..., E, F) synthetically generated surfaces which were translated coplanar to an assumed image plane. Besides the Horn-Schunck method other point-based differential methods (compare references in Section 5.4) were used.

where δt_{const} denotes the time difference between capturing of two pictures of the image sequence. The *SRE* functional was used for the experiments in Fig. 5.12. It reflects errors for motion vectors with small absolute value more sensitively than the *SAE* measure. *Point-based differential techniques* (the Horn-Schunck algorithm is one example of this class of algorithms) can only calculate correctly such "short" motion vectors (i.e. a maximum length of just a few pixels).

Figure 5.12 illustrates a general fact that the Horn-Schunck method is relatively tolerant with respect to different textures. Roughly speaking, a sufficiently structured texture secures "local stability" for the technique, where this texture should not periodically repeat itself in a distance below the length of the local displacement vectors. Figure 5.12 reports about experiments where in the calculated images of a sequence A, ..., E, or F the same homogeneously textured plane was shown with only small translations of this plane (in synthetic 3D space) between the different images of a sequence. The figure shows that the errors were above 5% in general. This figure and the specified error measures are given here for a brief illustration of possible approaches to more refined evaluations of different algorithms for local displacement calculation. Typically these algorithms may detect only relatively small motions. A special smoothness constraint can solve the uniqueness problem, but leads to essential errors at pixel positions with abrupt changes in the local displacement vector field. Motion parallel to object edges may be recognized by matching or optimization methods (regions or contours), but not with point-based differential methods. The local displacement vector field is discontinuous at borders between different motions, and the Taylor expansion approach fails with just a very few exceptions at these locations. However, often calculated vector fields allow rough estimates of 3D environments (see Section 5.3), and this may be appropriate, e.g., to support navigation solutions or obstacle detections. Also note that point-based differential techniques (as the discussed Horn-Schunck algorithm) can be implemented on parallel computing architectures allowing real-time solutions.

5.3   OBJECT ROTATION AND RECONSTRUCTION

Section 5.1 considered general theoretical fundamentals of relations between 3D motions and local displacement vectors without assuming calibration. Section 5.2 introduced a technique for approximate calculations of local displacement vectors. These calculated vector fields may be used for analyzing motion and object parameters (see Section 5.1.4).

In this section we assume geometric calibrations as discussed in Chapter 2. A special image acquisition set-up is studied, namely one static camera and objects on a turntable whose shapes have to be reconstructed. Two different approaches are discussed. At first we continue to focus on calculations of displacement vectors, and we describe how these vectors can be used to analyze 3D positions. The theoretical fundamentals of this approach resemble those of static stereo analysis. Instead of two images taken with two cameras now we have two images taken with the same camera but at different times. Again calibration, correspondence analysis, and triangulation define the whole sequence of reconstruction operations. Second we introduce a very different technique based on occluding boundaries. Here, just silhouettes are captured of objects on the turntable. These silhouettes provide the data to reconstruct surfaces of relatively high shape complexity. This approach has the advantage that local displacement vectors are not required.

5.3.1   World Coordinates from Point Correspondence

For the $X_w Y_w Z_w$ world coordinate system it is assumed that the Z_w-axis (compare Fig. 2.7 and Fig. 5.15) coincides with the rotation axis of a turntable and that the planar surface of the turntable (assumed to be an ideal plane) is parallel to the $X_w Y_w$-plane. This can be achieved by positioning a calibration object on the turntable (compare Fig. 2.6), and by calculating ideal turntable plane parameters during calibration. The objects for which surface data have to be reconstructed will be positioned on the turntable and at equidistant times $t = 0, 1, 2, \ldots$ (w.l.o.g.

$\delta t_{const} = 1$ is assumed again) recorded by a static camera. This results in captured image sequences E_0, E_1, E_2, ... Between the times $t = 0, 1, 2, ...$ the turntable is assumed to turn by a constant angle δ every time. The irradiance images E_t are given as measured values at image buffer coordinates (x_b, y_b).

We assume that a rotation matrix $\mathbf{R}$, a translation vector $\mathbf{T}$, the effective focal length f, the distortion coefficients κ_1 and κ_2, the principal point (c_x, c_y), and the scaling factor s_x are given as the result of a geometric calibration routine (compare Tsai's method in Section 2.1.5).

Consider an arbitrary surface point $\mathbf{P} = (X_w, Y_w, Z_w)$ of an object which is placed on the turntable. Assume that this surface point is at the point $\mathbf{P}^{(t)}$ at time t, and at the position

$$\mathbf{P}^{(t+1)} = \mathbf{R}_\delta \cdot \mathbf{P}^{(t)}$$

at the time $t + 1$ in world coordinates where $\mathbf{R}_\delta$ is the rotation matrix of the world coordinate system (i.e. rotation of the turntable) which corresponds to the angle δ. According to the affine transformation (compare Section 2.1.4) of the world coordinates into camera coordinates the positions $\mathbf{P}^{(t)}$ and $\mathbf{P}^{(t+1)}$ in camera coordinates are equal to

$$\mathbf{R} \cdot \mathbf{P}^{(t)} \; + \; \mathbf{T} \; = \; \mathbf{C}^{(t)} \quad \text{and} \quad \mathbf{R} \cdot \mathbf{R}_\delta \cdot \mathbf{P}^{(t)} \; + \; \mathbf{T} \; = \; \mathbf{C}^{(t+1)},$$

respectively. Because of $\mathbf{R}^{-1} = \mathbf{R}^T$ and $(\mathbf{R} \cdot \mathbf{R}_\delta)^{-1} = (\mathbf{R} \cdot \mathbf{R}_\delta)^T$ it follows that

$$\mathbf{R}^T \cdot \left(\mathbf{C}^{(t)} - \mathbf{T} \right) \; = \; \mathbf{P}^{(t)} \; = \; \left(\mathbf{R} \cdot \mathbf{R}_\delta \right)^T \left(\mathbf{C}^{(t+1)} - \mathbf{T} \right) \qquad (5.1)$$

and by a simple rearrangement of this equation we obtain

$$\left(\mathbf{R} \cdot \mathbf{R}_\delta \right)^T \mathbf{T} - \mathbf{R}^T \mathbf{T} \; = \; \left(\mathbf{R} \cdot \mathbf{R}_\delta \right)^T \mathbf{C}^{(t+1)} - \mathbf{R}^T \mathbf{C}^{(t)}. \qquad (5.2)$$

Let $\mathbf{C}^{(t)} = \left(X^{(t)}, Y^{(t)}, Z^{(t)} \right)^T$ be the representation of the position of the observed surface point in terms of camera coordinates, for an arbitrary value of t. According to the camera-centered projection model (compare Section 2.1.4) it holds that

$$x^{(t)} = \frac{f \cdot X^{(t)}}{Z^{(t)}} \quad \text{and} \quad y^{(t)} = \frac{f \cdot Y^{(t)}}{Z^{(t)}}$$

are the projection center coordinates (undistorted image coordinates). The relations between valid (distorted) coordinates $\left(x_v^{(t)}, y_v^{(t)} \right)$ and these undistorted coordinates are as follows,

$$x^{(t)} = x_v^{(t)} \left(1 + \kappa_1 \cdot r^{(t)2} + \kappa_2 \cdot r^{(t)4} \right) \quad \text{and} \quad y^{(t)} = y_v^{(t)} \left(1 + \kappa_1 \cdot r^{(t)2} + \kappa_2 \cdot r^{(t)4} \right),$$

where $r^{(t)} = \sqrt{x_v^{(t)2} + y_v^{(t)2}}$ is the distance between the valid coordinates and the origin of the image plane.

begin

transform the given image buffer coordinates using calibration parameters into undistorted image point coordinates (x_t, y_t) and (x_{t+1}, y_{t+1});

$$\mathbf{E}^{(t)} := \left(\frac{x^{(t)}}{f}, \frac{y^{(t)}}{f}, 1 \right)^T ; \qquad \mathbf{E}^{(t+1)} := \left(\frac{x^{(t+1)}}{f}, \frac{y^{(t+1)}}{f}, 1 \right)^T ;$$

$$\mathbf{b} := \left(\mathbf{R} \cdot \mathbf{R}_\delta \right)^T \mathbf{T} - \mathbf{R}^T \mathbf{T} ;$$

$$\left(c_1, c_2, c_3 \right)^T := \left(\mathbf{R} \cdot \mathbf{R}_\delta \right)^T \cdot \mathbf{E}^{(t+1)} ; \qquad \left(d_1, d_2, d_3 \right)^T := \mathbf{R}^T \cdot \mathbf{E}^{(t)} ;$$

solve the system of linear equations $\mathbf{b} = \begin{pmatrix} c_1 & -d_1 & 1 \\ c_2 & -d_2 & 0 \\ c_3 & -d_3 & 0 \end{pmatrix} \cdot \begin{pmatrix} z^{(t+1)} \\ z^{(t)} \\ 0 \end{pmatrix} ;$

use $\mathbf{P}^{(t)} := \mathbf{R}^T \left(z^{(t)} \mathbf{E}^{(t)} - \mathbf{T} \right)$ or $\mathbf{P}^{(t)} := \left(\mathbf{R} \cdot \mathbf{R}_\delta \right)^T \left(z^{(t+1)} \mathbf{E}^{(t+1)} - \mathbf{T} \right)$
for the final calculation

end

Figure 5.13: Calculation of world coordinates from a pair of corresponding points in two consecutive images in the image buffer.

The valid image point coordinates are finally determined in the image buffer by points $\left(x_b^{(t)}, y_b^{(t)} \right)$, where

$$x_v^{(t)} = \frac{d_x' \left(x_b^{(t)} - c_x \right)}{s_x} \quad \text{and} \quad y_v^{(t)} = d_y' \left(y_b^{(t)} - c_y \right) .$$

(Task 5.2): For a surface point $\mathbf{P} = (X_w, Y_w, Z_w)$ it is assumed that its motion from image E_t to image E_{t+1} (i.e. its local displacement) could be tracked exactly. In image E_t it is represented at position $\left(x_b^{(t)}, y_b^{(t)} \right)$ and in image E_{t+1} it is represented at position $\left(x_b^{(t+1)}, y_b^{(t+1)} \right)$. The rotation angle δ of the turntable is assumed to be known. The world coordinates X_w, Y_w, and Z_w of the point $\mathbf{P}$ have to be determined.

(Solution 5.2): First the valid coordinates $\left(x_v^{(t)}, y_v^{(t)} \right)$ and $\left(x_v^{(t+1)}, y_v^{(t+1)} \right)$ are determined using the given image buffer coordinates. Then the ideal (undistorted) image coordinates $\left(x^{(t)}, y^{(t)} \right)$ and $\left(x^{(t+1)}, y^{(t+1)} \right)$ are determined from these valid coordinates. Therefore the vectors

$$\mathbf{E}^{(t)} = \left(\frac{x^{(t)}}{f}, \frac{y^{(t)}}{f}, 1\right)^T \quad \text{and} \quad \mathbf{E}^{(t+1)} = \left(\frac{x^{(t+1)}}{f}, \frac{y^{(t+1)}}{f}, 1\right)^T$$

are known quantities for further calculations. It follows that

$$\mathbf{C}^{(t)} = \left(X^{(t)}, Y^{(t)}, Z^{(t)}\right)^T = \left(\frac{x^{(t)}Z^{(t)}}{f}, \frac{y^{(t)}Z^{(t)}}{f}, Z^{(t)}\right)^T = Z^{(t)} \cdot \mathbf{E}^{(t)}$$

and $\mathbf{C}^{(t+1)} = Z^{(t+1)} \cdot \mathbf{E}^{(t+1)}$. In equation (5.2) the vector

$$\mathbf{b} = \left(\mathbf{R} \cdot \mathbf{R}_\delta\right)^T \mathbf{T} - \mathbf{R}^T \mathbf{T}$$

can be assumed to be known for a particular given rotation angle δ. Thus, according to

$$
\begin{aligned}
\mathbf{b} &= \left(\mathbf{R} \cdot \mathbf{R}_\delta\right)^T \cdot \mathbf{C}^{(t+1)} - \mathbf{R}^T \cdot \mathbf{C}^{(t)} \\
&= \left(\mathbf{R} \cdot \mathbf{R}_\delta\right)^T \cdot Z^{(t+1)} \cdot \mathbf{E}^{(t+1)} - \mathbf{R}^T \cdot Z^{(t)} \cdot \mathbf{E}^{(t)} \\
&= Z^{(t+1)} \cdot \left(\mathbf{R} \cdot \mathbf{R}_\delta\right)^T \cdot \mathbf{E}^{(t+1)} - Z^{(t)} \cdot \mathbf{R}^T \cdot \mathbf{E}^{(t)} \\
&= Z^{(t+1)} \cdot \mathbf{c} \; - \; Z^{(t)} \cdot \mathbf{d} \\
&= \begin{pmatrix} c_1 & -d_1 & 1 \\ c_2 & -d_2 & 0 \\ c_3 & -d_3 & 0 \end{pmatrix} \cdot \begin{pmatrix} Z^{(t+1)} \\ Z^{(t)} \\ 0 \end{pmatrix} \; = \; \mathbf{A} \cdot \mathbf{z}
\end{aligned}
$$

a matrix $\mathbf{A}$ is defined, for the given vectors $\mathbf{c} = \left(\mathbf{R} \cdot \mathbf{R}_\delta\right)^T \cdot \mathbf{E}^{(t+1)} = \left(c_1, c_2, c_3\right)^T$ and $\mathbf{d} = \mathbf{R}^T \cdot \mathbf{E}^{(t)} = \left(d_1, d_2, d_3\right)^T$. This matrix enables us to calculate the Z_t-coordinates of the surface point $\mathbf{P} = \left(X_w, Y_w, Z_w\right)^T$ in camera coordinates.

Note that the derived system of linear equations $\mathbf{b} = \mathbf{A} \cdot \mathbf{z}$ is over-determined. We have three uncorrelated equations and only two unknowns. In general this points out that also a third unknown (e.g. the rotation angle δ) can be determined from one (!) pair of corresponding projections of the same surface point.

For a non-singular 3×3 matrix $\mathbf{A}$ it holds that $\mathbf{z} = \mathbf{A}^{-1} \cdot \mathbf{b}$. Generally the tracking of one surface point at several times $t, t+1, t+2, \ldots)$ leads to a $m \times 3$ matrix $\mathbf{A}$, and the Moore-Penrose inverse of $\mathbf{A}$ can be used for the calculation of

$$\mathbf{z} = \left(\mathbf{A}^T \mathbf{A}\right)^{-1} \mathbf{A}^T \cdot \mathbf{b}$$

in this general case. For 3×3 this general case starts with

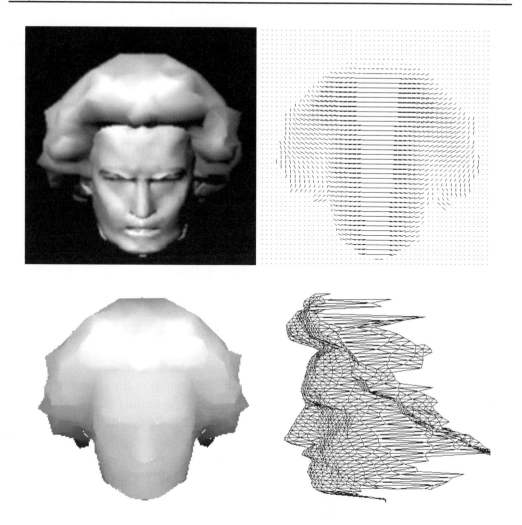

Figure 5.14: A rotation was carried out for a synthetic object (top left). The resulting local displacement vectors (top right) were used according to Algorithm 5.2 for the calculation of a height map (bottom left, height zero is also set to white). For a qualitative evaluation of the reconstruction result a grid representation of the calculated height map is shown below on the right.

$$
\mathbf{z} = \begin{pmatrix} c_1^2 + c_2^2 + c_3^2 & -c_1 d_1 - c_2 d_2 - c_3 d_3 & c_1 \\ -c_1 d_1 - c_2 d_2 - c_3 d_3 & d_1^2 + d_2^2 + d_3^2 & -d_1 \\ c_1 & -d_1 & 1 \end{pmatrix}^{-1} \begin{pmatrix} c_1 & c_2 & c_3 \\ -d_1 & -d_2 & -d_3 \\ 1 & 0 & 0 \end{pmatrix} \begin{pmatrix} b_1 \\ b_2 \\ b_3 \end{pmatrix}.
$$

Then, using equation (5.1) the position of the surface point $\mathbf{P} = (X_w, Y_w, Z_w)$ can be determined in world coordinates as

$$\mathbf{P}^{(t)} = \mathbf{R}^T \left(Z^{(t)} \mathbf{E}^{(t)} - \mathbf{T} \right) = \left(\mathbf{R} \cdot \mathbf{R}_\delta \right)^T \left(Z^{(t+1)} \mathbf{E}^{(t+1)} - \mathbf{T} \right),$$

where the two solutions given by these two equations can be compared to check the accuracy.

(**Algorithm 5.2**): The procedure is shown in Fig. 5.13.

(**Comment 5.2**): The reconstruction quality of the technique is illustrated in Fig. 5.14. Of course, for this synthetic object the calculated local displacements (i.e. the vectors between corresponding points in a pair of consecutive images) can be assumed to be correct in contrast to real world image sequences. The system $\mathbf{A} \cdot \mathbf{z} = \mathbf{b}$ of linear equations allows to determined the rotation angle δ between two consecutive images E_t and E_{t+1}, i.e. this angle does not have to be assumed to be known. This angle can also be determined from a pair of corresponding image points $\left(x_b^{(t)}, y_b^{(t)} \right)$ and $\left(x_b^{(t+1)}, y_b^{(t+1)} \right)$, and several pairs allow a more robust calculation. [7]

5.3.2 Constrained Search Space for Correspondence Analysis

The previous section has shown that analogously to the static stereo analysis depth values and world coordinates can also be calculated in the dynamic case in calibrated situations, using pairs or sequences of corresponding points. Absolute depth values could not be determined in non-calibrated situations (compare Section 5.1). In the case of static stereo analysis the search space for corresponding points can be reduced based on the epipolar geometry. In this case the search space shrinks to one line or even to a line segment. Analogous considerations can also be carried out for calibrated situations in the dynamic case. We illustrate this for the turntable situation (compare Fig. 5.15).

The turntable geometry can be considered in two different ways: the camera rotates around a static object or a static camera views an object on a turntable. For analyzing this geometry let us consider the first case, i.e. that the camera rotates in opposite direction to the turntable about the turntable center, and the turntable is now considered to be static (see Fig. 5.15). We believe that this way a better illustration of the process can be achieved. Notice that this assumed camera rotation is different compared to the one considered in Section 5.1.5.

Now assume that an object is placed on the turntable and consider one surface point $\mathbf{P}$ for such an object. This surface point is projected into the image point $\mathbf{p}^{(t)} = \left(x^{(t)}, y^{(t)} \right)$ in the undistorted image plane at time t. A cylindrical sur-

---

[7] R. Klette, D. Mehren, V. Rodehorst: *An application of surface reconstruction from rotational motion*. Real-Time Imaging **1** (1995), pp. 127 - 138.

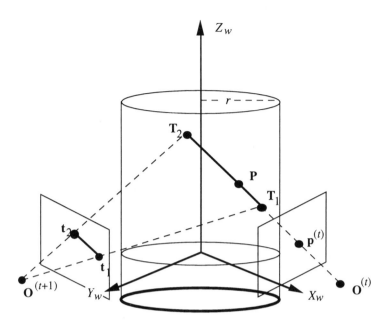

Figure 5.15: Assumed rotation of the camera about an assumed static turntable.

face is defined by an assumed translation of the circular turntable base along the rotation axis. The projection ray intersects this cylindrical surface in the points $\mathbf{T}_1$ and $\mathbf{T}_2$. At time $t+1$ these two points[8] are projected in the undistorted image plane into the image points $\mathbf{t}_1$ and $\mathbf{t}_2$. At the time $t+1$ the surface point $\mathbf{P}$ is projected onto a point on the line segment from $\mathbf{t}_1$ to $\mathbf{t}_2$ (if this surface point is projectively visible at all). This line segment is the restricted search space for a correspondence search which is defined uniquely with the point $\mathbf{p}^{(t)}$.

(Task 5.3): Consider a point $\mathbf{p}^{(t)}$ in the image plane t. Assume a constantly repeated rotation angle δ of the turntable. Calculate the points $\mathbf{t}_1$ and $\mathbf{t}_2$ of the image plane $t+1$ which specify the search space as illustrated in Fig. 5.15. The results of the camera calibration are given for image plane $t = 0$.

(Solution 5.3): Let $\mathbf{s}$ be the ray from $\mathbf{O}^{(t)}$ over $\mathbf{p}^{(t)}$ into the $X_w Y_w Z_w$-space. This ray intersects the cylinder surface

$$\left\{ (X_w, Y_w, Z_w) : \sqrt{X_w^2 + Y_w^2} = r \wedge Z_{min} \leq Z_w \leq Z_{max} \right\}$$

---

8 We refrain from a distinction of cases "two intersections, exactly one intersection, no intersection ...". But the special cases are taken into account in the algorithm.

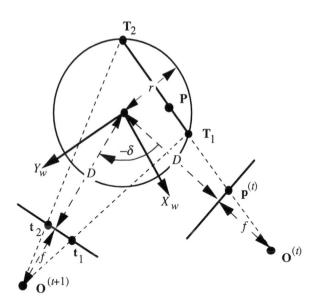

Figure 5.16: Representation of the assumed situation (turntable rotates counterclockwise about an angle δ, i.e., assumed camera rotation is clockwise about the Z_w-axis about an angle $-\delta$) in Fig. 5.15 where the viewing direction is opposite to the Z_w-axis.

in the points $\mathbf{T}_1$ and $\mathbf{T}_2$. Let $\mathbf{s}_i$ be the ray from $\mathbf{O}^{(t+1)}$ over $\mathbf{T}_i$ into the $X_w Y_w Z_w$-space, for $i = 1, 2$. These projection rays $\mathbf{s}_1$ and $\mathbf{s}_2$ intersect the image plane at time $t + 1$ in the sought-after points $\mathbf{t}_1$ and $\mathbf{t}_2$.

We assume that given calibration results correspond to the image acquisition situation at time $t = 0$. The projection center $\mathbf{O}^{(0)} = (0, 0, 0)^T$ is the origin of the calibrated camera-centered coordinate system. Accordingly, the world coordinates of the initial projection center can be calculated as

$$\mathbf{O}^{(0)} = \mathbf{R}^{-1} \cdot \left((0, 0, 0)^T - \mathbf{T} \right) = -\mathbf{R}^T \cdot \mathbf{T} = \left(X_z^{(0)}, Y_z^{(0)}, Z_z^{(0)} \right)^T .$$

Let $\mathbf{R}_{-\delta}$ be the rotation matrix specifying a $-\delta$ rotation about the Z_w-axis, i.e.

$$\mathbf{R}_{-\delta} = \begin{pmatrix} cos(\delta) & -sin(\delta) & 0 \\ sin(\delta) & cos(\delta) & 0 \\ 0 & 0 & 1 \end{pmatrix} .$$

Then it holds in world coordinates that

$$\mathbf{O}^{(t)} = \left(\mathbf{R}_{-\delta} \right)^t \cdot \mathbf{O}_0 = -\mathbf{R}_{-t\delta} \cdot \mathbf{R}^T \cdot \mathbf{T} = \left(X_z^{(t)}, Y_z^{(t)}, Z_z^{(t)} \right)^T ,$$

begin

transform the image buffer coordinates of $\mathbf{p}^{(t)}$ into undistorted image
point coordinates (x, y) or world coordinates (X, Y, Z);

let $\mathbf{O}^{(t)} = (a, b, c)$;

$$\lambda_{1,2} := \frac{-(2aX + 2bY) \pm \sqrt{(2aX + 2bY)^2 - 4(X^2 + Y^2)(a^2 + b^2 - r^2)}}{2(X^2 + Y^2)} \; ;$$

if λ_1 and λ_2 are complex valued **then**

no intersections with the cylinder surface exist (the projected
point $\mathbf{P}$ lies outside of the "bounded turntable cylinder")

else begin { if $\lambda_1 = \lambda_2$, then $\mathbf{T}_1 = \mathbf{T}_2 = \mathbf{P}$ }

$\mathbf{T}_1 := (a + \lambda_1 X, b + \lambda_1 Y, c + \lambda_1 Z)$;

$\mathbf{T}_2 := (a + \lambda_2 X, b + \lambda_2 Y, c + \lambda_2 Z)$;

{ if $c + \lambda_i Z$ is smaller than Z_{min} or larger than Z_{max},
then the corresponding intersections
with the cylinder surface can be used }

$\mathbf{T}_1 := \mathbf{R}_{-(t+1)\delta} \cdot \mathbf{R} \cdot \mathbf{T}_1 + \mathbf{T}$;

$\mathbf{T}_2 := \mathbf{R}_{-(t+1)\delta} \cdot \mathbf{R} \cdot \mathbf{T}_2 + \mathbf{T}$;

let $\mathbf{T}_i = (X_i, Y_i, Z_i)$, for $i = 1, 2$;

the desired line segment has end points $\mathbf{t}_1 := (f \cdot X_1/Z_1, f \cdot Y_1/Z_1)$
and $\mathbf{t}_2 := (f \cdot X_2/Z_2, f \cdot Y_2/Z_2)$

end {else}

end

Figure 5.17: Calculation of a line segment as search space in image $t + 1$ for the correspondence search process defined by image point $\mathbf{p}^{(t)}$, assuming the turntable situation.

for any arbitrary $t \geq 0$. Accordingly, for the image point $\mathbf{p}^{(t)} = \left(x^{(t)}, y^{(t)}\right)$ a representation in world coordinates is given in undistorted image coordinates with

$$\mathbf{p}^{(t)} = \mathbf{R}_{-t\delta} \cdot \mathbf{R}^T \cdot \left(\left(x^{(t)}, y^{(t)}, f\right)^T - \mathbf{T}\right) = \left(X_p^{(t)}, Y_p^{(t)}, Z_p^{(t)}\right)^T ,$$

at time $t \geq 0$. Now for the ray $\mathbf{s}$ the world coordinate representation

$$\mathbf{s} = \left\{\mathbf{O}^{(t)} + \lambda \cdot \mathbf{p}^{(t)} : \lambda \geq 0\right\} = \left\{\left(X_z^{(t)} + \lambda X_p^{(t)}, Y_z^{(t)} + \lambda Y_p^{(t)}, Z_z^{(t)} + \lambda Z_p^{(t)}\right) : \lambda \geq 0\right\}$$

can be used to determine the intersections $\mathbf{T}_1$ and $\mathbf{T}_2$ of $\mathbf{s}$ with the cylinder surface, for any arbitrary time $t \geq 0$. To do this the equation

$$\left(X_z^{(t)} + \lambda X_p^{(t)}\right)^2 + \left(Y_z^{(t)} + \lambda Y_p^{(t)}\right)^2 = r^2$$

has to be solved for λ. Two positive real solutions λ_1 and λ_2 allow the determination of the points $\mathbf{T}_1 = (X_1, Y_1, Z_1)^T$ and $\mathbf{T}_2 = (X_2, Y_2, Z_2)^T$ in world coordinates. These two points have to be projected into the image plane $t+1$. At time $t+1$ in the camera coordinate system these two points have the representation

$$\mathbf{T}_i^{(t+1)} = \mathbf{R}_{-(t+1)\delta} \cdot \mathbf{R} \cdot \mathbf{T}_i + \mathbf{T} = \left(X_i^{(t+1)}, Y_i^{(t+1)}, Z_i^{(t+1)}\right)^T .$$

After performing the central projection we receive the desired points

$$\mathbf{t}_i = \left(\frac{f \cdot X_i^{(t+1)}}{Z_i^{(t+1)}}, \frac{f \cdot Y_i^{(t+1)}}{Z_i^{(t+1)}}\right)^T, \text{ for } i = 1, 2,$$

in undistorted image plane coordinates. These coordinates still have to be transformed into image buffer coordinates (compare Table 2.1).

(**Algorithm 5.3**): The representation of the projection centers $\mathbf{O}^{(t)}$ in world coordinates can be separated into a preprocessing step. A selected image point $\mathbf{p}^{(t)}$ in image t initializes the subsequent procedure as given in Fig. 5.17.

(**Comment 5.3**): The cylinder parameters r, Z_{min}, and Z_{max} of the "bounded turntable cylinder", the constant rotation angle δ, and the camera calibration parameters are the variables of the technique. For the input point it can be assumed that it does not lie on the Z_w-axis (i.e. then $X^2 + Y^2 > 0$ is satisfied). In camera coordinates the inequalities $Z_i > f > 0$ are satisfied for both final point calculations.

5.3.3   Discussion

In the case of a calibrated image acquisition situation generally dynamic stereo analysis can be performed in such a way that first local displacement vectors are calculated, then the corresponding 3D surface point is determined for every vector (analog to Algorithm 5.2), and finally the individually reconstructed surface points are used for a reconstruction of the whole object surface.

Figure 5.18 represents a reconstruction result for this strategy for the discussed turntable situation. An object (plaster statue of Beethoven) is placed on the turntable. The local displacement field was approximately calculated as an

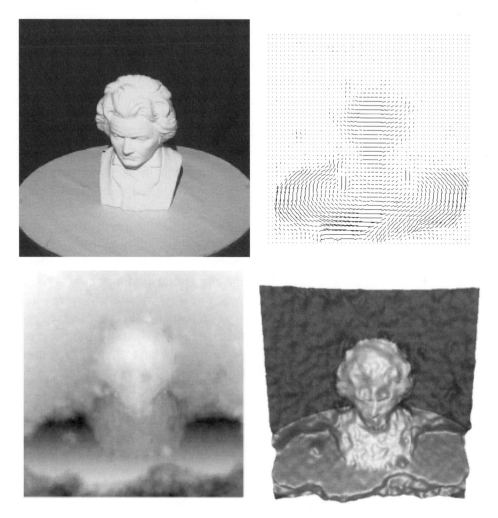

Figure 5.18: Plaster statue on a turntable (top left), calculated optical flow (top right) as an approximation of the local displacement field, reconstructed and smoothed height map (bottom left), and surface representation (with *texture mapping*) of the reconstruction result (bottom right).

optical flow [9] field. The reconstructed object surface is represented as a height map and as a textured 3D surface. Obviously such a rough approximation cannot be suggested to be used, e.g., for object modeling. However rough distance measurements between camera and object surface can, for example, support navigation solutions for which the object recognition of an obstacle is not essential.

---

[9] Following a procedure as suggested by P. Anandan: *Measuring visual motion from image sequences.* PhD, COINS TR 87-21, Univ. of Massachusetts, Amherst, 1987.

5.3.4   3D Models from Occluding Boundaries

This section deals with a shape reconstruction technique which is not based on analyzing local displacement vectors, and which allows better shape recovery results. It assumes that the objects are placed on a turntable, and that the occluding boundaries are captured for the different turntable positions. However for discussing the basic formulae of the technique we assume that the object is static, and that the camera rotates around the object. This rotation can be specified by an incremental angle δ between two consecutive images as in Section 5.3.2, or by a total angle θ which specifies an angular difference between a specified direction (e.g. negative Z_w-axis of a world coordinate system) and the direction of the optical axis. The angle θ defines a projection Π_θ of 3D points into the image plane.

The technique is based on analyzing geometric relations between object points $\mathbf{P}$ on the θ-rim and their projected points $\mathbf{p} = \Pi_\theta(\mathbf{P})$ on occluding boundaries in the image plane. The notions of the rim and occluding boundary (synonyms: occluding contours, apparent contours, profiles, silhouettes) were already defined at the end of Section 3.1.2. The θ-rim consists of all object surface points $\mathbf{P} = (X, Y, Z)$ with the property that the projection ray $\mathbf{v}_\theta(\mathbf{P})$ starting at the projection center and passing through point $\mathbf{P}$ is perpendicular to the surface normal $\mathbf{n}(\mathbf{P})$. The *occluding θ-boundary* is the θ-rim projected into the image.

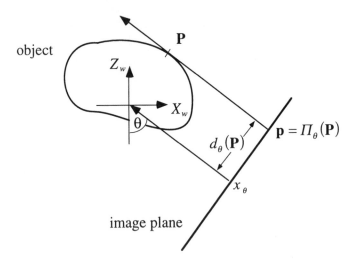

Figure 5.19: A sketch of the projection of a point $\mathbf{P}$ on the object rim into a point $\mathbf{p}$ on the occluding boundary in the image plane. The camera is assumed to rotate about the Y_w-axis of the world coordinate system where rotation axis and image plane are parallel. The Y_w-coordinates can be neglected for parallel projection. Let x_θ be the projection of the rotation axis into the image plane. The object is assumed to be static with respect to the world coordinate system. The rotation angle θ represents a viewing direction.

Central or parallel projection can be assumed to model the image acquisition process. Figure 5.19 illustrates the case of an assumed parallel projection. Note that the assumptions of a camera rotation about the Y_w-axis, and of an image plane parallel to the Y_w-axis allow to discuss the set-up for a 2D situation as shown in Fig. 5.19. Because the assumed camera rotation is dual to the turntable rotation it follows that

$$x_\theta = const, \text{ for all rotation angles } \theta.$$

Let x_0 be this constant value of the projected rotation axis into the image plane. The value $d_\theta(\mathbf{P})$ specifies the distance between x_0 and the projected point $\mathbf{p}$,

$$d_\theta(\mathbf{P}) = \mathbf{p} - x_0 \text{, for } \mathbf{p} = \Pi_\theta(\mathbf{P}) .$$

Note that $\mathbf{p}$ is just a real value because we neglected the Y_w-axis.

For the following discussions of the methodical fundamentals let us assume that the object surface is $C^{(1)}$, i.e. the surface normal $\mathbf{n}(\mathbf{P})$ is defined at each point $\mathbf{P}$ on a rim, and that each projected point $\mathbf{p} = \Pi_\theta(\mathbf{P})$ uniquely specifies point $\mathbf{P}$ on the object surface, i.e. the projections Π_θ of points on a θ-rim into the image plane are assumed to be bijective (i.e. one-to-one).

The ray $\mathbf{v}_\theta(\mathbf{P})$ passes through $\mathbf{p} = \Pi_\theta(\mathbf{P})$ and $\mathbf{P}$. In the case of a parallel projection it starts at a point at infinity, and in case of a central projection it starts at the optical center of the camera. Under the assumption that the camera coordinate system is properly calibrated with respect to the world coordinate system it follows that the ray $\mathbf{v}_\theta(\mathbf{P})$ can be calculated from a given image point $\mathbf{p} = \Pi_\theta(\mathbf{P})$. Let $\mathbf{t}_\theta(\mathbf{P})$ be a vector in the image plane starting at point $\mathbf{p} = \Pi_\theta(\mathbf{P})$ on the occluding θ-boundary which is tangential to the occluding θ-boundary passing through $\mathbf{p}$. Under the assumption that the occluding θ-boundary is properly calculated in the given image it follows that the vector $\mathbf{t}_\theta(\mathbf{P})$ can be calculated. For these vectors $\mathbf{t}_\theta(\mathbf{P})$ and $\mathbf{v}_\theta(\mathbf{P})$ it holds that

$$\mathbf{n}(\mathbf{P}) = \mathbf{v}_\theta(\mathbf{P}) \times \mathbf{t}_\theta(\mathbf{P}) .$$

This formula allows to calculate surface normals for points $\mathbf{P}$ on the θ-rim. However, the model also allows to calculate 3D world coordinates of such a point $\mathbf{P} = (X_w, Z_w)$. We prove this in detail for the case of assumed parallel projection:

From the situation illustrated in Fig. 5.19 it follows that $(cos\,\theta, sin\,\theta)^T$ is a vector in the image plane from point x_0 towards point $\mathbf{p} = \Pi_\theta(\mathbf{P})$, with

$$d_\theta(\mathbf{P}) = (X_w, Z_w) \cdot (cos\,\theta, sin\,\theta)^T \quad \text{and} \tag{5.3}$$

$$\left(\frac{\partial X_w}{\partial \theta}, \frac{\partial Z_w}{\partial \theta} \right) \cdot (cos\,\theta, sin\,\theta)^T = 0 . \tag{5.4}$$

Calculating the first derivatives of (5.3) with respect to θ leads to

$$\left(\frac{\partial X_w}{\partial \theta}, \frac{\partial Z_w}{\partial \theta}\right) \cdot (cos\theta, sin\theta)^T + (X_w, Z_w) \cdot (-sin\theta, cos\theta)^T = \frac{\partial d_\theta(\mathbf{P})}{\partial \theta} .$$

Together with (5.4) it follows that

$$\frac{\partial d_\theta(\mathbf{P})}{\partial \theta} = (X_w, Z_w)^T \cdot (-sin\theta, cos\theta)^T . \tag{5.5}$$

The combination of equations (5.3) and (5.5) into one matrix equation leads to

$$\begin{pmatrix} cos\theta & sin\theta \\ -sin\theta & cos\theta \end{pmatrix} \cdot \begin{pmatrix} X_w \\ Z_w \end{pmatrix} = \begin{pmatrix} d_\theta(\mathbf{P}) \\ d_\theta(\mathbf{P})/\partial\theta \end{pmatrix} .$$

For this orthogonal matrix it follows that

$$\begin{pmatrix} X_w \\ Z_w \end{pmatrix} = \begin{pmatrix} cos\theta & -sin\theta \\ sin\theta & cos\theta \end{pmatrix} \cdot \begin{pmatrix} d_\theta(\mathbf{P}) \\ \partial d_\theta(\mathbf{P})/\partial\theta \end{pmatrix} .$$

Because θ and $d_\theta(\mathbf{P})$ are known all depends upon calculations of good estimations of the change $\partial d_\theta(\mathbf{P})/\partial\theta$. Simple estimations can be based on two consecutive images. This concludes our theoretical discussion how to calculate world coordinates (X_w, Z_w) for points $\mathbf{P}$ on a rim.

In case of central projection we cannot neglect the Y_w coordinate. Here the general case $\mathbf{P} = (X_w, Y_w, Z_w)$ has to be discussed. It is possible to derive the formula

$$(X_w, Y_w, Z_w)^T = \frac{f \cdot D}{xys + f \cdot \frac{\partial x}{\partial \theta} - f^2 - x^2} \cdot \begin{pmatrix} x \cdot cos\theta - (xys + f \cdot \frac{\partial x}{\partial \theta} - x^2) \cdot sin\theta \\ y \\ x \cdot sin\theta + (xys + f \cdot \frac{\partial x}{\partial \theta} - x^2) \cdot cos\theta \end{pmatrix}$$

where $\mathbf{p} = (x, y)$, f denotes the effective focal length, D is the distance of the rotation axis to the image plane, and $s = \partial x/\partial y$ denotes the slope of the occluding boundary. Note that the image coordinate x corresponds to $d_\theta(\mathbf{P})$ above.

These formulae support the design of a shape reconstruction procedure where projected occluding boundaries in subsequent images (during the rotation of the given object on a turntable) are used to calculate 3D object surface positions.

Occluding boundaries can also be used to "carve out the given object from an a-priori specified 3D bounding volume". Such a process can be based on calculating projection rays for all the points at the given occluding boundaries, and on subsequent restrictions ("object points can only be on one side of the projection

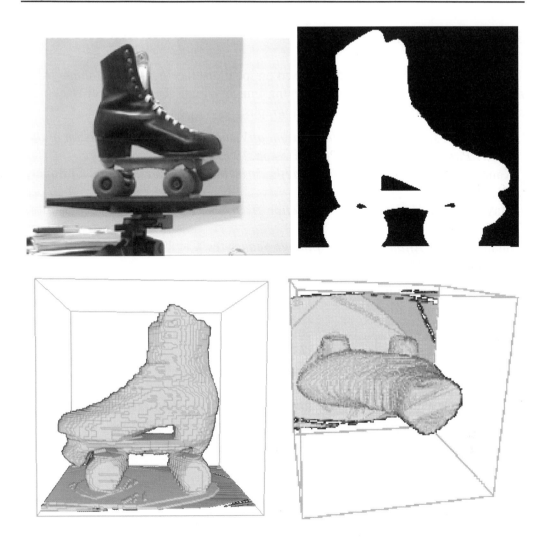

Figure 5.20: An object on a turntable (top left) generates a sequence of occluding boundaries (top right) which may be transformed into a 3D model of the rotating object. The bottom row shows the given object in reconstructed form (different viewing directions) where the visualized reconstruction resolution is about 1/64 of the actually achieved accuracy.

ray towards a surface point on a rim") of the remaining volume which finally may contain the given object. Figure 5.20 illustrates a reconstruction result for such a volume based approach.

These techniques fail for the reconstruction of surface concavities with respect to the projection direction. However these techniques may be combined with others, e.g. multi-source shading based approaches (see Chapter 8).

5.4 REFERENCES

The topics of shape reconstruction based on local displacement fields (*shape from motion*), and of interpreting time-varying imagery (e.g. also for object tracking) are, for example, discussed in the monographs

Aloimonos, J., Shulman, D.: *Integration of Visual Modules: An Extension of the Marr Paradigm*. Academic Press, Boston, 1990,

Kanatani, K.: *Group-Theoretical Methods in Image Understanding*. Springer, Berlin, 1990,

Maybank, S.: *Theory of Reconstruction from Image Motion*. Springer, Berlin, 1993, and

Shapiro, L. S.: *Affine Analysis of Image Sequences*. Cambridge University Press, Cambridge 1995.

For the approximate calculation of local displacement fields using optical flow techniques we refer to

Barron, J.L., Fleet, D.J., Beauchemin, S.S.: *Performance of optical flow techniques*. Int. J. Computer Vision **12** (1994), pp. 43 - 77,

Fleet, D.J., Jepson, A.D.: *Measurement of Image Velocity*. Kluwer, Boston 1992,

Handschack, P., Klette, R.: *Quantitative comparisons of differential methods for measuring of image velocity*. in: *Aspects of Visual Form Processing*, C. Arcelli, L.P. Cordella, G. Sanniti di Baja (eds.), World Scientific, Singapore, 1994, pp. 241 - 250, and

Horn, B.K.P.: *Robot Vision*. McGraw-Hill, New York 1986.

The two cited articles deal with the evaluation problem of these approximate calculations. The outlined Horn-Schunck method was published in

Schunck, B.G., Horn, B.K.P.: *Constraints on optical flow computation*. Proc. Pattern Recognition and Image Processing Conf., Dallas, 1981, pp. 205 - 210.

The given iterative technique converges if it specifies a contraction (compare Banach's fix point theorem in mathematical analysis). Several optical flow algorithms were designed as modifications of the Horn-Schunck method over the years, compare for example

Willick, D., Yang, Y.-H.: *Experimental evaluation of motion constraint equations*. CVGIP: Image Understanding, **54** (1991), pp. 206 - 214

for a comparative discussion, and

Martin, W.N., Aggarwal, J.K. (eds.): *Motion Understanding - Robot and Human Vision*. Kluwer, Boston, 1988 for a compilation of publications about motion analysis. The calibrated turntable situation and the related shape reconstruction problem (Sections 5.3.1, 5.3.2, and 5.3.3) were discussed in

Mehren, D., Rodehorst, V.: *Gestaltsanalyse komplexer Objekte bei kontrollierter Bewegung*. Diplomarbeit, TU Berlin, Fachbereich Informatik, 1994.

Moving light displays (marks on a human body) were suggested and studied in

Johannson, G.: *Perception of motion and changing form*. Scandinavian J. Psychology **5** (1964), pp. 181 - 208.

Shape from occluding boundaries is reported in

Giblin, P., Weiss, R.: *Reconstruction of surfaces from profiles*. 1st Int. Conf. on Computer Vision (ICCV'87), 1987, pp. 136 - 144,

Zheng, J. Y.: *Acquiring 3-D models from sequences of contours*. IEEE Trans. Pattern Analysis and Mach. Intell. **PAMI-16** (1994), pp. 163 - 178,

Zheng, J. Y., Fukagawa, Y., Abe, N.: *3D surface estimation and model construction from specular motion in image sequences*. IEEE Trans. Pattern Analysis and Mach. Intell. **PAMI-16** (1997), pp. 513 - 520, and

Zhao, C. S., Mohr, R.: *Global three-dimensional surface reconstruction from occluding contours*. Computer Vision and Image Understanding **64** (1996), pp. 62 - 96.

For motion analysis in the context of specific (engineering) applications we refer to

Aloimonos, J. (ed.): *Active Perception*. Lawrence Erlbaum, Hillsdale 1993, and

Zhang, Z., Faugeras, O.: *3D Dynamic Scene Analysis*. Springer, Berlin, 1992.

The latter book deals, for instance, with visual navigation and the analysis of image sequences.

5.5 EXERCISES

(1) Sketch local displacement fields (a) for the translation of a rectangle within a translation plane which is slanted to the image plane, and (b) for a rotation of a rectangle about one of its corner points where the rotation plane is parallel to the image plane (analogously to Fig. 5.2, for assumed parallel projection).

(2) How do the equations in Theorem 5.1 have to be modified if the camera-centered projection model is assumed?

Figure 5.21: Results of Algorithm 5.1 for two images of the sequence TREES (compare Fig. 5.11). These images are enlargements of the lower middle part of the original sequence. Optical flow was calculated with 100 iterations. Different weighting factors λ were used: $\lambda = 0.01$ (top left), $\lambda = 0.1$ (top right), $\lambda = 1$ (bottom left), and $\lambda = 10$ (bottom right). A stronger smoothing effect can be observed in the upper row. The motion vectors of scene objects which are closer to the (passing) camera have a tendency to be longer than for objects within a larger distance to the camera.

(3) Prove the coordinate transformations

$$x' = \frac{f \cdot X'}{Z'} = f \cdot \frac{r_{11}x + r_{12}y + r_{13}f}{r_{31}x' + r_{32}y' + r_{33}f} \quad \text{and} \quad y' = \frac{f \cdot Y'}{Z'} = f \cdot \frac{r_{21}x + r_{22}y + r_{23}f}{r_{31}x + r_{32}y + r_{33}f}$$

that were given in Section 5.1.5 for the mapping of image point coordinates caused by a camera rotation (the projection center and rotation center are assumed to be identical).

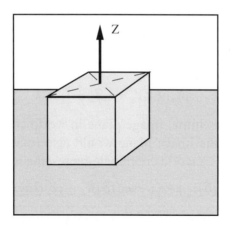

(4 - Assignment) Calculate the optical flow for two subsequent pictures of an image sequence using the Horn-Schunck method (Algorithm 5.1). Use the suggested initial values and local difference operations as specified in Solution 5.1. Discuss the influence of the parameter λ (compare Fig. 5.21) and the influence of the number of iterations (compare Table 5.1).

(5) What is the intersection of the line $u \cdot E_x + v \cdot E_y = -E_t$ with that straight line which is defined by the direction vector

$$\left(E_x, E_y \right)^T$$

(compare Fig. 5.6). Use this point of intersection as the initial value for the technique that was implemented in Exercise (4). Compare the speed of convergence for different image pairs of input image sequences.

(6) Apply the simple difference operations in Example 5.1 to the technique implemented in Exercise (4). Compare the convergence velocity and the calculated results of this modified technique with the convergence velocity and the calculated results of the original algorithm.

Figure 5.22: Cube in initial position (before rotation about the Z-axis).

(7) Consider a "small rotation" of the cube given in Fig. 5.22 about the Z-axis. Sketch the resulting local displacement field and the expected optical flow field if the Horn-Schunck method is used for calculation.

(8) The points $\mathbf{t}_i$ in Algorithm 5.3 could also be determined on rays $\mathbf{s}_i$, with

$$\mathbf{s}_i = \left\{ \left(X_z^{(t+1)} + \lambda X_i, Y_z^{(t+1)} + \lambda Y_i, Z_z^{(t+1)} + \lambda Z_i \right) : \lambda \geq 0 \right\}$$

in world coordinates, where $i = 1, 2$, without a final central projection. For this, the two rays have to be intersected with the image plane $t + 1$. At time $t = 0$ the image plane is given by the equation $Z = f$ in camera coordinates. According to the calibration results

$$r_7 X_w + r_8 Y_w + r_9 Z_w + T_z = f$$

is a representation of this initial image plane in world coordinates. With the assumed camera rotation the image plane would also rotate accordingly. At time $t \geq 0$ the image plane has a world coordinate representation

$$r_7 \big(cos(t\delta) X_w + sin(t\delta) Y_w \big) + r_8 \big(-sin(t\delta) X_w + cos(t\delta) Y_w \big) + r_9 Z_w + T_z = f \ .$$

What are the explicit representations of $\mathbf{t}_1$ and $\mathbf{t}_2$ which correspond to this solution strategy?

6   REFLECTION MODELS

The amount of light encoded into the gray value of a particular pixel of a digital image can be seen as the result of interactions between surface materials and light sources. This chapter deals with a number of laws and models which are fundamental for the analysis of images with the goal of extracting three-dimensional features of surfaces. All methods described in this textbook are influenced by the lighting and by the reflection characteristics of the observed objects. Therefore it is necessary to model the properties of both the illumination and the object materials. This leads to a theoretical basis for the interpretability of image information.

Almost every method for the recovery of three-dimensional object features such as depth values or surface orientations assumes certain reflection characteristics of the object surface. Many techniques do not work properly if the object surface shows highlights, for instance. This is true for most of the approaches introduced in Chapters 4, 5, and 9. These methods generally do not model the reflection properties of the object explicitly and often assume that the object surface has completely matte finish. An explicit modeling is the precondition to reconstruct three-dimensional object surfaces for all methods introduced in Chapters 7 and 8. In principle, the CCD cells of the imaging sensor (compare Section 2.2) can be seen as radiometric measurement sensors for these techniques.

Section 6.1 describes some radiometric quantities and laws which are important to describe reflection properties of surfaces. A general standardized representation of reflection properties used in computer vision and computer graphics is subject of Section 6.2. Under certain conditions reflection properties can be represented relatively easy as so-called reflectance maps. Section 6.3 describes this representation which is often employed in shading based shape recovery approaches.

If it is more convenient to describe the reflection characteristics of object surfaces with a small number of parameters a mathematical description of the reflection characteristics has to be found. Such analytical reflection models are easy to use if the reflection parameters are known. They are discussed in Section 6.4. Section 6.5 relates the reflection characteristics that were up to now consid ered as being independent from the sensor to a simple sensor model leading to the image irradiance equation.

6.1   RADIOMETRIC QUANTITIES AND LAWS

As already mentioned some *radiometric quantities* will be introduced at the beginning of this chapter. They are helpful for the derivation and representation of reflection properties. It should be mentioned that equivalent *photometric quantities* exist which refer to the interpretation with the human eye and are usually used in illuminating engineering and sometimes adapted in computer vision. The symbols and the basic relationships do correspond but names and units differ. Table 6.1 lists basic radiometric and photometric terms.

radiometric quantity	photometric quantity	symbol	radiometric unit
radiant energy	luminous energy	Q	W·s
radiant power, radiant flux	luminous power, luminous flux	Φ	W
irradiance	illuminance	E	$\mathrm{W \cdot m^{-2}}$
radiant emittance, radiant exitance	luminous emittance, luminous exitance	M	$\mathrm{W \cdot m^{-2}}$
radiant intensity	luminous intensity	I	$\mathrm{W \cdot sr^{-1}}$
radiance	luminance	L	$\mathrm{W \cdot sr^{-1} \cdot m^{-2}}$

Table 6.1: Radiometric and photometric quantities.

6.1.1   Quantities Independent from Solid Angles

The existence of optical electromagnetic radiation (light) is always associated with the transmission of energy. This energy is emitted by a light source and is partly reflected by one or more object surfaces. Finally part of the energy is received and interpreted by an imaging sensor (camera) and encoded into a gray value.

It is known that the *radiant energy Q* of a light quantum has a direct proportional relationship to the frequency of the light radiation where Planck´s constant *h* represents the proportionality factor of this relationship. The *radiant power* or *radiant flux Φ* expressed in W (watt) is the radiant energy *Q* per unit time, so the radiant power is given by the formula

$$\Phi = \frac{dQ}{dt} .$$

If the radiant power *Φ* is related to a radiating surface area A_1 (source) we get the differential quotient

$$M = \frac{d\Phi}{dA_1}$$

which is called *radiant emittance* or *radiant exitance M*. To differentiate between emitting and incoming radiation it is common to mark the quantities related to emitting radiation with index 1 and to mark the quantities associated with incoming radiation with index 2. This will be maintained when the relationship is not obvious from the context. If a surface receives radiation the radiant power *Φ* can also be related to the illuminated surface area A_2 (receiver). This is called the *irradiance E*

$$E = \frac{d\Phi}{dA_2}$$

and is expressed in $W \cdot m^{-2}$ (watts per square meter). The irradiance is of great importance for computer vision since the irradiance is the quantity which is measured by the imaging sensor and is encoded into a gray value for every pixel. Therefore it is often called *image irradiance* in computer vision. If a surface patch does not absorb any radiation and if no transmission of radiation occurs then it reflects the entire incoming radiation and hence the irradiance *E* is equal to the radiant emittance *M*.

6.1.2 Quantities Dependent on Solid Angles

The following quantities relate the radiant power *Φ* to a surface area *A* and to a solid angle *Ω*. The solid angle *Ω* can be determined analogously to the radian measure as described in Section 3.1.4. These definitions are now used to describe the quantities radiant intensity *I* and radiance *L*. If we relate the outgoing radiant power *Φ* to the solid angle $Ω_1$ in which radiation is emitted then we get the *radiant intensity I*

$$I = \frac{d\Phi}{d\Omega_1}$$

which is expressed in $W \cdot sr^{-1}$ (watts per steradian). The radiant intensity can be interpreted as the solid angular "density" of the radiant power. The radiant power which is emitted by a surface can also be related to both the solid angle Ω_1 and to the surface area A. The resulting quantity is called *radiance L* with

$$L = L_1 = \frac{d^2\Phi}{dA_1 \cdot cos(\theta_1) d\Omega_1} \quad .$$

The radiance is expressed in $W \cdot m^{-2} \cdot sr^{-1}$ (watts per square meter per steradian). θ_1 denotes the angle between the surface normal and the emittance direction. Thus the surface area A is foreshortened and the effective surface area is merely $dA_1 \cdot cos(\theta_1)$.

A similar definition of the radiance can be given for an illuminated surface A_2 and an associated solid angle θ_2. This leads to the formula

$$L = L_2 = \frac{d^2\Phi}{dA_2 \cdot cos(\theta_2) d\Omega_2} \quad .$$

For the purpose of better differentiation between these two different radiance terms the first is also called *reflected radiance* or *scene radiance*. By making some assumptions we will show in Section 6.5.1 that an approximately proportional relationship exists between the scene radiance which is reflected by a surface patch and the image irradiance measured by the camera sensor.

6.1.3   A Fundamental Relationship

The quantities of outgoing radiation and incoming radiation were considered separately in the above definitions. A fundamental relationship connects the quantities and describes the radiation exchange between two differential surface patches dA_1 and dA_2:

$$d^2\Phi = L \cdot \frac{dA_1 \cdot cos(\theta_1) \cdot dA_2 \cdot cos(\theta_2)}{r^2} \quad .$$

$d^2\Phi$ is the radiant power emitted from surface patch dA_1 and received by surface patch dA_2 if the surface patch dA_1 has the radiance L in direction of surface patch dA_2. The angles θ_1 and θ_2 refer to the light direction which is shown in Fig. 6.1 as a dotted line. The distance between the surface patches is r.

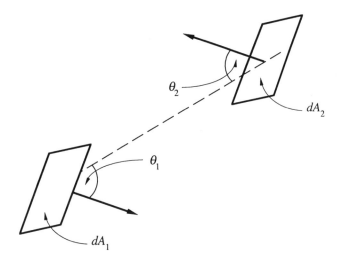

Figure 6.1: Relationship between two radiation exchanging surface patches.

It follows from the symmetry of the formula that the meanings of the emitting and the receiving quantities can be exchanged. It does not matter for the mathematical consideration which surface patch emits and which surface patch receives radiation assuming equal radiance L. This property which is called *law of reciprocity* is also important for the description of form factors of *radiosity*-algorithms in computer vision and computer graphics. If we apply the definition of the solid angle as stated in Section 3.1.4

$$d\Omega_1 = \frac{dA_2 \cdot cos(\theta_2)}{r^2}$$

the just introduced fundamental relationship takes the form

$$d^2\Phi = L dA_1 \cdot cos(\theta_1) d\Omega_1 \ .$$

Furthermore, it holds

$$d\Phi = \int_{\Omega_1} L dA_1 \cdot cos(\theta_1) d\Omega_1$$

for the differential radiant power over the entire solid angle Ω_1.

6.1.4   Inverse Square Law

By using the definition of the radiant intensity I in conjunction with the previous formula the radiant intensity I of a surface area A_1 is given as

$$I = \frac{d\Phi}{d\Omega_1} = \int_{A_1} L \cdot cos(\theta_1) dA_1 \ .$$

The differential portion of radiant intensity dI in surface patch dA_1 is

$$dI = L \cdot cos(\theta_1) dA_1 \ .$$

Applying the definition of the irradiance and the fundamental relationship introduced in the previous section leads to the differential portion of irradiance dE of the same surface patch dA_1:

$$dE = L \cdot \frac{cos(\theta_1) \cdot dA_1 \cdot cos(\theta_2)}{r^2} \ .$$

By substituting $dI = L \cdot cos(\theta_1) dA_1$ into this formula it follows

$$dE = dI \cdot \frac{cos(\theta_2)}{r^2} \ .$$

Under the assumption of a constant quotient the differential irradiance dE can be integrated and we get

$$E = I \cdot \frac{cos(\theta_2)}{r^2} \ , \ \text{with} \ \frac{cos(\theta_2)}{r^2} = \text{const} \ .$$

This relationship is called the *inverse square law*. It describes the relationship between a radiating source with radiant intensity I and the irradiance E of a slanted surface patch at distance r. The required conditions are not exactly fulfilled in practice hence the inverse square law can be applied only if the distance r does not fall below a certain limit which depends among other things on the size of the radiating source and on the spatial distribution of the radiant intensity as well.

6.2   REFLECTANCE-DISTRIBUTION FUNCTION

If we consider reflection properties of different surface materials the important question arises how the reflection properties can be represented. In computer vision as well as in computer graphics the *bidirectional reflectance-distribution function* (*BRDF*) is used as a fundamental tool to describe reflection characteristics. The *BRDF* was defined by the National Bureau of Standards, a standardization authority of the USA for the standardization of reflection representations in 1977.

6.2.1 Definition of BRDF

The BRDF describes how "bright" the differential surface dA of a material appears when it is observed from a general direction and illuminated from a particular direction. We define the BRDF as the ratio between the reflected differential radiance dL_1 in viewer direction and the differential irradiance dE_2 coming from an illumination direction:

$$f_r(\theta_2,\phi_2;\theta_1,\phi_1) = \frac{dL_1(\theta_2,\phi_2;\theta_1,\phi_1;E_2)}{dE_2(\theta_2,\phi_2)} \ .$$

The symbol f_r is standard and should not be mixed up with the focal length f. The BRDF is expressed in sr^{-1} (1 / steradian). The term "direction" in the above definition should be interpreted as a differential solid angle in a direction given by spherical coordinates. The letter θ denotes the slant angle and the letter ϕ stands for the tilt angle.

Note that we used different symbols for the representation of slant and tilt in Section 3.1.4. The spherical coordinates of the *BRDF* refer to a right-handed coordinate system where the origin coincides with the surface point and whose Z-axis coincides with the surface orientation[1]. The tilt angle is taken counterclockwise by looking onto the surface patch. Using these definitions the local geometry can be represented as shown in Fig. 6.2.

If the differential irradiance dE_2 is described in the foreshortened portion of the illumination over the differential solid angle $d\Omega_2$ by using the radiance which is received by the surface the BRDF can be formulated as

$$f_r(\theta_2,\phi_2;\theta_1,\phi_1) = \frac{dL_1(\theta_2,\phi_2;\theta_1,\phi_1;E_2)}{L_2(\theta_2,\phi_2)\cdot\cos(\theta_2)d\Omega_2} \ .$$

If we integrate over the entire observed solid angle Ω_2 of the incoming radiation the reflected radiance L_1 is represented by the equations

$$L_1 = \int_{\Omega_2} dL_1(\theta_2,\phi_2;\theta_1,\phi_1;E_2)$$

$$= \int_{\Omega_2} f_r(\theta_2,\phi_2;\theta_1,\phi_1)\,dE_2(\theta_2,\phi_2)$$

$$= \int_{\Omega_2} f_r(\theta_2,\phi_2;\theta_1,\phi_1)\cdot L_2(\theta_2,\phi_2)\cdot\cos(\theta_2)d\Omega_2 \ .$$

---

[1] Contrary to this the spherical coordinates which were introduced in Section 3.1.4 refer to a coordinate system whose Z-axis coincides with the line of sight (optical axis, compare Fig. 3.3).

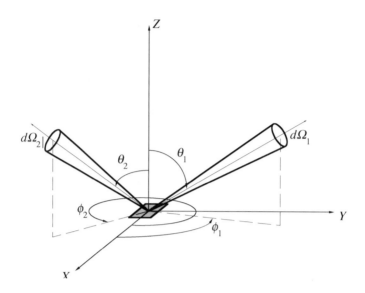

Figure 6.2: Geometry of the bidirectional reflectance-distribution function (BRDF).

The irradiance E was defined in Section 6.1.1 as a quantity independent from any direction. Now the irradiance dE_2 depends on a direction since it holds

$$dE_2(\theta_2,\phi_2) = L_2(\theta_2,\phi_2) \cdot \cos(\theta_2)\, d\Omega_2 \ .$$

This is a more detailed characterization of the irradiance.

6.2.2 BRDF of a Perfect Diffuse Surface

A *perfectly diffuse* reflecting surface appears equally bright when observed from any arbitrary direction. Furthermore, this feature is also independent from the type of illumination. If a surface emits the entire incoming energy through reflection then it is called a *Lambertian reflector* and neither absorption nor transmission of radiation takes place. It follows that the entire radiance L_1 which is reflected over the visible hemisphere is equal to the incoming irradiance E_2. A Lambertian reflector has three important properties:

1. The reflected radiance L_1 does not depend on the direction (isotropic) and is constant, i.e. $L_1(\theta_1,\phi_1) = L_1 = \text{const}$.

2. The BRDF is constant, i.e. $f_r(\theta_2,\phi_2,\theta_1,\phi_1) = f_r = \text{const}$.

3. The radiant emittance M is equal to the irradiance E_2, i.e. $M = E_2$.

The radiant emittance M can now be expressed as the integral of the reflected radiance L_1 over the visible hemisphere:

$$M = \int_{\Omega_1} L_1 \, d\Omega_1 = L_1 \, \pi = E_2 \ .$$

From this it follows that

$$f_r = \frac{L_1}{E_2} = \frac{1}{\pi}$$

holds for the Lambertian reflector. If the Lambertian reflector is illuminated by a light source which has the radiance $L_2(\theta_2, \phi_2)$ we get

$$L_1 = \frac{1}{\pi} \int_{\Omega_2} L_2(\theta_2, \phi_2) \cdot cos(\theta_2) \, d\Omega_2$$

as reflected radiance. This equation contains Lambert´s cosine law which will be explained in the following.

6.2.3 Lambert´s Cosine Law

A differential radiance falling on a Lambertian reflector is reflected as radiance which is proportional to the cosine of the angle between the normal at the illuminated point and the illumination direction (*Lambert´s cosine law*). Assume we would approximate the above integral as a finite sum then every radiance that was assumed to be constant in the finite solid angle contributes as factor

$$\frac{1}{\pi} \cdot cos(\theta_2)$$

to the totally reflected radiance. For a parallel radiating light source (i.e. all light rays are parallel) the radiance falling on a surface is different from zero for exact one direction but zero for all other directions. Without going into details it is just mentioned that this radiance can be modeled as an integrable mathematical function. Then the reflected radiance L_1 of a Lambertian reflector illuminated by a parallel radiating light source of irradiance E_0 is described by the equation

$$L_1 = \frac{E_0}{\pi} \cdot cos(\theta_2).$$

In this context the index 0 usually denotes a quantity related to the light source. It is assumed that illumination directions outside of the interval

$$0 \le \theta_2 < \frac{\pi}{2}$$

do not cause reflections since the light cannot reach the observed surface patch.

6.2.4 Albedo

According to its definition the Lambertian reflector does not absorb any radiation for any wavelength. The so-called *albedo* ρ is used to describe surfaces which possess all properties of a Lambertian reflector apart from a partial absorption of the incoming radiation (*Lambertian surfaces*).

It describes the relative portion of the radiation which is reflected by the surface. The albedo can be seen as a scaling factor which lies usually in the interval [0,1]. The definition of the albedo can be extended to non-Lambertian surfaces.

6.2.5 BRDF Measurement

To determine the BRDF of a specimen which possesses unknown reflection properties it is illuminated from a large number of different directions. For each illumination direction measurements for a large number of reflection directions are taken. The motions of the light source and of the measuring device are usually done automatically. Such a device for measuring the BRDF is called a *gonio-reflectometer*.

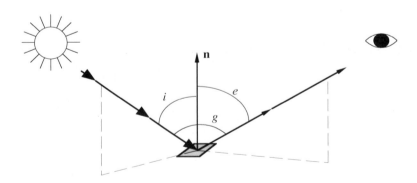

Figure 6.3: Definition of the three photometric angles i, e, and g. Each arrow marks the direction of one light ray.

Most materials have the property that their reflection characteristics are invariant to rotations of the surface about its normal. Such materials are called *isotropic*. Materials not having this characteristic are called *anisotropic*. Some materials that show anisotropic reflection characteristics are for example the mineral tiger eye, velvet, varnished wood, and unfinished aluminum. Anisotropic reflections can also be seen on wheel rims. Anisotropic materials can be recognized by having asymmetric highlights in spite of a symmetric surface with symmetric illumination. This is particularly noticeable for spherical objects which can, for instance, have a half-moon-shaped highlight. The reflection model of the BRDF covers anisotropic reflection since the angles ϕ_1 and ϕ_2 are independent (compare Fig. 6.2).

For isotropic materials the geometric relationship between the surface normal, the illumination direction, and the reflection direction simplifies because the angular difference $\phi_1 - \phi_2$ is constant. In this case the reflection geometry can be directly related to the surface normal. The originally four independent angles for the description of the BRDF reduce to three angles.

It is convenient to define the three photometric angles i, e, and g with respect to the surface normal **n** (see Fig. 6.3) where i is the angle between the surface normal and the illumination direction (*incident angle*), e is the angle between the surface normal and the reflection direction (*emittance angle, emergent angle*), and g is the angle between the illumination direction and the reflection direction (*phase angle*). Without loss of generality the reflection direction can be aligned to the viewer direction (optical axis) because only the radiation falling on the sensor has to be considered for our purposes.

6.3   REFLECTANCE MAPS

It is often assumed that the viewer direction does not change over the surface. This is only true for an (idealized) parallel projection. If the distance between the sensor and the object is large and if the object size does not exceed a certain level and if a large focal length is chosen then this approximates a parallel projection. The *viewer direction* is described by a vector **v** which points to the viewer (camera). Generally, an orthographic projection is assumed so that the viewer direction reduces to $\mathbf{v} = (0, 0, -1)$. This viewer direction is used as the standard viewer direction in Chapters 6, 7, and 8 when there is nothing different noted. Similarly the *illumination direction* can be described by a vector **s** which points to the light source. The vectors **n**, **s**, and **v** are related by

$$i = \angle\,(\mathbf{n},\mathbf{s})\ ,\quad e = \angle\,(\mathbf{n},\mathbf{v})\quad \text{and}\quad g = \angle\,(\mathbf{s},\mathbf{v})$$

to the photometric angles (see Section 6.2.5). Considering surface reflection properties and assuming non-varying illumination directions **s** and viewer directions **v** variations in the reflected radiation are solely caused by changes of the surface orientation. B.K.P. Horn (1977) introduced the so-called *reflectance map* to model this relationship between the reflected radiance and the surface orientation.

6.3.1   Definition and Representation

We can define reflectance maps as continuous or discrete functions. As known from Section 3.4.1 the surface orientation can be represented in different ways. Usually the gradient space representing the surface gradients (p, q) is chosen for reflectance maps because of its simplicity. In this case the reflectance map function is

$$R(p, q) \, .$$

Another useful representation are the stereographic coordinates f and g:

$$R_s(f, g) \, .$$

Furthermore, a general reflectance map can be defined by using the unit surface normal $\mathbf{n}^\circ$

$$R_n(\mathbf{n}^\circ)$$

(compare Section 3.1.2). The reflectance maps R and R_s can be seen as functions from the domain set $\Re^2$ to the range set $\Re$:

$$R, \, R_s : \Re^2 \to \Re.$$

They can be displayed by various visualization techniques, for example contour plots showing isoradiance curves which is the most common visualization type for reflectance maps.

6.3.2   Linear Reflectance Maps

During research work of reflection properties of the Maria of the moon (dark formations on the moon when observed from earth) it was found that the relationship between the reflected radiance and the gradient of the illumination direction can be modeled as being approximately linear under certain incident angles. The measured radiance is constant for the ratio between the cosine of the photometric angle i and the cosine of the photometric angle e. It follows that the reflectance map in gradient representation has the form

$$R(p,q) = E_0 \cdot \rho \cdot \frac{p_s \cdot p + q_s \cdot q + 1}{\|(p_s, q_s, -1)\|} \; .$$

In this reflectance map the illumination direction **s** is represented by its *illumination gradient* (p_s, q_s) where E_0 is the irradiance of the light source (the sun) and ρ is the albedo (see Section 6.2.4). Note that according to Section 3.1.2 three-dimensional vectors also allow a definition of gradients. *Linear reflectance maps* can be represented in the general form

$$R(p,q) = h(a \cdot p + b \cdot q).$$

The components p and q of the surface gradient are linearly combined using the coefficients a and b. The function h is arbitrary and generally strictly monotonic.

For a linear reflectance map represented in gradient space the points of equal radiance lie on parallel straight lines. As known from Section 3.4.2, the orientations which are represented in the gradient space by a straight line are parallel to a fixed plane in the three-dimensional space. In the case of linear reflectance all surface orientations which lie coplanar to such a plane are associated with the same (scene) radiance. Since the isoradiance lines are parallel their associated planes have a certain relationship to each other, in fact all planes have the same line of intersection which can be considered as a rotation axis for generating the planes.

How does the shading of a sphere look like that has linear reflectance? If we move the described rotation axis in such a way that it intersects the center of the sphere, then it defines a pencil of planes and each of these planes intersects the

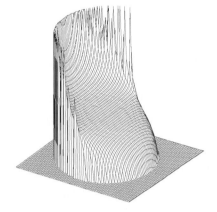

Figure 6.4: Irradiance image of a linearly shaded sphere (using the illumination gradient $(p_s, q_s) = (-0.5, 0)$) and three overlaid isoirradiance curves (left) and a grid representation of the irradiances (right).

sphere in a circle (great circle). All points of such a great circle on the sphere show the same scene radiance values (neglecting shadows).

The left picture in Fig. 6.4 shows the irradiance image[2] of a linearly shaded sphere. The gradient $(p_s, q_s) = (-0.5, 0)$ was used as illumination direction. Three isoirradiance curves are overlaid onto the irradiance image. Each curve describes locations of equal irradiance. The right picture of Fig. 6.4 shows a three-dimensional plot of the irradiance image where the irradiances were coded directly as height values.

Sections 7.2.1 and 8.2 describe shading based methods for recovering surface normals of surfaces whose reflection properties can be modeled by linear reflectance maps.

6.3.3   Lambertian Reflectance Maps

The radiance equation for a Lambertian reflector as defined in Sections 6.2.2 and 6.2.3 can be extended for a general Lambertian surface not being necessarily a Lambertian reflector. Let us assume that the surface has albedo ρ and is illuminated by a parallel radiating light source with irradiance E_0 under the incident angle i. Then the corresponding radiance equation is

$$L_1 = \frac{E_0}{\pi} \cdot \rho \cdot cos(i).$$

If the reflection geometry is described by the surface normal $\mathbf{n}$ and by the illumination direction $\mathbf{s}$ we get the equation

$$L_1 = \frac{E_0}{\pi} \cdot \rho \cdot cos \sphericalangle (\mathbf{n}, \ \mathbf{s}) \ .$$

Constant scaling factors are usually eliminated from the representation of reflectance maps. We will do so and omit the factor $1/\pi$ for the *Lambertian reflectance maps*. Consequently, the reflectance map

$$R_n(\mathbf{n}^\circ) = E_0 \cdot \rho \cdot \cos \sphericalangle (\mathbf{n}^\circ, \ \mathbf{s}) = E_0 \cdot \rho \cdot \cos \sphericalangle (\mathbf{n}, \ \mathbf{s})$$

corresponds to the above equation for a Lambertian surface. The cosine function can be eliminated by using the *scalar product*

$$\mathbf{a}^T \mathbf{b} = \|\mathbf{a}\| \cdot \|\mathbf{b}\| \cdot cos \sphericalangle (\mathbf{a}, \mathbf{b}) \ , \text{ with } \mathbf{a}, \mathbf{b} \ \in \ \Re^3.$$

---

[2] As already mentioned in Section 6.1.2 the scene radiance L and the image irradiance E can approximately be related by a scaling factor. This relation is discussed in Section 6.5.

Then the reflectance map takes the form

$$R_n(\mathbf{n}^\circ) = E_0 \cdot \rho \cdot \mathbf{n}^{\circ T} \mathbf{s}^\circ \ , \ \text{with} \ \mathbf{n}^\circ = \frac{\mathbf{n}}{\|\mathbf{n}\|} \ \text{and} \ \mathbf{s}^\circ = \frac{\mathbf{s}}{\|\mathbf{s}\|} \ .$$

If we represent the Lambertian reflectance map in gradient space it has the form

$$R(p,q) = E_0 \cdot \rho \cdot \cos \measuredangle \left((p, \ q, \ -1), \ \mathbf{s}\right).$$

The vector $(p, q, -1)$ describes the surface normal $\mathbf{n}$ (compare Section 3.1.2). If, in addition, the illumination direction is given as illumination gradient (p_s, q_s) the reflectance map can be represented as the scalar product

$$R(p,q) = E_0 \cdot \rho \cdot \frac{(p, \ q, \ -1)(p_s, \ q_s, \ -1)^T}{\|(p, \ q, \ -1)\| \cdot \|(p_s, \ q_s, \ -1)\|}$$

$$= E_0 \cdot \rho \cdot \frac{p \cdot p_s + q \cdot q_s + 1}{\sqrt{p^2 + q^2 + 1} \cdot \sqrt{p_s^2 + q_s^2 + 1}} \ .$$

Due to the known disadvantages of the gnomonic projection discussed in Section 3.4.1 it is sometimes convenient to represent Lambertian reflectance maps in stereographic coordinates. The above reflectance map can be formulated in stereographic coordinates using the normalized illumination direction $\mathbf{s}^\circ$ as

$$R_s(f,g) = E_0 \cdot \rho \cdot \frac{\left(4f, \ 4g, \ f^2 + g^2 - 4\right) \cdot \mathbf{s}^\circ}{4 + f^2 + g^2} \ .$$

One special case of the Lambertian reflectance map, the so-called *rotationally symmetric Lambertian reflectance map*, is of particular interest for shading based shape recovery methods that will be discussed Section 7.2.2 because it allows to solve the corresponding mathematical equations in a simpler way. If the illumination direction $\mathbf{s}$ is identical to the viewer direction $\mathbf{v}$, i.e. it holds that

$$\mathbf{s} = \mathbf{s}^\circ = \mathbf{v} = \mathbf{v}^\circ = (0, \ 0, \ -1)^T$$

the Lambertian reflectance map simplifies to

$$R(p,q) = E_0 \cdot \rho \cdot \frac{1}{\|(p, \ q, \ -1)\|} \ .$$

This reflectance map has some interesting properties. The maximal radiance of the reflectance map occurs for gradient $(p,q) = (0,0)$. All gradients in distance $r = \|(p,q)\|$ to the origin possess the same radiance value hence the reflectance map is rotationally symmetric. The value zero does not have a valid orientation

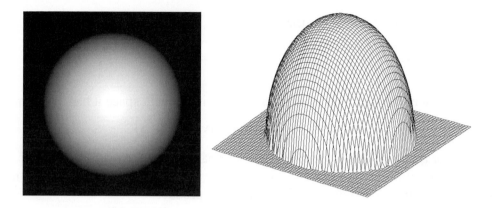

Figure 6.5: Irradiance image of a Lambertian shaded sphere using illumination gradient $(p_s, q_s) = (0, 0)$ and a three-dimensional plot of the image irradiances.

associated with it since orientations orthogonal to the orientation $\mathbf{n} = (0, 0, -1)$ lie at infinity in the gradient space and hence cannot be represented. Figure 6.5 shows on the left an irradiance image of a sphere that was shaded using a rotationally symmetric Lambertian reflectance map. A three-dimensional plot of the sphere image is shown on the right in Fig. 6.5.

If we use the stereographic coordinates f and g to represent the surface orientations the value zero is assigned to all orientations which lie on a circle with radius 2 and center located at the origin (compare Section 3.4.1). The property of the rotational symmetry holds for this representation as well. Figure 6.6 shows the reflectance map using the stereographic coordinates f and g. The values of the

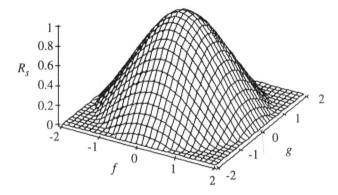

Figure 6.6: Rotationally symmetric reflectance map of a Lambertian surface under parallel illumination of direction $\mathbf{s} = \mathbf{v} = (0, 0, -1)$. Stereographic coordinates were chosen for representing the orientations.

reflectance map in the plot are normalized to $E_0 \cdot \rho$. Lambertian reflectance maps with $\mathbf{s} \neq \mathbf{v}$ are not rotationally symmetric but have nevertheless a common structure. If we consider $R(p,q)$ for an arbitrary but fixed radiance value c, i.e.

$$c = R(p,q) \, ,$$

a set of gradients (p, q) is associated with each c.

From an algebraic point of view a *conic section* corresponds to a radiance value c in the gradient space since the Lambertian reflectance map defines a second order algebraic curve (quadratic curve) for a fixed value of c. This can easily be shown by rearranging the equations. A second order curve has the form

$$a_{20} \cdot p^2 + a_{02} \cdot q^2 + 2a_{11} \cdot p \cdot q + 2a_{10} \cdot p + 2a_{01} \cdot q + a_{00} = 0 \, .$$

Figure 6.7 shows two different plots of the same reflectance map. The domain sets for both plots have to be restricted for visualization. Here, the interval [-12,12] was chosen for both p and q. $(p,q) = (\pm 12, 0)$ and $(p,q) = (0, \pm 12)$ represent orientations that have an angle of approximately $85.2°$ to the viewer direction $\mathbf{v}$. The angle is about $1.4°$ larger at the four corner points of the domain set, i.e. $(p,q) = (\pm 12, \pm 12)$ and $(p,q) = (\pm 12, \mp 12)$.

The second order curve as given above describes a point, a circle, an ellipse, a parabola, a hyperbola, or a straight line depending on the coefficients a_{ij}. Some of these conic sections occur only once in a reflectance map. Figure 6.7 shows the reflectance map (using the gradient space) of a Lambertian surface and

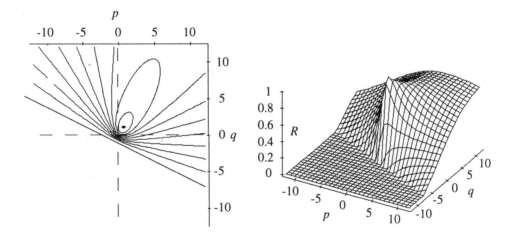

Figure 6.7: Reflectance map of a Lambertian surface in gradient space with illumination direction $\mathbf{s} = (0.5, 1, -1)$. The left picture shows an isoradiance contour plot. Every curve shows locations of equal radiance values. The picture on the right shows a three-dimensional plot of the Lambertian reflectance map.

gradient $(p_s, q_s) = (0.5, 1)$. The left hand side of Fig. 6.7 shows the reflectance map as isoradiance plot thus every curve shows orientations of equal scene radiance values (*isoradiance curves*). As we will see in Section 6.5 every isoradiance curve defines the location of equal irradiances in the image as well (compare footnote in Section 6.3.2). Consequently, these curves are also called *isoirradiance curves*.

The point in the isoradiance plot represents that gradient which is identical to the gradient (p_s, q_s) of the illumination direction and hence takes the maximal radiance value. The gradients lying on the straight line represent those surface normals which are orthogonal to the illumination direction (compare Section 3.4.2). The function value zero is assigned to them since surface patches oriented in this way cannot receive light from the light source.

The straight line is dual to the illumination gradient (p_s, q_s) (dual straight line, compare Section 3.4.2) and separates the gradient space into two half spaces. One half space represents orientations of surface points that can be illuminated by the chosen illumination direction. The other half space represents gradients of surface points that cannot be illuminated. The straight line separates the set of orientations into those which form an angle with the illumination direction which is smaller than 90° respectively greater than or equal to 90°. This line is therefore called *self-shadow line*. The relationship between the illumination gradient and the self-shadow line can be derived from the properties of the gradient space discussed in Section 3.4.2.

The distance between the illumination gradient (p_s, q_s) and the origin is reciprocal to the distance between the self-shadow line and the origin. Additionally, the illumination gradient and the self-shadow line are located on different sides of the origin. The self-shadow line is uniquely defined by the illumination gradient. The larger the declination of the illumination direction the closer the self-shadow line moves towards the origin of the gradient space.

Figure 6.8 shows a Lambertian reflectance map for illumination direction $\mathbf{s} = (0.5, 1, -1)$ using stereographic coordinates f and g. The domain set $[-2,2]$ was chosen for f and g. Note that the reflectance map contains orientations which are not visible from the viewer direction $\mathbf{v} = (0, 0, -1)$ (compare exercises in Section 6.7).

6.3.4   Generation of Reflectance Maps

We introduce two different algorithms to generate a reflectance map. The first algorithm assumes Lambertian reflection and a known illumination direction. This leads to an analytical description of the reflection. The second algorithm assumes

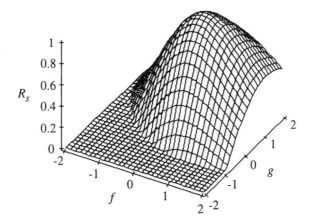

Figure 6.8: Reflectance map (in stereographic coordinates) of a Lambertian surface with illumination direction **s** = (0.5, 1, -1).

---

procedure *gen_lambertian_rmap*(p_s, q_s: **real**; *maxpq*: **real**; **var** *R*: *byteimage*);
    { domain set of the reflectance map in gradient space:
      $p,q \in$ [*-maxpq,+maxpq*],   *R* is the calculated reflectance map
      represented as byte image of size $M \times N$ }
function *xylin*(*xs,xe*: **real**; *ys,ye*: **real**; *x*: **real**): **real**;
    { linear transformation of a value *x* from interval [*xs,xe*] to [*ys,ye*] }
begin
    return *ys* + (*x-xs*)·(*ye-ys*)/(*xe-xs*)
end; { *xylin* }

var *p, q, h*: **real**;
begin
  for *y* := 1 **to** *N* **do for** *x* := 1 **to** *M* **do begin**
    p := *xylin*(1, *M*, -*maxpq*, *maxpq*, *x*); *q* := *xylin*(1, *N*, -*maxpq*, *maxpq*, *y*);
    $h := Gmax \cdot \dfrac{p \cdot p_s + q \cdot q_s + 1}{\left\| (p, \; q, \; -1) \right\| \cdot \left\| (p_s, \; q_s, \; -1) \right\|}$;
    call *ADJUST*(*h*, *R*(*x,y*)); { see Section 1.2.2 }
  end
end; { *gen_lambertian_rmap* }

Figure 6.9: Generation of a Lambertian reflectance map in gradient space for a given illumination direction **s** = (p_s, q_s, -1).

isotropic but not necessarily Lambertian reflection. It measures image irradiance values by using a calibration object of known shape leading to an empirical description of a reflectance map (*empirical reflection model*). Note once again we can make the assumption that image irradiance and scene radiance are equal up to scaling factor (see Section 6.5).

Figure 6.9 shows an algorithm to generate reflectance maps of a Lambertian surface for an arbitrary but fixed illumination gradient (p_s, q_s). This algorithm was used to calculate the reflectance map illustrated in Fig. 6.7. For real object scenes the illumination direction can be estimated with the method described later on in Section 8.3.3 if not already known. The radiance values are scaled so that the brightest value is 255.

For isotropically reflecting surface materials with unknown reflection characteristics the mapping of an orientation to a radiance value can be determined using a calibration object. We make the following assumptions. The calibration object has the same surface material as the surface we want to reconstruct later on by using a shading based shape recovery method (see Chapter 7 and 8). Note that only one surface material can be characterized by a single reflectance map.

The calibration object should have a simple and known geometry since we are to assign surface normals to all illuminated surface points projected in the image. The calibration object should contain as many different surface orientations as possible since we try to cover a large "area" of the new reflectance map. Therefore it is recommended to use a sphere as calibration object. The illumination direction is not needed for this empirical generation of a reflectance map. Figure 6.10 shows the algorithm for a spherical calibration object.

Figure 6.11 illustrates a calibration sphere of a surface material that approximately satisfies Lambert´s cosine law (compare Section 6.2.3). The left image shows the calibration sphere acquired with a CCD camera (see Section 2.2). A distant light source was used and leads to an approximately parallel illumination over the sphere. The light source was positioned to the left of, and slightly below, the camera. This sphere image could be taken as input for the algorithm shown in Fig. 6.10.

The picture on the right shows an isoirradiance plot of the sphere image. Each of the white "circle-shaped" curves represents points having identical irradiance values. These circles are not ideal since the image of the sphere is also influenced by projective foreshortening. Hence the curves become thinner towards the rim of the sphere. Additionally, the surface geometry is not smooth. Moreover, the surface of the sphere does not show a perfectly uniform and matte surface finish. The influence of noise which is introduced by the image acquisition system is good visible.

```
procedure gen_real_rmap( maxpq: real; E: byteimage; var R: byteimage);
        { domain set of the reflectance map in the gradient space:
          p,q∈ [-maxpq,+maxpq]. E is a byte image of the calibration
          sphere, image E is of size M× N,  R defined as in Fig. 6.9 }
var     p, q, r, cx, cy: integer;
        z: real;
        n : real_vector3;
begin
        calculate radius r and center (cx, cy) of the sphere in pixels;
        for y := -r to r do for x := -r to r do begin
                z := root(r·r - x·x - y·y); { compare Section 3.1.4 }
                n := (x, y, z) / r ; { orientation of sphere in (x,y) }
                p := xylin(-maxpq, maxpq, 1, M, −nₓ /n_z); {image coord.}
                q := xylin(-maxpq, maxpq, 1, N, −n_y /n_z); {image coord.}
                if p < 1 or p > M or q < 1 or q > N then
                        { slant angle of the orientation too large }
                else R(p, q) := E(x+cx, y+cy) { irradiance at (p,q) }
        end {for}
        fill gaps of R by interpolation;
end; {gen_real_rmap}
```

Figure 6.10: Generating a reflectance map in gradient space using a calibration sphere.

 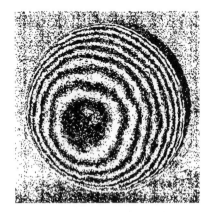

Figure 6.11: The left side shows an image of a real approximately Lambertian sphere. The sphere was illuminated by a single, approximately parallel radiating light source. The light source was positioned to the left of, and slightly below, the camera. The right side of the figure illustrates some isoirradiance curves of the sphere.

6.4   REFLECTION COMPONENTS

The previous section has explained how the reflection properties of surface materials in conjunction with parallel illumination can be described using reflectance maps. The simple reflection representation in the form of reflectance maps allows the description of the large class of isotropic reflecting materials which is of major advantage. If the reflection behavior is known as for Lambertian surfaces the knowledge of the albedo and the illumination direction is sufficient to generate a reflectance map since Lambertian reflection can be formulated analytically.

On the other hand, the generation of empirical reflectance maps is not easy since sampling and resolution insufficiencies arise as discussed in the previous section. High-quality data are required for an empirical description of reflection properties. Furthermore, a sample of the unknown reflecting material must exist and has to be mounted onto a spherical surface. This is practically impossible in many cases or would lead to high costs. For example, consider the attempt to describe the reflection properties of the surface of a watering can. Either metal can or plastic can - it is difficult to find a calibration object with a suitable geometry showing the same reflection properties as the watering can.

Although the watering can contains a large number of different orientations which could be used for constructing a reflectance map, this approach would contradict the goal of the subsequent surface reconstruction. A known geometry of the object is required for the analysis of the reflection properties but we actually want to recover the surface geometry of the watering can. This difficulty is reducible to a certain degree if the characterized reflection can be described by a small number of parameters.

Therefore it is necessary to formulate *analytical reflection models* in a more general way than already done for the Lambertian reflection. An analytical reflection model should satisfy the requirements of simplicity and should be physically plausible as much as possible. In general, it is assumed that the reflection is an additive composition of two *reflection components*, namely the diffuse reflection L_b and the specular reflection L_s: $L = L_s + L_b$.

Object surfaces showing such a kind of reflection can be called *hybridly reflecting surfaces*. In the following several relevant models will be introduced that comprise both reflection components.

6.4.1   Diffuse Reflection

The *diffuse reflection component* L_b (also called body reflection component) is modeled as uniformly reflected radiation caused by penetration of light into the surface with internal, multiple light-material interactions and subsequent emittance. The internal scattering arises from microscopic inhomogeneities in the surface medium which is, e.g., caused by color particles. Reflection, refraction, and scattering are the major light-material interactions inside the surface. This process is called *internal scattering*. The uniformity of the undirected reflected radiation is independent from the direction of the incoming light.

Because of its properties the diffuse reflection component is usually modeled by Lambert´s cosine law (see Section 6.2.3) though there exists no complete physical explanation of Lambert´s cosine law. The assumption of diffusely reflecting surfaces is made by most computer vision methods including binocular stereo analysis and motion analysis, but some methods belonging to these classes exist which are especially designed for non-diffusely reflecting objects. For the sake of simplicity it is also useful to make this assumption for shading based methods described in the following chapters.

However even for objects showing an apparently matte surface finish certain limitations exist for using Lambert´s cosine law. In particular for rough surfaces such as sand, rough plaster and rough sandpaper the diffuse reflection is not independent from the viewer direction. Moreover, it can be observed that surfaces showing the mentioned characteristics appear in total brighter when the viewer direction approaches the illumination direction.

For example, a cylindrically shaped object would appear flatter than expected. Its brightness decreases slower towards the rim of the object than Lambert´s cosine law would predict. A number of models are known for the description of these characteristics. Such generalizations of Lambert´s cosine law are only possible when additional parameters are introduced. This leads again to the problem that it is difficult to calculate these parameters for an object of unknown geometry in advance.

6.4.2 Specular Reflection

In contrast to the diffuse reflection component many models exist for the description of the *specular reflection component* L_s (also called interface reflection component). In principle there are two different ways to describe specular reflection, approaches that use physical optics (wave optics) and approaches which apply models from *geometrical optics*. Approaches of *physical optics* use the electromagnetic theory for the analysis of the reflection where the Maxwell equations constitute the mathematical basis. The application of geometrical optics is a lot simpler, but it can be used only if the wavelength of the incoming light is small compared to the roughness of the material. Consequently, reflection models which are derived from geometrical optics can always be approximations of the wave-optical reflection models.

Two general representatives of these approaches are the *Beckmann-Spizzichino model* (physical optics) and the *Torrance-Sparrow model* (geometrical optics). Simplifications of both reflection models are used in computer vision and computer graphics to describe the specular component.

The Beckmann-Spizzichino model describes the specular reflection by two additively overlapping components usually called *specular spike* and *specular lobe*. The *specular spike*-component models a portion of the reflection which only occurs in a very narrow range of angles around the direction of perfect specular (mirror-like) reflection. The diffuse portion of the specular reflection is modeled by the lobe component. It describes the scattering reflection caused by the surface roughness.

The larger the roughness the more the light scatters around the direction of perfect specular reflection. For a perfect mirror the lobe component is zero and the spike component is very large. Both rough surfaces and smooth surfaces can be modeled with the Beckmann-Spizzichino model. But, in general, there is the limitation to electrically conducting materials. Moreover, it should be mentioned that a combination of both components is only of significance for a small range of roughness values.

The Torrance-Sparrow model describes the specular reflection for surfaces whose roughness is large compared to the wavelength of the light. It models the surface by planar, perfectly specular reflecting microfacets whose orientations are normally distributed around the macroscopic surface orientation which is visually inferable. The mathematical formula mainly comprises a Fresnel term, the geometrical attenuation factor, and a Gaussian normal distribution. The Fresnel term describes the reflection behavior depending on the illumination direction **s**, on the viewer direction **v**, and on the refraction index of the surface material. Note that the refraction index depends on the wavelength.

The Torrance-Sparrow model has a by far greater significance than the Beckmann-Spizzichino model. One reason for this is the good approximation of the lobe component of the Beckmann-Spizzichino model by the Torrance-Sparrow model. On the other hand, the spike component is not of great importance for the majority of surface materials.

Details of the general Torrance-Sparrow model can be found in the extensive literature of computer graphics (see Section 6.6 for a few references). In computer vision a simplified version of the Torrance-Sparrow model is used to describe the specular reflection component. The Fresnel term and the geometric attenuation factor are usually assumed to be constant for this simplified model. This assumption holds for many configurations of objects, light sources, and

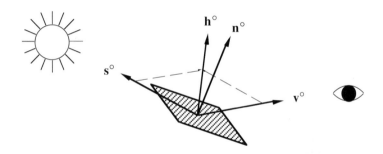

Figure 6.12: Geometric relationships between the surface normal $\mathbf{n}°$, the illumination direction $\mathbf{s}°$, the viewer direction $\mathbf{v}°$, and the halfway-vector $\mathbf{h}°$.

viewer directions without a significant loss of accuracy in computer vision. The simplified specular reflection term of the Torrance-Sparrow model,

$$L_{s,\,Torrance-Sparrow} = k \cdot e^{-\left(\frac{\arccos(\mathbf{n}°\mathbf{h}°)}{m}\right)^2} \quad , \text{ with } \mathbf{h}° = \frac{\mathbf{s}° + \mathbf{v}°}{\|\mathbf{s}° + \mathbf{v}°\|}$$

contains only the following unknown parameters: the normalized surface orientation $\mathbf{n}°$, the root mean square (rms) m of the microfacet normals, a scaling factor k and the normalized illumination direction $\mathbf{s}°$. The parameter m is the surface roughness parameter of the surface and describes to what extent a normal of a microfacet deviates from the average (macroscopic) surface normal.

The vector $\mathbf{h}°$ is usually called *halfway*-vector and represents the normalized vector sum between the illumination direction $\mathbf{s}°$ and the viewer direction $\mathbf{v}°$. If the incident angle $\measuredangle\,(\mathbf{s}°,\mathbf{n}°)$ and the emittance angle $\measuredangle\,(\mathbf{v}°,\mathbf{n}°)$ are equal the above term takes its maximum value. In this case the exponent is zero since the vectors $\mathbf{h}°$ and $\mathbf{n}°$ coincide. Figure 6.12 illustrates the relationship between the four vectors $\mathbf{n}°$, $\mathbf{s}°$, $\mathbf{v}°$, and $\mathbf{h}°$. Because of the reciprocal exponential term the observed reflection decreases quickly when the angle $\measuredangle\,(\mathbf{h}°,\mathbf{n}°)$ increases. The parameter m controls how fast this decrease should occur globally. For smooth surfaces the decrease is faster than for rough surfaces.

Besides the simplified Torrance-Sparrow model the *Phong model* is used in computer vision and in computer graphics. The specular term

$$L_{s,\,Phong1} = k \cdot (\mathbf{n}°\mathbf{h}°)^n$$

of the Phong model can also be adapted for surfaces of varying roughness. This is done by changing the exponent n. The larger n the smoother the surface will be. The left diagram of Fig. 6.13 shows an irradiance profile (cross-section) through the image of a synthetically shaded sphere by using a Lambertian reflectance map

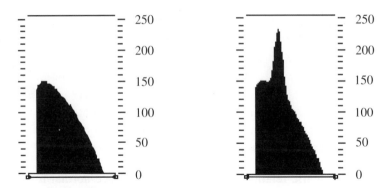

Figure 6.13: Irradiance profiles (cross-sections) through a diffusely reflecting sphere (left) and a hybridly reflecting sphere (right).

with illumination direction $s = (1, 1, -1)$. The linear profile was "drawn" by using an angle of 45° from the north-east to the south-west going through the center of the sphere. Hence, the profile has the same direction as the tilt of the illumination direction s.

The right picture of Fig. 6.13 displays the irradiance image of the same sphere, but here the reflectance map was extended by the Phong term shown above. A roughness value of $n = 100$ was chosen. The ratio between the diffuse and the specular component is 3:2. The irradiance values were scaled to the interval [0,255]. Alternatively to the above representation the Phong term can be given without the *halfway*-vector by the slightly more complex formula

$$L_{s,Phong2} = k \cdot ((2\mathbf{n}°(\mathbf{n}°\mathbf{s}°) - \mathbf{s}°)\mathbf{v}°)^n \quad .$$

Note that identical exponents n of the two Phong terms do not model the same surface roughness.

6.4.3 Dichromatic Reflection Model

A model that describes hybrid reflection properties without specifying the diffuse and the specular reflection component explicitly is the so-called *Dichromatic Reflection Model* (*DRM*). This model can be used for inhomogeneous dielectric materials whose surface structure can be modeled as being composed of an interface and an optically neutral medium containing color pigments. Figure 6.14 illustrates the principal structure of such an inhomogeneous dielectric.

The interface separates the surface from the environment which is usually air. If the distribution of the color pigments is uniform and the pigments display the same optical behavior then it can assumed that the penetrating light does not have a specific direction when it leaves the surface. The reflection associated with this is called *body reflection* and models the diffuse reflection component as introduced in Section 6.4.1. Part of the radiation falling on the object surface does not penetrate the medium and is reflected by the interface which is called *interface reflection*. It models the specular reflection component with microfacets as shown in the previous section. Mathematically, the Dichromatic Reflection Model can be formulated in the following way:

$$L(\lambda, \mathbf{n}, \mathbf{s}, \mathbf{v}) = L_s(\lambda, \mathbf{n}, \mathbf{s}, \mathbf{v}) + L_b(\lambda, \mathbf{n}, \mathbf{s}, \mathbf{v})$$

$$= m_s(\mathbf{n}, \mathbf{s}, \mathbf{v}) \cdot c_s(\lambda) + m_b(\mathbf{n}, \mathbf{s}, \mathbf{v}) \cdot c_b(\lambda) \ .$$

The modeled scene radiance L is a quantity that depends on the wavelength λ. As known from the previous sections the scene radiance further depends on the surface normal $\mathbf{n}$, on the illumination direction $\mathbf{s}$, and on the viewer direction $\mathbf{v}$. L is an additive composition of the radiance of the *interface reflection* L_s and of the *body reflection* L_b.

The essential assumption of the Dichromatic Reflection Model is that both reflection components can be factorized into a geometrical component and a spectral component as given in the above formula. The geometrical components are m_s and m_b. The spectral components are c_s and c_b. The factor c_s is called *interface reflection color* and c_b *body reflection color*. The factorization of the interface reflection only holds when the same assumptions are made as in the case of the simplified Torrance-Sparrow model introduced in the previous section. The factorization of the body reflection is feasible without any further significant restrictions.

With the additional assumption of a neutral reflecting interface c_s describes the spectral distribution (color) of the light source. This special case of the Dichro-

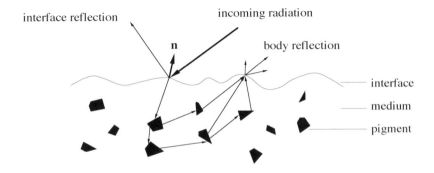

Figure 6.14: Simple model of an inhomogeneous dielectric material.

matic Reflection Model is called *Neutral Interface Reflection Model* (*NIRM*). The geometrical component m_s can be made explicit by the formulas of the simplified Torrance-Sparrow model, the Phong model or other models. But the particular advantage of the DRM is that the geometric component of the specular reflection does not have to be modeled explicitly to apply the DRM for various tasks. The scaling factor m_b can be usually modeled by Lambert´s cosine law as discussed in Section 6.4.1.

If the description of the scene radiance L is restricted to three narrow wavelength bands in the red, green, and blue spectral range of the visible light then the scene radiance can be represented as a three-dimensional color vector $\mathbf{L}$ (compare Section 2.2):

$$
\begin{aligned}
\mathbf{L} &= \begin{pmatrix} L(\mathrm{Re}\,d, \mathbf{n}, \mathbf{s}, \mathbf{v}) \\ L(Green, \mathbf{n}, \mathbf{s}, \mathbf{v}) \\ L(Blue, \mathbf{n}, \mathbf{s}, \mathbf{v}) \end{pmatrix} \\
&= \mathbf{L}_s + \mathbf{L}_b \\
&= m_s(\mathbf{n}, \mathbf{s}, \mathbf{v}) \cdot \mathbf{c}_s + m_b(\mathbf{n}, \mathbf{s}, \mathbf{v}) \cdot \mathbf{c}_b \\
&= m_s(\mathbf{n}, \mathbf{s}, \mathbf{v}) \cdot \begin{pmatrix} c_{s,R} \\ c_{s,G} \\ c_{s,B} \end{pmatrix} + m_b(\mathbf{n}, \mathbf{s}, \mathbf{v}) \cdot \begin{pmatrix} c_{b,R} \\ c_{b,G} \\ c_{b,B} \end{pmatrix}.
\end{aligned}
$$

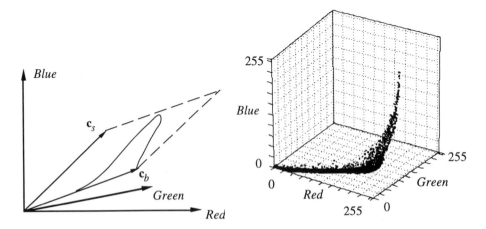

Figure 6.15: Left: Dichromatic plane of a curved, hybridly reflecting object showing one color. Right: An *L*-shaped color cluster of a real, orange watering can (see Fig. 6.16, left) represented as color histogram.

Figure 6.16: The left side shows the image of a real, orange watering can showing a large highlight (compare Color Image 4 in the Appendix). The right side shows a picture of the watering can after removal of the specular reflection. The six gray patches of the GretagMacbeth ColorChecker® was used to linearize the camera (compare Section 2.3.2).

Since, from the mathematical point of view, m_s and m_b represent arbitrary scaling factors the vectors $\mathbf{c}_s$ and $\mathbf{c}_b$ form a two-dimensional sub-space (a plane) in the RGB color space (*dichromatic plane, color-signal plane*).

It can be observed that the colors in the dichromatic plane form *T*- and *L*-shaped clusters if the object has sufficiently many and different surface orientations.

Figure 6.15 shows on the left the outline of a typical *L*-shaped cluster and on the right the cluster for the real orange watering can (see Fig. 6.16, left). If the object shows several hybridly reflecting materials one cluster arises for every material. The representations shown in Fig. 6.15 are called *color histograms*. Contrary to gray value histograms color histograms only have binary values. Color histograms only code whether a certain color exists in the image or not. Both the DRM and the NIRM are of great importance in physics-based computer vision. For example, it is possible to separate the reflection components and hence to remove the specular reflection component (highlights) from images by analyzing color histograms.

Figure 6.16 displays an example of such a highlight removal. The left picture shows the original image of a watering can. The right picture shows the watering can after the elimination of the specular reflection component using the DRM. These reflection models can also be used to remove interreflections (see next section), color image segmentation, color classification, and color object recognition. Publications exist that show how good DRM and NIRM model the reflection properties for many materials.

6.4.4   Interreflections

Up to now it was assumed that every object surface point is illuminated only by one light source. However, this only holds when the object has a convex shape and no other objects are in the environment. As soon as the object contains concavities every surface point that is visible from other surface points receives secondary radiation hence *interreflections* (also called *mutual illuminations*) arise. If the environment comprises more objects they will influence each other as secondary light sources as well. We also speak of intra-object and inter-object interreflections to distinguish between the two kinds of interreflections.

Interreflections are independent from the viewer direction and therefore do not negatively influence binocular stereo and motion based methods (Chapters 4 and 5). However they affect shading based methods since the reflection models that they use usually describe the interactions between light and surfaces only locally. There exist some approaches which treat the effects of interreflections as post processing step or iteratively. Figure 6.17 illustrates interreflections by means of the synthetically shaded section of a Mozart statue which contains several concavities. The Mozart statue was shaded using a rotationally symmetric Lambertian reflectance map and hence illumination direction $s° = (0, 0, -1)$. The right picture of Fig. 6.17 shows the calculated intra-object interreflections. The gray values of the image were scaled for better visualization since the intensity of interreflections is low compared to the primary light source.

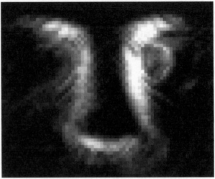

Figure 6.17: The left picture shows a section of a synthetically shaded Mozart statue. The right image displays the interreflections as scaled gray values.

6.5 IMAGE IRRADIANCE EQUATION

Up to now (apart from some anticipating exceptions in the previous sections) we did not take the relation between the scene radiance and the image irradiance as well as the characteristics of the image acquisition system into account. It remains to relate the radiance reflected from the object surfaces (scene radiance) to its counterpart, the *measured image irradiance* of the imaging sensor.

6.5.1 Image Formation

It can be shown that the relation between the reflected radiance L and the image irradiance E can be represented with certain simplifications by

$$E = L \cdot \frac{\pi}{4} \cdot \frac{d^2}{f^2} \cdot cos^4(\alpha)$$

(Horn and Sjoberg (1979)), where d is the diameter of the lens, f is its focal length and α is the angle between the optical axis and the light ray going through the center of the observed small solid angle (see Fig. 6.18). For the sake of clarity the illustration only shows the central ray of the solid angle. The above relationship was derived by making the following assumptions.

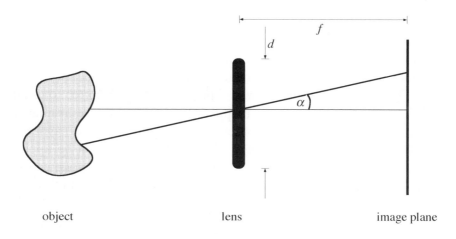

object   lens   image plane

Figure 6.18: Simple model of the image formation process (according to Horn and Sjoberg (1979)).

1. The projection system is focused.

2. The irradiance E is only caused by the radiance L. There is no other radiation.

3. There is no vignetting (no reduction of image irradiance with an increasing off-axis angle)

4. There is no light reduction as a result of transmission.

5. The influence of refraction can be neglected.

If it can also be assumed that the influence of the angle α is constant over the whole image, then the relationship between the image irradiance E and the scene radiance L can be defined by a simple proportionality (scaling factor).

6.5.2   General Equation

This relationship in conjunction with a reflectance map R leads to the *image irradiance equation*

$$E(x,y) = c \cdot R(p,q) \; ,$$

where c is the mentioned scaling factor. Since the surface gradient (p,q) depends on the world coordinates X and Y but the image irradiance E is given in terms of the image coordinates x and y, this equation implicitly contains the assumption of an orthographic projection as it was already assumed for defining the reflectance map in Section 6.3.

If, additionally, the image irradiance is proportional to the values measured by the imaging sensor and the digitization system then the relationship between the scene radiance and the measured image irradiance (gray value) of the image is linear, too. Normal video cameras have a built-in gamma recorrection (compare Section 2.3.1) which is a non-linear mapping between the image irradiances and the gray values. Therefore a photometric calibration must be carried out to linearize the camera before the image irradiance equation can be applied. As already mentioned in Section 6.3.3, for simplification purposes we can usually neglect scaling factors and the image irradiance equation is often represented in the literature by

$$E(x,y) = R(p,q) \; .$$

Therefore the function $E(x, y)$ in this equation can be regarded as image irradiance function and as measured image irradiance function, and we will not further distinguish between image irradiances and measured image irradiances in the following chapters.

The image irradiance equation is the most important tool to describe the relationship between irradiances, scene radiances, and surface gradients. The image irradiance equation is the basis for the shading based shape recovery methods which will be discussed in the following chapters.

6.6   REFERENCES

A discussion of radiometric and photometric quantities which are relevant for computer vision is offered by

Haralick, R.M., Shapiro, L.G.: *Computer Vision and Robot Vision*. Vol. I and II, Addison-Wesley, Reading, Massachusetts, 1993.

The bidirectional reflectance-distribution function (BRDF) was defined by F.E. Nicodemus et al. at the National Bureau of Standards of the U.S.A. in 1977 in

Nicodemus, F.E., Richmond, J.C., Hsia, J.J., Ginsberg, I.W., Limperis, T.: *Geometrical Considerations and Nomenclature for Reflectance (Monograph 160)*. U.S. Department of Commerce, National Bureau of Standards, Washington, 1977.

The reflectance map was introduced in the paper

Horn, B.K.P.: *Understanding image intensities*. Artificial Intelligence **8** (1977), pp. 201-231.

The derivation of reflectance maps for various kinds of materials using the corresponding BRDF and various illumination distributions is explained in

Horn, B.K.P., Sjoberg, R.W.: *Calculating the reflectance map*. Applied Optics **18** (1979), pp. 1770-1779 and in
Horn, B.K.P.: *Robot Vision*. The MIT Press, Cambridge, Massachusetts, 1986.

General models for reflectance maps can be found in

Tagare, H.D., deFigueiredo, R.J.P.: *A framework for the construction of reflectance maps for machine vision*. CVGIP: Image Understanding **57** (1993), pp. 265-282.

A good description of geometrical optics and physical optics can be found in

Hecht, E.: *Optics*. 3rd Ed, Addison-Wesley, Reading, Massachusetts, 1997.

The generalization of the Lambertian model to rough surfaces is given in

Nayar S.K., Oren, M.: *Generalization of the Lambertian Model and Implications for Machine Vision*. Int. Journal of Computer Vision **14** (1995), pp. 227-251.

A comprehensive comparison of the Beckmann-Spizzichino model and the Torrance-Sparrow model (Section 6.4) is presented in

Nayar, S.K., Ikeuchi, K., Kanade, T.: *Surface reflection: physical and geometrical perspectives*. IEEE Transactions on Pattern Analysis and Machine Intelligence **13** (1991), pp. 611-634.

A detailed description of general reflection models (Section 6.4) can be found in computer graphics books such as

Foley, J.D., van Dam, A., Feiner, S.K., Hughes, J.F.: *Computer Graphics: Principles and Practice*. 2nd Ed, Addison-Wesley, Reading, Massachusetts, 1990,

Watt, A., Watt, M.: *Advanced Animation and Rendering Techniques: Theory and Practice*, ACM Press, New York, 1993, and

Hall, R.: *Illumination and Color in Computer Generated Imagery*. Springer-Verlag, New York, 1989.

A survey of different reflection models is given in

Schlick, C.: *A survey of shading and reflectance models*. Computer Graphics Forum **13** (1994), pp. 121-131.

An extended discussion of the Dichromatic Reflection Model (Section 6.4.3) can be found in

Klinker, G.J., Shafer, S.A., Kanade, T.: *The measurement of highlights in color images*. Int. Journal of Computer Vision **2** (1988), pp. 7-32

where the author takes also the necessary sensor characteristics into consideration. The above article as well as

Klinker, G.J., Shafer, S.A., Kanade, T.: *A physical approach to color image understanding*. Int. Journal of Computer Vision **4** (1990), pp. 7-38

contain an approach to separate reflection components in color images. An efficient method for separating the reflection components in color images as shown in Fig. 6.16 is presented in

Schlüns, K., Teschner, M.: *Fast separation of reflection components and its application in 3D shape recovery*. Proc. IS&T/SID 3rd Color Imaging Conference, Scottsdale, Arizona, USA, 1995, pp. 48-51.

6.7 EXERCISES

(1) An illumination direction is given in terms of the stereographic coordinates $(f, g) = (0.5, 1)$. Describe the corresponding Lambertian reflectance map in gradient space.

(2) Assume a given linear reflectance map. The angle between the parallel lines and the p-axis is ϑ. Which orientation does the rotation axis of the isoradiance planes have? Hint: Use the properties of points and lines in the gradient space as discussed in Section 3.4.2.

(3) Show that besides the rotationally symmetric Lambertian reflectance map represented in the gradient space the corresponding reflectance map represented by stereographic coordinates is rotationally symmetric as well.

(4) How does the shape of the reflectance map from Fig. 6.8, which is represented in terms of stereographic coordinates, change when it is restricted to visible orientations? Would there be a change for the rotationally symmetric reflectance map in Fig. 6.6, too?

(5 - Assignment) Extend the algorithm for the generation of synthetic reflectance maps (Fig. 6.9) with the simplified Torrance-Sparrow model as discussed in Section 6.4.2.

6.7   EXERCISES

7 SHAPE FROM SHADING

The reconstruction of non-planar surfaces from a single irradiance image is one of the classic tasks in scene analysis. This goal is theoretically as well as practically challenging: How can we determine the three-dimensional shape of an object from its irradiances in a single image by using its reflection properties? This problem is called *Shape from Shading* (*SFS*).

The goal can be outlined easily but the search for suitable methods and restrictions of the problem is all the harder. SFS is one of the classic ill-posed problems of scene analysis (see Section 1.1.2). As we can imagine there is not sufficient information contained in an arbitrary irradiance image to reconstruct the object surface unambiguously.

Firstly, this chapter states some restrictions of SFS (Section 7.1) to specify an approach to SFS. Each of the subsequent sections (7.2 - 7.4) covers a selected class of SFS methods. All techniques assume a known reflectance map which models the illumination and the reflection properties of the object surface (see Section 6.3).

7.1 INTRODUCTION

Chapters 2, 3, and 6 have discussed a number of factors that influence the measured irradiances of an image. Firstly, the image which is acquired by the sensor depends on the geometrical and spectral distribution of the light source which illuminates the observed scene. The individual objects of the scene are characterized by their geometry and by their reflection properties. The geometry and the reflection properties affect the light falling on the imaging sensor. The imaging system converts the light to measured image irradiances. Therefore, it also has a considerable influence on the measured image irradiance values. Summarized, four different scene factors interact with each other:

measured image irradiance =

illumination (Chapter 6) $\oplus$ reflection (Chapter 6) $\oplus$

geometry (Chapter 3) $\oplus$ sensor (Chapter 2) .

At this stage a comparison with computer graphics is useful to illustrate the information contained in a measured image irradiance value. A considerable amount of information is required to generate a realistic computer graphical picture. First, a spectral illumination model has to be chosen which should be based on the Torrance-Sparrow model (see Section 6.4). Furthermore, shadows and surface textures have to be generated. Raytracers and radiosity-methods are necessary for realistic generation of multiple reflections. Each of these components of a computer graphics system depends on a number of parameters which have to be known in advance to generate the image. Now we have to study the inverse process.

7.1.1 SFS Constraints

SFS methods try to infer the geometry of an object from a single image. For this inversion, the above mentioned factors and their influences have to be considered for the conceptual design of a SFS method. Thus, compared to computer graphics we have to solve the above equation with respect to the geometry (compare Section 1.1.2). The only a-prioi constraint is that only the geometry has to be extracted from the image.

An additional goal could be to extract the reflection properties from the given image, as well, to obtain a more complete description of the visible surface. In this case the above equation for the measured image irradiance must be solved for the geometry and the reflection properties.

This discussion should clarify that it would never be possible to infer unambiguous geometrical properties of objects from image irradiances without restricting the problem. In the following the most common assumptions of SFS methods are summarized to improve the ability of getting an unambiguous surface reconstruction from a single image. However, it has to be stressed that many SFS methods, even with very restrictive assumptions, conceptually do not allow to reconstruct an unambiguous surface. The design of SFS methods, that allow a mathematical proof of existence and uniqueness of a solution, is still a subject of research .

Now let us briefly discuss which constraints arise if one or several scene factors in the measured irradiance equation are known.

Illumination: The irradiance and the direction of the illumination are known. There are no intra-object or inter-object interreflections, i.e. scene objects do not act as secondary light sources. In general a light source is assumed which emits parallel light of a constant irradiance from a constant and known illumination direction **s**. If the illumination direction **s** coincides with the viewer direction **v**, SFS simplifies significantly. Some SFS methods exist that assume a close point light source, hence the light rays cannot be modeled as parallel. Approaches that assume diffuse illumination (e.g. sky illumination) form another special case. Furthermore, the effects of the inverse square law are usually disregarded (see Section 6.1.4).

Reflection: The reflection properties of the object surfaces are known. For additional simplification, linearly reflecting surfaces (see Section 6.3.2) or Lambertian surfaces (see Section 6.2.3) are often assumed where the albedo ρ is constant and known for the entire object.

Illumination + Reflection: The interaction between a light source and reflection properties can be described by a reflectance map (see Section 6.3), hence a unique scene radiance value is assigned to each surface orientation. In general the reflectance map has to be known. Sometimes it is assumed that the reflectance map can be approximated as being locally or globally linear (see Section 6.3.2).

Geometry: The reconstructed surface is continuous or continuously differentiable (see Section 3.1.1). Some methods exist which are especially designed to reconstruct polyhedral objects. In general it has to be assumed that height values respectively orientations are known in certain (singular) points in advance. Of special interest are boundary points showing zero-irradiances (occluding boundaries, see Section 4.2.4) and points of maximal irradiance. Sometimes it is assumed that the surface can be locally approximated as a plane (facet model, see Section 3.1.1) or as a sphere.

Sensor: The sensor is linear (see Section 2.3). This assumption is made throughout Chapters 7 and 8.

Projection: SFS methods usually assume an orthographic projection. But there exist also methods that assume perspective projection.

After stating this list of possible constraints two comments are appropriate: First, the above assumptions can be reduced by extracting some parameters from the scene which were expected to be known. For example, usually only the product of the irradiance E_0 of the light source and the albedo ρ has to be determined and not their individual values. If parallel illumination, a Lambertian reflection, and an orientation $\mathbf{n}^*$ in the scene which coincides with the illumination direction $\mathbf{s}$ are assumed ($\mathbf{n}^* = \mathbf{s}$) then the product $E_0\rho$ can be read from the maximal irradiance value.

Second, in practice many of the constraints (except two of them) prove to be rather uncritical restrictions. One exception is the condition of an albedo ρ that is constant over the whole object which corresponds to a uniform coloring. The problem is reduced when only few albedo values occur on the surface since the

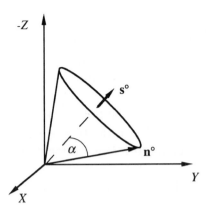

Figure 7.1: For a Lambertian surface the surface normals $\mathbf{n}^\circ$ which are consistent with the image irradiance E form the lateral area of a right circular cone.

albedo can be extracted from the image under certain conditions. Chapter 8 will show how independence from the albedo can be achieved using several light sources. The other critical assumption is the limitation to Lambertian surfaces since beside the diffuse component many materials exhibit a considerable amount of specular reflection.

In spite of all the assumptions, SFS remains extremely complicated. This is illustrated with a formal example making the following assumptions: parallel and constant illumination from direction $\mathbf{s}^\circ$, Lambertian surface, constant albedo ρ, and a known product $E_0\rho$. According to Lambert's cosine law and the image irradiance equation it holds

$$E = E_0\rho \cdot cos(\alpha), \text{ with } \alpha = \measuredangle\,(\mathbf{n}^\circ,\mathbf{s}^\circ)$$

for the irradiance E and an orientation $\mathbf{n}^\circ$ (compare Sections 6.3.3 and 6.5.2). Now we try to calculate the local surface orientation at an image point of irradiance E. The term $cos(\alpha)$ and hence the angle α can be calculated from the known quantities. All vectors which subtend the angle α with the illumination direction are solutions to the above equation.

The Gaussian sphere is useful to represent these solutions (see Section 3.4.1). Without loss of generality we can restrict the surface orientations to unit surface normals $\mathbf{n}^\circ$. Then the solution vectors $\mathbf{n}^\circ$ form the lateral area of a right circular cone. The vertex of the cone lies at the center of the Gaussian sphere. The orientation of the cone (vector of the cone axis) is determined by the illumination direction $\mathbf{s}^\circ$. Figure 7.1 illustrates the cone.

The boundary of the circular base of the cone touches the surface of the Gaussian sphere. These points on the Gaussian sphere are surface orientations satisfying the equation for the image irradiance E. When using the gradient space representation (see Section 3.4) the valid gradients are represented by conic sections (see Section 6.3.3). We see that usually an infinite number of solutions exist. If the measured image irradiance E is identical to the product $E_0\rho$, then a singularity occurs. In this case $\alpha = 0°$ which implies that $\mathbf{n}° = \mathbf{s}°$.

Therefore, the surface orientation and the value of the product $E_0\rho$ can be uniquely determined. If we assume that there exists at least one such orientation in the image then we only have to search for the maximal image irradiance to find these points.

7.1.2   Classification of SFS Methods

SFS methods can be classified into three classes. Propagation methods develop the object surface over its domain area of projection in the image starting from points of known height values. Such methods are discussed in Section 7.2.

Global minimization methods have in common that they look at the image information as a whole. The formulation of a functional and the choice of a suitable minimization approach are the most important issues for these approaches. For example, there exist calculus of variations methods (Section 7.3.3) as well as minimization approaches such as conjugate gradient methods. Global minimization based methods are presented in Section 7.3.

Local methods are the third class of SFS approaches. They can be regarded as the opposite pole to the global minimization methods since they calculate the surface geometry from a small neighborhood of each image point. Clearly, such techniques can only recover surface orientations and not height values. Section 7.4 explains a representative of this class of SFS techniques.

The above classification is one possible way to group SFS methods. The transitions are often fuzzy. Alternatively, the classification can also be carried out by assigning other attributes to the methods, such as:

(a)   The method works iteratively or non-iteratively.

(b)   The method uses only one resolution or a resolution hierarchy (multi-grid methods).

(c)   The method calculates surface orientations, height values or both simultaneously.

(d)   The method needs (or does not need) a set of known orientations or height values for initialization.

(e)   The method assumes perspective projection or parallel projection.

(f) The method recovers (or does not recover) the illumination direction.

We make the following assumptions throughout this chapter: parallel light rays, constant illumination over the object surface, a continuously differentiable surface, an orthographic projection, and a linear sensor. Additionally, all assumptions apply that were already made prior to the introduction of the image irradiance equation (see Section 6.5).

7.1.3   Direct Interpretation of Image Irradiances

Before discussing the three different classes of SFS methods, let us look at a curious phenomenon of the three-dimensional interpretation of image irradiances. Under certain conditions irradiance images can be directly interpreted as gray value encoded height maps (compare Section 3.2.1). The real images that are shown in Fig. 7.2 illustrate to what extent such a simple interpretation is possible. These four images are part of set of images that are often used in the literature to evaluate SFS methods.

We assume a rotationally symmetric Lambertian reflectance map. According to these assumptions the illumination direction $\mathbf{s}° = \mathbf{v}° = (0, 0, -1)$ is orthogonal to the image plane and the object surface exhibits a perfectly diffuse reflection with a uniform albedo ρ (Lambertian surface). Then, the following theorem holds for a spherical surface.

Theorem 7.1: Under the assumption of a (rotationally symmetric) Lambertian reflectance map with $p_s = q_s = 0$ the irradiance image of a sphere corresponds (up to a known scaling factor) to its relative height map.

Proof: Assume that the center of the sphere is located at the point (a,b,c) in the three-dimensional space. Let r be the radius of the sphere. The points of the visible surface of the sphere are described by the position vectors

$$\mathbf{x} = \begin{pmatrix} X_t \\ Y_t \\ Z_t(X_t, Y_t) \end{pmatrix} = \begin{pmatrix} X + a \\ Y + b \\ c - \sqrt{r^2 - X^2 - Y^2} \end{pmatrix}, \text{ with } X^2 + Y^2 \leq r^2$$

(compare Example 3.2). The normal $\mathbf{n}°$ at a point of the sphere is equal to

$$\mathbf{n}° = \frac{1}{r} \cdot \begin{pmatrix} X \\ Y \\ -\sqrt{r^2 - X^2 - Y^2} \end{pmatrix}, \text{ with } X^2 + Y^2 \leq r^2 .$$

Figure 7.2: Irradiance images of SFS test images: Lenna (above left), mannequin (above right), mask (below left), and vase (below right).

The generated irradiance image $E(x, y)$ under orthographic projection ($x = X$, $y = Y$) has the form

$$E(x = X, y = Y) = E_0\rho \cdot \mathbf{n}°\mathbf{s}° = E_0\rho \cdot \frac{\sqrt{r^2 - X^2 - Y^2}}{r} \ , \ \text{with} \ \mathbf{s}° = \begin{pmatrix} 0 \\ 0 \\ -1 \end{pmatrix} .$$

The surface function $Z_t(X_t, Y_t)$ of the sphere can be related to the image irradiance function $E(x = X_t, y = Y_t)$ by the equation

$$c - Z_t(X_t, Y_t) = \frac{r}{E_0\rho} \cdot E(x = X_t, y = Y_t) .$$

The scaling factor is therefore

$$r/(E_0\rho) \ .$$

Q.E.D.

The constant c can be chosen arbitrarily because absolute height values cannot be recovered. Theorem 7.1 states that the image of a sphere corresponds to its relative height map under the made assumptions. The sphere is not the only object showing this nice property. Another example is the irradiance image of a torus whose axis of rotational symmetry is orthogonal to the projection plane (see Exercise (2) in Section 7.6).

Furthermore, all objects of a subclass of the generalized cylinders have the described property. This subclass contains generalized cylinders whose generating space curve (called axis, compare Footnote 1 in Section 3.1.1) is coplanar to the projection plane.

In addition, the cross-sections of the generalized cylinders are circular with a constant radius and perpendicular to the tangent to the axis (right uniform circular generalized cylinders).

The three-dimensional plots of the irradiances belonging to the images shown in Fig. 7.2 are presented in Fig. 7.3. The three-dimensional impression is quite surprising. This impression can be achieved although these images belong by no means to the image class discussed above. The Lenna face has no uniform albedo which even increases the pseudo three-dimensional effect, for example at the eyes.

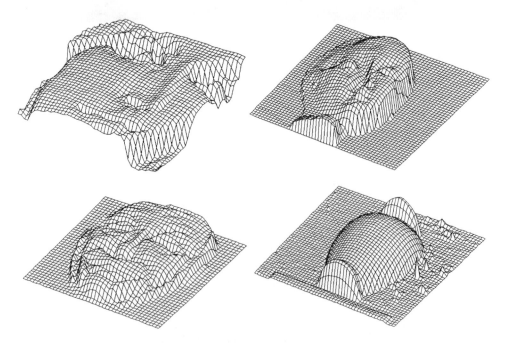

Figure 7.3: Three-dimensional plots of the images shown in Fig. 7.2. In particular for the vase (bottom right) the 3D-effect is rather good.

7.2 PROPAGATION METHODS

SFS methods which develop the surface over the object region by starting from points of known orientation or height values are called *propagation methods*. The growing process is performed iteratively or along certain linear or curved paths in the image. These paths can depend on the image content, i.e. on the image irradiances. This section follows the excellent description of propagation methods as given in B.K.P. Horn (1986).

7.2.1 Linear Reflectance Maps

In the case of linear reflection the reflectance map R in gradient space is formulated

$$R(p,q) = h(a \cdot p + b \cdot q)$$

as already presented in Section 6.3.2. The function h is assumed to be arbitrary but strictly monotonic, hence it has an inverse function h^{-1}. All points of equal scene radiance form a straight line in the gradient space (see Section 3.4). All these straight lines are perpendicular to the straight line $\ell : b \cdot p - a \cdot q = 0$ which passes through the origin and through the point (a,b). Figure 7.4 illustrates such a reflectance map.

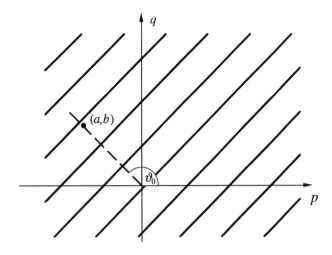

Figure 7.4: Contour plot of a linear reflectance map in the gradient space. The isoradiance curves are parallel lines. These lines are perpendicular to the straight line defined by the origin and the point (a,b).

Furthermore, it is assumed that the function h as well as the parameters a and b are known. These are the results of the modeling phase of the reflectance map where the surface material is studied under specific illumination. The modeling process can be based on approximating straight lines to the gradient space. It follows from the image irradiance equation (see Section 6.5) that the surface gradients (p, q) consistent with a measured image irradiance $E(x, y)$ can be described by the straight line

$$a \cdot p + b \cdot q = h^{-1}(E(x,y)) .$$

The following method was described by B.K.P. Horn (1986) to recover the surface of an object based on this equation. Let $m(\vartheta)$ be the slope of the surface in an arbitrary direction ϑ with respect to the image $E(x,y)$. The slope could be determined using the directional derivative (see Section 3.1.2)

$$m(\vartheta) = p \cdot cos(\vartheta) + q \cdot sin(\vartheta)$$

if p and q were already known for the image point (x, y). If we choose a special direction $\vartheta = \vartheta_0$ then p and q do not have to be known to calculate $m(\vartheta = \vartheta_0)$. The normalized direction vector of this direction is

$$\left(cos(\vartheta_0),\ sin(\vartheta_0)\right) = \left(\frac{a}{\sqrt{a^2 + b^2}},\ \frac{b}{\sqrt{a^2 + b^2}} \right) ,\ \text{with}\ \vartheta_0 = \arctan\!\left(\frac{b}{a}\right) .$$

This direction is identical to the direction of the straight line ℓ which was defined above. Therefore, the slope $m(\vartheta_0)$ of the surface in this particular direction can be calculated by

$$m = m(\vartheta_0) = \frac{a \cdot p + b \cdot q}{\sqrt{a^2 + b^2}} = \frac{h^{-1}(E(x,y))}{\sqrt{a^2 + b^2}} .$$

Since the right most term of this equation contains exclusively known parameters, the slope of the surface in the particular direction $\vartheta = \vartheta_0$ can be determined from the irradiance at an image point (x, y). The slopes p and q in direction of the coordinate axes x and y of the image still remain unknown, but we are able to propagate the relative height values of the surface along the direction $\vartheta = \vartheta_0$ as it will be shown now.

If we take a small step $\delta\chi$ in direction $\vartheta = \vartheta_0$ in the image starting from an image point (x_0, y_0), then this step is associated with a change in height $\delta Z = m \cdot \delta\chi$ on the surface. In particular this holds for an infinitesimal small step $d\chi$:

$$\frac{dZ}{d\chi} = m(\vartheta_0) = \frac{h^{-1}(E(x_0, y_0))}{\sqrt{a^2 + b^2}} .$$

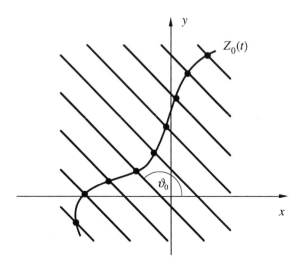

Figure 7.5: Propagation of a surface along characteristic curves starting at a curve $Z_0(t)$ of known Z values. For a linear reflectance map the characteristic curves are parallel lines.

If the height value Z_0 at the point (x_0, y_0) is known in advance, then all Z values can be determined along the direction $\vartheta = \vartheta_0$ by calculating a line integral:

$$Z(\chi) = Z_0 + \int_0^\chi \frac{dZ}{d\chi} \, d\chi$$

$$= Z_0 + \frac{1}{\sqrt{a^2 + b^2}} \int_0^\chi h^{-1}(E(x_0 + \chi \cdot \cos(\vartheta_0), \ y_0 + \chi \cdot \sin(\vartheta_0))) \, d\chi \ .$$

If only a single height value Z_0 is known, then the surface can only be reconstructed along this particular linear path. This path is usually called a *characteristic curve* or just a *characteristic*. The surface can be completely reconstructed if starting values are known along a curve $Z_0(t)$ which is not parallel to the direction $\vartheta = \vartheta_0$. Figure 7.5 shows the propagation paths of a surface starting at such a curve. The direction $\vartheta = \vartheta_0$ depends on the parameters of the reflectance map.

Example 7.1: We consider the irradiance image of size 256×256 shown in Fig. 6.4 which is given by

$$E(x, y) = \begin{cases} \dfrac{E_0 \rho}{\sqrt{1.25}} \left(\dfrac{-0.5x}{\sqrt{100^2 - (x - 128)^2 - (y - 128)^2}} + 1 \right) & , \text{ for } x^2 + y^2 < 100^2 \\ 0 & , \text{ otherwise.} \end{cases}$$

Let us assume that the object in the image shows a linear shading (what is the case for Fig. 6.4) and the equation of the reflectance map is

$$R(p,q) = \frac{E_0\rho}{\sqrt{1.25}} \cdot (-0.5p + 1) \ .$$

When we define the function

$$h(x) = \frac{E_0\rho}{\sqrt{1.25}} \cdot x + 1$$

the linear reflectance map can be represented in its standard form

$$R(p,q) = h(a \cdot p + b \cdot q) \ ,$$

where the parameters are $a = -0.5$ and $b = 0$. The inverse function of $h(x)$ is

$$h^{-1}(x) = \frac{\sqrt{1.25}}{E_0\rho} \cdot x - 1 \ .$$

From the parameters a and b we see that the particular image direction is $\vartheta_0 = 0°$. By using the outlined method we assume the position

$$P_0 = (x_0 = X_0, y_0 = Y_0, Z_0)$$

as starting point with depth value Z_0 for the propagation process of the surface along the straight line

$$\ell: \quad y = \frac{\sin(\vartheta_0)}{\cos(\vartheta_0)} \cdot (x - x_0) + y_0 = y_0$$

in the image. It is assumed that the starting point in the image is inside the object region. The line integral

$$Z(\chi) = Z_0 + \frac{1}{\sqrt{a^2 + b^2}} \int_0^\chi h^{-1}(E(x_0 + \chi \cdot \cos(\vartheta_0), \ y_0 + \chi \cdot \sin(\vartheta_0))) \, d\chi$$

$$= Z_0 + 2 \int_0^\chi h^{-1}(E(x_0 + \chi, y_0)) \, d\chi$$

$$= Z_0 + 2 \int_0^\chi \frac{\sqrt{1.25}}{E_0\rho} \frac{E_0\rho}{\sqrt{1.25}} \left(\frac{-0.5(x_0 + \chi)}{\sqrt{100^2 - (x_0 + \chi - 128)^2 - (y_0 - 128)^2}} + 1 \right) - 1 \, d\chi$$

can be simplified to

$$Z(\chi) = Z_0 - \int\limits_{0}^{\chi} \frac{(x_0 + \chi)}{\sqrt{100^2 - (x_0 + \chi - 128)^2 - (y_0 - 128)^2}}\, d\chi$$

and solved by using some substitutions and the integration rule

$$\int \frac{x}{\sqrt{\alpha - x^2}}\, dx = -\sqrt{\alpha - x^2} \; .$$

This leads to

$$Z(\chi) = Z_0 + \sqrt{100^2 - (x_0 + \chi - 128)^2 - (y_0 - 128)^2} \; \Big|_0^\chi$$

$$= \Delta Z + \sqrt{100^2 - (x_0 + \chi - 128)^2 - (y_0 - 128)^2}$$

with

$$\Delta Z = Z_0 - \sqrt{100^2 - (x_0 - 128)^2 - (y_0 - 128)^2} \; .$$

The function $Z(\chi)$ describes semi-circles of radius

$$r = \sqrt{100^2 - (y_0 - 128)^2}$$

which are parallel to the $Z=0$-plane. The projections of their centers are located at the image points $(128, y_0)$. If an initial image curve

$$(x_0(t), y_0(t)) = (128, t)$$

and the corresponding height values

$$Z_0(t) = c - \sqrt{100^2 - (128 - t)^2}$$

with an arbitrary constant c are known then the integration along the base characteristics leads to the shape of a sphere. { end of Example 7.1 }

7.2.2   Rotationally Symmetric and General Reflectance Maps

The general case of a rotationally symmetric reflectance map, where the center of rotation is located at the origin of the gradient space, is given by the equation

$$R(p, q) = h(p^2 + q^2)$$

(see Section 6.3.3). Let the function h be strictly monotonic like in the previous section so that it has an inverse function h^{-1}. Additionally, assume that h is differentiable:

$$h'(x) = \frac{dh(x)}{dx} \; .$$

The locations of equal radiance in the gradient space are concentric circles. For rotationally symmetric reflectance maps the slopes m can be calculated in direction of the gradient of the surface by the formula

$$m = \sqrt{p^2 + q^2} = \sqrt{h^{-1}(E(x, y))} \; , \quad \text{with} \quad E(x, y) = R(p, q) \; .$$

Similar to the previous section, the surface slope can be recovered and the gradient direction cannot be recovered. The direction of the gradient of the unknown surface $Z(x=X, y=Y)$ at an image point (x, y) can be represented as the unit vector

$$grad^{\circ}(Z(x = X, y = Y)) = (\frac{p}{\sqrt{p^2 + q^2}}, \frac{q}{\sqrt{p^2 + q^2}}) \; .$$

If we take a step of length $\sqrt{p^2 + q^2} \cdot \delta\chi$ in the direction of the gradient then this results in the following changes in the directions x, y, and Z:

$$\delta x = p \cdot \delta\chi \; ,$$

$$\delta y = q \cdot \delta\chi \; ,$$

$$\delta Z = (p^2 + q^2) \cdot \delta\chi = h^{-1}(E(x, y)) \cdot \delta\chi \; .$$

The changes δp and δq in p and q can be linearly estimated with the equation

$$\delta p = \frac{E_x}{2 \cdot h'} \cdot \delta\chi \quad \text{and} \quad \delta q = \frac{E_y}{2 \cdot h'} \cdot \delta\chi$$

by using the first partial derivatives E_x and E_y of the image irradiance function. Now, if we let $\delta\chi \to 0$ then the following five equations of χ arise

$$\frac{dx(\chi)}{d\chi} = \dot{x}(\chi) = p \; , \qquad \frac{dy(\chi)}{d\chi} = \dot{y}(\chi) = q \; ,$$

$$\frac{dZ(\chi)}{d\chi} = \dot{Z}(\chi) = p^2 + q^2 , \quad \frac{dp(\chi)}{d\chi} = \dot{p}(\chi) = \frac{E_x}{2 \cdot h'} \; , \quad \text{and}$$

$$\frac{dq(\chi)}{d\chi} = \dot{q}(\chi) = \frac{E_y}{2 \cdot h'} \; ,$$

which is a system of ordinary differential equations. This system can be solved numerically by using known starting values. The arising curves which are generated by the parameter χ are called characteristic curves, too. Since the characteristic curves have the direction of the irradiance gradient (E_x, E_y) they are perpendicular to the isoheight curves of the surface.

B.K.P. Horn (1986) shows that this approach can be further generalized to arbitrary reflectance maps of the form $R(p,q)$. Again, five ordinary differential equations of χ arise:

$$\frac{dx(\chi)}{d\chi} = \dot{x}(\chi) = \frac{\partial R(p,q)}{\partial p} \ , \quad \frac{dy(\chi)}{d\chi} = \dot{y}(\chi) = \frac{\partial R(p,q)}{\partial q} \ ,$$

$$\frac{dZ(\chi)}{d\chi} = \dot{Z}(\chi) = p \cdot \frac{\partial R(p,q)}{\partial p} + q \cdot \frac{\partial R(p,q)}{\partial q} \ ,$$

$$\frac{dp(\chi)}{d\chi} = \dot{p}(\chi) = E_x \ , \quad \text{and}$$

$$\frac{dq(\chi)}{d\chi} = \dot{q}(\chi) = E_y \ .$$

Note that all right sides of the five equations can be calculated from the reflectance map and from the irradiances of the image $E(x,y)$. This set of differential equations can be solved when initial values are given.

7.2.3   More Robust Methods

The propagation techniques from the beginnings of SFS research which were introduced up to now grow an object surface starting with known points along certain characteristic curves. Unfortunately, this means that the errors in the reconstructed Z values can grow along the characteristic curves, as well. The reason for this lies in the strongly local determination of the Z values because only a single known Z value is used for the calculation of the next Z value on the characteristic curve. The remaining information for the change of the Z value is contained completely in the local image irradiances.

More recent propagation approaches try to determine the Z value of a particular image point **p** using a small neighborhood of **p**. The method by M. Bichsel and A.P. Pentland (1992) initially determines possible surface slopes in various directions of the image (directional derivatives, see Section 3.1.2) in a pre-processing step. The facet model from Section 3.1.1 is used for modeling of the surface geometry. As already known, a set of surface orientations which satisfy the image irradiance equation can be assigned to every image irradiance value E. If a direction ϑ is given in the image, then a corresponding set of slopes in direction ϑ can be determined using the directional derivative.

```
begin
        initialize the height map;
        rotate the irradiance image by the angle α;
        generate M×N×8 image with directional derivatives in 8-neighborhood;
        for n:= 1 to number of iterations do begin
                for every image point do
                        increment Z value with optimal directional derivative;
                change scanning direction of the image;
        end; {for}
        rotate irradiance image back by the angle -α
end;
```

Figure 7.6: Iterative propagation according to M. Bichsel and A.P. Pentland (1992).

This set of slopes usually has two extreme values. From this pair of slopes that particular slope is chosen for which the surface develops in inverse illumination direction -s. The complete set of slopes consists of eight values because the directions are defined by an 8-neighborhood.

With this approach a slope can be assigned to every image point and to each of the eight directions. To avoid infinite slopes in the neighboorhood of small irradiances, the image should be rotated by an angle α. This angle is chosen in such a way that one of the discrete directions (for example a diagonal direction) approximately coincides with the tilt angle of the illumination direction.

The actual reconstruction process starts after this pre-processing operation. In every step of the iterative process it is assumed that the surface has already

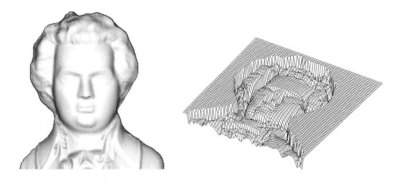

Figure 7.7: Lambertian shaded image with $s°=v°=(0, 0, -1)$ of the height map of a Mozart statue and a three-dimensional plot of the irradiances of the Mozart image.

been constructed to some degree. For the calculation of a new Z value it is checked which one of the eight calculated slopes of the surface would propagate the surface most strongly into the illumination direction. The old Z value is incremented with the maximal slope. This propagation rule ensures that the iteration converges after a certain number of steps.

For the initialization of the iteration it is assumed that the Z values are known for a certain set of singular points or for the object boundary. The number of required points depends on the complexity of the object. One to twelve singular points were used in the publication by M. Bichsel and A.P. Pentland (1992). If the initial points are given at the object boundary, then the number of required points depends on the shape of the contour. Because of the rotation in the pre-processing step the height map has to be rotated back by the angle $-\alpha$ after the last iteration. Figure 7.6 shows a sketch of the algorithm. Note that the image irradiances only contribute to the calculation of the maximum slopes during the pre-processing step. For the iterative calculation of the height values they are not needed anymore.

The left picture of Fig. 7.7 shows the synthetic irradiance image of a Mozart statue which represents a popular test object for SFS algorithms like the images in Fig. 7.2. The image was generated by shading of a height map using a rotationally symmetric Lambertian reflectance map. The picture on the right of Fig. 7.7 shows the three-dimensional plot of the Mozart image. Figure 7.8 shows the reconstruction of the Mozart statue using the method by M. Bichsel and A.P. Pentland (1992). Eight iterations were carried out. The Z value of a single (singular) point located at the tip of the nose was used to initialize the iteration sequence of the method. No further information was supplied.

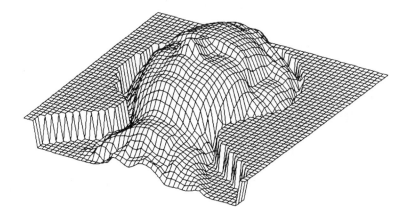

Figure 7.8: Three-dimensional plot of the height map of a synthetic Mozart statue, reconstructed with the method by M. Bichsel and A.P. Pentland (1992).

7.3   GLOBAL MINIMIZATION APPROACHES

The topic of this section are SFS methods which incorporate the entire set of an image's irradiances into the surface reconstruction through minimizing a functional[1] without propagating the reconstruction along certain paths. The functional can be represented in various forms. Beside a formulation of suitable restrictions the choice of an appropriate approach to determine the minimum is an important aspect of global SFS methods. Calculus of variations which solve associated differential equations and techniques of optimization theory are typical classical approaches.

7.3.1   Formulation of Constraints

First, some constraints are described which often occur in SFS functionals. The so-called *irradiance constraint (brightness constraint)* is the most important constraint on the surface variety supplied by the irradiance image.

For a representation of the surface orientations in the gradient space the irradiance constraint has the form

$$\mathbf{F}b_1(p,q) = \iint_\Omega \big(E(x,y) - R(p(x,y),q(x,y))\big)^2 \; dxdy \; .$$

This condition is used in almost all global minimization techniques. Ω is the image region where the object is located which has to be reconstructed. $E(x,y)$ is the image irradiance function. The function $R(p(x,y),q(x,y))$ represents the reflectance map (see Section 6.3). Note that $x = X$ and $y = Y$ (orthographic projection). The irradiance constraint associates ("compares") the image irradiance function with the reflectance map and reflects that for reconstructed gradients (p,q) the radiances (respectively irradiances) in the reflectance map have to be as similar as possible to the corresponding measured irradiances for all region points. The optimal case is an equality where the functional is equal to zero. The term E-R is squared to emphasize differences and to ensure non-negative values.

Two further formulations of the irradiance constraint with other representations of the surface orientations are

$$\mathbf{F}b_2(f,g) = \iint_\Omega \big(E(x,y) - R_s(f(x,y),g(x,y))\big)^2 \; dxdy \; ,$$

where the orientations are represented as stereographic coordinates (see Section 3.4.1), respectively

---

[1] A functional $\mathbf{F}$ is a mapping $\mathbf{F}(f_1, f_2, ..., f_n)$ into the range of real numbers which has the functions $f_1, f_2, ..., f_n$ as arguments. In this book the arguments describe the surface function.

$$\mathbf{F}b_3(\mathbf{n}^\circ) = \iint_\Omega \left(E(x, y) - R_n(\mathbf{n}^\circ) \right)^2 \; dxdy \; ,$$

where the orientations are represented by unit normals. The reflectance maps R_s and R_n are already defined in Section 6.3.1.

It is obvious that the irradiance constraint alone is not sufficient for a unique determination of the surface normally since a set of infinitely many surface orientations is consistent with each measured irradiance. The ambiguity of the surface can be restricted further by the conditions stated in the following.

One way of further restriction is the comparison of the similarity of neighboring orientations. This is also called *regularization* of the SFS problem. The more different two neighboring orientations are, the more unlikely it is that the reconstructed surface does not contain any discontinuities, i.e. the surface would not be smooth. Therefore this restriction is called *smoothness constraint*. The smoothness constraint is formulated differently depending on the representation of the surface orientations. Four derivatives have to be examined to control the smoothness in all directions. These derivatives are the two partial derivatives of the surface gradients in x- direction and in y-direction. The functional

$$\mathbf{F}s_1(p_x, p_y, q_x, q_y) = \iint_\Omega \left(p_x^2(x, y) + p_y^2(x, y) + q_x^2(x, y) + q_y^2(x, y) \right) \; dxdy$$

evaluates these four derivatives. The argument functions of the functional are related to the surface $Z(x,y)$ through the terms

$$p_x(x, y) = \frac{\partial p(x, y)}{\partial x} = \frac{\partial^2 Z(x, y)}{\partial x^2} \; ,$$

$$p_y(x, y) = \frac{\partial p(x, y)}{\partial y} = \frac{\partial^2 Z(x, y)}{\partial x \partial y} \; ,$$

$$q_x(x, y) = \frac{\partial q(x, y)}{\partial x} = \frac{\partial^2 Z(x, y)}{\partial y \partial x} \; , \quad \text{and}$$

$$q_y(x, y) = \frac{\partial q(x, y)}{\partial y} = \frac{\partial^2 Z(x, y)}{\partial y^2} \; .$$

The above smoothness constraints weights each of the four variations in the surface gradient equally where the second partial derivatives are squared for the already mentioned reasons. The functional "prefers" surfaces which contain only small orientation changes in a small neighborhood. The optimal case would be a single planar surface patch.

For SFS methods that include image points with orientations orthogonal to the optical axis (occluding boundaries, see Section 3.1.2) the gradient space representation cannot be applied for specifying an additional constraint since the gradient is undefined for occluding boundaries. The stereographic projection (see Section 3.4.1) is defined for these orientations, and the functional has the form

$$\mathbf{F}s_2(f_x, f_y, g_x, g_y) = \iint_\Omega \left(f_x^2(x, y) + f_y^2(x, y) + g_x^2(x, y) + g_y^2(x, y) \right) \, dxdy \ ,$$

where

$$f_x(x, y) = \frac{\partial f(x, y)}{\partial x}, \quad f_y(x, y) = \frac{\partial f(x, y)}{\partial y}, \quad g_x(x, y) = \frac{\partial g(x, y)}{\partial x}, \quad g_y(x, y) = \frac{\partial g(x, y)}{\partial y}$$

are the partial derivatives. The stereographic coordinates f and g are related to the gradients (p, q) of the surface through the equation

$$f(x, y) = \frac{2p(x, y)}{1 + \sqrt{1 + p^2(x, y) + q^2(x, y)}} \quad \text{and} \quad g(x, y) = \frac{2q(x, y)}{1 + \sqrt{1 + p^2(x, y) + q^2(x, y)}}$$

(see Section 3.4.1). Alternatively to the smoothness condition $\mathbf{F}s_1$ the functional

$$\mathbf{F}s_3(p_x, q_y) = \iint_\Omega \left(p_x^2(x, y) + q_y^2(x, y) \right) \, dxdy$$

is also used. In comparison to $\mathbf{F}s_1$ it constrains the surface less since it does not include the mixed partial derivatives. If the orientations are represented as unit normals, then the smoothness condition takes the following form:

$$\mathbf{F}s_4(\mathbf{n}_x, \mathbf{n}_y) = \iint_\Omega \left(\|\mathbf{n}_x(x, y)\|^2 + \|\mathbf{n}_y(x, y)\|^2 \right) \, dxdy \ .$$

In this case the derivatives

$$\mathbf{n}_x(x, y) = \frac{\partial \mathbf{n}(x, y)}{\partial x} \quad \text{and} \quad \mathbf{n}_y(x, y) = \frac{\partial \mathbf{n}(x, y)}{\partial y}$$

are the variations in the surface orientation in x-direction and in y-direction. Note that somehow the functionals $\mathbf{F}s_1$ and $\mathbf{F}s_3$ are more comparable with each other than the functionals $\mathbf{F}s_3$ and $\mathbf{F}s_4$, even though they have a similar form. This is caused by the fact that the surface orientation

$$\mathbf{n}(x, y) = \begin{pmatrix} p(x, y) \\ q(x, y) \\ -1 \end{pmatrix}$$

already contains the first partial derivatives. The smoothness constraint can also
be formulated in the frequency domain with the equation

$$\mathbf{F}s_5(Z) = \tfrac{1}{2\pi} \iint_\Omega \left((u^2 + v^2) \| F(Z(x,y)) \|^2 \right) \, dudv \ ,$$

where $F(Z)$ is the Fourier transform of the surface $Z(x,y)$ and (u,v) are the frequencies in x-direction and in y-direction, respectively. The higher the frequencies
u and v become, the larger is the output of the above functional. Beside the
positive regularization effect, the smoothness constraint unfortunately tends to
lead to over-smoothed surfaces. This is very undesirable since it results in a loss
of information in the surface reconstruction process.

Now, another very important restriction of the surface orientations inside a
small neighborhood is shown. Without any further constraints the gradients of the
reconstructed surfaces can be inconsistent with respect to each other even if the
smoothness constraint is satisfied. Inconsistency in this context means that the
first derivatives of the surface are not continuous. For such gradient vector fields
the equations

$$\frac{\partial^2 Z(x,y)}{\partial x \partial y} = \frac{\partial^2 Z(x,y)}{\partial y \partial x} \quad \text{respectively} \quad \frac{\partial p(x,y)}{\partial y} = \frac{\partial q(x,y)}{\partial x}$$

are not satisfied.

As a result, the integration process (see Section 3.3) can lead to different Z
values for the same image point when using different integration paths. Therefore,
there is no unique relationship between the gradient field of the surface and the
relative Z values of the surface anymore. The so-called *integrability constraint*
can be employed to take this problem into account as it was introduced in Section
3.1.1. Depending on the approach whether the SFS method generates a gradient
field or directly calculates Z values (respectively both at the same time) two
different formulations

$$\mathbf{F}i_1(p_y, q_x) = \iint_\Omega \left(p_y(x,y) - q_x(x,y) \right)^2 \, dxdy \quad \text{and}$$

$$\mathbf{F}i_2(Z_x, Z_y, p, q) = \iint_\Omega \left((Z_x(x,y) - p(x,y))^2 + (Z_y(x,y) - q(x,y))^2 \right) \, dxdy$$

are possible. The functional $\mathbf{F}i_1$ describes the integrability using gradients, whereas the comparison of the derivative of the reconstructed Z values with the reconstructed gradients is performed by functional $\mathbf{F}i_2$.

If we compare the derivative of the reflectance map and the derivative of
the image irradiance function then the irradiance constraint takes the form

$$\mathbf{F}d(p,q) = \iint_{\Omega} \left(\begin{array}{c} \left(R_x(p(x,y),q(x,y)) - E_x(x,y) \right)^2 \\ -\left(R_y(p(x,y),q(x,y)) - E_y(x,y) \right)^2 \end{array} \right) dxdy$$

which is called *irradiance gradient constraint* (*intensity gradient constraint*). This condition is sometimes used to substitute the smoothness condition and to get around the already described disadvantages. Another constraint that can be taken to design a global SFS method is the *unit normal constraint*. This constraint enforces that the reconstructed orientations are normalized:

$$\mathbf{F}n(\mathbf{n}) = \iint_{\Omega} \left(\|\mathbf{n}(x,y)\|^2 - 1 \right) dxdy \ .$$

On one hand, the length of a reconstructed normal can vary if small variations in the albedo occur. On the other hand, the length can deviate from unity if all three components of the normal vector are estimated at the same time. The unit normal constraint tries to cope with these variations.

7.3.2   Combination of Constraints

As already mentioned, the described functionals can be combined with each other, for example

$$\mathbf{F}k_{Ikeuchi\ and\ Horn}(f,g,f_x,f_y,g_x,g_y) = \mathbf{F}s_2(f_x,f_y,g_x,g_y) + \lambda \cdot \mathbf{F}b_2(f,g) \ .$$

The arguments of the double integrals are added in such a way that the functional $\mathbf{F}k_{Ikeuchi\ and\ Horn}$ can be described by the integral

$$\iint_{\Omega} \left(\begin{array}{c} f_x^2(x,y) + f_y^2(x,y) + g_x^2(x,y) + g_y^2(x,y) + \\ \lambda \cdot \left(E(x,y) - R_s(f(x,y),g(x,y)) \right)^2 \end{array} \right) dxdy.$$

The scaling factor λ models the weighting of the irradiance constraint and the smoothness constraint, where the smoothness constraint has implicitly the weighting factor 1. Thus, λ can control what influence the two constraints should have on the reconstruction process. The choice of such a factor has to be carried out carefully. In general it can only be determined by doing experiments. To understand the influence of λ it can be helpful to look at the extreme cases.

If $\lambda = 0$, then the irradiance constraint does not affect the reconstruction process at all and therefore the entire image irradiance information is lost and the SFS problem degenerates. The minimum is achieved by a plane.

If $\lambda \gg 0$, the smoothness term (which can now be disregarded in relation to the irradiance condition) does not have any influence on the reconstruction process. Every orientation which satisfies the image irradiance function at a certain image point is a local optimum. Therefore, an arbitrary set of locally consistent orientations minimizes the functional.

Now, we present some combinations of functionals that can be found in the literature. The first functional contains the combination of three constraints:

$$\mathbf{Fk}_{Brooks\,and\,Horn} = \mathbf{F}b_3 + \lambda \cdot \mathbf{F}s_4 + \mu \cdot \mathbf{F}n \ .$$

The factors λ and μ again reflect the weighting of the constraints. The functional

$$\mathbf{Fk}_{Horn\,and\,Brooks} = \mathbf{F}b_1 + \lambda \cdot \mathbf{F}i_1$$

offers an example for the application of an integrability constraints. Other functionals used in SFS methods are

$$\mathbf{Fk}_{Horn} = \mathbf{F}b_1 + \lambda \cdot \mathbf{F}g_1 + \mu \cdot \mathbf{F}i_2 \ ,$$

$$\mathbf{Fk}_{Zheng\,and\,Chellappa} = \mathbf{F}b_1 + \mathbf{F}d + \mu \cdot \mathbf{F}i_2 \ , \text{ and}$$

$$\mathbf{Fk}_{Zhang\,and\,Shah} = \mathbf{F}b_1 + \lambda \cdot \mathbf{F}s_1 \ .$$

The functional of R. Zhang and M. Shah has a certain similarity to the functional by B.K.P. Horn. R. Zhang and M. Shah approximate the gradients with simple differences of the Z values of the reconstructed surface. For the minimization of the functional the surface is completely represented by its Z values and therefore without any gradient information.

All listed functionals of this subsection are ordered chronologically according to the date of publication (1981-1994).

7.3.3   SFS as a Variational Problem

The previous section described a number of functionals for constraining the surface. Now, we show ways to minimize functionals. Thus, assume a task where a surface has to be found which minimizes a given functional. The aim is to find an absolute minimum. Therefore, an extremal problem has to be solved. In this extremal problem we do not search for a real number that minimizes a function but instead we search for a function that minimizes a functional. This is the fundamental problem of calculus of variations.

In *calculus of variations* (certain) integrals are minimized by initially reformulating the problem. In principle there are two numerical approaches which differ in the moment when the discretization takes place in the solution process (see Section 5.2.2):

1. Initially the integral which is to be minimized is transformed into one or more corresponding Eulerian differential equations where the differential equations are formulated in a continuos form. Subsequently, a numerical approach has to be found for solving the differential equations.

2. Another way is to discretize the functional directly. Afterwards the problem is addressed of finding a numerical approach to solve the discrete form.

These approaches (see K. Ikeuchi and B.K.P. Horn (1981), B.K.P. Horn (1986)) are described in the following by taking the functional $Fk_{Ikeuchi\,and\,Horn}$ from the previous section as an example[2]. The functional $Fk_{Ikeuchi\,and\,Horn}$ depends on the functions $f(x,y)$ and $g(x,y)$ and their first derivatives which is formally represented by the functional:

$$\iint_\Omega F(f,g,f_x,f_y,g_x,g_y)\ dxdy\ .$$

As already known, f and g are the stereographic coordinates of the orientations we are to reconstruct. The corresponding Eulerian differential equations are

$$\frac{\partial F(f,g,f_x,f_y,g_x,g_y)}{\partial f} - \frac{\partial F_{f_x}(f,g,f_x,f_y,g_x,g_y)}{\partial x} - \frac{\partial F_{f_y}(f,g,f_x,f_y,g_x,g_y)}{\partial y} = 0\ ,$$

$$\frac{\partial F(f,g,f_x,f_y,g_x,g_y)}{\partial g} - \frac{\partial F_{g_x}(f,g,f_x,f_y,g_x,g_y)}{\partial x} - \frac{\partial F_{g_y}(f,g,f_x,f_y,g_x,g_y)}{\partial y} = 0\ .$$

By performing the differentiations the first equation turns into

$$2\lambda(E - R_s(f,g))\frac{-\partial R_s(f,g)}{\partial f} - 2f_{xx} - 2f_{yy} = 0\ ,$$

$$\text{with }\ f_{xx} = \frac{\partial^2 f(x,y)}{\partial x^2}\ \text{ and }\ f_{yy} = \frac{\partial^2 f(x,y)}{\partial y^2}\ .$$

All functions depend on the image coordinates x and y which are not explicitly shown in the equations for the sake of clarity. The second equation gives

$$2\lambda(E - R_s(f,g))\frac{-\partial R_s(f,g)}{\partial g} - 2g_{xx} - 2g_{yy} = 0\ ,$$

$$\text{with }\ g_{xx} = \frac{\partial^2 g(x,y)}{\partial x^2}\ \text{ and }\ g_{yy} = \frac{\partial^2 g(x,y)}{\partial y^2}\ .$$

---

[2] An elaborate explanation of the formulation of an iterative approach for the solution of a functional was already given in Section 5.2.2.

After simplifying the equations the two second order partial differential equations have the form

$$\nabla^2 f = \lambda(E - R_s(f,g))\frac{-\partial R_s(f,g)}{\partial f} \quad \text{and}$$

$$\nabla^2 g = \lambda(E - R_s(f,g))\frac{-\partial R_s(f,g)}{\partial g} \quad,$$

$$\text{with} \quad \nabla^2 = \frac{\partial^2}{\partial x^2} + \frac{\partial^2}{\partial y^2} \quad.$$

The symbol ∇^2 denotes the Laplace operator. The solvability of the set of partial differential equations represents a necessary condition for the existence of an extreme value (minimum or maximum) of the functional. Note that a found extreme value is not necessarily a global minimum. If initial values for f and g are known at the object boundary, then a numerical technique can be used to solve the differential equations. Various methods, e.g. the Jacobi method, the Gauß-Seidel method, and multiple grid methods can be found, for example in the book "Numerical Recipes" (see References in Section 7.5).

The second mentioned way for minimization is to discretize the functional. A very simple discretization of the smoothness condition $\mathbf{F}g_2$ with consideration of just one neighboring pixel for each image point (i,j) is as follows:

$$s(i,j) = \tfrac{1}{4}((f(i+1,j) - f(i,j))^2 + (f(i,j+1) - f(i,j))^2$$
$$- (g(i+1,j) - g(i,j))^2 + (g(i,j+1) - g(i,j))^2) \quad.$$

Now, the functions $f(i,j)$ and $g(i,j)$ are defined with respect to discrete image points. The differences in the above equation represent a forward difference approximation scheme of the partial derivatives. The irradiance constraint $\mathbf{F}b_2$ changes only slightly in the discrete case:

$$b(i,j) = (E(i,j) - R_s(f(i,j),g(i,j)))^2 \quad.$$

Now, the aim is to minimize the discrete error term

$$e = \sum_i \sum_j (s(i,j) + \lambda \cdot b(i,j))$$

of the functional $\mathbf{F}k_{Ikeuchi\ and\ Horn}$ comprising the two just described discrete SFS constraints.

A necessary condition for the minimization is that the first partial derivatives are zero. It is assumed that this is the global minimum. The function depends on the same number of variables $f(i,j)$ and $g(i,j)$ as there are image points (i,j) in

$$4-\text{average}: \quad \frac{1}{4} \cdot \begin{array}{|c|c|c|} \hline 0 & 1 & 0 \\ \hline 1 & 0 & 1 \\ \hline 0 & 1 & 0 \\ \hline \end{array} \quad , \quad 8-\text{average}: \quad \frac{1}{20} \cdot \begin{array}{|c|c|c|} \hline 1 & 4 & 1 \\ \hline 4 & 0 & 4 \\ \hline 1 & 4 & 1 \\ \hline \end{array}$$

Figure 7.9: Averaging masks of the SFS method according to K. Ikeuchi and B.K.P. Horn (1981).

the considered object region. Every image point has two variables for which the minimal value e has to be found. Thus, e can be regarded as a function and has to be differentiated with respect to its variables $f(i,j)$ and $g(i,j)$:

$$\frac{\partial e}{\partial f(i,j)} = 2(f(i,j) - \bar{f}(i,j)) - 2\lambda(E(i,j) - R_s(f(i,j),g(i,j)))\frac{\partial R_s}{\partial f} \text{ , with}$$

$$\bar{f}(i,j) = \tfrac{1}{4}(f(i+1,j) + f(i,j+1) + f(i-1,j) + f(i,j-1)) \text{ and}$$

$$\frac{\partial e}{\partial g(i,j)} = 2(g(i,j) - \bar{g}(i,j)) - 2\lambda(E(i,j) - R_s(f(i,j),g(i,j)))\frac{\partial R_s}{\partial g} \text{ , with}$$

$$\bar{g}(i,j) = \tfrac{1}{4}(g(i+1,j) + g(i,j+1) + g(i-1,j) + g(i,j-1)) \text{ .}$$

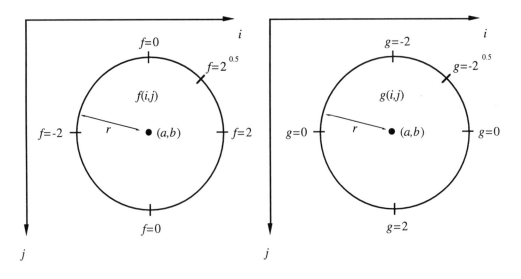

Figure 7.10: Initialization of the data arrays of f and g at the occluding boundaries of a sphere with radius r. These values are used as boundary conditions for the method by K. Ikeuchi and B.K.P. Horn (1981).

The discrete functions $f(i,j)$ and $g(i,j)$ notated with overbars are the local averages of the stereographic coordinates in a 4-neighborhood, see Fig. 7.9 (left picture). After the equations were set equal to zero, a large, sparse system of linear equations has to be solved. A simple approach is to use the iteration scheme

$$f^{n+1}(i,j) = \bar{f}^n(i,j) + \lambda(E(i,j) - R_s(\bar{f}^n(i,j), \bar{g}^n(i,j)))\frac{\partial R_s}{\partial f} \ ,$$

$$g^{n+1}(i,j) = \bar{g}^n(i,j) + \lambda(E(i,j) - R_s(\bar{f}^n(i,j), \bar{g}^n(i,j)))\frac{\partial R_s}{\partial g} \ .$$

The superscript n denotes the nth iteration. The evaluation of the partial derivatives of the stereographic reflectance maps is done with the averaged f- and g values in a certain neighborhood taken from the nth iteration. A significant improvement of the results can be achieved when the above mentioned 4-neighborhood is substituted by the mask shown in the right picture of Fig. 7.9.

To initialize the iteration a set of known orientations has to be found at singular points (e.g. at the boundary) and assigned to the data arrays of f and g. Figure 7.10 shows the initial values for a sphere. The remaining points are initialized with an arbitrary orientation. Figure 7.11 and Fig. 7.12 describe an algorithm for the SFS method by K. Ikeuchi and B.K.P. Horn (1981).

The algorithm consists of two parts. In the first part which is illustrated in Fig. 7.11 the initialization of the data arrays of f and g is shown for a sphere. In

```
begin
        { Initialization of the arrays f and g of the stereographic coordinates for a
            sphere with radius r at the center point position (a,b,c) with n points }

        assign the value 0 to all fg values; { i.e., n°=(0, 0, -1) }
        for k:= 1 to n do
                begin
                        t:= 2π·k/n;
                        i:= r·cos(t)+ a; j:= r·sin(t) + b;
                        f(i,j):= 2(i-a)/r;
                        g(i,j):= 2(j-b)/r
                end
end;
```

Figure 7.11: Initialization of an iterative SFS method by K. Ikeuchi and B.K.P. Horn (1981) for a sphere.

begin

        choose the weighting factor λ;

        while an improvement of the reconstruction can be expected **do**

            for $j := 1$ **to** N **do for** $i := 1$ **to** M **do begin**

                $fa :=$ average of f in the point (i,j);

                $ga :=$ average of g in the point (i,j);

                { calculation of the derivatives of $R_s(f, g)$

                in the point (fa,ga): $\left.\dfrac{\partial R_s(f,g)}{\partial f}\right|^{(fa,ga)}$, $\left.\dfrac{\partial R_s(f,g)}{\partial g}\right|^{(fa,ga)}$ }

$$Rsf := \frac{4s_x + 2fa \cdot s_z - 2fa \cdot R_s(fa, ga)}{4 + fa^2 + ga^2};$$

$$Rsg := \frac{4s_y + 2ga \cdot s_z - 2ga \cdot R_s(fa, ga)}{4 + fa^2 + ga^2};$$

                { calculation of the new values f and g }

                $f(i,j) := fa - \lambda \cdot (E(i,j) - R_s(fa, ga)) \cdot Rsf$;

                $g(i,j) := ga - \lambda \cdot (E(i,j) - R_s(fa, ga)) \cdot Rsg$

        end {for}

end;

Figure 7.12: Iterative SFS method with functional minimization developed by K. Ikeuchi and B.K.P. Horn (1981).

the second part (see Fig. 7.12) the orientations are iteratively refined starting from the initialization. The direction to the light source is represented by the vector $s° = (s_x, s_y, s_z)$. The calculation of surface orientations is feasible for any Lambertian reflectance map with the algorithm which is illustrated in Fig. 7.12.

    To a certain degree the second part of the algorithm is independent from the initialization of a particular object. But note that the initialization influences which (local) minimum is found. The selection of the weighting factor λ is crucial for the quality of the reconstruction (see Section 7.3.2). The smaller λ is, the smoother the reconstructed surface will be. If λ is chosen too small then information could be lost. If we select λ too large, then the orientations satisfy the image irradiance equation but globally seen there is no physically plausible relation between the reconstructed surface (except for singular orientations) and the reconstructed surface anymore.

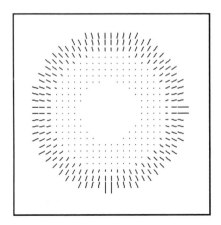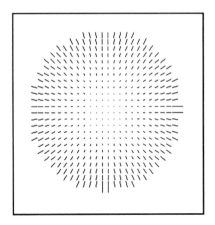

Figure 7.13: Needle maps of the reconstruction results of a synthetic sphere for the method by K. Ikeuchi and B.K.P. Horn (1981). The left image shows the result after 50 iterations. The right image shows the result after 300 iterations.

Note that the iteration takes place "in the array", i.e. the calculated new values in the arrays of stereographic coordinates are immediately used for the current iteration what is sometimes called a sequential iteration. It improves the convergence behavior of the algorithm[3] and reduces the amount of required memory. A disadvantage is that it can lead to a small distortions.

Despite sequential iteration usually several hundred iterations have to be carried out to achieve a satisfactory solution. Figure 7.13 shows the result of the method by K. Ikeuchi and B.K.P. Horn (1981) for a synthetic sphere after 50 and after 300 iterations. The value $\lambda = 1.0$ was chosen as the weighting factor.

The input sphere was rendered with a rotationally symmetric Lambertian reflectance map (see Fig. 6.5). Orientations at occluding boundaries of the sphere were used as boundary conditions according to the algorithm in Fig. 7.11. The needle map representation was chosen for the visualization of the results (see Section 3.2.3). The maximal needle length (scaling factor s in the algorithm for needle map generation in Section 3.2.3) was chosen such that the ratio of s and the edge length of the image of the needle map is 1:32.

Orientations which still point towards the viewer according to the initialization of the fg arrays ($f = g = 0$) are not represented in the needle maps so that we can better recognize the growing process of the surfaces. The influence of the weighting factor on the reconstruction result is visualized for a small factor ($\lambda = 0.0$) and a large factor ($\lambda = 10.0$) in Fig. 7.14. Both needle maps show the

---

[3] This corresponds approximately to the properties of the Gauß-Seidel method in comparison with the Jacobian method for solving partial differential equations.

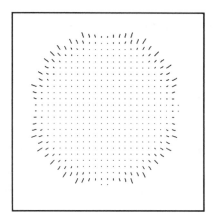
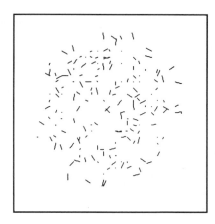

Figure 7.14: Needle maps of the reconstruction results of a synthetic sphere for the method by K. Ikeuchi and B.K.P. Horn (1981). The left image shows the result where $\lambda=0$ was chosen as the weighting factor. The right needle map shows the result with $\lambda=10$. Both times 300 iterations were carried out.

result after 300 iterations. A rotationally symmetric Lambertian reflectance map was used for the generation of the sphere image.

The reconstruction result for the synthetic Mozart image in Fig. 7.7 is shown in Fig. 7.15. The weighting factor λ was set to 1.0 and 300 iterations were required. The rough geometry of the Mozart statue could be recovered well from a single image. But finer structures were lost due to the smoothness constraint. The

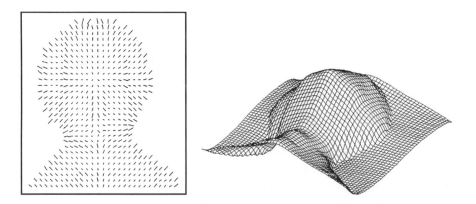

Figure 7.15: Needle map and three-dimensional plot of a reconstruction result of the synthetic Mozart statue by using the method by K. Ikeuchi and B.K.P. Horn (1981). The value $\lambda = 1$ was chosen as the weighting factor and 300 iterations were carried out.

method by R.T. Frankot and R. Chellappa (1988, see Section 3.3.2) was used for the conversion to a height map.

7.4   LOCAL SHAPE FROM SHADING

This section will give an example of a SFS method where the shape at an image point is calculated by using the image irradiances only in a small neighborhood of that image point. Local methods have the advantage of time efficiency because the influence on the determination of the shape is locally restricted and the approaches are generally of non-iterative nature. Furthermore, the realization of the algorithms is often easier than for global methods. However, non-iterative local SFS methods can only determine surface orientations and therefore have to rely on a subsequent integration step (see Section 3.3).

7.4.1   Spherical Approximation and Calculation of Tilt

A SFS approach by C.-H. Lee and A. Rosenfeld (1985) will be described in the following. The idea of the method is to approximate the object in every surface point as a sphere to resolve the ambiguity of the orientations associated with an image irradiance E over the locally known geometry of the surface.

For this, a coordinate transformation is performed from the right-handed Cartesian sensor coordinate system XYZ (Z axis in viewing direction) to a coordinate system $X^*Y^*Z^*$. This new coordinate system is defined by the illumination direction $\mathbf{s}°$. The new Z^*-axis is aligned with the illumination direction $\mathbf{s}°$ and the rotation about the Z^*-axis can be defined arbitrarily. In this new coordinate system the "optical axis" coincides with the illumination direction, hence the new, corresponding reflectance map is rotationally symmetric. C.-H. Lee and A. Rosenfeld (1985) could show that the tilt of the surface orientation in the new coordinate system $X^*Y^*Z^*$ can be calculated in a simple way. The tilt can be determined directly from the linearly transformed partial derivatives of the image irradiance function $E(x,y)$ if the geometry of the surface is locally approximated as a sphere.

In the following σ will denote the slant and θ the tilt of the illumination direction $\mathbf{s}°$, ς is the slant and ϑ the tilt of the surface orientation $\mathbf{n}°$. This means that the orientations are represented as spherical coordinates[4] (see Section 3.4.1).

---

[4] The slant at this point is denoted by the lower case Greek letter sigma which is denoted by the symbol σ as well as by the symbol ς. The same is true for the tilt (lower case Greek letter theta) which is denoted by the symbol θ as well as by ϑ.

These quantities are defined in the coordinate system XYZ. A superscript asterix denotes their transformations into the coordinate system $X^*Y^*Z^*$, i.e. for example σ^* or $s^{*\circ}$. The transformation between the coordinate systems from a point $\mathbf{P}$ into a point $\mathbf{P}^*$ is described by the 3×3 rotation matrix $\mathbf{T}_1$:

$$\begin{pmatrix} X^* \\ Y^* \\ Z^* \end{pmatrix} = \mathbf{T}_1 \cdot \begin{pmatrix} X \\ Y \\ Z \end{pmatrix}, \text{ with } \mathbf{T}_1 = \begin{pmatrix} \cos(\sigma)\cos(\theta) & \cos(\sigma)\sin(\theta) & -\sin(\sigma) \\ -\sin(\theta) & \cos(\theta) & 0 \\ \sin(\sigma)\cos(\theta) & \sin(\sigma)\sin(\theta) & \cos(\sigma) \end{pmatrix}.$$

If we assume that the center of the approximating sphere is located at the origin of both coordinate systems and that it has radius r then the sphere can be defined in the coordinate system XYZ by the function

$$Z(X,Y) = \sqrt{r^2 - X^2 - Y^2} , \text{ with } X^2 + Y^2 \le r^2.$$

The orientation $\mathbf{n}^\circ$ at (X, Y) is given by

$$\mathbf{n}^\circ = \frac{1}{r} \cdot (X, Y, Z)^T.$$

The relationship between the representation of the illumination direction $\mathbf{s}^\circ$ by a unit vector and the representation by spherical coordinates (σ, θ) is given by the equation

$$\mathbf{s}^\circ = (\sin(\sigma)\cos(\theta), \ \sin(\sigma)\sin(\theta), \ \cos(\sigma))^T.$$

Therefore, the image irradiances

$$E(x = X, y = Y) = E_0\rho \cdot (\mathbf{n}^\circ \mathbf{s}^\circ)$$

of the sphere can be described by

$$E(x = X, y = Y) = \frac{E_0\rho}{r}(X \sin(\sigma)\cos(\theta) + Y \sin(\sigma)\sin(\theta) + Z(X,Y)\cos(\sigma)).$$

The first partial derivatives of the image irradiance function are

$$E_x(x = X, y = Y) = \frac{E_0\rho}{r}\left(\sin(\sigma)\cos(\theta) - \frac{X \cdot \cos(\sigma)}{Z(X,Y)} \right) \text{ and}$$

$$E_y(x = X, y = Y) = \frac{E_0\rho}{r}\left(\sin(\sigma)\sin(\theta) - \frac{Y \cdot \cos(\sigma)}{Z(X,Y)} \right).$$

If $\sigma = 0$, i.e. if the illumination direction coincides with the optical axis, then the above partial derivatives simplify.

If the system is rotated by using the above transformation $\mathbf{T}_1$ then the transformed derivatives of the image irradiances are

$$\begin{pmatrix} E^*_x (x = X, y = Y) \\ E^*_y (x = X, y = Y) \end{pmatrix} = \mathbf{T}_2 \cdot \begin{pmatrix} E_x (x = X, y = Y) \\ E_y (x = X, y = Y) \end{pmatrix},$$

with $\mathbf{T}_2 = \begin{pmatrix} cos(\sigma)cos(\theta) & cos(\sigma)sin(\theta) \\ -sin(\theta) & cos(\theta) \end{pmatrix}$,

which corresponds to the rotation of the X-coordinates and the Y-coordinates in the above described coordinate transformation $\mathbf{T}_1$. It can be shown that the direction of the calculated vector corresponds to the direction of the tilt of the surface orientation at the considered image point.

7.4.2   Calculation of Slant

What remains is the calculation of the slants ς of the surface orientations $\mathbf{n}^\circ$ for the image points. The equation

$$E = E_0\rho \cdot (\mathbf{n}^{*\circ}\mathbf{s}^{*\circ}) = E_0\rho \cdot cos(\varsigma^*)$$

holds in the transformed coordinate system $X^*Y^*Z^*$. It represents the relationship of the rotated vectors $\mathbf{n}^{*\circ}$ and $\mathbf{s}^{*\circ}$ to the image irradiances. If the product $E_0\rho$ is known, then

$$\varsigma^* = arccos\left(\frac{E(x = X, y = Y)}{E_0\rho} \right).$$

The product $E_0\rho$ of the illumination irradiance and the albedo can be determined very easily if it can be assumed that one orientation of the examined object coincides with the illumination direction (see Section 7.1.1). Then the scalar product of the illumination direction and this singular surface normal is 1, hence $E = E_0\rho$. Finally, the slant ς^* of the surface orientation $\mathbf{n}^{*\circ}$ has to be transformed back into the coordinate system XYZ.

The back transformation of the angles ς^* and ϑ^* can be done by calculating $\mathbf{n}^{*\circ}$ and transforming this vector by using the matrix $\mathbf{T}_1^T$:

$$\mathbf{n}^\circ = \mathbf{T}_1^T \cdot \mathbf{n}^{*\circ}, \quad \text{with } \mathbf{n}^{*\circ} = \begin{pmatrix} sin(\varsigma^*)cos(\vartheta^*) \\ sin(\varsigma^*)sin(\vartheta^*) \\ cos(\varsigma^*) \end{pmatrix}.$$

The angles ς and ϑ can be calculated from $\mathbf{n}^\circ$ as follows:

$$\varsigma = \arccos(n_z) \text{ and } \vartheta = \arctan\left(\frac{n_y}{n_x}\right), \text{ with } (n_x, n_y, n_z) = \mathbf{n}^\circ \text{ and } n_x \neq 0 .$$

Figure 7.16 shows the complete local SFS algorithm for an arbitrary illumination direction. The described technique has the interesting property of "quasi" albedo independence of the calculated tilt ϑ because the albedo is eliminated from the quotient of the partial irradiance derivatives. Furthermore, no initial 3D information needs to be known for this method.

---

begin

        determine the product $E_0\rho$;

        for every image point (x,y) **do begin**

                calculate gradient $(E_x(x, y),\ E_y(x, y))$;

                calculate by $\mathbf{T}_2$ the rotated gradient $(E\,{}^*_x(x, y), E\,{}^*_y(x, y))$;

                { calculation of the tilt ϑ^* of the surface orientation n*° }

                $\vartheta^* :=$ direction of $(E\,{}^*_x(x, y),\ E\,{}^*_y(x, y))$;

                { calculation of the slant ς^* of n*° }

$$\varsigma^* := arccos\left(\frac{E(x = X, y = Y)}{E_0\rho}\right) ;$$

                { rotated the calculated orientation back }

$$\mathbf{n}^\circ := \mathbf{T}_1^T \cdot \begin{pmatrix} sin(\varsigma^*)cos(\vartheta^*) \\ sin(\varsigma^*)sin(\vartheta^*) \\ cos(\varsigma^*) \end{pmatrix} ;$$

                { calculate the slant ς and the tilt ϑ of the surface orientation }

                $\begin{pmatrix} n_x & n_y & n_z \end{pmatrix} := \mathbf{n}^\circ$;

                $\varsigma := arccos(n_z)$;

                $\vartheta := arctan(n_y / n_x)$;

        end {for}

end;

Figure 7.16: Example of the local SFS technique published by C.-H. Lee and A. Rosenfeld (1985).

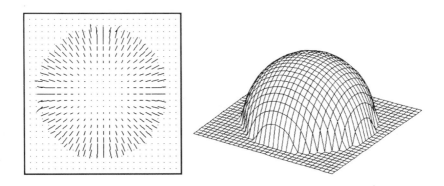

Figure 7.17: Needle map and three-dimensional plot of a sphere reconstructed with the local SFS method by C.-H. Lee and A. Rosenfeld (1985).

Figure 7.17 illustrates the reconstructed needle map of a synthetic sphere whose orientations were calculated using the above method. The photometric properties of the sphere were modeled through a rotationally symmetric Lambertian reflectance map (sphere image see Fig. 6.5). With the exception of errors at the boundaries the reconstruction of the orientations corresponds to the model. This is not surprising since a sphere satisfies the assumption of a locally spherical surface in every point.

The right picture of Fig. 7.17 shows the surface calculated from the reconstructed orientations. The illustrated local method can also determine adequate results for some surfaces which do not satisfy the geometrical assumptions at all. Figure 7.18 shows the reconstructed needle map of the synthetic Mozart image in Fig. 7.7. The irradiance image was again generated under the assumption of a rotationally symmetric Lambertian reflectance map. The calculated slant of the

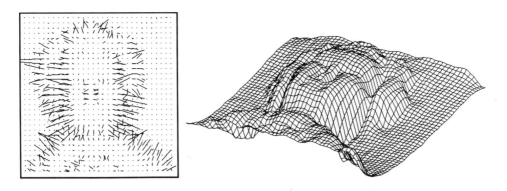

Figure 7.18: Needle map and height map of the synthetic Mozart image which were reconstructed with the local SFS method by C.-H. Lee and A. Rosenfeld (1985).

orientations was too small compared to the correct slant which can be recognized by very short needles, for example in the face. The ratio between the maximal needle length and the edge length of the needle map is 1:8 in Fig. 7.18.

The right picture of Fig. 7.18 shows the reconstructed height map of the synthetic Mozart image. The method of R.T. Frankot and R. Chellappa was used to calculate the height values. Because of the wrong slant angles the *Z* values of the height map were rectified by using a certain scaling. It can be seen that the tilt angles were mostly calculated correctly.

7.5   REFERENCES

A good overview on SFS can be found in

> Horn, B.K.P.: *Height and gradient from shading.* Int. Journal of Computer Vision **5** (1990), pp. 37-75.

A textbook with an excellent description of propagation methods and global minimization approaches is

> Horn, B.K.P.: *Robot Vision.* The MIT Press, Cambridge, Massachusetts, 1986.

The book

> Shirai, Y.: *Three-dimensional Computer Vision.* Springer, Berlin, 1987

contains a short description of the SFS topic and related areas. A collection of important and fundamental SFS articles (up to the year 1989) is given in the book

> Horn, B.K.P., Brooks, M.J.: *Shape from Shading.* The MIT Press, Cambridge, Massachusetts, 1989

which also contains the method by K. Ikeuchi and B.K.P. Horn (1981, see Section 7.3.3) as well as the method by R.T. Frankot and R. Chellappa (1988) which was described in Section 3.3.2.

An experimental comparison of eight different SFS methods from the three classes introduced in this chapter is carried out in

> Zhang, R., Tsai, P.-S., Cryer, J.E., Shah, M.: *Analysis of shape from shading techniques.* Proc. Computer Vision and Pattern Recognition 94, Seattle, Washington, USA, 1994, pp. 377-384.

It is interesting that all techniques were tested using the same synthetic and real scenes which means that a direct comparison of the methods can be carried out. The source code of the method by M. Bichsel and A.P. Pentland (see Section 7.2.3) can be found in

Bichsel, M., Pentland, A.P.: *A simple algorithm for shape from shading*. Proc. Computer Vision and Pattern Recognition 92, Champaign, Illinois, USA, 1992, pp. 459-465.

The global SFS approach described in Section 7.3.3 can be found in the above mentioned book by B.K.P. Horn and M.J. Brooks (1989) and in

Ikeuchi, K., Horn, B.K.P.: *Numerical shape from shading and occluding boundaries*. Artificial Intelligence **17**, 1981, pp. 141-184.

The same is true for the local approach described in Section 7.4.1 which was originally published in

Lee, C.-H., Rosenfeld, A.: *Improved methods of estimating shape from shading using the light source coordinate system*. Artificial Intelligence **26** (1985), pp. 125-143.

The book by B.K.P. Horn and M.J. Brooks (1989) contains a revised version of this article.The article of C.-H. Lee and A. Rosenfeld (1985) also contains the proofs of the used theorems and a method for determining the illumination direction. Furthermore, an alternative method is described. It can be used to determine the product of the illumination irradiance and the albedo. Other SFS approaches can, for example, be found in

Kimmel, R., Bruckstein, A.M.: *Global shape from shading*. Computer Vision and Image Understanding **62** (1995), pp. 360-369 and in

Kimmel, R., Siddiqi, K., Kimia, B.B, Bruckstein, A.M.: *Shape from shading: level set propagation and viscosity solution*. Int. Journal of Computer Vision **16** (1995), pp. 107-133.

The SFS approaches often employ standard techniques from numerics and from optimization theory. The book

Press, W.H., Teukolsky, S.A., Vetterling, W.T., Flannery, B.P.: *Numerical Recipes in C (FORTRAN, PASCAL)*. 2nd Edition, Cambridge University Press, Cambridge, USA, 1992

contains such techniques and their source code in C notation. A description of a selection of these techniques with respect to SFS techniques can be found in

Szeliski, R.: *Fast shape from shading*. CVGIP: Image Understanding **53** (1991), pp. 129-153.

The article

Kozera, R., Klette, R.: *Finite difference based algorithms for a linear shape from shading*. Machine Graphics & Vision **6** (1997), pp. 157-201.

presents a convergence analysis of finite difference schemes for solving linear Shape from Shading.

   An approach that assumes diffuse illumination can be found in

   Stewart, A.J., Langer, M.: *Toward Accurate Recovery of Shape from Shading Under Diffuse Lighting.* IEEE Transactions on Pattern Analysis and Machine Intelligence **19** (1997), pp. 1020-1025

which is also known as "Shape from Shading on a Cloudy Day".

7.6   EXERCISES

(1) Show that the direct 3D interpretation of local image irradiances (Section 7.1.3) is only approximately true for an ellipsoid.

(2) Show that beside the sphere we can also interpret a torus as a height map if its rotation axis is orthogonal to the projection plane. Hint: The parameter representation of a torus is

$$\begin{pmatrix} X(u,v) \\ Y(u,v) \\ Z(u,v) \end{pmatrix} = \begin{pmatrix} cos(u) & -sin(u) & 0 \\ sin(u) & cos(u) & 0 \\ 0 & 0 & 1 \end{pmatrix} \cdot \begin{pmatrix} cos(v) \\ 0 \\ sin(v) \end{pmatrix}.$$

(3) Calculate (as far as possible) the values of the functionals $\mathbf{Fg_1}$, $\mathbf{Fg_2}$ and $\mathbf{Fg_3}$ which were described in Section 7.3.2 for the surfaces

   plane : $Z_1(x,y) = a \cdot x + b \cdot y + c$,

   paraboloid of revolution : $Z_2(x,y) = x^2 + y^2$ and

   hyperbolic paraboloid : $Z_3(x,y) = x \cdot y$.

(4) Why do the reconstructed orientations $\mathbf{n}°$ in Fig. 7.13 start to grow to the center of the sphere image not from the first iteration but after a certain number of iterations?

(5) Which result do you expect when the orientations of a polyhedral scene are calculated using the method by C.-H. Lee and A. Rosenfeld (see Section 7.4.1)?

(6 - Assignment) Implement the algorithms which were described in Sections 7.3.3 and 7.4.1. The calculated orientations can be visualized by a needle map (see Section 3.2.3). Extend the initialization procedure in Fig. 7.11 to a torus (for torus equation refer to Exercise (2)).

8   PHOTOMETRIC STEREO

The term *photometric stereo method* (*PSM*) or just *photometric stereo* refers to the extension of Shape from Shading (Chapter 7) to a class of methods that use two or more images for shading based 3D shape reconstruction. The previous chapter discussed techniques which recover surface orientations and/or relative height values from a single irradiance image using known reflection properties and known illumination parameters. SFS methods can be extended if several irradiances are known for every image point and the corresponding surface point. Because of the larger amount of data an improvement of the reconstruction results and furthermore a reduction of the necessary assumptions can be expected. The photometric stereo method firstly recovers surface orientations and can be combined with an integration method (compare Section 3.3) to calculate a height map. Even without a subsequent integration step the surface orientations can be used, for example to determine curvature parameters of object surfaces or to recognize objects.

In photometric stereo the recovery of surfaces is based on their photometric properties whereas static and dynamic stereo analyses (Chapters 4 and 5) use geometric models to reconstruct surfaces. All methods in the Chapters 4, 5, and 8 have in common that they use several images of the object scene for surface reconstruction. In the case of the static stereo analysis the scene is observed from different positions where pose and orientation of object and illumination remain unchanged.

To acquire images for photometric stereo the object is consecutively illuminated by several light sources. Each image is taken with only one light source being switched on. A movement inside the system consisting of the object, the light sources, and the sensor is not allowed. Therefore, more than one irradiance value can be assigned to a projected surface point without encountering a correspondence problem (which has to be solved for the methods in Chapters 4 and 5). Each acquired image corresponds to one light source.

The first section of this chapter discusses the limitations of SFS methods. Section 8.2 deals with photometric stereo methods which use two light sources and hence analyze two irradiances per surface point. We distinguish between albedo dependent methods and albedo independent methods. The property of *albedo dependent methods* is that the albedo ρ of the surface material or the product $E_0\rho$ has to be known for every image point. This is especially true for SFS methods. *Albedo independent methods* have the property that the albedo has theoretically no influence on the reconstruction of orientations or height values. Therefore it is no required to know the albedo.

In Section 8.3 three light sources are used for surface reconstruction and hence three irradiance values are available at each image point. Similarly to Section 8.2, albedo dependent methods and albedo independent methods will be discussed.

8.1 LIMITATIONS OF SFS

SFS methods as they were introduced in the previous chapter require a strong restriction of the object surfaces because the problem to recover a surface from a single image is extremely underdetermined. Therefore, SFS is an ill-posed problem (compare Section 1.1.2). Assumptions on the surface properties support to find a unique solution to a certain extent. But with every additional restriction the practical use of such methods declines as well. Very critical simplifications are the following three assumptions.

1. The term $E_0\rho$ is known and constant, compare Section 7.1.1.

2. The surfaces are at least $C^{(1)}$-continuous, compare Section 3.1.1.

3. 3D coordinates of singular points and/or singular orientations are known.

The first assumption means that the product of the irradiance of the illumination E_0 and the albedo ρ has to be known for every image point. If the product $E_0\rho$ is unknown then the set of possible orientations cannot be constrained sufficiently by a single measured positive image irradiance value. All orientations being consistent with an irradiance value and the known illumination direction $\mathbf{s}^\circ$ subtend angles smaller than 90°. This corresponds to a half plane[1] in gradient space or to a Gaussian hemisphere on the Gaussian sphere.

If the product $E_0\rho$ is known for an assumed Lambertian reflectance map, then the set of solutions reduces to a conic section in gradient space or to the corresponding circle on the Gaussian sphere (compare Section 7.1.1). We see that knowing the term $E_0\rho$ is of particular help for SFS. The term $E_0\rho$ can be deter-

---

[1] If the illumination direction $\mathbf{s}^\circ$ is not equal to the viewer direction $\mathbf{v}^\circ = (0, 0, -1)$ then the orientations are restricted to a half plane. If $\mathbf{s}^\circ = \mathbf{v}^\circ$ then the set of possible solutions for a given irradiance value is the entire gradient space.

mined for a Lambertian reflectance map if a surface orientation $\mathbf{n}°$, with $\mathbf{n}° = \mathbf{s}°$, exists and if this orientation is visible. It is obvious that the knowledge of the individual quantities E_0 and ρ satisfies the assumption of a known term $E_0\rho$, too. Regarding the irradiance of the illumination E_0 it can be generally assumed that it is constant over the whole scene and if necessary it can be calculated by a calibration procedure.

If the albedo is unknown and not constant over the entire surface, then SFS methods assume that image regions of constant albedo values can be segmented. Furthermore, only if each of the segmented regions r contains a singular orientation $\mathbf{n}°$, with $\mathbf{n}° = \mathbf{s}°$, the term $E_0\rho_r$ can be extracted from the image without additional information. An individual reflectance map has to be assigned to each region. Of course, the reflectance maps are equal up to the scaling factors $E_0\rho_r$. The more different albedo values occur in the image the smaller the segmented regions will be and the probability of finding a singular orientation for every region would decrease. Hence a large number of different albedo values or even color transitions must not occur in the image.

Some SFS techniques try to estimate the term $E_0\rho$ and the illumination direction $\mathbf{s}°$ before starting the actual reconstruction. But this estimation usually needs even more assumptions and the problem of required limitations is only transformed onto another level.

The problems discussed for the Lambertian surfaces similarly exist for surfaces exhibiting other reflection properties. For hybridly reflecting surfaces additional parameters have to be determined. Besides the surface roughness, the ratio of the diffuse reflection component and the specular reflection component has to be known (compare Section 6.4).

The second assumption in the above list permits no polyhedral objects to be subject of common SFS methods[2]. Since the continuity condition must hold for every image point, it is difficult to reconstruct objects which are composed of a set of non-fitting curved surface segments which lead to orientation edges. The latter problem can be avoided if the discontinuous points are detectable with an edge operator and if the reconstruction can be done segmentwise. But if $C^{(2)}$-continuity is assumed, discontinuities are not easily detectable.

The third assumption in the above list refers partly to the fundamental problem of SFS methods how to decide whether a surface is convex or concave. The top half of Fig. 8.1 shows the irradiance image of a hemisphere which was rendered by using a rotationally symmetric Lambertian reflectance map, compare Section 6.3.3. Hence $\mathbf{v}° = \mathbf{s}° = (0, 0, -1)$ and identical irradiance values are assigned to all orientations having identical slants. As known from Section 7.1.3,

---

2 However special SFS approaches exist to analyze polyhedrons.

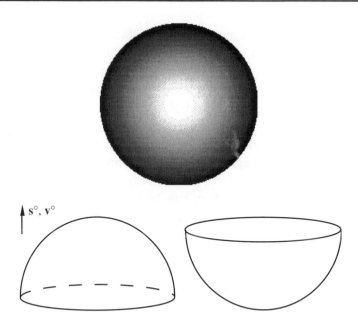

Figure 8.1: The irradiance image of a hemisphere and an oblique view of the convex and concave hemispheres which are consistent with the irradiance image.

the irradiance image is identical to the height map of the sphere. Even if we know that the image shows a hemisphere, it cannot be distinguished whether it is a convex hemisphere or a concave hemisphere. An oblique view of the outline of two possible surfaces for this image is shown at the bottom of Fig. 8.1. In the following this ambiguity shall be called *concave-convex conflict*.

Uniqueness can only be achieved by integrating further knowledge about the object. If the SFS method by K. Ikeuchi and B.K.P. Horn (1981) as described in Section 7.3.3 is initialized with correctly oriented occluding boundaries the intended solution would be obtained for the image. For the convex sphere the normals at the occluding boundaries have to point away from the object center, and for the concave shape the normals at the occluding boundaries have to point towards the sphere center.

The correctly oriented normals at the occluding boundaries cannot be determined from the irradiance image alone. As discussed in the previous chapter the alternative way of initializing SFS methods is to provide singular height values. For the discussed sphere we have to know at least two different height values in order to solve the concave-convex conflict. The SFS method by C.-H. Lee and A. Rosenfeld (1985), see Section 7.4.1, would determines the convex solution for the sphere. The reason is that the geometric model assumes a convex sphere and the method does not employ any initial values. A correct solution can only be achieved by methods which classify the singular points of the sphere $(\mathbf{n}^\circ = \mathbf{s}^\circ)$ as being convex or concave.

Example 8.1: For a further illustration of the concave-convex conflict we consider a simple *ruled surface* whose normal vectors are coplanar to the *XY*-plane of the coordinate system *XYZ* for all surface points. We assume that the reflection can be described by a rotationally symmetric Lambertian reflectance map. Thus, it is $\mathbf{s}^\circ = \mathbf{v}^\circ = (0, 0, -1)$ and the illumination direction is coplanar to the *XZ*-plane of the coordinate system *XYZ*, too. Therefore, the discussions can be made independently of the *Y*-axis at any arbitrary cross-section that is coplanar to the *XZ*-plane because all *Y*-components are zero. The *Y*=0-plane shall be used as the cross-section in the following.

First, consider the cross-section curve C_1 of the sine-shaped periodic ruled surface shown in Fig. 8.2. At the points of inflection of the curve the surface normals and the illumination direction subtend an angle of 45° or $\pi/4$. At the minima and the maxima of the curve C_1 the angle is 0°. Therefore, if we assume $E_0\rho = 1$, the image irradiance interval is equal to $[cos(\pi/4), 1]$. The irradiance curve $E = C_5$ is the image of the cross-section curve C_1 assuming a parallel projection, i.e. $x = X$. The curve $E = C_5$ describes another ruled surface having its minima at the points of inflection because in those points C_1 has its maximal slopes. The maxima of the irradiance curve $E = C_5$ are reached at the minima and at the maxima of C_1.

When we try to recover the intended curve C_1 from the irradiance curve $E = C_5$, then for every measured irradiance value E the number of possible orientations is two. This is a result of the assumption that the surface normals lie in the *XZ*-plane. The angle subtended by the surface normal and the illumination direction $\mathbf{s}$ can be assigned to every irradiance E by using the known product $E_0\rho = 1$. In the plane exactly two normals subtend this angle with respect to the illumination direction $\mathbf{s}$. Figure 8.2 shows this ambiguity for the surface normal pair $(\mathbf{n}_2, \mathbf{n}_3)$ at a point of inflection of the curve C_1. The two normals only coincide at singular points, where $\mathbf{n}_1 = \mathbf{s}$. At these points an unambiguous orientation can be recovered. In this example we call a resulting normal having a positive *X*-component "positive solution" and a solution normal with a negative *X*-component "negative solution".

To integrate a correct solution for the curve C_1 (compare Section 3.3) we have to alternate between the positive and the negative solution at each singular point when we move along the *x=X*-axis. Furthermore, it has to be assumed that the correct orientation is known for the starting point to find the intended solution C_1. The starting point must not be singular, too. In the example we have to start with the negative solution when the surface is integrated from left to right. If we

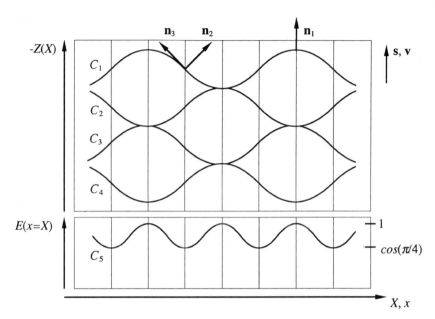

Figure 8.2: Irradiance curve $E(x{=}X)$ and surfaces consistent with it. The points of contact of the curves are switches between the possible surfaces.

started with a positive solution, then the not intended curve C_2 would be recovered. The initial height value can be chosen arbitrarily. Therefore, the curves C_3 and C_4 are also consistent with the irradiance curve. If the solution at each singular point is not alternated periodically between the positive solution and the negative solution during the integration process, several solution curves can be determined each being still consistent with the irradiance curve $E = C_5$. To illustrate this ambiguity consider the points of contact of the curves C_1 to C_4 in Fig. 8.2 as switches where we can change our way on the curve. Every path that can be taken on the curves is consistent with the irradiance curve! { end of Example 8.1 }

The illustrations given here for the two-dimensional case can be transferred to the 3D space. Note that smoothness assumptions do not always lead to a reduction of the ambiguity problem as can be seen from the example in Fig. 8.2. The intended surface can only be recovered when some additional information about the surface is known in advance. As we have seen the knowledge whether a singular point is a convex point, a concave point, a saddle point, or has a known height value is helpful in this respect. Providing the mentioned attributes is generally difficult for an unknown object.

The generalization of the image acquisition set-up to two or more light sources is an option to overcome the dilemma between the ambiguity on the one hand and the reduction of applicability caused by additional information on the other hand.

8.2   ANALYSIS OF IRRADIANCE PAIRS

As a first extension of SFS methods one additional parallel light source shall be used now to accomplish the task of unique surface recovery. We assume that the illumination directions s_1 and s_2 of the two light sources are not collinear. In order to prevent an interference of the irradiances of the two light sources, the two pictures have to be taken consecutively. The object and the camera have a fixed position and orientation. Thus, two irradiances are assigned to each image point and the corresponding surface point. These measured irradiances are to be called an *irradiance pair*. Techniques which employ the described image acquisition set-up are called *two source methods* or for short *2S methods* in the context of photometric stereo.

In general, it is assumed that both measured irradiances are positive. If one of the irradiances is zero (*zero-irradiance*), then the considered surface point is not illuminated by the corresponding light source when we assume that the albedo is not equal to zero. Each of the two light sources can illuminate those surface points of a convex object having orientations which belong to a Gaussian hemisphere defined by the corresponding illumination direction. The remaining orientations lie in the self-shadow of the light source. A single light source can illuminate the entire set of orientations of visible points only in such a case if the viewer direction v coincides with the illumination direction s, i.e. if $s = v$. If the object is not convex then a zero-irradiance can further be caused by cast-shadows.

Since 2S methods analyze two irradiances at every surface point, the recoverable surface portion is limited to those orientations which are illuminated by both light sources. The portion of the Gaussian sphere that is illuminated depends on the angle γ that is subtended by the illumination directions s_1 and s_2. The smaller the angle γ, the more orientations can be recovered. The cardinality of orientations illuminated by both light sources can be represented as the surface area of a lune on the Gaussian sphere. The area of the respective lune (for definition refer to Section 3.1.4) depends on the angle $\alpha = \pi - \gamma$ subtended by the great circles of the Gaussian hemispheres (see Fig. 8.3).

The larger the angle γ, the more robust 2S methods are with respect to noise in the measured irradiances and the estimation of parameters, for example the illumination directions. Hence there is no optimal choice of illumination directions with respect to the number of recoverable orientations and the recon-

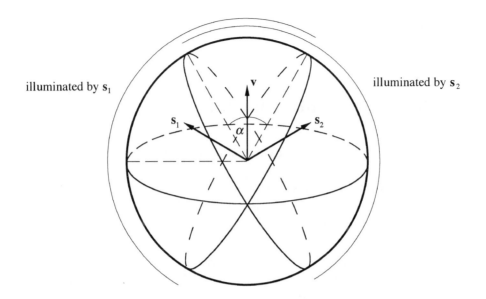

Figure 8.3: Intersection of two Gaussian hemispheres which represent the orientations illuminated by two light sources. The half circles drawn as fine lines show the regions that are covered by the corresponding light source.

struction quality. For the choice of illumination directions it has to be kept in mind that all orientations which are illuminated by the two light sources should be visible from the viewer direction **v**. This holds if the vector **v** can be represented by a linear combination

$$\mathbf{v} = a \cdot \mathbf{s}_1 + b \cdot \mathbf{s}_2$$

with two positive scalars a and b. Otherwise, some orientations would be illuminated that are not visible for the camera. The reconstruction of surfaces using 2S methods with different assumptions about the reflection properties is described in the following sections.

8.2.1 Linear Reflectance Maps

If linear reflection with respect to the gradient space can be assumed (compare Sections 6.3.2 and 7.2.1), then a positive irradiance E_1 measured at an image point **p** reduces the set of possible gradients to a straight line

$$h \ : \ q = h(p) = m(\mathbf{s}_1) \cdot p + b(\mathbf{s}_1, E_1)$$

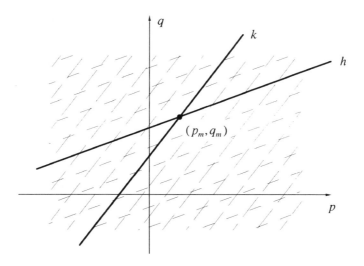

Figure 8.4: Intersection of two straight lines h and k of linear reflectance maps in the gradient space.

in gradient space. The slope m of this straight line depends on the direction $\mathbf{s}_1$ of the first light source [3]. The q-intercept b depends on $\mathbf{s}_1$ and on the irradiance E_1. When we change the illumination direction and measure an irradiance E_2 at the image point $\mathbf{p}$ through a further image acquisition process, then another straight line

$$k \; : \; q = k(p) = m(\mathbf{s}_2) \cdot p + b(\mathbf{s}_2, E_2)$$

arises for the linear reflectance map of the new illumination direction $\mathbf{s}_2$. Since the two measured irradiances E_1 and E_2 belong to the same surface point $\mathbf{P}$ the intersection (p_m, q_m) of the lines h and k represents the orientation that is consistent with both irradiances. This orientation is uniquely determined for the image point $\mathbf{p}$ (compare Fig. 8.4). A system of linear equations can be formulated. Thus, the surface normal $\mathbf{n} = (p_m, q_m, -1)$ can be calculated from the equations by

$$\begin{pmatrix} p_m \\ q_m \end{pmatrix} = \begin{pmatrix} -m(\mathbf{s}_1) & 1 \\ -m(\mathbf{s}_2) & 1 \end{pmatrix}^{-1} \cdot \begin{pmatrix} b(\mathbf{s}_1, E_1) \\ b(\mathbf{s}_2, E_2) \end{pmatrix}$$

where the superscript "-1" denotes the inverse of the matrix. This equation shows that for two linear reflectance maps having different slopes a unique surface normal can be recovered for each irradiance pair since the matrix containing the slopes is invertible (not singular).

---

[3] The slope of vertical straight lines is undefined, thus the equation must be defined in terms of q.

In the following 2S methods are discussed which assume diffuse reflecting (Lambertian) surfaces.

8.2.2   Albedo Dependent Analysis

The above approach for linear reflectance maps cannot be directly transferred to Lambertian reflectance maps. As known from Section 6.3.3 a Lambertian image irradiance value constrains the gradient (p,q) to a conic section, i.e. to a second order curve (quadratic curve). For a Lambertian reflecting surface at most two valid orientations can be assigned to an image irradiance pair since two isoradiance curves have no more than two intersections. Note that up to four solutions exist for two general conic sections, for example when two ellipses intersect.

Theorem 8.1: *If the reflection properties of an object surface can be described by two Lambertian reflectance maps (i.e. one for each light source) then 2S methods constrain the set of possible solutions at each image point. If two positive irradiances are assigned to an image point then at most two orientations exist.*

Proof: Assume we have measured the irradiances E_1 and E_2 at an image point **p** using the illumination directions $\mathbf{s}_1$ and $\mathbf{s}_2$, respectively. Let us further assume that gradient space representations of $\mathbf{s}_1$ and $\mathbf{s}_2$ are given by

$$p_{si} = p(\mathbf{s}_i) \quad \text{and} \quad q_{si} = q(\mathbf{s}_i), \quad \text{with} \quad i = 1, 2 .$$

Note that the functions p and q were defined in Section 3.4.1. The two image irradiance equations

$$E_1 = E_{01}\rho \frac{p \cdot p_{s1} + q \cdot q_{s1} + 1}{\sqrt{p^2 + q^2 + 1} \cdot \sqrt{p_{s1}^2 + q_{s1}^2 + 1}} \quad \text{and}$$

$$E_2 = E_{02}\rho \frac{p \cdot p_{s2} + q \cdot q_{s2} + 1}{\sqrt{p^2 + q^2 + 1} \cdot \sqrt{p_{s2}^2 + q_{s2}^2 + 1}}$$

specifying mathematical relations between the gradient (p,q) of the surface orientation **n** and the irradiance pair (E_1, E_2) follow from the Lambertian reflectance maps (compare Sections 6.3.3 and 6.5.2). The equations are nonlinear in p and q where ρ is the albedo and the parameters E_{01} and E_{02} represent the irradiances of the two light sources.

The illumination directions $\mathbf{s}_1$ and $\mathbf{s}_2$ can be considered as position vectors in the *XYZ* coordinate system as shown in Fig. 8.5. First, we rotate both vectors by using a 3×3 rotation matrix **R** which is defined in such a way that the *Y*-compo-

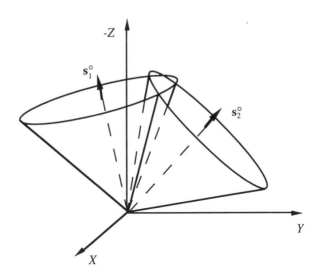

Figure 8.5: Illustration of the set of solutions of an albedo dependent 2S method represented by two right circular cones. The intersections (or the contact points) represent the orientations which are consistent with the corresponding irradiance pair.

nents of the two rotated illumination directions $\mathbf{s}_{1'}$ and $\mathbf{s}_{2'}$ become zero. After the transformation

$$\mathbf{s}_{i'} = \mathbf{R} \cdot \mathbf{s}_i \ , \quad \text{with} \ \ i = 1, 2 \ ,$$

the illumination directions $\mathbf{s}_{1'}$ and $\mathbf{s}_{2'}$ lie in the XZ-plane of the XYZ coordinate system. The rotated illumination directions can be represented in the gradient space by

$$p_{si'} = p(\mathbf{s}_{i'}) \quad \text{and} \quad q_{si'} = q(\mathbf{s}_{i'}) = 0 \ .$$

The surface orientation $\mathbf{n}$ at the image point $\mathbf{p}$ can be subjected to the same rotation $\mathbf{R}$. After rotation the new gradient components of $\mathbf{n}$,

$$p' = p(\mathbf{n}') = p(\mathbf{R} \cdot \mathbf{n}) \quad \text{and} \quad q' = q(\mathbf{n}') = q(\mathbf{R} \cdot \mathbf{n}) \ ,$$

are consistent with the rotated illumination directions. As a result, the image irradiance equations simplify to

$$E_1 = E_{01}\rho \frac{p' \cdot p_{s1'} + 1}{\sqrt{p'^2 + q'^2 + 1} \cdot \sqrt{p_{s1'}^2 + 1}} \quad \text{and}$$

$$E_2 = E_{02}\rho \frac{p' \cdot p_{s2'} + 1}{\sqrt{p'^2 + q'^2 + 1} \cdot \sqrt{p_{s2'}^2 + 1}} \ .$$

Note that the image irradiances do not change due to the coordinate transformation. By eliminating the length

$$\sqrt{p'^2 + q'^2 + 1}$$

of the surface orientation $\mathbf{n}'$ the two equations can be reduced to one equation:

$$E_2 \cdot E_{01}\rho(p' \cdot p_{s1'} + 1)\sqrt{p_{s2'}^2 + 1} = E_1 \cdot E_{02}\rho(p' \cdot p_{s2'} + 1)\sqrt{p_{s1'}^2 + 1} \ .$$

In this equation p' is the only unknown. Since it only appears as a linear term, p' can be recovered uniquely from the irradiance pair (E_1, E_2). The variable q' can be determined by substituting p' into one of the two image irradiance equations. The equation

$$E_1^2 E_{02}^2 \rho^2 (p'^2 + q'^2 + 1)(p_{s1'}^2 + 1) = (p' \cdot p_{s1'} + 1)^2$$

is quadratic in q'. Therefore, there exist at most two possible solutions $q'_{1,2}$. Finally, the pair of orientations can be calculated easily through an inverse rotation by using the matrix $\mathbf{R}^{-1} = \mathbf{R}^T$. Q.E.D.

To illustrate the set of surface orientations that are consistent with a single irradiance value E a right circular cone was used in Section 7.1.1. When two irradiances E_1 and E_2 are known the set of solutions reduces to the intersection of two right circular cones as illustrated in Fig. 8.5.
    If the illumination directions are different and the cones do not just touch, then there exist two intersections for a consistent (physically plausible) irradiance pair. A unique solution exists if the cones touch each other. No solution exists if the two image irradiances are not consistent with each other.

Theorem 8.2: *If a pair of solutions exists under the assumptions of Theorem 8.1 then these orientations are symmetric with respect to that plane which is spanned by the two illumination directions* $\mathbf{s}_1$ *and* $\mathbf{s}_2$ *in the XYZ coordinate system.*

Proof: In equation

$$E_1^2 E_{02}^2 \rho^2 (p'^2 + q'^2 + 1)(p_{s1'}^2 + 1) = (p' \cdot p_{s1'} + 1)^2$$

of the proof of Theorem 8.1 the variable q' appears only in the quadratic term q'^2. Therefore, the q'-components of the two rotated solutions of the quadratic equation only differ in their sign. It follows that the rotated orientations are symmetric to the XY-plane. Furthermore, the orientations are symmetric to the plane spanned by the rotated illumination directions $\mathbf{s}_{1'}$ and $\mathbf{s}_{2'}$ since they lie in the XY-plane. After applying the inverse rotation $\mathbf{R}^T$ the illumination directions still define the symmetry plane for both orientations. Q.E.D.

Theorem 8.3: *If a unique solution normal* **n** *exists under the assumptions of Theorem 8.1 then the three position vectors* **n**, $\mathbf{s}_1$, *and* $\mathbf{s}_2$ *are coplanar in the XYZ coordinate system.*

Proof: According to Theorem 8.2 the two possible q'-values only differ in their sign. Thus, the solution is unique if $q' = 0$. The rotated surface normal **n'** is coplanar to the rotated illumination directions $\mathbf{s}_{1'}$ and $\mathbf{s}_{2'}$ because the Y-components of the vectors are equal to zero. Thus, the surface orientation **n** and the illumination directions $\mathbf{s}_1$ and $\mathbf{s}_2$ are coplanar. Q.E.D.

From Theorem 8.3 it follows that for certain surface geometries a unique surface orientation can be recovered from an irradiance pair without taking the neighborhood of the considered image point into account if Lambertian reflectance maps can be used to model the reflection properties. All visible orientations of such a surface have to be coplanar. This holds for a subset of the ruled surfaces (compare Example 8.1) which do not necessarily even have to be $C^{(1)}$ continuous. For example, cylinders and right prisms can be described as such ruled surfaces. The light sources have to be arranged in such a way that their directions $\mathbf{s}_1$ and $\mathbf{s}_2$ are always parallel to the surface normals of the object.

As an important result we see that the problem is no longer ill-posed due to the strong geometric constraints (compare Section 1.1.2). Note that this surface geometry was also used in Example 8.1. Hence all ambiguities that were discussed in Example 8.1 can now be resolved by using two light sources. Surface normals can be recovered locally, i.e. without considering adjacent points or introducing additional constraints.

But there exist image acquisition set-ups where the geometric relation between the surface normals **n** and the illumination directions $\mathbf{s}_1$ and $\mathbf{s}_2$ will not lead to any improvements in comparison to SFS. If the plane defined by the illumination directions is orthogonal to the plane which is parallel to all visible surface normals, then no reduction of the set of possible solutions can be obtained with respect to the ruled surfaces discussed in Example 8.1.

Example 8.2: This example compares the two extreme cases just mentioned above. The surface of a half cylinder will be employed as object geometry since it shows the feature of coplanarity for all surface normals. If additionally the illumination directions $\mathbf{s}_1$ and $\mathbf{s}_2$ and the surface normals **n** are parallel to a plane, then the orientation of every surface point which is illuminated by both light sources can be uniquely calculated by an irradiance pair (compare Fig. 8.6).

When we rotate the illumination directions $\mathbf{s}_1$ and $\mathbf{s}_2$ by 90° about the viewer direction **v** which is coplanar to $\mathbf{s}_1$ and $\mathbf{s}_2$ as well as orthogonal to the plane where the half cylinder lies on, we obtain the image acquisition set-up as illustrated in Fig. 8.7. According to Theorem 8.1 and Theorem 8.2 two orienta-

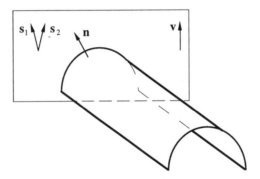

Figure 8.6: Unique and albedo dependent reconstruction of the surface orientations of a half cylinder using irradiance pairs. The illumination directions and the surface normals have to be parallel to a plane. In this case, the reconstruction of the surface normals can be done point-locally for all points.

tions are possible for each irradiance pair. Assume that for point **P** in Fig. 8.7 the two solutions are $\mathbf{n}_1$ and $\mathbf{n}_2$. Similarly to the hemispheres in Fig. 8.1 we cannot distinguish between a convex and a concave (negative) half cylinder. In this case a second light source does not help to resolve the concave-convex conflict. { end of Example 8.2 }

Now it will be shown how the two solutions can be calculated that exist for an image irradiance pair. For example, the strategy that was used in the proof of Theorem 8.2 can be applied. But it is easier to calculate the possible orientations from an explicit formula.

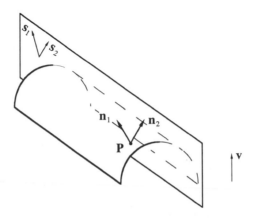

Figure 8.7: Example of a half cylinder for which the concave-convex conflict cannot be resolved through the analysis of irradiances pairs. Here, the plane defined by the illumination directions is orthogonal to the plane which is parallel to all surface normals.

The two orientations can be described by a system of vector equations which has the solutions

$$\mathbf{n}_{1,2}^{\circ} = \frac{u_{1,2} \cdot \mathbf{s}_1 + u_{2,1} \cdot \mathbf{s}_2 \pm w \cdot \mathbf{s}_1 \times \mathbf{s}_2}{\|\mathbf{s}_1 \times \mathbf{s}_2\|^2},$$

see B.K.P. Horn (1986). The scaling factors $u_{i,j}$ and w are given by the equations

$$u_{i,j} = \hat{E}_i \|\mathbf{s}_j\|^2 - \hat{E}_j \cdot \mathbf{s}_i^T \mathbf{s}_j \quad \text{and} \quad w = \sqrt{\|\mathbf{s}_1 \times \mathbf{s}_2\|^2 - \|\hat{E}_2 \cdot \mathbf{s}_1 - \hat{E}_1 \cdot \mathbf{s}_2\|^2},$$

with $\hat{E}_a = \dfrac{E_a \|\mathbf{s}_a\|}{E_{0a}\rho}$ and $a, i, j = 1, 2$.

From the equations it follows immediately that not every irradiance pair represents a valid orientation, since the irradiances are inconsistent with the two image irradiance equations. For such pairs the radicand (term under the root sign) is negative. If the radicand is zero, we obtain a unique solution since then

$$w = 0 \quad \text{and} \quad \mathbf{n}_1^{\circ} = \mathbf{n}_2^{\circ}.$$

Two solutions exist, if the radicand is positive. In the following, the solution vector

$$\mathbf{n}_1^{\circ} = \frac{u_{1,2} \cdot \mathbf{s}_1 + u_{2,1} \cdot \mathbf{s}_2 + w \cdot \mathbf{s}_1 \times \mathbf{s}_2}{\|\mathbf{s}_1 \times \mathbf{s}_2\|^2}$$

is referred to as the *positive solution*. The solution

$$\mathbf{n}_2^{\circ} = \frac{u_{1,2} \cdot \mathbf{s}_1 + u_{2,1} \cdot \mathbf{s}_2 + (-w) \cdot \mathbf{s}_1 \times \mathbf{s}_2}{\|\mathbf{s}_1 \times \mathbf{s}_2\|^2}$$

is referred to as the *negative solution*. If we know one of the two solution vectors, the other solution vector can be determined using the illumination vectors $\mathbf{s}_1$ and $\mathbf{s}_2$ even if the initial image irradiances are unknown.

For many curved surfaces possessing a simple geometry the image points with a unique solution, i.e. $\mathbf{n}_1^{\circ} = \mathbf{n}_2^{\circ}$ lie on a single, open curve C. This especially holds for convex surfaces. According to Theorem 8.2 the surface points which correspond to the image curve C have orientations which are parallel to the plane of the illumination directions $\mathbf{s}_1$ and $\mathbf{s}_2$. For the sphere in Fig. 8.8 the curve C coincides with the great circle defined by $\mathbf{s}_1$ and $\mathbf{s}_2$ which is projected into the image plane.

The curve C divides the image into two regions R_1 and R_2. For two close points $\mathbf{p}$ and $\mathbf{q}$ in the regions R_1 and R_2, respectively, the four combination

$$\left(\mathbf{n}_1^\circ(\mathbf{p}),\ \mathbf{n}_1^\circ(\mathbf{q})\right),\ \left(\mathbf{n}_1^\circ(\mathbf{p}),\ \mathbf{n}_2^\circ(\mathbf{q})\right),$$

$$\left(\mathbf{n}_2^\circ(\mathbf{p}),\ \mathbf{n}_1^\circ(\mathbf{q})\right),\ \left(\mathbf{n}_2^\circ(\mathbf{p}),\ \mathbf{n}_2^\circ(\mathbf{q})\right)$$

of possible pairs of solutions exist. As already known there exist a positive and a negative solution for both points $\mathbf{p}$ and $\mathbf{q}$. One of the above solution pairs describes a convex situation in the neighborhood of $\mathbf{p}$ and $\mathbf{q}$. Another pair describes a concave situation. For the two remaining pairs both orientations point in the same half space with respect to the symmetry plane defined by $\mathbf{s}_1$ and $\mathbf{s}_2$. Thus, $\mathbf{p}$ and $\mathbf{q}$ would lie in the neighborhood of a saddle point on the curve C. Figure 8.9 illustrates the four different cases by showing cross-sections of surfaces which are consistent with the surface normal pairs. All points on the curve C (in the cross-section just a point) are similar to the points of contact (switches) in Fig. 8.2.

An example of a possible location of the cross-section is shown in Fig. 8.8 as a curve segment passing through the image points $\mathbf{p}$ and $\mathbf{q}$. The cross-section was chosen as being orthogonal to the symmetry plane. In Fig. 8.9 the surface normals which are drawn in bold display the intended orientations for the four possible local surface structures.

It can be shown that inside the regions R_1 and R_2, which are separated by the curve C, the surface normal of a smooth object cannot change from a negative to a positive solution, or vice versa. R. Onn and A. Bruckstein (1990) could show that each region contains only such orientations which point into one half space with respect to the symmetry plane. Formally, this means that the scalar product

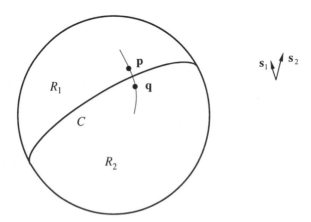

Figure 8.8: Segmented image of a sphere. The locations of uniquely recoverable orientations lie on the curve C. The thin curve segment passing through the points $\mathbf{p}$ and $\mathbf{q}$ identify the surface cross-section used in Fig. 8.9.

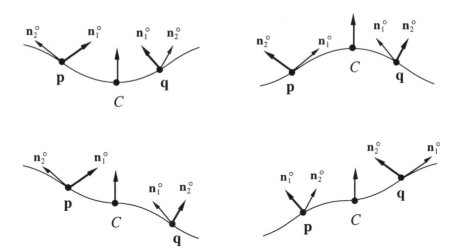

Figure 8.9: Ambiguities of a recovered surface caused by two solution normals at each image point. The four subfigures illustrate cross-sections of the surface shown in Fig. 8.8. The cross-sections are orthogonal to the symmetry plane defined by the illumination directions.

of the vectors $\mathbf{n}$ and $\mathbf{s}_1 \times \mathbf{s}_2$,

$$\mathbf{n}^T(\mathbf{s}_1 \times \mathbf{s}_2),$$

does not change its sign inside a region. This property is very important with respect to the calculation of a unique surface. It implies that the solutions cannot change independently between being positive and negative in a local neighborhood.

8.2.3 Uniqueness by Integrability

This section shows how a unique surface can be recovered despite the mentioned ambiguities. This can be achieved in different ways.

Direct SFS extension. A simple approach to recover a unique surface is to extend SFS methods. The global minimization approaches (compare Section 7.3) are particularly suitable for this because the functionals can be extended by introducing additional conditions based on the second image. However, the fact that the set of solutions is already point-locally constrained to at most two surface normals can generally not be taken into account.

Convexity assumption. Following the discussion in the previous section, another way to seek for a unique solution is to restrict the object scenes to convex or concave surfaces. As shown above, the solution can be determined uniquely.

Integrability constraint. Furthermore, we can try to recover a unique surface by constraining the set of solutions through an integrability condition as already described in the previous chapter. R. Onn and A. Bruckstein (1990) as well as R. Kozera (1991, 1992) use the integrability constraint

$$\frac{\partial p(x, y)}{\partial y} = \frac{\partial q(x, y)}{\partial x} \, ,$$

which was applied to formulate the functional $\mathbf{F}i_1$ in Section 7.3.1 (see also Section 3.1.1).

From Example 8.2 it can be seen that in spite of applying an integrability constraint a unique reconstruction of the surfaces is not possible for arbitrary configurations of objects and light sources. However, it is sensible to include an integrability constraint in the reconstruction process since it helps to detect gradient regions that do not correspond to a valid height map. This will be illustrated by using the example of a convex half cylinder once again.

Example 8.3: Assume the situation in the first part of Example 8.2 as the initial configuration (see Fig. 8.6). If we rotate the illumination directions $\mathbf{s}_1$ and $\mathbf{s}_2$ by the angle α, with $\alpha \in (0°, 90°)$, about the viewer direction $\mathbf{v}$, then according to Theorem 8.2 the symmetry plane of the surface normal pairs is also subjected to this rotation. Figure 8.10 shows the half cylinder as it appears after applying an orthographic projection from a viewer direction $\mathbf{v}$ which is orthogonal to the plane on the page. The illumination directions were rotated by $\alpha = 22.5°$ from the initial configuration (compare Fig. 8.6).

The left hand side of Fig. 8.10 shows a needle map (compare Section 3.2.3) of the negative solutions [4]. On the straight line segment C those orientations $\mathbf{n}$ are located, for which a unique solution can be determined. In the example it holds $\mathbf{n} = \mathbf{v}$. The orientations on C are invariant with respect to the chosen rotation angle α. The set of positive solutions is shown in Fig. 8.10 on the right.

In the following it is shown that the set of gradients on the left hand side of C in the left needle map (region R_{11}) and the set of gradients right of C in the right hand needle map (region R_{22}) do not satisfy the condition of the integrability constraint. Figure 8.11 shows an enlarged part of the left needle map of Fig. 8.10. It can be tested whether the condition of the integrability constraint is satisfied. The given gradient map (compare Section 3.2.1) can be described formally as a vector field

$$\mathbf{K}(\mathbf{v}) \, : \, \Re^2 \to \Re^2$$

---

[4] For definition of the terms "negative solution" and "positive solution" refer to the end of Section 8.2.2.

which has to be conservative to have a physically plausible meaning. The intgration of a conservative vector field is independent of the integration path between two arbitrary points **p** and **q** (compare Section 3.1.1). Two different paths from **p** to **q** are shown in Fig. 8.11. Assume that the path from **p** to **u** is parallel to the surface gradients, i.e. parallel to the orientations of the shown needles. Assume that the path from **u** to **q** is perpendicular to the surface gradients. The line integral

$$\int_{pq} \mathbf{K}\,d\mathbf{r}$$

over the linear path from **p** to **q** of the gradient map is qual to zero. Since all orientations on the curve C point towards the viewer no height change occurs (i.e. no change in Z). The question is whether the line integral sum

$$\int_{pu} \mathbf{K}\,d\mathbf{r} + \int_{uq} \mathbf{K}\,d\mathbf{r}$$

is equal to zero, as well. The second summand is equal to zero because the path direction is perpendicular to the surface gradients. However, the first summand is obviously not equal to zero. Thus, it could be shown that the condition of the integrability constraint is not satisfied for region R_{11}.

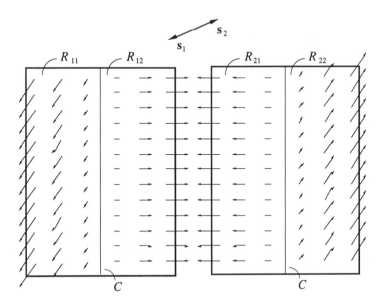

Figure 8.10: Needle maps for an image pair of a half cylinder. The gradient pairs were calculated albedo dependently. The left needle map shows the negative solutions. The needle map on the right shows the positive solutions. The straight line segment C describes locations having unique solutions.

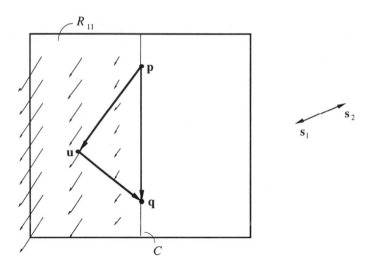

Figure 8.11: Needle map of a non-integrable gradient map and two integration paths from point **p** to **q**. The straight line segment C shows locations of unique solutions.

The same can be shown for region R_{22} whereas the gradient maps of the regions R_{12} and R_{21} are conservative vector fields. Finally, we have to merge R_{12} and R_{21}. The condition of the integrability constraint for the half cylinder cannot be satisfied with respect to a rotation with $\alpha \in (0°, 90°)$ for the regions R_{12} and R_{21}. { end of Example 8.3 }

This example has demonstrated that the application of an integrability constraint can support the recovery of unique gradient maps enormously.

(Task 8.1) A unique gradient map shall be recovered from a pair of irradiance images of a Lambertian reflecting object by using the integrability constraint. The illumination directions s_1 and s_2 associated with the irradiance images and the irradiances E_{01}, E_{02} of the two light sources are assumed to be known. Furthermore, the albedo ρ is known and assumed to be constant over the object surface.

(Solution 8.1) The surface normal pairs are determined for every image point and stored in the gradient maps $(p_1(x, y), q_1(x, y))$ and $(p_2(x, y), q_2(x, y))$, as the first step. R. Onn and A. Bruckstein (1990) provide methods to segment the image and to calculate the integrability condition. The next step is to prepare the segmentation. Therefore, singular image points are labeled where a surface normal can be uniquely recovered. Furthermore, image regions are labeled where at least one of the irradiances is zero or invalid. Both sets of labels define a binary mask. Then, the inverse mask is used to segment the image into regions Ω consisting of either positive or negative solutions. This can be done by applying a standard connected components algorithm.

As shown in Example 8.3, often only one of the two gradient images satisfies the condition of the integrability constraint in each segmented region. The integral Fi_1 which is defined in Section 7.3.1 is used as the integrability constraint. In order to select the correct solution in a region Ω the integrals

$$e_1 = \iint_{\Omega} \left(\frac{\partial p_1(x, y)}{\partial y} - \frac{\partial q_1(x, y)}{\partial x} \right)^2 dxdy \text{ and}$$

$$e_2 = \iint_{\Omega} \left(\frac{\partial p_2(x, y)}{\partial y} - \frac{\partial q_2(x, y)}{\partial x} \right)^2 dxdy$$

are calculated. The gradient image which possesses the smaller error value is interpreted as the correct solution for the region Ω. But note that for the images of the half cylinder in the second part of Example 8.2 both integrals would become zero which indicates that the ambiguity cannot be resolved.

(Algorithm 8.1) The first part of a possible realization of the described method is illustrated in Fig. 8.12. The employed functions $p(\mathbf{n})$ and $q(\mathbf{n})$ were defined in Section 3.4.1. The subalgorithm *Calculation* contains the determination of the solution pairs and the labeling process. In the second subalgorithm *Selection* which is illustrated in Fig. 8.13 the integrability constraint is applied for every segmented region Ω and the selected resulting gradients are assigned to the output gradient map $(p_{result}(x, y), q_{result}(x, y))$.

(Comment 8.1) The method uses only a few assumptions on the geometry of the surface. As already mentioned it has to be assumed that the second partial derivatives of the surface are not equal to zero. However, some further aspects have to be considered to apply the method.

Firstly, discrete partial derivatives have to be calculated. This can only be done approximately (compare Exercise (8) in Section 8.5). Because of the necessary discretization the integrability constraint not only "evaluates" the partial derivatives but "evaluates" the discretization error, as well. The discretization error of the partial derivatives distorts the values e_1 and e_2 of the error integrals. Hence it is difficult to distinguish them from the actual values which describe the integrability.

Secondly, the validity of the calculated criterion also depends on the size of the regions Ω. The larger the regions, the more accurately the criterion can be calculated. The size of the regions depends on the object geometry as well as on the illumination directions. Thirdly, the locations of unique solutions are found by applying a threshold that can be used to control which orientations are classified as belonging to the symmetry plane.

begin

    for every image point (x,y) **do**

        if $(E_1(x, y) \neq 0)$ **and** $(E_2(x, y) \neq 0)$ **then begin**

$$\hat{E}_1 := \frac{E_1(x, y)\|\mathbf{s}_1\|}{E_{01}\rho} ; \quad \hat{E}_2 := \frac{E_2(x, y)\|\mathbf{s}_2\|}{E_{02}\rho} ;$$

$$u_{1,2} := \hat{E}_1 \|\mathbf{s}_2\|^2 - \hat{E}_2 \cdot \mathbf{s}_1^T \mathbf{s}_2 \; ; \; u_{2,1} := \hat{E}_2 \|\mathbf{s}_1\|^2 - \hat{E}_1 \cdot \mathbf{s}_2^T \mathbf{s}_1 \; ;$$

$$h := \|\mathbf{s}_1 \times \mathbf{s}_2\|^2 - \left\| \hat{E}_2 \cdot \mathbf{s}_1 - \hat{E}_1 \cdot \mathbf{s}_2 \right\|^2 \; ; \; \{ \, h = w^2 \, \}$$

        if $h < 0$ **then**

            label image point (x,y) as being invalid

        else begin

$$\mathbf{n}_1^\circ = \frac{u_{1,2} \cdot \mathbf{s}_1 + u_{2,1} \cdot \mathbf{s}_2 + \sqrt{h} \cdot \mathbf{s}_1 \times \mathbf{s}_2}{\|\mathbf{s}_1 \times \mathbf{s}_2\|^2} \; ;$$

$$\mathbf{n}_2^\circ = \frac{u_{1,2} \cdot \mathbf{s}_1 + u_{2,1} \cdot \mathbf{s}_2 - \sqrt{h} \cdot \mathbf{s}_1 \times \mathbf{s}_2}{\|\mathbf{s}_1 \times \mathbf{s}_2\|^2} \; ;$$

        if h is close to zero **then begin**

            label image point (x,y) as being singular ;

$$P_{result}(x, y) := p(\mathbf{n}_1^\circ + \mathbf{n}_2^\circ) \; ;$$

$$q_{result}(x, y) := q(\mathbf{n}_1^\circ + \mathbf{n}_2^\circ)$$

        end else begin

$$p_1(x, y) := p(\mathbf{n}_1^\circ) \; ; \; q_1(x, y) := q(\mathbf{n}_1^\circ) \; ;$$

$$p_2(x, y) := p(\mathbf{n}_2^\circ) \; ; \; q_2(x, y) := q(\mathbf{n}_2^\circ)$$

        end

      end $\{ \, h \geq 0 \, \}$

    end else label image point (x,y) as being invalid

end;

Figure 8.12: Subalgorithm *Calculation* for the 2S photometric stereo method by R. Onn and A. Bruckstein (1990).

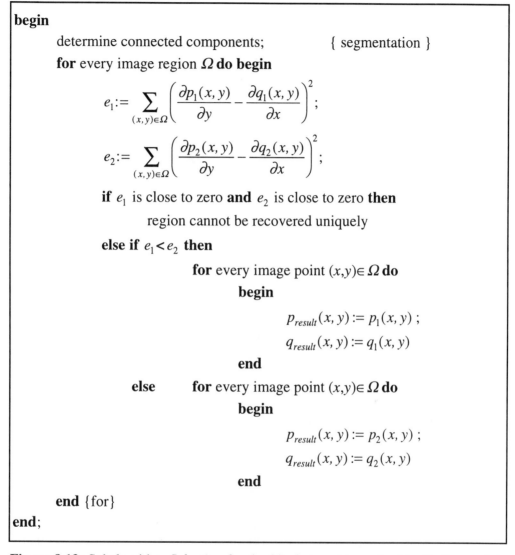

begin

  determine connected components;   { segmentation }

  for every image region Ω **do begin**

$$e_1 := \sum_{(x,y)\in\Omega} \left(\frac{\partial p_1(x,y)}{\partial y} - \frac{\partial q_1(x,y)}{\partial x} \right)^2 ;$$

$$e_2 := \sum_{(x,y)\in\Omega} \left(\frac{\partial p_2(x,y)}{\partial y} - \frac{\partial q_2(x,y)}{\partial x} \right)^2 ;$$

  if e_1 is close to zero **and** e_2 is close to zero **then**

    region cannot be recovered uniquely

  else if $e_1 < e_2$ **then**

      for every image point $(x,y) \in \Omega$ **do**

       begin

        $p_{result}(x,y) := p_1(x,y)$;

        $q_{result}(x,y) := q_1(x,y)$

       end

  else **for** every image point $(x,y) \in \Omega$ **do**

       begin

        $p_{result}(x,y) := p_2(x,y)$;

        $q_{result}(x,y) := q_2(x,y)$

       end

  end {for}

end;

Figure 8.13: Subalgorithm *Selection* for the 2S photometric method by R. Onn and A. Bruckstein (1990).

Figure 8.14 shows the needle maps of the positive solutions (left picture) and the negative solutions (right picture) for a synthetic sphere with a radius of 100 pixels. The orientation pairs were calculated by subalgorithm *Calculation* of Algorithm 8.1 (see Fig. 8.12). Lambertian reflectance maps having the illumination directions

$$\mathbf{s}_1 = (-0.3, \ -0.3, \ -1) \text{ and } \mathbf{s}_2 = (0.3, \ 0.3, \ -1)$$

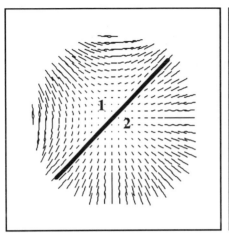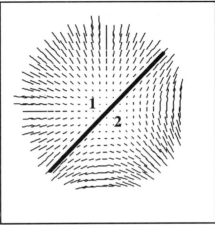

Figure 8.14: Needle map pair illustrating the surface normal pairs of a sphere calculated as the first step in an albedo dependent 2S photometric stereo method. The left needle map shows the positive solutions. The negative solutions are presented on the right. The straight line segment drawn in bold illustrates locations of unique solutions. The labels identify the segmented regions.

were selected to render the two input images of the sphere. Using these illumination directions the symmetry plane graphically sketched in the needle map transforms into a diagonal straight line segment (see Fig. 8.14).

These straight line segments correspond to the curve C in Fig. 8.8. In region 1 lying left of the straight line segment the negative solutions are the correct gradients, whereas in region 2 the positive solutions correspond to the intended solution. The other solutions are not integrable (compare Exercise (7) in Section 8.5), respectively. When a symmetric difference quotient[5] is used to calculate the integrability constraint, then the error variables e_1 and e_2 in the algorithm *Selection* (see Fig. 8.13) have a ratio of about 1:100 for the sphere. Each of the two regions contains approximately 12,000 image points. Thus, for the synthetic sphere we can robustly distinguish between the integrable and the non-integrable solution.

For image pairs of more complex objects such as the synthetic Lambertian Mozart statue that was already used in the previous chapter the selection of the correct solution is more difficult because some of the segmented regions contain only a few image points. Illumination directions s_1 and s_2 having the spherical coordinates

$$\sigma(s_1) = \sigma(s_2) = 20°, \quad \theta(s_1) = -150° \quad \text{and} \quad \theta(s_2) = -30°$$

---

[5] See Exercise (8) in Section 8.5.

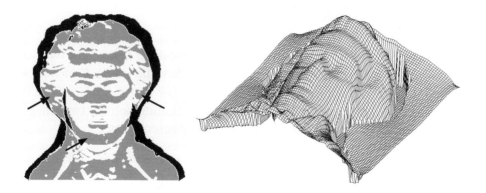

Figure 8.15: Left: Labeled image of a synthetic Mozart statue. For the coding of the four gray values refer to the text. The arrows indicate regions with incorrectly selected surface normals. Right: 3D plot of the recovered Mozart statue.

were chosen to render the statue[6]. The two irradiance images of the Mozart statue are displayed in Fig. 8.22 (center and right picture).

For a discrete image a certain threshold has to be defined that indicates which orientations are considered as belonging to the symmetry plane. A simple and useful criterion is to measure the angle which is subtended by the symmetry plane and the examined orientation. If the angle is smaller than a threshold, then the solution is classified as being unique. A threshold of 10° was applied for the Mozart statue.

The left picture of Fig. 8.15 shows the labeled segmentation result. In the black regions one of the two irradiances is zero so that no orientation can be determined. The light gray regions characterize locations whose orientations were classified as belonging to the symmetry plane. Dark gray regions represent locations for which the integrability criterion could be calculated. White regions indicate locations which were left untouched because they are too close to the boundary, the irradiances are too low, or the gradients are too steep.

A wrong selection of a positive or negative solution occurs in some regions. The largest areas where the wrong solution was selected are indicated by arrows. The right hand picture of Fig. 8.15 shows the recovered surface of the Mozart statue. Since for integration of the surface the method introduced in Section 3.3.2 was used the incorrectly recovered surface normals have only a minor effect on the overall result. Visible errors occur at the chin where a double chin appears. The recovery result can be improved by an adaptive segmentation.

---

6 The functions σ and θ were defined in Section 3.4.1.

8.2.4   Albedo Independent Analysis

As proved in Theorem 8.1 the number of solutions can be reduced to two with an irradiance pair of consistent surface orientations when the terms $E_{01}\rho$ and $E_{02}\rho y$ are known. In the following it will be examined how many solutions we obtain when the albedo ρ stays unknown. Under parallel illumination the two image irradiance equations of a Lambertian surface can be represented as

$$E_1 = E_{01}\rho\frac{\mathbf{n}^T\mathbf{s}_1}{\|\mathbf{n}\|\cdot\|\mathbf{s}_1\|} \quad , \quad E_2 = E_{02}\rho\frac{\mathbf{n}^T\mathbf{s}_2}{\|\mathbf{n}\|\cdot\|\mathbf{s}_2\|}.$$

To eliminate the denominator the two equations can be subtracted in the following way (compare proof of Theorem 8.1)

$$
\begin{array}{c|c|}
E_{01}\,\rho\cdot\mathbf{n}^T\mathbf{s}_1 = E_1\|\mathbf{n}\|\cdot\|\mathbf{s}_1\| & \cdot E_2\|\mathbf{s}_2\| \\
E_{02}\,\rho\cdot\mathbf{n}^T\,\mathbf{s}_2 = E_2\|\mathbf{n}\|\cdot\|\mathbf{s}_2\| & \cdot E_1\|\mathbf{s}_1\|
\end{array} \; -
$$

resulting in the equation

$$\rho\cdot\mathbf{n}^T(E_{01}\cdot E_2\|\mathbf{s}_2\|\|\mathbf{s}_1\| - E_{02}\cdot E_1\|\mathbf{s}_1\|\|\mathbf{s}_2\|) = 0 \; ,$$

which can be interpreted as a scaled scalar product. If $\rho \neq 0$, then the albedo can be eliminated from the equation which leads to albedo independence. By collecting the known quantities in

$$E_{0a,b} = E_{0a}\cdot E_b\|\mathbf{s}_b\|$$

the equation can be represented as the simplified scalar product

$$\mathbf{n}^T(E_{01,2}\cdot\mathbf{s}_1 - E_{02,1}\cdot\mathbf{s}_2) = 0 \; .$$

The representation

$$\mathbf{n}^T(\mathbf{s}_{1,2} - \mathbf{s}_{2,1}) = 0 \; , \quad \text{with } \mathbf{s}_{a,b} = E_{0a,b}\cdot\mathbf{s}_a = E_{0a}\cdot E_b\|\mathbf{s}_b\|\mathbf{s}_a$$

is even more compact. The vector difference $\mathbf{s}_{1,2} - \mathbf{s}_{2,1}$ consists of known quantities and lies in the symmetry plane defined by the illumination directions $\mathbf{s}_1$ and $\mathbf{s}_2$. For a given illumination geometry the variables of the vector difference $\mathbf{s}_{1,2} - \mathbf{s}_{2,1}$ are just the two image irradiances E_1 and E_2. The vector $\mathbf{s}_1 \times \mathbf{s}_2$ is perpendicular to the set of vectors defined by $\mathbf{s}_{1,2} - \mathbf{s}_{2,1}$. The solutions of the above equation are vectors $\mathbf{n}$, for which the scalar product becomes zero. From this it follows that all those vectors $\mathbf{n}$ satisfy the equation which are oriented orthogonal to the vector difference $\mathbf{s}_{1,2} - \mathbf{s}_{2,1}$ (compare Fig. 8.16).

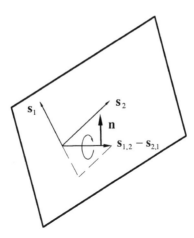

Figure 8.16: Illustration of the orientations which are consistent with an albedo independent irradiance pair. These are all the vectors which are perpendicular to a fixed linear combination of the illumination directions.

The gradients of the possible vector differences $s_{1,2} - s_{2,1}$ lie in the gradient space on a determinable straight line h which is constant for a given illumination geometry. The straight line h is the line which is dual to the gradient

$$(p_s, q_s) = (p(s_1 \times s_2), q(s_1 \times s_2))$$

(compare Section 3.4.2). A unique point on h is assigned to each irradiance pair (E_1, E_2). From the relationship

$$n^T (s_{1,2} - s_{2,1}) = 0$$

it follows that each gradient G on the straight line h has a dual straight line k which represents the possible solutions n of the above equation (compare Fig. 8.17). The straight line h can be described explicitly by the equation

$$q_h = h(p_h) = -\frac{p_s}{q_s} \cdot p_h - \frac{1}{q_s}$$

(compare Section 3.4.2). The set of straight lines generated by the straight line h can be represented explicitly by

$$q_k = k(p_k) = \frac{q_s}{1 + p_s \cdot p_h} \cdot (1 + p_h \cdot p_k) \, .$$

The variable p_h itself depends on the measured image irradiance pair (E_1, E_2) and can be calculated by

$$p_h = p(\mathbf{u}) , \text{ with } \mathbf{u} = E_{01} \cdot E_2 \|\mathbf{s}_2\| \mathbf{s}_1 - E_{02} \cdot E_1 \|\mathbf{s}_1\| \mathbf{s}_2.$$

Thus, all gradients which are consistent with any arbitrary irradiance pair can be calculated by using this equation. It can be shown that the gradient (p_s, q_s) lies on the straight line k. The albedo p can be found for every gradient by substituting a solution into any of the two image irradiance equations.

If we look at the corresponding points on the Gaussian sphere, then every pair of positive irradiances restricts the orientations to a half of a great circle because the latter is represented in the gradient space by a straight line (compare Section 3.4.2). In contrast to the gradient space the representation of orientations using the Gaussian sphere is independent from the viewer direction $\mathbf{v}$. Therefore, the number of solutions reduces implicitly from a great circle to a half of a great circle since only those orientations are relevant.

8.2.5 Uniqueness By Spherical Approximation

In principle, the albedo independent reconstruction of orientations starting from a single irradiance pair can be compared with SFS. In both cases the irradiance information restricts the orientations to circles on the Gaussian sphere. The dependence on the viewer direction $\mathbf{v}$ is ignored in the following.

The perimeter of the circles can be seen as a measure of the cardinality of the orientations which are consistent with the irradiances. For SFS methods the

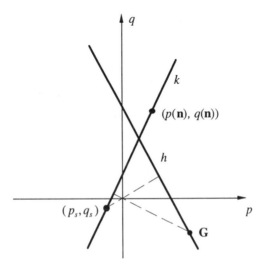

Figure 8.17: Representation of these gradients which are consistent with an irradiance pair by a straight line k in gradient space.

perimeter of the circle is always smaller than 2π for positive irradiances. The larger the irradiance value, the smaller the perimeter of the circle. The irradiance E and the perimeter U of the circle are related through the equation

$$U = 2\pi \cdot \left(1 - \left(\frac{E}{E_0 \rho}\right)^2\right).$$

On the other hand, the perimeter of the circle of albedo independent 2S methods remains always equal to 2π for all irradiance pairs and therefore it is in general larger than the circles in SFS methods while keeping the viewer direction and the restriction of the orientations by the illumination directions in mind. Besides the surface orientation another unknown variable, the albedo ρ, exists for 2S methods. As discussed before, neighboring orientations on the surface are often linked together through smoothness assumptions. From a formal point of view such assumptions would also be sensible for the albedo. But for real-world objects discontinuous albedo changes are more likely. Usually discontinuous albedo variations occur more often than smooth color value changes or gray value changes.

(Task 8.2) Assume that a unique gradient map of a Lambertian surface has to be recovered from a pair of irradiance images without knowing the albedo value ρ. Assume that the two illumination directions $\mathbf{s}_1$ and $\mathbf{s}_2$ are known associated with the irradiance images.

(Solution 8.2) C.-H. Lee and A. Rosenfeld (1984) propose a 3D shape recovery method for Lambertian surfaces that can be approximated locally by spheres. The same restriction was already used for the local SFS method in Section 7.4.1. Under the assumption of a locally spherical surface it can be shown that the possible orientations can be restricted to a straight line in the gradient space for a given a single image irradiance value E. This is even possible without knowledge of the $E_0 \rho$ term. The restriction to a straight line follows like in Section 7.4.1 by using the irradiance changes for the considered image point. It can be shown that this straight line can be represented by the equation

$$E_y \cdot p - E_x \cdot q = tan(\sigma(\mathbf{s})) \cdot \left(cos(\theta(\mathbf{s})) \cdot E_y - sin(\theta(\mathbf{s})) \cdot E_x\right),$$

$$\text{with } E_x = \frac{\partial E(x, y)}{\partial x} \text{ and } E_y = \frac{\partial E(x, y)}{\partial y}.$$

As for linear reflectance maps (compare Section 8.2.1) two irradiances are sufficient to recover the gradient (p, q) uniquely by intersecting two straight lines.

(**Algorithm 8.2**) The gradient (p, q) can be calculated for each image point with the equation

$$\begin{pmatrix} p \\ q \end{pmatrix} = \begin{pmatrix} E_{1y} & -E_{1x} \\ E_{2y} & -E_{2x} \end{pmatrix}^{-1} \cdot \begin{pmatrix} tan(\sigma(\mathbf{s}_1)) \cdot \left(cos(\theta(\mathbf{s}_1)) \cdot E_{1y} - sin(\theta(\mathbf{s}_1)) \cdot E_{1x} \right) \\ tan(\sigma(\mathbf{s}_2)) \cdot \left(cos(\theta(\mathbf{s}_2)) \cdot E_{2y} - sin(\theta(\mathbf{s}_2)) \cdot E_{2x} \right) \end{pmatrix}$$

with $E_{ix} = \dfrac{\partial E_i(x, y)}{\partial x}$ and $E_{iy} = \dfrac{\partial E_i(x, y)}{\partial y}$, $i = 1, 2$,

using the irradiance pair (E_1, E_2). For simplification we assume that the light sources have identical irradiances, i.e. $E_{01} = E_{02}$. Figure 8.18 shows the entire algorithm (compare Exercise (5) in Section 8.5).

(**Comment 8.2**) The above equation is not only independent of the albedo ρ, it can be reformulated so that the equation becomes independent of the absolute irradiances of the light sources, as well. In practice this makes the the determination of the illumination parameters easier. As a conclusion the knowledge of the

---

begin
    { Let (p_{s1}, q_{s1}) and (p_{s2}, q_{s2}) be the gradients of the
    illumination directions $\mathbf{s}_1$ and $\mathbf{s}_2$. }

  for every image point with positive irradiances E_1 and E_2 **do**
    begin
      calculate the partial derivatives E_{1x}, E_{2x}, E_{1y}, and E_{2y}.
      $h_1 := E_{1y} \cdot p_{s1} - E_{1x} \cdot q_{s1}$;
      $h_2 := E_{2y} \cdot p_{s2} - E_{2x} \cdot q_{s2}$;
      $det := E_{1x} \cdot E_{2y} - E_{1y} \cdot E_{2x}$;
      if det is close to zero **then**
        gradient (p,q) cannot be determined
      else begin

$$p := \frac{E_{1x} \cdot h_2 - E_{2x} \cdot h_1}{det} \ ;$$

$$q := \frac{E_{1y} \cdot h_2 - E_{2y} \cdot h_1}{det} \ ;$$

      end
    end
end;

Figure 8.18: Albedo independent 2S method by C.-H. Lee and A. Rosenfeld (1984).

ratio E_{01}/E_{02} of the irradiances values is sufficient. For the numerical determination of the partial derivatives of the image irradiance function $E(x,y)$ it has to be assumed that the albedo ρ does not change in the immediate neighborhood of an image point.

8.3 ANALYSIS OF IRRADIANCE TRIPLETS

Section 8.2 discussed ways for shading based surface reconstruction when the analyzed objects are illuminated consecutively by two light sources. Subsequently such methods are introduced where the scene is illuminated by three light sources. Similar to Section 8.2 it is assumed that no motion occurs inside the system consisting of the object, the light sources, and the sensor. Therefore, three irradiances (*an irradiance triplet*) can be assigned to every object point that is projected into the image plane. Approaches which use three light sources are called *three source methods* or for short *3S methods*. It is assumed that all irradiances are positive which means that shadows are excluded from the analysis.

The smaller the angle between the illumination directions, the more object portions are covered simultaneously by all light sources. On the other hand, with smaller angles the sensitivity with respect to noise in the measurements of the irradiances during the image acquisition increases. The same holds for the sensitivity with respect to the inaccurate estimation of other fixed parameters, for example the illumination directions. Thus, similar to the 2S methods no optimal choice of illumination directions exists for 3S methods.

8.3.1 Albedo Dependent Analysis

As described in Section 8.2, the solution manifold of the orientations can be restricted to at most two by using an irradiance pair of a Lambertian surface. However, this requires the assumption that for both light sources the products $E_{0i}\rho$ of the light source irradiances and the albedo are known. On the Gaussian sphere the two orientations are represented by the intersection of two circles (i.e. by two right circular cones touching the Gaussian sphere, compare Fig. 8.5).

When a third light source is added to the reconstruction process, then another circle arises on the Gaussian sphere. For three consistent image irradiances the three circles must have at least one common point of intersection. If we chose the illumination direction s_3 of the third light source coplanar to the directions s_1 and s_2 of the existing light sources, then the third circle would intersect the two others at the intersections that are already known. By considering the symmetry properties of the resulting orientations (compare Section 8.2.2) this property can be proven easily. Hence, if the three illumination directions are coplanar, then the additional light source cannot resolve the ambiguity of the solutions.

However, if the three illumination directions are not coplanar and the three image irradiances are consistent with each other, then adding a third light source leads to a unique solution. Because of the symmetry properties of the orientations it is impossible that the solution remains ambiguous.

The previous paragraph contains an important conclusion: The orientation of a point on a Lambertian surface can be recovered uniquely with three image irradiances independent of the neighborhood of the considered image point. We do not have to introduce smoothness assumptions or integrability constraints. The reconstruction of the surface orientations is carried out point-locally by analyzing irradiance triplets.

Analytic intersection of isoirradiance curves. Besides the Gaussian sphere the above discussion can be carried out for other representations of the surface orientations. For a Lambertian surface the pair of gradients of an irradiance pair is given by the intersection of two conic sections in the gradient space.

The left picture in Fig. 8.19 illustrates the intersection of two conic sections. When an additional light source is introduced which generates the image irradiance E_3, then the three conic sections intersect at a unique point (see Fig. 8.19, right). The intersection (p,q) in gradient space represents the desired orientation.

When the irradiances are measured for a real surface point, then basically there never exists a unique intersection due to noise and other errors. But even in

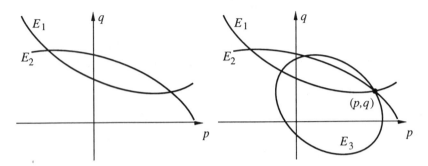

Figure 8.19: Isoirradiance curves in the gradient space. The points of intersection of the curves on the left represent the gradients of the two valid orientations of an irradiance pair. In the right hand picture a third irradiance curve is introduced which determines uniquely the desired gradient (p,q).

this case the two gradients would exist for each consistent pair of irradiances. If the three possible irradiance pairs are used to calculate the solution pairs, then six intersections occur. The irradiance pairs can be calculated with the formula from Section 8.2.2. Three of the six intersections should represent orientations which point approximately in the same direction like the sought-after surface normal $\mathbf{n} = (p, q, -1)$. Due to the properties of the gradient space (compare Section 3.4.1) not the gradients themselves but the orientations should be compared to determine an approximate orientation.

Non-analytic intersectiom of isoirradiance curves. Furthermore, the recovery of the solution could be achieved without explicitly calculating the solution candidates, simply by generating the intersection curves non-analytically. For this approach the reflectance maps are represented as image matrices. For this purpose the generation of the discrete reflectance maps can be performed by using the procedures described in Section 6.3.4. Using a calibration object has the advantage that neither the illumination directions nor the products $E_{0i}\rho$ have to be known.

The selection of the orientations could be carried out through a simple threshold segmentation of the reflectance maps. The three irradiances measured in the image are taken to select the thresholds. The segmentation result consists of three regions which represent the orientations that are consistent with the image irradiances.

As a next step, the binarized reflectance maps are intersected (binary AND operation). The centroid of the resulting region can be used to represent approximately the orientation at the considered image point. The stereographic projection (see Section 3.4.1) is a more convenient two-dimensional representation of the orientations since it causes less distortions. The width W of the segmentation interval $\left[E_i - W/2, E_i + W/2\right]$, with $i = 1,2,3$, can be adapted to the noise level in the image acquisition system and to expected variations in the albedo.

The described robust approach has the advantage that it is easily applicable to surfaces which have no Lambertian reflection properties since we do not have to solve a system of nonlinear equations. For reflectance maps that are synthetically generated and parameterized by a set of real parameters ambiguous solutions can easily be detected for a certain accuracy without a uniqueness proof. If the reflectance maps are generated by using a calibration object, then we do not have to determine the reflection parameters, i.e. the surface roughness and the ratio of the diffuse and the specular reflection component.

Look-up tables. An irradiance triplet that is measured in the image can be regarded as a point in a Cartesian coordinate system $E_1 E_2 E_3$ where each of the three axes (irradiance axis) represents the image irradiances of one light source. A surface orientation is uniquely assigned to every possible irradiance triplet, thus the generation of a three-dimensional look-up table is possible (compare Section 2.3.2).

The generation of the look-up table can be carried out in two different ways. If the illumination directions and irradiances of the light sources are known, then the look-up table can be built by applying explicit equations. Besides, a calibration object can be employed for the generation. Again it is of advantage that the directions and irradiances of the light sources as well as the reflection parameters do not have to be known explicitly.

A surface orientation is determined by looking up the entry which corresponds to the measured irradiance triplet. The look-up table entry contains either a two-dimensional representation of the surface orientation or it is empty. If the image irradiances are digitized with 8-bit accuracy and the surface orientations are encoded with 2×4 Bytes, then the look-up table needs 128MB of memory.

Figure 8.20 and Fig. 8.21 illustrate four different views of a look-up table for a real sphere showing Lambertian reflection characteristics. The estimated illumination directions for the sphere are

$$\mathbf{s}_1 = (-0.312, -0.231, -1) \, , \; \mathbf{s}_2 = (0.049, 0.304, -1), \; \text{and} \; \mathbf{s}_3 = (0.411, -0.236, -1).$$

The estimated ratios of the light source irradiances are $1.0 : 1.022 : 0.772$. A total number of 41717 triplets with positive 8-bit irradiances were measured on the sphere having a radius of 123 pixels. For the sake of clarity the illustrations only

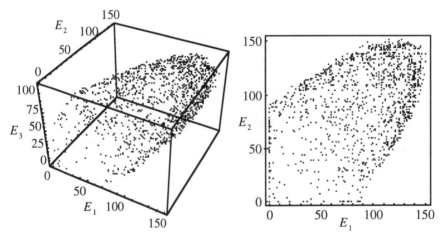

Figure 8.20: The left hand picture shows the three-dimensional oblique view of a real look-up table in a coordinate system which is spanned by three irradiances originating from three different light sources. On the right the look-up table is illustrated as an orthogonal view with projection along the irradiance axis E_3.

display 1303 irradiance triplets. Figure 8.20 on the right and all subfigures of Fig. 8.21 show orthographic projections of the look-up table. It can easily be seen that the irradiances describe a certain surface. In this example, the density of the look-up table is only approximately 3% with respect to the number of its entries. It can be shown that in the ideal case this point distribution can be described by the surface of an ellipsoid (R.J. Woodham (1994)).

The center of this ellipsoid is located at the origin of the $E_1 E_2 E_3$ coordinate system. The ellipsoid is restricted to the first octant of the coordinate system because only positive irradiances make sense. Each irradiance restricts the other two irradiance values to an ellipse in the $E_1 E_2 E_3$ space. Hence a unique solution is found by intersecting the three orthogonal ellipses.

The lengths of the three semiaxes of the ellipsoid are proportional to the albedo of the surface material. Moreover, the orientation of the ellipsoid is albedo independent and determined by the three illumination directions. Every ray in the $E_1 E_2 E_3$ space passing through the origin represents a unique orientation. From the mentioned properties it follows that the look-up table can be made albedo independent by propagating each entry along a ray. Thus, a valid surface orientation is assigned to every look-up table entry.

8.3.2 Albedo Independent Analysis

As known from Section 8.2.4, a pair of irradiances constrains the gradients of a Lambertian surface with unknown albedo to a straight line in gradient space. If a third light source is added, then the three irradiance pairs and therefore three straight line equations can be formulated. It can easily be shown that the three

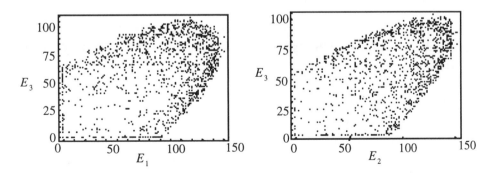

Figure 8.21: Orthographic projections of a real look-up table for 3S photometric stereo. The projection was performed along the irradiance axis E_2 to generate the left hand picture and along the irradiance axis E_1 to generate the right hand picture.

straight lines always have a common point of intersection under the assumption of consistent irradiances.

Section 8.2.4 provided an equation for calculating a vector that is perpendicular to the sought-after surface orientation $\mathbf{n}$. The vector equation

$$\mathbf{n}^T (E_{01} \cdot E_2 \|\mathbf{s}_2\| \mathbf{s}_1 - E_{02} \cdot E_1 \|\mathbf{s}_1\| \mathbf{s}_2) = 0$$

is given once again for the image irradiance pair (E_1, E_2). Similar equations can be formulated for the irradiance pairs (E_1, E_3) and (E_2, E_3). For the pair (E_1, E_3) the equation

$$\mathbf{n}^T (E_{01} \cdot E_3 \|\mathbf{s}_3\| \mathbf{s}_1 - E_{03} \cdot E_1 \|\mathbf{s}_1\| \mathbf{s}_3) = 0$$

arises, which can now be combined with the equation for the image irradiance pair (E_1, E_2). The terms in parentheses are vectors which are orthogonal to the desired surface orientation $\mathbf{n}$. After calculating the vector product

$$\mathbf{u} = (E_{01} \cdot E_2 \|\mathbf{s}_2\| \mathbf{s}_1 - E_{02} \cdot E_1 \|\mathbf{s}_1\| \mathbf{s}_2) \times (E_{01} \cdot E_3 \|\mathbf{s}_3\| \mathbf{s}_1 - E_{03} \cdot E_1 \|\mathbf{s}_1\| \mathbf{s}_3)$$

a vector results which is collinear to the surface normal $\mathbf{n}$. Therefore,

$$\mathbf{n} = s \cdot \mathbf{u} .$$

The scaling factor s must have such a sign that the surface normal $\mathbf{n}$ obtains a negative Z-component. Besides the surface normal the albedo can be point-locally recovered by substituting the normalized vector $\mathbf{n}^\circ$ into one of the three image irradiance equations. When the equation is divided by one of the three irradiances of the light sources, for example by E_{03}, then the direction of the calculated vector

$$\mathbf{u}^* = (\frac{E_{01}}{E_{03}} \cdot E_2 \|\mathbf{s}_2\| \mathbf{s}_1 - \frac{E_{02}}{E_{03}} \cdot E_1 \|\mathbf{s}_1\| \mathbf{s}_2) \times (\frac{E_{01}}{E_{03}} \cdot E_3 \|\mathbf{s}_3\| \mathbf{s}_1 - E_1 \|\mathbf{s}_1\| \mathbf{s}_3)$$

does not change with respect to $\mathbf{u}$. This property is helpful for the realization of an albedo independent photometric stereo method since it means that only the ratios of the irradiances of the light sources have to be known. This leads to a different scaling of the albedo value.

Figure 8.22 shows three input images of the synthetic Mozart statue for the described photometric stereo method. The images were generated by using Lambertian reflectance maps. A light source set-up having the slant angles

$$\sigma(\mathbf{s}_1) = \sigma(\mathbf{s}_2) = \sigma(\mathbf{s}_3) = 20°$$

and the tilt angles

$$\theta(\mathbf{s}_1) = 90°, \ \theta(\mathbf{s}_2) = -150°, \ \theta(\mathbf{s}_3) = -30°$$

Figure 8.22: Image triplet of a synthetic Mozart statue for 3S photometric stereo. In the text the indices 1, 2, and 3 are assigned to the images (from left to right).

was chosen for rendering. Relatively small slant angles for the illumination directions guarantee that no strong self-shadows arise. The ratios of the irradiance values E_{0i} of the light sources are equal to one.

Figure 8.23 illustrates the shape recovery results for the Mozart statue. The integration of the height map was carried out using the global method introduced in Section 3.3.2. The left picture of Fig. 8.23 shows a grid representation of the reconstruction. Since detail information gets lost in this representation the right hand picture presents the same surface by using texture mapping. The texture image was calculated from the recovered surface normals by using a Lambertian reflectance map with the illumination direction $\mathbf{s} = (1, \ 1, \ -1)$.

The image triplet of the real hand shown in Fig. 8.24 is an example of an object with a non-constant albedo (different blood circulation). The ratios of the light source irradiances were estimated as 1.0 : 0.638 : 0.640. Estimations for the illumination directions of the three hand images are

$$\mathbf{s}_1 = (\text{-}0.370, \text{-}0.028, \text{-}1), \ \mathbf{s}_2 = (0.044, 0.472, \text{-}1), \text{ and } \mathbf{s}_3 = (0.420, 0.043, \text{-}1).$$

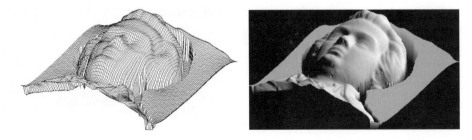

Figure 8.23: Surface reconstruction using irradiance triplets of a synthetic Mozart statue. On the left a grid representation and on the right a representation with texture mapping was used for the visualization. The texture was generated from the recovered normals.

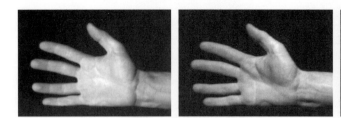

Figure 8.24: An image triplet of a real hand used as input for a 3S photometric stereo method. The images 2 and 3 were brightened for visualization purposes where the indices 1, 2, and 3 are assigned to the images from left to right.

The 3D plots presented in Fig. 8.25 show that a good surface reconstruction is possible by using 3S photometric stereo. Artifacts can occur when the hand is not entirely still and when the specular reflection component (caused by the transpiration) is not taken into account by the reflection model. In the right picture of Fig. 8.25 the first input image is mapped onto the 3D reconstruction.

Figure 8.26 shows a further 3S photometric stereo result. The left picture shows one of three input images. The plot on the right illustrates the recovered surface which was rendered by using texture mapping. The estimated illumination directions used for the 3D shape recovery are

$$\mathbf{s}_1 = (-0.345, -0.292, -1), \ \mathbf{s}_2 = (0.057, 0.312, -1), \text{ and } \mathbf{s}_3 = (0.446, -0.308, -1).$$

The ratios of the light source irradiances were estimated as $1.0 : 0.552 : 0.926$. The two sets of real images were acquired under non-ideal illumination conditions because the irradiances of the light sources are rather different.

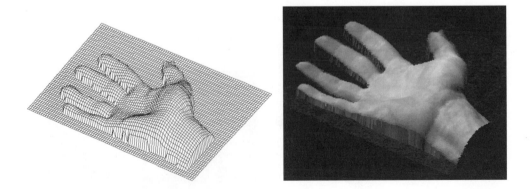

Figure 8.25: Surface reconstruction obtained by analyzing irradiance triplets of a real hand. On the left a grid representation and on the right a plot with texture mapping (first input image) was chosen for display.

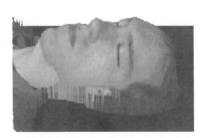

Figure 8.26: The left picture shows one of the input images for 3S photometric stereo of the scene KARSTEN. The picture on the right illustrates the surface reconstruction with texture mapping (compare Color Image 5 in the Appendix).

Linear mapping. The system of image irradiance equations

$$E_1 = E_{01}\rho \cdot \mathbf{n}^{\circ T} \mathbf{s}_1^{\circ} \ ,$$

$$E_2 = E_{02}\rho \cdot \mathbf{n}^{\circ T} \mathbf{s}_2^{\circ} \ , \ \text{and}$$

$$E_3 = E_{03}\rho \cdot \mathbf{n}^{\circ T} \mathbf{s}_3^{\circ}$$

for a Lambertian surface is bascially a set of scaled scalar products. Since the normalized surface normal $\mathbf{n}^{\circ}$ is part of all equations we can represent the equations in matrix form. First, the image irradiances E_1, E_2, and E_3 are written as a vector

$$\mathbf{E} = (E_1, \ E_2, \ E_3)^T$$

and the light source irradiances E_{01}, E_{02}, and E_{03} are represented as the diagonal matrix

$$\mathbf{D} = diag(E_{01}, \ E_{02}, \ E_{03}) = \begin{pmatrix} E_{01} & 0 & 0 \\ 0 & E_{02} & 0 \\ 0 & 0 & E_{03} \end{pmatrix}.$$

Furthermore, the illumination directions $\mathbf{s}_1^{\circ}$, $\mathbf{s}_2^{\circ}$, and $\mathbf{s}_3^{\circ}$ are described by the matrix

$$\mathbf{S} = \begin{pmatrix} \mathbf{s}_{1x}^{\circ} & \mathbf{s}_{1y}^{\circ} & \mathbf{s}_{1z}^{\circ} \\ \mathbf{s}_{2x}^{\circ} & \mathbf{s}_{2y}^{\circ} & \mathbf{s}_{2z}^{\circ} \\ \mathbf{s}_{3x}^{\circ} & \mathbf{s}_{3y}^{\circ} & \mathbf{s}_{3z}^{\circ} \end{pmatrix}.$$

Using the three defined quantities $\mathbf{E}$, $\mathbf{D}$, and $\mathbf{S}$ the system of image irradiance equations can be rewritten in a compact form as

$$\mathbf{E} = \rho \cdot \mathbf{D} \cdot \mathbf{S} \cdot \mathbf{n}°.$$

The relationship between $\mathbf{E}$ and $\mathbf{n}°$ is a *linear mapping*. After inverting the matrices $\mathbf{D}$ and $\mathbf{S}$ the unit vector of the surface normal

$$\rho \cdot \mathbf{n}° = \mathbf{S}^{-1} \cdot \mathbf{D}^{-1} \cdot \mathbf{E}$$

which is still scaled by the albedo ρ can be determined point-locally. The inversion of the matrix $\mathbf{S}$ is possible if the illumination directions are not coplanar. The matrix $\mathbf{D}$ can be inverted, if none of the irradiances becomes zero. The albedo ρ can be recovered by calculating the length of the vector

$$\mathbf{S}^{-1} \cdot \mathbf{D}^{-1} \cdot \mathbf{E} .$$

The above formulation is very similar to the original representation chosen by R.J. Woodham (1978, 1980) who developed the photometric stereo method based on three light sources.

8.3.3   Calculation of the Illumination Direction

The classical photometric stereo approach shown above can also be employed for the *calculation of an illumination direction*. Assume that we have acquired the irradiance image of a curved calibration object having a Lambertian surface of known geometry and a uniform albedo (compare Section 6.3.4).

Furthermore, assume that the calibration object was illuminated by a parallel light source of unknown direction $\mathbf{s}$. The photometric stereo method described in Section 8.3.2 assumes that three positive irradiance values can be measured for every image point with respect to the three illumination directions $\mathbf{s}_1°$, $\mathbf{s}_2°$, and $\mathbf{s}_3°$. A surface normal $\mathbf{n}°$ is calculated from the irradiance triplet by using the known illumination parameters.

For the calculation of an illumination direction with the calibration object the previous meaning of the surface normal $\mathbf{n}°$ being to the unknown and of the illumination directions $\mathbf{s}_1°$, $\mathbf{s}_2°$, and $\mathbf{s}_3°$ being the given data can be exchanged. The unkown illumination direction $\mathbf{s}°$ can be calculated from the irradiances E_1, E_2, and E_3 by using a calibration object which has (at least) three different surface normals $\mathbf{n}_1°$, $\mathbf{n}_2°$, and $\mathbf{n}_3°$. The three known surface normals can be combined into a matrix

$$
\mathbf{N} = \begin{pmatrix} \mathbf{n}_{1x}^{\,\circ} & \mathbf{n}_{1y}^{\,\circ} & \mathbf{n}_{1z}^{\,\circ} \\ \mathbf{n}_{2x}^{\,\circ} & \mathbf{n}_{2y}^{\,\circ} & \mathbf{n}_{2z}^{\,\circ} \\ \mathbf{n}_{3x}^{\,\circ} & \mathbf{n}_{3y}^{\,\circ} & \mathbf{n}_{3z}^{\,\circ} \end{pmatrix}.
$$

The new matrix $\mathbf{D}$ contains the irradiance values of the light source at the considered image points. We can assume that these values are constant over the object. The corresponding system of image irradiance equations in vector notation is

$$
\mathbf{E} = \rho \cdot \mathbf{D} \cdot \mathbf{N} \cdot \mathbf{s}^{\circ} .
$$

The unit vector of the illumination direction which is scaled by the albedo ρ can be determined with

$$
\rho \cdot \mathbf{s}^{\circ} = \mathbf{N}^{-1} \cdot \mathbf{D}^{-1} \cdot \mathbf{E}
$$

after calculating the inverses of the matrices $\mathbf{D}$ and $\mathbf{N}$. Since the illumination direction can be scaled by an arbitrary factor (which is not equal to zero) in practice the matrix $\mathbf{D}$ is simply the identity matrix.

Because the meaning of being given or unknown data was exchanged for the surface normal and the illumination direction this method is also referred to as *inverse photometric stereo method*. The robustness should be improved by including more than three surface normals. A closed form representation of the solution can be found in B.K.P. Horn (1986).

8.4   REFERENCES

Textbooks containing the photometric stereo method with three light sources are

Horn, B.K.P.: *Robot Vision*. The MIT Press, Cambridge, 1986 and
Shirai, Y.: *Three-dimensional Computer Vision*. Springer, Berlin, 1987.

A 2S method which is based on a convexity assumption (compare Section 8.2.3) is presented in

Yang, J., Ohnishi, N., Sugie, N.: *Two image photometric stereo method*. Intelligent Robots and Computer Vision XI, SPIE **1826** (1992), pp. 452-463.

A photometric stereo approach which is based on the extension of a SFS method (compare Section 8.2.3) is given in

Lee, K.M., Kuo, C.-C.J.: *Surface reconstruction from photometric stereo images*. Journal Optical Society America A **10** (1993), pp. 855-867.

The albedo dependent 2S method which was also presented in Section 8.2.3 can be found in the publication

Onn, R., Bruckstein, A.: *Integrability disambiguates surface recovery in two-image photometric stereo*. Int. Journal of Computer Vision **5** (1990), pp. 105-113.

A mathematical discussion of the integrability condition is represented in a thorough manner in

Kozera, R.: *Existence and uniqueness in photometric stereo*. Applied Mathematics and Computation **44** (1991), pp. 1-104 and
Kozera, R.: *On shape recovery from two shading patterns*. Int. Journal of Pattern Recognition and Artificial Intelligence **6** (1992), pp. 673-698.

Necessary and sufficient conditions for the existence of a unique solution can be found in these publications by R. Kozera. The albedo independent 2S method which is explained in Section 8.2.5 was inroduced in

Lee, C.-H., Rosenfeld, A.: *An approximation technique for photometric stereo*. Pattern Recognition Letters **2** (1984), pp. 339-343.

This publication includes mathematical proofs related to the method.
The original photometric stereo method was developed by R.J. Woodham. The fundamental ideas are discussed in the publications

Woodham, R.J.: *Photometric stereo: a reflectance map technique for determining surface orientation from image intensity*. Image Understanding Systems & Industrial Applications, SPIE **155** (1978), pp. 136-143 and
Woodham, R.J.: *Photometric method for determining surface orientations from multiple images*. Optical Engineering **19** (1980), pp. 139-144.

The treatment of interreflections (compare Section 6.4.4) in conjunction with the photometric stereo method can be found in, e.g.,

Nayar, S.K., Ikeuchi, K., Kanade, T.: *Shape from interreflections*. Int. Journal of Computer Vision **6** (1991), pp. 173-195 and
Rumpel, D., Schlüns, K.: *Szenenanalyse unter Berücksichtigung von Interreflexionen und Schatten*. Proc. DAGM-Symposium, Bielefeld, 1995, pp. 218-227.

Approaches which generalize the photometric stereo method to more than three light sources are presented in, e.g.,

Nayar, S.K., Ikeuchi, K., Kanade, T.: *Determining shape and reflectance of hybrid surfaces by photometric sampling*. IEEE Transactions on Robotics and Automation **6** (1990), pp. 418-431 and

Sato, Y., Ikeuchi, K.: *Temporal-color space analysis of reflection.* Journal Optical Society America A **11** (1994), pp. 2990-3002.

A time-efficient realization of the photometric stereo method where three colored (red, green, blue) light sources are used for image acquisition is represented in

Woodham, R.J.: Gradient and curvature from the photometric-stereo method, including local confidence estimation. Journal Optical Society America A **11** (1994), pp. 3050-3068.

This implementation does not include the recovery of a height map. Other publications in which the object scene is illuminated by colored light sources are

Drew, M.S.: *Robust specularity detection from a single multi-illuminant color image.* CVGIP: Image Understanding **59** (1994), pp. 320-327 and

Drew, M.S., Kontsevich, L.L.: *Closed-form attitude determination under spectrally varying illumination.* Proc. Computer Vision and Pattern Recognition 94, Seattle, Washington, USA, 1994, pp. 985-990.

The integration of shadow information in the surface recovery using photometric stereo can be found in

Solomon, F., Ikeuchi, K.: *Extracting the Shape and Roughness of Specular Lobe Objects Using Four Light Photometric Stereo.* IEEE Transactions and Pattern Analysis and Machine Intelligence **18** (1996), pp. 449-454 and in

Schlüns, K.: *Shading Based 3D Shape Recovery in the Presence of Shadows.* Proc. First Joint Australia & New Zealand Biennial Conference on Digital Image & Vision Computing: Techniques and Applications, Albany, Auckland, 1997, pp. 195-200.

An approach that employs a sequence of images that are taken by using extended light sources can be found in

Nayar, S.K., Ikeuchi, K., Kanade, T.: *Determining Shape and Reflectance of Hybrid Surfaces by Photometric Sampling.* IEEE Transactions on Robotics and Automation **6** (1990), pp. 418-431.

8.5   EXERCISES

(1) How many solution curves exist that are consistent with the irradiance curve $E(x=X)$ in Example 8.1?

(2) Show that the set of all lines k generated by the dual straight line h defined in Section 8.2.4 covers the entire gradient space for general illumination directions.

(3) What influence does a scaling of the image irradiances have on the albedo independent 2S method described in Section 8.2.4?

(4) Student Albado has developed an albedo independent 2S photometric stereo method. According to Section 8.2.4 a vector can be determined for every irradiance pair which is orthogonal to the sought-after surface normal. He restricts the analysis to surfaces which only have a slight height difference in a small neighborhood of an image point. His idea is as follows: Two vectors **a** and **b** oriented orthogonal to the sought-after surface normal can be determined in a small environment of an image point. If we calculate the vector product **a** × **b**, a vector results which is perpendicular to both vectors. This is the sought-after surface normal. Will student Albado be successful with his approach? Give reasons for your decision.

(5) Show that the two equations

$$tan(\sigma(\mathbf{s})) \cdot cos(\theta(\mathbf{s})) = p(\mathbf{s}) \text{ and } tan(\sigma(\mathbf{s})) \cdot sin(\theta(\mathbf{s})) = q(\mathbf{s})$$

hold (compare Section 8.2.5). The vector **s** describes the illumination direction. The functions p, q, σ and θ used in the equations were defined in Section 3.4.1. Hint: The trigonometric relationships

$$cos(arctan(a)) = \frac{1}{\sqrt{1+a^2}} \text{ and } sin(arctan(a)) = \frac{a}{\sqrt{1+a^2}} \text{ , for } a \in \Re,$$

can be employed.

(6) Can the method described in Section 8.3.3 which determines the illumination direction be used when the calibration object has a texture (no uniform albedo)?

(7) Show that region 1 of the gradient map which is shown on the left of Fig. 8.14 cannot be integrated. First show that the negative solution can be transformed into a positive solution by mirroring at the symmetry plane which has the equation $(1,-1,0)(X,Y,Z)^T = 0$. Hint: The negative solution in region 1 can be calculated from the equation of a sphere (see Section 3.1.4) by calculating the first partial derivatives.

(8 - Assignment 1) Implement the 2S method described in Section 8.2.3 using Algorithm 8.1. Compare different numerical approximations for differentiation in the subalgorithm *Selection* for testing the integrability condition. Compare the results of a forward difference quotient and of a symmetric difference quotient.

The forward difference quotient in direction of the i-axis (x-axis) of a spatially discrete function $f(i, j)$ is determined for the point (i,j) by the difference $f(i+1, j) - f(i, j)$. The symmetric difference quotient in direction of the i-axis is determined for the point (i,j) by the difference $(f(i+1, j) - f(i-1, j))/2$. The approximations of the partial derivatives in direction of the j-axis (y-axis) are derived in a similar way.

(9 - Assignment 2) Section 8.3.1 described a method how the orientations of surfaces can be recovered that show a specular reflection component without solving a system of nonlinear equations.

Generate three non-Lambertian reflectance maps whose specular reflection components could be described with the simplified Torrance-Sparrow model (see Section 6.4.2). Lambert´s cosine law should be used as the model for the diffuse reflection component (compare Section 6.4.1). Calculate three input images for the photometric stereo method by using the generated reflectance maps. The geometry of the surface could be modeled with the equation of a torus that was given in Exercise (2) of Section 7.6. Recover the surface orientations of the specular torus. Afterwards apply the global integration method presented as Algorithm 3.2 in Section 3.3.2.

9 STRUCTURED LIGHTING

The projection of light patterns into a scene is called *structured lighting*. The light patterns are projected onto the objects which lie in the field of view of the camera. The distance of an object to the camera or the location of an object in space can be determined through analyzing the observed light patterns in the images. The active manipulation of the scene by using light patterns simplifies the 3D reconstruction task enormously as described in this chapter.

Notice that the location (x, y) of a pixel in the image (this is a grid square or grid rectangle) constrains the 3D location of the corresponding object point (X, Y, Z) to a certain sub-space in the scene. This sub-space contains all those scene points which project onto the grid square (x, y) and can be modeled as a four-sided infinite pyramid [1]. If the intrinsic parameters of the camera are known then this sub-space can be described with respect to the camera coordinate system. The apex of the pyramid lies at the projection center of the camera. The four edges of the pyramid pass through the corners of the grid square (x, y).

In the following we regard the grid square as a point which is defined as lying at the center of the grid square. The infinite pyramid shrinks to a ray ℓ in the scene. This ray ℓ can be interpreted as the projection ray corresponding to the object point (X, Y, Z) and the image point (x, y). Therefore, we can constrain the search space for (X, Y, Z) to ℓ which is one of the basic ideas of all structured lighting approaches.

A further general idea of structured lighting consists in intersecting the ray ℓ with an additional ray ℓ' or an additional plane Π which leads to a unique reconstruction of the object point (X, Y, Z). The goal of structured lighting is to introduce the ray ℓ' or the plane Π in such a way that a correspondence analysis is not necessary.

Note, in Chapter 4 the result of the correspondence analysis was a set of matched image points. Since the two matched points correspond to the same object point (X, Y, Z) the intersection of their projection rays leads to the reconstruction of (X, Y, Z). Thus, a second ray ℓ' was found by means of a correspondence analysis. In structured lighting the ray ℓ' or the plane Π are projected

---

[1] An infinite pyramid is a pyramid having no base.

actively into the scene, and it is assumed that their equations (or equivalent information) are available, e.g. by a geometrical calibration as presented in Chapter 2. For the sake of simplicity the light rays and planes are modeled by straight lines and plane equations, respectively. Hence, the diameter or thickness of the projected light patterns is normally not part of the mathematical models.

As a result of the above discussion structured lighting methods can be regarded as a modification of static binocular stereo. One of the cameras is replaced by a light source which projects the light pattern into the scene. The correspondence problem in the stereo vision pipeline (see the beginning of Chapter 4) does not exist any more since the triangulation is carried out by intersecting the projection ray (camera) and the light ray/plane (light source).

Almost all previously discussed 3D shape recovery methods assumed not very complex requirements for image acquisition. The solution of the reconstruction problem was found by analyzing theoretical, mathematical, and algorithmical issues. Structured lighting simplifies the task by increasing the engineering prerequisites, hence the complexity of the surface reconstruction task is shifted to another level in structured lighting.

Various shapes of light patterns exist, e.g. spot patterns, stripe patterns or color-coded patterns. The position, orientation and shape of the light patterns can be changed or remain static during the image acquisition process.

Structured lighting is especially applied in those fields where the automated three-dimensional measurement of an object has to be carried out with high precision. Of course, this class of techniques is restricted to environments allowing the active projection and detection of light patterns. Even outdoor scenes are recoverable without introducing artificial illumination. For example, sunlight in conjunction with a thin pole produces a stripe of shadow on the objects which yields equivalent information.

Laser light sources, special light stripe projectors, or slide projectors are employed to generate the light patterns. Structured lighting systems which are often called *3D scanners* or *range scanners* exist for a wide range of object sizes and applications. For example, small hand-held 3D scanners are available for reconstructing single teeth, and larger ones are used for "whole human body" reconstructions employing several light sources and cameras.

The 3D coordinates of the scene points in the images are recovered by assuming a known image acquisition geometry and using triangulation which is explained in Section 9.1.1. The methods of 3D object acquisition using structured lighting can be divided into methods which use simple geometric light patterns such as light spots or light stripes and methods which are based on spatial and/or temporal coding of the light patterns. Both classes will be introduced in the following sections.

9.1 PROJECTION OF SIMPLE GEOMETRIC PATTERNS

The motivation for using structured lighting is based on the expectation of precise detection of the projected light patterns in the acquired images. The 3D coordinates can be triangulated directly as soon as the acquisition geometry is known and the light pattern is located in the image. The simplest and best recognizable light patterns are light spots and light stripes.

In practice the precise detection of these simple geometric patterns is essential because they determine the achievable accuracy of the 3D reconstruction. One way to obtain a pixel accurate (or subpixel accurate) location of the patterns in the image is to calculate the first moments of those image segments which depict the projected light patterns (compare Exercise 3 in Section 2.5).

9.1.1 Light Spot Projection

The *light spot projection technique* is the simplest method to measure distances between the image acquisition system and points on object surfaces in the scene. A single light beam which is modeled as a ray (or line) is projected into the scene. The projection ray and the ray of the light beam are intersected to find the position of the illuminated object point in the 3D space.

(Task 9.1) Let us assume that an object surface is illuminated pointwise by a collimated laser beam and the reflected light is received by the camera. Determine the distance between the receiver and the illuminated object point using *triangulation*.

(Solution 9.1, 2D) For the sake of simplicity, at first the discussion is carried out for a plane, i.e. for a "2D object scene" having no vertical dimension (no Y-axis). This allows a simpler illustration of the fundamental principles. Object, light source, and camera lie in one plane (see Fig. 9.1). The goal is to recover the position of the object (i.e. the illuminated object point) in the plane. The angle α is given by the calibration and can be controlled using the deflection system of the laser. The angle β is defined by the projection geometry (compare Exercise (1) in Section 9.4) of the camera. The camera has to be regarded as an one-dimensional device since a 2D image acquisition set-up is assumed.

Let **O** be the projection center of the camera and the origin of the camera coordinate system. The base distance b is assumed to be constant and known. The distance d between the camera and the object point $\mathbf{P} = (X_0, Z_0)$ is calculated by using the law of sines:

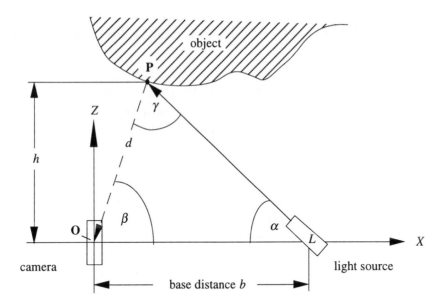

Figure 9.1: Triangulation with a light spot projector.

$$\frac{d}{sin(\alpha)} = \frac{b}{sin(\gamma)} \; .$$

From $\gamma = \pi - (\alpha + \beta)$ and $sin(\pi - \gamma) = sin(\gamma)$ it follows that

$$\frac{d}{sin(\alpha)} = \frac{b}{sin(\pi - \gamma)} = \frac{b}{sin(\alpha + \beta)} \; .$$

Thus, the distance d is given as

$$d = \frac{b \cdot sin(\alpha)}{sin(\alpha + \beta)} \; .$$

The location of the point $\mathbf{P} = (X_0, Z_0)$ can be represented in the camera coordinate system by the two-dimensional polar coordinates (d, β). The transformation into Cartesian coordinates is carried out by

$$X_0 = d \cdot cos(\beta) \quad \text{and} \quad Z_0 = h = d \cdot sin(\beta) \; .$$

The Z-axis coincides with the optical axis of the camera and the image plane lies at $Z = f$. Thus the distance coordinate Z can be determined using the angle β.

(Solution 9.1, 3D) The general case of a 3D triangulation requires to include the vertical dimension, in our case the Y-axis (compare Fig. 9.2). A camera centered

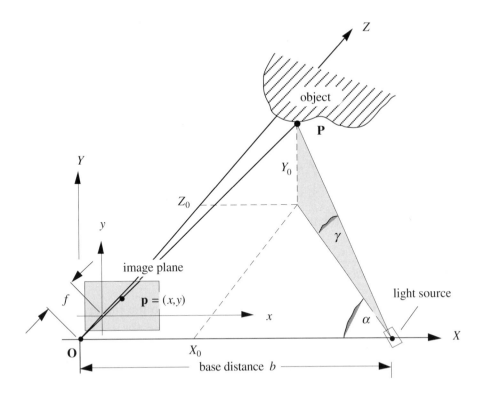

Figure 9.2: Illustration of the light spot projection technique in three dimensions.

XYZ-coordinate system and an image plane lying at $Z = f$ are assumed. The considered object point $\mathbf{P} = (X_0, Y_0, Z_0)$ is projected onto a point $\mathbf{p} = (x, y)$ in the image plane.

In the 3D case the camera and the light source can be arranged in an arbitrary way. Again, the Z-axis is the optical axis of the camera. We assume that the optical center of the light source is located on the X-axis. In contrast to the 2D case the laser beam is no longer restricted to the XZ-plane. The beam can be modeled by a segment of a straight line starting at point $(b, 0, 0)$ and ending at point $\mathbf{P}$.

The angles α and γ define the direction of the laser beam in 3D space (see Fig. 9.2). According to the ray theorem it holds that

$$\frac{X_0}{x} = \frac{Z_0}{f} = \frac{Y_0}{y} \; ,$$

for the chosen camera centered coordinate system. Using the trigonometry of right triangles it follows that

$$tan(\alpha) = \frac{Z_0}{b - X_0}$$

and

$$Z_0 = \frac{X_0}{x} \cdot f = tan(\alpha) \cdot (b - X_0)$$

resulting in

$$X_0 \left(\frac{f}{x} + tan(\alpha) \right) = tan(\alpha) \cdot b .$$

The 3D position of point **P** can be calculated by

$$X_0 = \frac{tan(\alpha) \cdot b \cdot x}{f + x \cdot tan(\alpha)}, \quad Y_0 = \frac{tan(\alpha) \cdot b \cdot y}{f + x \cdot tan(\alpha)}, \quad \text{and} \quad Z_0 = \frac{tan(\alpha) \cdot b \cdot f}{f + x \cdot tan(\alpha)} .$$

The distance $d_2(\mathbf{P}, \mathbf{O}) = \|(X_0, Y_0, Z_0)\|$ can be assigned to the range image at point (x, y). Notice that the angle γ is not used to calculate the scene point **P**. The reason is that the light beam is regarded as being a plane when the point **P** is calculated. This plane is oriented perpendicular to the XZ-plane (compare Fig. 9.2). The X-axis and this plane subtend the angle α.

(**Algorithm 9.1**) The procedure in Fig. 9.3 can be taken as a basis for calculating a range image (compare Section 3.2.1) by using the light spot technique.

---

calibrate image acquisition system;
begin
    for angle $\alpha := \alpha_{min}$ **to** α_{max} **do**
        for angle $\gamma := \gamma_{min}$ **to** γ_{max} **do**
            if (**p** is visible and detectable) **then**
                begin
                    determine position $\mathbf{p} = (x, y)$;
                    calculate coordinates X_0, Y_0, Z_0 for **P**;
                    assign distance $d_2(\mathbf{P}, \mathbf{O})$ to point (x, y) of the range image
                end {*if*}
end

Figure 9.3: Generation of a range image employing the light spot projection technique.

(**Comment 9.1**) For the practical application of this technique the accuracy of the results is influenced by several factors. Problems in practice are

a) the limitation to incomplete range images or depth maps caused by shadows and invisibility, see Fig. 9.4, since a distance measurement is not possible inside the shaded areas when either the camera does not see this area or the laser point does not reach the object surface,

b) the speed of the measurement process which depends on the deflection system and the light spot detection,

c) the accurate calibration of the image acquisition system (see Chapter 2), and

d) the precise detection of the light spot in the image.

These influencing factors apply to a certain degree to the more advanced techniques described later in this chapter as well.

9.1.2 Light Spot Stereo Analysis

The method of *light spot stereo analysis* is based on the combination of the light spot technique with a method of static stereo analysis (compare Chapter 4). A laser spot is projected at a chosen location onto the object surface, and this spot is acquired with two cameras from different directions (compare Fig. 9.5).

Models of the geometry of a stereo image acquisition system as discussed in Chapter 4 can be used for the two cameras. The three-dimensional position of the spot in the scene can be determined analogously to the static stereo analysis namely based on the positions of the projected laser spot in the two image planes. Notice that for both methods, static stereo analysis and light spot projection, this

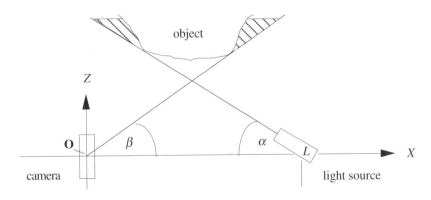

Figure 9.4: Visibility problems of the light spot projection technique.

determination of the 3D scene point is called triangulation since it is the same type of calculation from a geometrical point of view.

The advantage of the light spot stereo analysis technique is that the correspondence analysis is considerably simplified in both images compared to the static stereo analysis. The image of the laser spot on the object surface is assumed to be the brightest point in both images. Therefore, these two image points can be matched as corresponding points without any ambiguity problem.

The influence of the scene illumination on the laser point detection can be reduced by using special laser light filters for the image acquisition and by using image subtraction. For image subtraction the scene is taken at the beginning of the image acquisition process. This image is subtracted from the current image containing the laser spot. Under utilizing the epipolar geometry described in Section 4.1 the search space for the corresponding point in the second image can be reduced to an one-dimensional search interval along the epipolar line. Contrary to an "ordinary" method of the static stereo analysis a stereo image has to be generated and analyzed for each object point. Alternatively the detection of the laser spot can be achieved by using special hardware which provides directly the x- and y-position without a software based search process.

The advantage of the light spot stereo analysis technique compared to the light spot technique is that no calibration of the laser deflection system is necessary. The precision of the positioning of the laser beam does not influence

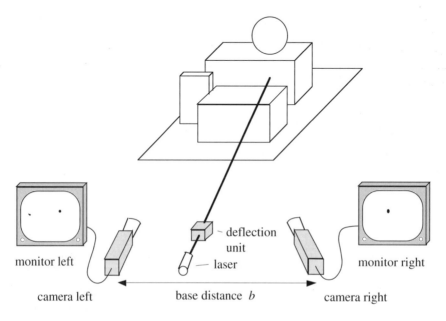

Figure 9.5: General arrangement for a method based on light spot stereo analysis.

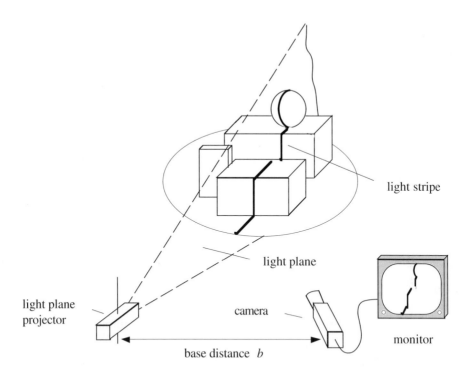

light stripe

light plane

light plane
projector

camera

monitor

base distance *b*

Figure 9.6: Image acquisition set-up for the light stripe projection technique.

the accuracy of the reconstruction because the orientation of the laser beam does not affect the calculation. Therefore, less requirements with respect to the light projection system are necessary which leads to a considerable reduction of the expenses for the realization of the image acquisition set-up.

For the software implementation of the technique a rough calibration of the deflection system is suggested because the search space in both images can be minimized with that rough knowledge of the geometry of the projected light spot in the image planes.

9.1.3 Light Stripe Projection

The *light stripe projection technique* or *light striping technique* represents an extension of the light spot projection technique (compare Section 9.1.1). This technique projects a light plane into the object scene (see Fig. 9.6). The idea is to intersect the projection ray of the examined image point with the light plane. The intersection of the light plane with the object surface is visible as a light stripe in the image. Therefore, a larger set of depth values can be recovered from a single image which results in a faster reconstruction process compared to the single spot techniques. A light plane can be generated, for example, by using laser light in conjunction with a cylindrical lens, a laser plane projector, or a slide projector with a slit mask.

The use of laser light leads to a very bright and narrow light stripe which is important for an appropriate depth resolution. When employing a slide projector the slit has to be sufficiently wide so that the light stripe is sufficiently bright in the image. The slit mask is cheaper than the laser and in contrast to the laser no eye safety requirements are necessary.

(**Task 9.2**) Determine the distances between the illuminated object points in the scene and a reference plane using a light stripe projection technique. The reference plane is defined by the vertical axes (Y-axes) of the coordinate system of the light plane projector and the camera which are assumed to be parallel.

(**Solution 9.2**) The light plane is perpendicular to the reference plane and perpendicular to the plane spanned by the optical axes of the light plane projector and the camera. The optical axes are assumed to be coplanar but must not be parallel. The angle α_{opt} subtended by the optical axes will be estimated later. We assume that the camera image is digitized as a matrix of size $M \times N$ and that the

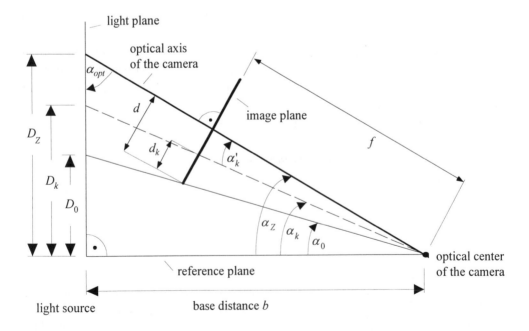

Figure 9.7: Schematic representation of a particular geometry for the light stripe technique which simplifies the calibration significantly.

column indices of this matrix are $x = 0, 1, ..., M - 1$. The described technique follows an approach given in K.S. Fu et al. (1987).

As an initial step a calibration has to be carried out to calculate the depth values. A goal is to make the calibration process as simple as possible. Firstly, the length b is measured which is the distance between the optical centers of the light plane projector and the camera. Without using a special calibration procedure this can only be done approximately.

Let us define two angles α_Z and α_0. The angle α_Z which is subtended by the reference plane and the optical axis of the camera (compare Fig. 9.7) can be estimated as follows. It is assumed that a planar calibration object which is oriented parallel to the reference plane can be shifted along the optical axis of the light plane projector. Hence the calibration object stays parallel to the reference plane during the movement. The calibration object is shifted in such a way that the light stripe is projected onto the center column $x = M / 2$ in the image.

Next, the distance D_Z between the calibration object and the reference plane is measured and the angle α_Z is determined by

$$\alpha_Z = arctan\left(\frac{D_Z}{b}\right).$$

(9.1)

The two optical axes subtend an angle of $\alpha_{opt} = 90° - \alpha_Z$.

The angle α_0 is subtended by the reference plane and the plane which is defined by the first (left) image column and the optical center of the camera. Notice that every image column can be modeled as a straight line segment in 3D space (compare Fig. 9.7). For the determination of the angle α_0 the distance between the calibration object and the reference plane is reduced until the light stripe is projected into column $x = 0$ in the image plane. The distance D_0 is measured, and it follows that α_0 is determined by

$$\alpha_0 = arctan\left(\frac{D_0}{b}\right).$$

(9.2)

As soon as the angles α_Z and α_0 are known it follows that the horizontal length $2 \cdot d$ of the image plane can be determined by

$$2 \cdot d = 2 \cdot f \cdot tan(\alpha_Z - \alpha_0) ,$$

(9.3)

where f is the effective focal length of the camera.

The length $2 \cdot d$ describes the width of the visible portion of the CCD-sensor. Equation (9.3) can be simplified by applying the addition formula

$$tan(x \pm y) = \frac{tan(x) \pm tan(y)}{1 \mp tan(x) \cdot tan(y)}$$

(9.4)

giving

$$tan(arc\,tan(x) \pm arctan(y)) = \frac{x \pm y}{1 \mp x \cdot y}$$

and resulting in

$$d = f \cdot \frac{(D_Z - D_0) \cdot b}{b^2 + D_Z \cdot D_0} \qquad . \tag{9.5}$$

It was assumed that the digital image has M columns hence the distance d_k between column k and column 0 can be calculated by

$$d_k = k \frac{d}{M/2} = \frac{2kd}{M}. \tag{9.6}$$

The angle α_k which is subtended by an arbitrary image column (the projection of an arbitrary stripe) and the reference plane (compare Fig. 9.7) can be easily determined since it holds that

$$\alpha_k = \alpha_Z - \alpha'_k \tag{9.7}$$

with

$$tan(\alpha'_k) = \frac{d - d_k}{f} .$$

Using equation (9.6) it follows that

$$\begin{aligned} tan(\alpha'_k) &= \frac{d \cdot (M - 2k)}{M \cdot f} \\ &= \frac{(D_Z - D_0) \cdot b \cdot (M - 2k)}{M \cdot (b^2 + D_Z \cdot D_0)} \end{aligned} \tag{9.8}$$

with $0 \le k \le M - 1$. Hence, if the point on the light stripe belonging to scene point **P** is detected in a column k then the angle α'_k and α_k can be recovered. Finally, the distance D_k between the reference plane and the scene point **P** is given by

$$\begin{aligned} D_k &= b \cdot tan(\alpha_k) \\ &= b \cdot tan\left(\alpha_Z - arctan\left(\frac{d \cdot (M - 2k)}{M \cdot f}\right)\right) \\ &= b \cdot tan\left(\alpha_Z - arctan\left(\frac{(D_Z - D_0) \cdot b \cdot (M - 2k)}{M \cdot (b^2 + D_Z \cdot D_0)}\right)\right) \end{aligned} \tag{9.9}$$

or

$$D_k = \frac{D_Z - \dfrac{(D_Z - D_0) \cdot b^2 \cdot (M - 2k)}{M \cdot (b^2 + D_Z \cdot D_0)}}{1 + \dfrac{D_Z \cdot (D_Z - D_0) \cdot (M - 2k)}{M \cdot (b^2 + D_Z \cdot D_0)}}$$

(9.10)

$$= \frac{(D_Z^2 + b^2)MD_0 + 2k(D_Z - D_0)b^2}{(D_Z^2 + b^2)M - 2k(D_Z - D_0)D_Z}$$

for $0 \le k \le M - 1$. Equations (9.9) and (9.10) state that a distance can be calculated by detecting the image column of the projected scene point **P**. Notice that equation (9.7) does not contain the effective focal length f of the camera.

(**Algorithm 9.2**) The realization of the algorithm is trivial since it just consists in implementing equation (9.10). After the calibration is carried out the distance value for every column can be stored in a look-up table.

(**Comment 9.2**) An advantage of the above described arrangement is the simple way to calibrate the system and to determine the distance values. As a drawback we have the assumption that the vertical axes of the light plane projector and the camera are coplanar. Furthermore, the optical axes have to be coplanar and the calibration plane has to be moved exactly parallel to the reference plane. Deviations from these assumptions limit the accuracy.

Example 9.1: Figure 9.8 shows on the left the look-up table entries for three different image acquisition set-ups of the above method where the angle α_{opt} was varied. Therefore, the curves refer to different camera orientations. The parameters of the first image acquisition set-up are presented in Table 9.1.

The angles α_{opt} of the two other curves are 36.56° and 46.56°. The parameters M, b, f, and d were left unchanged. Of course, the values of D_Z and D_0 change. They can be read from the curves. The curves demonstrate that the range of recoverable distances decreases when the angle α_{opt} is increased. On the other hand, the depth resolution is improved in this case.

The right hand plot of Fig. 9.8 shows the differences $D_{k+1} - D_k$ between adjacent distance entries in the look-up tables. If the light stripe in the image is not detected in subpixel accuracy then the shown values represent the best achievable depth resolution. The closer the object point to the reference plane the higher is the depth resolution. Todays 3D scanners can achieve a much higher resolution by incorporating subpixel accuracy and interpolation (compare Section 9.2.1). { end of Example 9.1 }

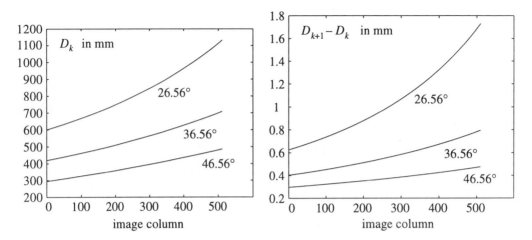

Figure 9.8: The left hand plot shows a graphical representation of the three look-up tables used in Example 9.1 for the light stripe projection technique. The graphics on the right depicts the differences of adjacent distance entries in the look-up tables.

Alternatively to the calibration method discussed above the curves shown in Fig. 9.8 could be found by curve fitting. The underlying model of the curve is given in equation (9.10). The control points for the curve fitting are measured by positioning the calibration plane at a suitable number of distances. The x-component of each control point is the detected image column. The y-component is the current position (distance) of the calibration plane to the reference plane. The advantage of this approach is that the base distance b does not have to be known in advance. Moreover, the position of the reference plane can be chosen arbitrarily, however notice that its orientation must not be changed from the initial definition. Altogether, this leads to a simpler calibration set-up.

Up to now the light stripe projection technique can recover distance values D_k for object points which are illuminated by the light plane. To obtain a 3D reconstruction the object can be rotated on a turntable. Each rotation leads to a *3D*

Calibration parameters				Calculated parameters		
M	b	D_Z	D_0	α_{opt}	f	d
512	40 cm	80 cm	60 cm	26.56°	30 mm	3.75 mm

Table 9.1: Calibration parameters and calculated parameters of a typical image acquisition set-up for the light stripe projection technique.

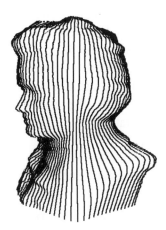

Figure 9.9: Left: Beethoven plaster statue. Right: Recovered 3D profiles on the statue using the light stripe projection technique.

profile of distance values. If the axis of rotation is oriented in such a way that it is parallel to the reference plane and lies "inside" the light plane then the 3D object can be easily represented in cylindrical coordinates.

Figure 9.9 and Fig. 9.10 illustrate reconstruction results of a Beethoven plaster statue which was rotated on a turntable. The 360°-reconstruction was obtained by using 81 rotation steps. Hence a number of 81 3D profiles were reconstructed.

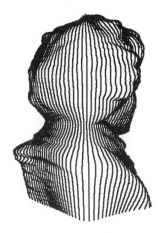

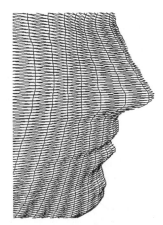

Figure 9.10: Left: Rear view of the recovered 3D profiles of the Beethoven statue shown on the left of Fig. 9.9. Right: Recovered triangular mesh around nose and mouth of the statue.

The left image of Fig. 9.9 shows the input object. The right image of Fig. 9.9 and the left image of Fig. 9.10 illustrate the recovered 3D profiles along the detected light stripes. After the 3D profiles are calculated a surface has to be fitted to the data. One way to derive a surface model is to generate triangles between adjacent 3D profiles and adjacent points on the 3D profiles. The plot shown on the right hand side of Fig. 9.10 presents the recovered triangular mesh around nose and mouth of the statue.

9.1.4   Static Light Pattern Projection

Instead of using single light rays or planes we can project several rays or planes at the same time on the examined object surfaces (*static light pattern projection technique*, see Fig. 9.11) to reduce the number of images. These light rays or planes are visible as a set of light spots or stripes in the image. The fundamental principle is based on the techniques described in the previous sections. Popular patterns are dotted lines, parallel lines, dot matrices, as well as concentric circles.

The main question is how to uniquely identify and index the light stripes in the camera image when several light rays or planes are projected simultaneously into the scene. It has to be determined which pattern element corresponds to which illuminated point in the image in order to compute the triangulation. Using

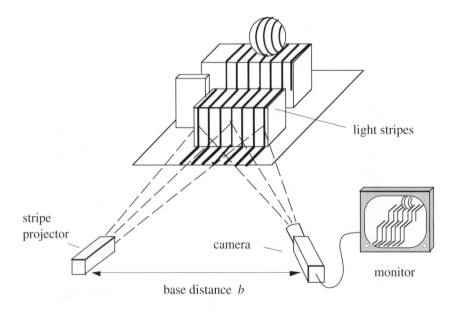

Figure 9.11: The principle of simultaneously projecting several light stripes.

smoothness assumptions the elements of a regular pattern can be addressed by taking neighborhood relations into account.

The projection of static light patterns can also be used to carry out planarity checks on smooth surfaces for industrial quality control, for example. Indexing of the pattern elements and a subsequent depth value calculation are not required for this application. The planarity check could be realized by comparing the measured image positions with the image of a highly planar surface.

9.2   PROJECTION OF ENCODED PATTERNS

If a simple geometric pattern, for example a light spot or a light stripe, is projected onto an object, then a large number of images has to be generated for determining the surface geometry of the object. When dealing with complex surfaces several light patterns cannot be simultaneously projected into a scene because a unique matching between the projected pattern and the pattern visible in the camera image cannot be ensured, for example due to possible occlusions. However, a unique matching can be obtained by a spatiotemporal or spatial coding of the patterns. In the following the calculation of depth values by means of the analysis of binary encoded and color encoded patterns will be described. The main principle of triangulation underlying the depth recovery will not be changed.

9.2.1   Binary Encoded Light Stripes and Phase Shifting

For the *binary encoded light stripe projection technique* a set of light planes is projected onto the examined objects. The individual light planes are indexed by an encoding scheme for the light patterns. These light patterns lead to a unique code for every plane. In principle every (unique) binary code could be employed. Then, 2^n light planes are uniquely encodable by using n patterns, i.e. taking n images.

The so-called *Gray code* (named after Frank Gray) is often used as a simple and robust indexing scheme. To avoid confusion notice that we are not dealing with a gray value code. A Gray code $G(i)$ is a binary code where i is an integer, and the binary representations of $G(i)$ and $G(i+1)$ differ exactly in one bit. Therefore, a code error in neighboring light planes can be easily detected. Figure 9.12 illustrates the principle of coding.

By applying a threshold operation to the images the scene areas which are illuminated by the current pattern are detectable. The obtained binary images are bit-planes which form a so-called *bit-plane stack*. After completing the image

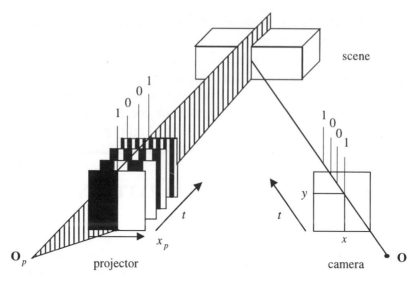

Figure 9.12: Principle of binary encoded light stripe technique.

acquisition process the bit-plane stack contains a sequences of n bits for all projected scene points and the corresponding image points (x, y).

Figure 9.13 shows an image sequence of a cube that were taken to create a Gray code bit-plane stack of 256 light planes. The light planes were horizontally projected onto the object unlike in the previous examples. The first image of the figure (upper left) shows the object scene where all light planes are switched on, hence an usual intensity image was acquired. The remaining $n = 8$ images of Fig. 9.13 are necessary to encode the $2^n = 256$ planes. The images are arranged row-wise in the order they were taken during image acquisition.

For example, the first image in this sequence (middle image in the top row) was acquired when the upper half of the light planes were switched on and the lower half of the light planes were switched off. For a better illustration of the projected patterns Fig. 9.14 visualizes the status (on or off) of the light planes. A depicted signal level "high" refers to "light plane on" and "low" refers to "light plane off". The left hand part of each binary curve in Fig. 9.14 corresponds to the upper region of the images, and the right hand part corresponds to the lower region.

During the surface reconstruction process the bit-plane-stack is used to uniquely address the light plane corresponding to every image point. A calibration procedure has to be performed for obtaining the equations of all light planes. Notice that the simple calibration scheme discussed in Section 9.1.3 is not suitable for the binary encoded light stripe technique. One reason is that the light planes cannot be regarded as lying parallel to each other.

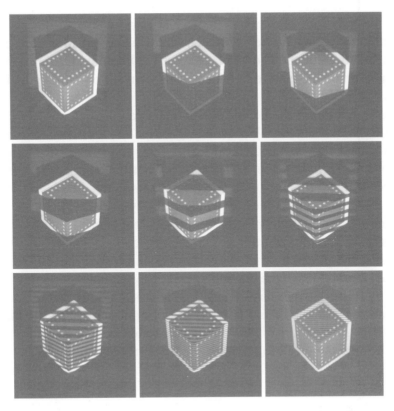

Figure 9.13: Binary encoded illumination. The entirely illuminated scene CUBE is shown at the top left. The other images show the generated images for different projected light patterns (with kind permission by A. McIvor, Industrial Research Ltd., Auckland).

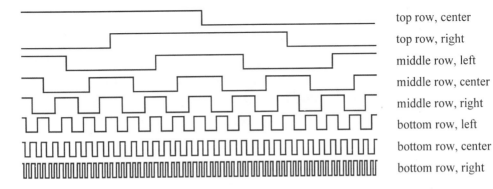

Figure 9.14: "On/off" status of the light planes during the image acquisition process. The eight different signals refer to the image sequence shown in Fig. 9.13. The signal level "high" refers to "light plane on" and "low" refers to "light plane off".

An alternative way for calibration is to place at least two planar objects of known orientation and position in the scene. The light plane equations are calculated from the light stripes on the known planes. After calibration the 3D coordinates of the examined object points are obtained using conventional triangulation (compare Section 9.1.1).

The resolution of the depth measurement can be increased by employing the so-called *phase shift method* which is based on the idea of interpolating between adjacent light planes. One possible way is to fuse two adjacent light planes to one macro light plane, as a first step. Thus the number of projected light planes is reduced by a factor of 2. The task of this initial step is to compute the indices of all macro light planes by using the Gray code technique as described above. Then the macro light planes are shifted four times by the width of one single light plane and four additional images are acquired (see Fig. 9.15).

During the preparation of the interpolation process the shifted pattern is regarded as a continuous sine shaped signal. The parameters of this signal are calculated by fitting the measured image irradiances to a sine model. The obtained phase parameter describes the relative depth information inside the macro light planes. The determination of the phase parameter is very sensitive to noise. Therefore a large number of (actually) identical images are taken in every step

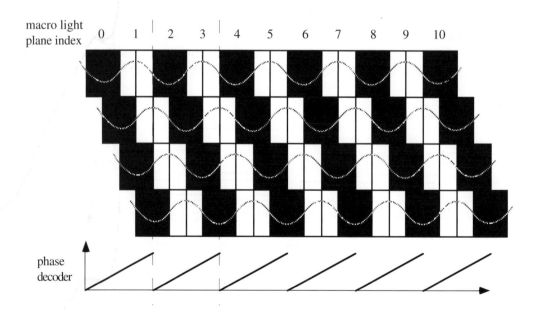

Figure 9.15: Sketch of the spatial arrangement of light patterns used to implement a simple phase shift method.

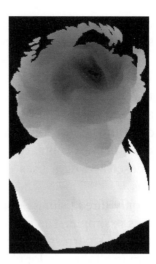

Figure 9.16: Beethoven plaster statue and a recovered range image. The surface recovery result was obtained by using the binary encoded light stripe technique and an LCD-projector which produces 320 light planes.

and an average is calculated. Notice that phase shifts can also be achieved by a mechanical movement of the projection unit.

The advantage of the binary encoded light stripe projection compared to the "ordinary" light stripe projection is that much less images are required for the same number of measured object points in the scene. Furthermore, we obtain a dense depth map or range image, and a rotation of the object is not required. Of course, a rotation is mandatory to recover a complete *3D model* of the object. However a more complete 3D model can be calculated from a set of dense depth maps or range images.

Usually computer controllable *LCD-projectors* (liquid crystal display projectors) are used to generate the light planes. There exist special projectors for structured lighting that are manufactured with high precision and can generate more than 1000 very bright light planes. Fig. 9.16 illustrates on the right a recon-structed range image of a Beethoven plaster statue (shown on the left) by using an LCD-projector which generates 320 light planes.

9.2.2 Color Encoded Light Stripe Projection

With exception of the static light pattern technique all structured lighting approaches discussed so far were based on a sequential acquisition of a set of images. The reconstruction of moving or non-rigid objects is not possible when several images have to be taken consecutively. In principle the static light pattern technique can cope with this class of objects but there exists no way for a direct measurement of dense depth information. The idea of the binary encoded light stripe technique combined with the additional utilization of color leads to the projection of a single color pattern. This approach is used to recover depth data from a single color image. It is obvious that many more distinguishable states can be coded by colors than by a binary code. The *color encoded light stripe projection technique* described here uses patterns consisting of red, green, blue, and white light planes.

Because only three primary colors and white are utilized the segmentation of the light stripes is simple. The primary colors should produce maximum image irradiance values in the corresponding color channels, and the white plane should cause a maximum in all three color channels. Without making further assumptions this condition is only fulfilled if the examined object surfaces have no color, i.e. the objects are white or gray.

Keep in mind that the spectral power distribution $E(\lambda)$ of the illumination and the spectral reflectance factor $R(\lambda)$ of the surface material are only "seen" as an integral of the product $E(\lambda) \cdot R(\lambda)$ by the three sensors of a color camera (compare Section 2.2.2). If the object color is white or gray then its spectral reflectance factor $R(\lambda)$ can be modeled as being constant. If the object is colored then it depends on $E(\lambda)$, $R(\lambda)$ and the spectral sensitivity of the camera whether the four colors can be disentangled or not. In this respect surface colors having a low saturation are more suitable than surfaces showing pure colors.

The actual problem of the color encoded light stripe projection is the unique indexing of the light stripes in the image (compare Section 9.1.4). If all light planes are visible in the image and if each light stripe is completely visible then indexing would be trivial. However, in general, some light stripes are invisible or only partially visible due to occlusions. In this case it has to be ensured that each light stripe can be uniquely assigned to the corresponding light plane by incorporating the local neighborhood of the stripe.

For the color encoded light stripe technique the knowledge about the arrangement (coding) of the color pattern is used to solve this problem. The color pattern is divided into several distinguishable subpatterns (color codes). For the generation of the color pattern,

> the entire number of projected stripes (i.e. the width of the light planes),

> the number of light planes in every subpattern,

> the number of subpatterns, and

> the number of colors

have to be taken into account. A color code is selected that neighboring stripes have different colors. This restriction reduces the possible arrangements of the color code. Let L be the entire number of used colors and K the number of stripes of every subpattern, then the number M_0 of possible codes is

$$M_0(K, L) = L \cdot (L-1)^{K-1}.$$

The formula is derived as follows. For the first stripe in a subpattern we can choose among L colors. For the remaining $K - 1$ positions we can choose among $L - 1$ colors. If the colors red (R), green (G), blue (B), and white (W) are used for the color stripes ($L = 4$) and if every subpattern shall consist of $K = 6$ stripes, then $M_0 = 972$ different subpatterns can be generated according to the above formula. If the scene shall be illuminated with 512 stripes, then only 86 of these subpatterns are needed because $6 \cdot 86 \geq 512$. Bear in mind that the colors at the borders of two adjacent subpatterns have to be different. The designed color stripe code could be physically realized as a slide by using a film recorder attached to a computer. Then the slide is projected onto the object with a common slide projector.

The algorithm for finding the correct index of the color stripes in the image searches along a path orthogonal to the stripes. If an entire subpattern is visible then the index of each light stripe belonging to the subpattern can be found using its position in the complete color pattern. Starting with this information the color stripes in the remaining incompletely projected subpatterns are recognized. For instance, if the subpattern (GBWRWG) was completely found, then it is known from the chosen order of the subpatterns that the subpattern (RWBGRB) should lie next to it on the left. If instead only the pattern (RWRB) is visible in the image, then it follows that the blue and the green color stripes are occluded. The three-dimensional coordinates of the object points are calculated by a triangulation (compare Section 9.1.1).

The advantage of the color encoded light stripe projection is that the geometry of an object can be reconstructed from only one color image. The disadvantage is that the colors of recoverable objects are constrained to a certain extent.

9.2.3   Active Color Stereo Analysis

The main problem of the technique described in the previous section is the robust identification of the color pattern. One way to avoid this problem is to employ a second camera. As for the color encoded light stripe technique a color pattern is projected onto the objects. The scene is taken by two cameras placed at two different positions (stereo image acquisition). Therefore ambiguous color patterns

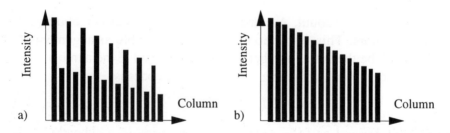

Figure 9.17: Contrasting illumination (a) and continuous illumination (b).

are no longer a problem since the patterns do not change between the two views. The color stripes can be matched by a correspondence analysis (compare Section 4.3). The advantage of this *active color stereo analysis* compared to a normal static stereo analysis consists in the possibility of matching corresponding points even if the surfaces show no texture.

By using two cameras actually any arbitrary color code can be used. However, the choice of the suitable color pattern is of great importance to assure a robust matching of the points in the two images. There exist two different ways how to design the color pattern. The pattern can be generated such that a high contrast arises between neighboring stripes (*contrasting illumination*) or such that continuous stripes arise between the stripes (*continuous illumination*).

Figure 9.17 illustrates the spatial arrangement of one color component inside a subpattern with contrasting or continuous illumination where a vertical projection of the color pattern is assumed. Neighboring color stripes can be distinguished well with contrasting illumination and smooth changes of the distances in the scene. However, for depth discontinuities, i.e. at object edges, the contrasting

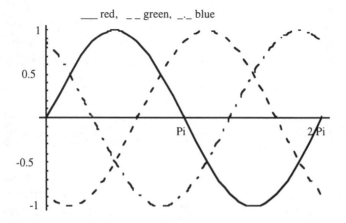

Figure 9.18: Sketch of the intensities of the three color components in a subpattern.

illumination can lead to a lower contrast between neighboring stripes in the image. On the other hand, for continuous illumination the contrast is generally low but high at object edges.

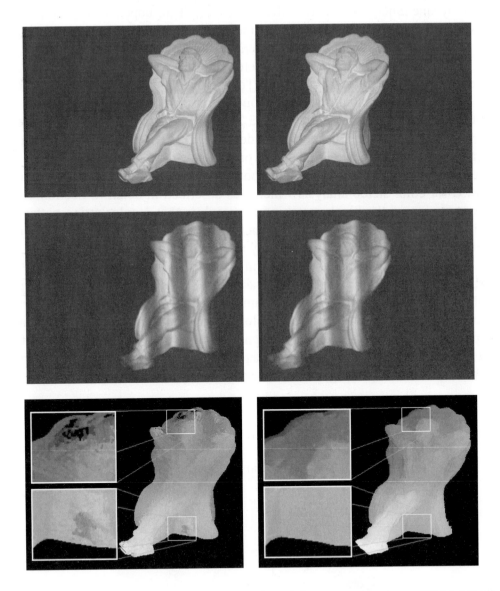

Figure 9.19: Top row: Gray value representation of the stereo color image TOM. Middle row: Gray value representation of the stereo image with projection of a color code (original images see Color Images 7 and 8). Lower left: Disparity map calculated without the projected color code. Lower right: Disparity map calculated by using the projected color pattern.

For the generation of a continuous illumination the intensity in the color components can be modeled by "sawtooth functions" or sine functions. Figure 9.18 shows a subpattern in which the intensity of the three color components are determined by sine functions that are shifted by $2/3\ \pi$. The subpattern is generated by a combination of the three components (see Color Image 6). The total color code is a periodical arrangement of several identical subpatterns.

The color stripe pattern is projected into the scene and a stereo image is generated from two different positions. To improve the color quality in both images a white balance should be carried out for the two cameras before the image acquisition starts (compare Section 2.3.2). With the standard stereo geometry (compare Section 4.1) the correspondence analysis simplifies considerably because corresponding pixels always lie on the same rows in the images.
One approach to match corresponding points is, for instance, the block matching method for color stereo analysis which was described in detail in Section 4.3.2. The extension of the block matching approach is that a color stripe pattern is projected onto the examined objects. Then the method from Section 4.3.2 can be applied to the stereo images (without any modifications) .

In the following the achievable improvement of the surface reconstruction will be illustrated. In Fig. 9.19 a gray value representation of a stereo image pair TOM is shown in the top row and the same scene with an overlaid color pattern is shown in the middle row (compare Color Images 7 and 8). The dense disparity maps calculated by using the block matching method are visualized in the bottom row of Fig. 9.19. The left and right image illustrate the recovered disparity map without and with employing active illumination, respectively.

Figure 9.20: Left: Differences (scaled) between the two disparity maps in Fig. 9.19. Right: Shaded plot of the scene TOM which is reconstructed using the projected color pattern.

Errors in the disparity map on the left are visible for instance, around the head and the foot of TOM. Two enlargements are superimposed to underline the differences between the disparity maps. Another representation of the differences is shown on the left of Fig. 9.20 where darker intensities represent higher errors. The right hand side of Fig. 9.20 visualizes a 3D plot of the recovered geometry reconstructed from the stereo image pair by overlaying the color pattern.

The advantage of color active stereo analysis compared to the color encoded light stripe projection is that on the one hand no knowledge about the projected color code is required and on the other hand in principle no assumptions are made on the object colors. Usual stereo analysis methods are not able to determine the correct dense depth maps in homogeneous image regions. This problem is solved by the (active) projection of the color pattern into the scene.

9.3   REFERENCES

General overviews about scene analysis techniques using structured lighting can, for example, be found in

Jarvis, R.A.: *A perspective on range finding techniques for computer vision.* IEEE Transact. on Pattern Analysis and Machine Intelligence **5** (1983), pp. 122-139, and

Shirai, Y.: *Three-Dimensional Computer Vision.* Springer-Verlag, Berlin, 1987.

Descriptions about the geometrical background of the techniques are given in

Fu, K.S., Gonzalez, R.C., Lee, C.S.G.: *Robotics: Control, Sensing, Vision, and Intelligence.* McGraw-Hill, Singapore, 1987,

Suk, M, Bhandarkar, S.M.: *Three-Dimensional Object Recognition from Range Images.* Springer-Verlag, Tokyo, Japan, 1992, and

Wechsler, H.: *Computational Vision.* Academic Press, Boston, USA, 1990.

The technique of the light spot stereo analysis is described in

Gerhardt, L.A., Kwak, W.I.: *An improved adaptive stereo ranging method for three-dimensional measurements.* Proc. International Conference on Computer Vision and Pattern Recognition, Miami Beach, 1986, pp. 21-26.

The binary encoded light approach is introduced in

Wahl, F.: *A coded light approach for depth map acquisition.* Proc. 8. DAGM-Symp. Musterkennung, G. Hartmann (Ed.), Paderborn, Germany, 1986, pp. 12-17, and

Stahs, T., Wahl F.: *Fast and robust range data acquisition in a low-cost environment.* Proc. of SPIE **1395**, Close-Range Photogrammetry Meets Machine Vision, Zurich, Switzerland, 1990, pp. 496-503.

If an LCD-projector is used for structured lighting, then besides the lens distortion of the camera (compare Section 2.1.4) also the lens distortion of the projector has to be modeled. A calibration technique which takes both lens distortions into account is given in

Valkenburg, R.J., McIvor, A.M.: *Accurate 3D measurement using a structured light system.* Image and Vision Computing **16** (1998), pp. 99-110.

Investigations about the theoretically and practically achievable accuracy using light stripe techniques can be found in

Lin, J.C., Chi, Z.-C.: *Accuracy analysis of a laser/camera based 3-d measurement system.* Proc. of SPIE **449**, 3rd International Conference on Robot Vision and Sensor Controls, Cambridge, Massachusetts, 1983, pp. 158-170,

McIvor, A.M.: *The accuracy of range data from a structured light system.* Report 190, Industrial Research Limited, Auckland, New Zealand, 1994.

Yang, Z.M., Wang, Y.F.: *Error Analysis of 3D Shape Construction from Structured Lighting.* Pattern Recognition **29** (1996), pp. 189-206.

Techniques for active color stereo analysis (Section 9.2.3) can be found in

Chen, C.-S., Hung, Y.-P., Chiang, C.-C., Wu, J.-L.: *Range data acquisition using color structured lighting and stereo vision.* Image and Vision Computing **15** (1997), pp. 445-456, and in

Koschan, A., Rodehorst, V., Spiller, K.: *Color stereo vision using hierachical block matching and active color illumination.* Proc. Int. Conference on Pattern Recognition ICPR´96, Vienna, Austria, 1996, pp. 835-839.

The first article employs dynamic programming for the correspondence analysis (see Section 4.3.2) and the second one uses a block matching approach (compare Section 4.3.3).

9.4   EXERCISES

(1) Section 9.1.1 described the 2D triangulation using two known angles α and β. Now, consider the calculation of the angle β. Let f be the effective focal length of the camera. The point **P** is projected onto a point **p** in the image plane $Z = -f$ of the camera which has the X-coordinate x. The optical center is **O** (compare Fig.

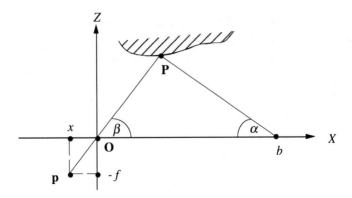

Figure 9.21: Determination of the angle β.

9.21). Derive the formula to determine the angle β from the position of the projected scene point **p** in the image plane.

(2) As described in Section 9.1.1 the angle γ is not taken into account when the range data is calculated (3D case). How can γ be used to verify the reconstruction result?

(3) Discuss ways to improve the achievable depth resolution of the method introduced in Section 9.1.3.

(4) A light plane is projected into a scene consisting of two polyhedral objects

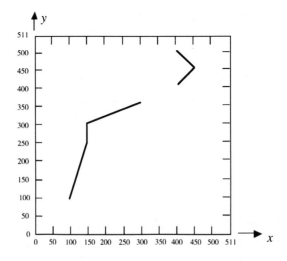

Figure 9.22: Light stripes visible in the image.

using a projector. The light stripes represented in Fig. 9.22 are visible in the image. The geometry of the image acquisition system corresponds to the arrangement in Fig. 9.7 with $M = 512$, $D_0 = 30\,\text{cm}$, $D_Z = 60\,\text{cm}$, $b = 20$ cm, and $f = 15$ mm. Determine the corresponding 3D profile, i.e. the distances between the objects and the reference plane. Notice that the effective focal length f is not needed to recover the 3D profile. Use f to calculate the value d (compare Equation (9.3)).

(5 - Assignment) Implement a modified version of Algorithm 9.2 which is based on a parallel projection model. How does the formula that calculates D_k changes if parallel projection is assumed? Fit a "curve" according to the model of the function $D_k(k)$ to the data. Use a ray tracer to generate synthetic images or take images with a camera.

(6) Assume that concentric circles are projected onto the scene objects as structured illumination. Some circles are assumed to be projected completely onto planar surfaces. We suppose that they can be detected as ellipses in the acquired image. Describe a technique to obtain the slopes of the planar faces from these detected ellipses.

APPENDIX: COLOR IMAGES

Color Image 1: A reproduction of the GretagMacbeth ColorChecker® (see Fig. 1.8).

Color Image 2: Color stereo image pair showing polyhedral objects (see Fig. 1.20).

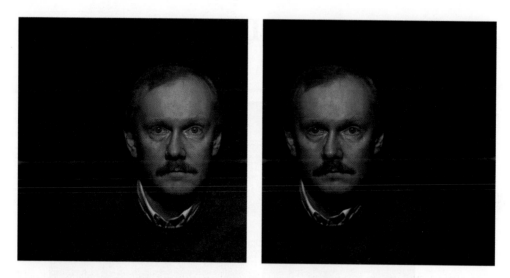

Color Image 3: Color stereo image pair ANDREAS (see Fig. 4.14).

Color Image 4: Real orange watering can with and without its specular reflection component (see Fig 6.16).

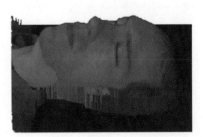

Color Image 5: Color image KARSTEN (one of the input images for 3S photometric stereo) and a shading based surface reconstruction (see Fig. 8.26). The eyes are closed to avoid specularities in the input images.

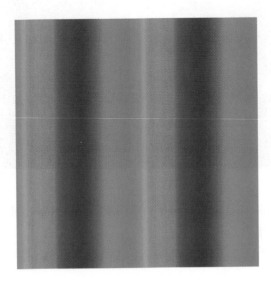

Color Image 6: Color code for active stereo analysis (see Figs. 9.18 and 9.19).

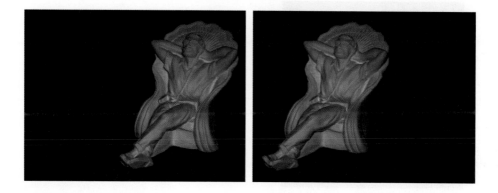

Color Image 7: Color stereo image pair TOM (see Fig. 9.19).

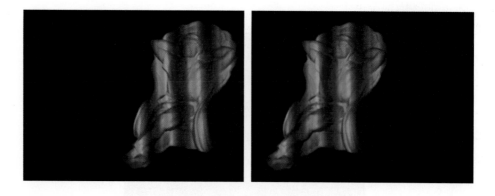

Color Image 8: Color stereo image pair TOM with projection of the color code shown in Color Image 6 (see Fig. 9.19).

LIST OF ALGORITHMS

These algorithms are explained in detail in this textbook:

INDEX